SELF-STUDY WORKBOOK

Version 7.2 for UNIX® and Windows NT®

Understanding GIS

The ARC/INFO® Method

ENVIRONMENTAL SYSTEMS RESEARCH INSTITUTE, INC.

Published by
Environmental Systems Research Institute, Inc.
380 New York Street
Redlands, California 92373-8100, USA

First edition 1990. Second edition 1992. Third edition 1995.
Fourth edition 1997.

Library of Congress Cataloging-in-Publication Data
A CIP record for this book is available from the Library of Congress.

ISBN 1-879102-01-3

Address inquiries relating to ARC/INFO® software to Environmental Systems
Research Institute, Inc., 380 New York Street, Redlands, California 92373-8100,
USA, or to your local international distributor.

Preface

Almost 30 years ago, a number of geographers conceived a system for storing and organizing spatial information in a computer. Over the past decade, this growing technology has come to be known as geographic information systems (GIS). Paralleling advancements in the technology has been the growth of GIS applications. From high-quality cartography to land use planning, natural resource management, environmental assessment and planning, tax mapping, ecological research, emergency vehicle dispatch, demographic research, utilities, business applications, and more, GIS promises to be one of the largest computer applications ever to emerge.

Why the growing interest in GIS? Because, GIS technology provides a means of integrating information in a way that helps us understand and address some of the most pressing problems we face today— tropical deforestation, acid rain, rapid urbanization, overpopulation, hunger, spread of disease, and impacts from changes in our global climate, to name a few. GIS helps us to organize data about these problems and to understand their spatial relationships, providing a basis for making more sensitive and intelligent decisions.

Understanding GIS—The ARC/INFO Method provides a hands-on introduction to this technology and a methodology for implementing it. While specific to a particular project, the approach presented in this workbook can be modified to apply to many of the functions for which GIS is used.

This workbook is meant primarily for beginning ARC/INFO® software users; however, GIS managers will find the first three lessons a useful introduction to the field, and more experienced users may use the book as a reference at various stages in their GIS projects. We also designed *Understanding GIS* to provide the basis for a computer lab component for university GIS courses.

We hope this book provides the background you need to make a difference in the way your organization applies geographic information and, ultimately, in the way we live.

Special acknowledgement to David Rhind, Teresa Connolly, and Birkbeck College, University of London, who compiled portions of this book. And for their helpful comments, a special thanks to the Regional Research Laboratories of the U.K. Economic and Social Research Council.

Contents

Lesson 5 Making spatial data usable

Lesson 6 Getting attribute data into ARC/INFO

Lesson 7 Managing the database

Lesson 8 Performing geographic analysis

Lesson 9 Presenting the results of the analysis

Lesson 10   Customizing ARC/INFO

What next?

Glossary

Index

Introduction

Welcome to *Understanding GIS—The ARC/INFO Method.* This workbook teaches the basics of geographic information systems (GIS) in the context of completing an ARC/INFO project. During the training, you will complete a small GIS project. You'll design and develop a digital spatial database, perform spatial analysis, create a map, and generate a report.

This workbook introduces some of the basic concepts of GIS and overviews the functions and capabilities of ARC/INFO. It is not a comprehensive guide to ARC/INFO software. Mastery of the software requires additional education through instructor-led courses and practical experience.

intended audience

This training is designed for people with little or no experience using ARC/INFO. Before you begin, read *Getting Started,* one of the ARC/INFO user's guides that comes with the software. *Getting Started* contains an online tutorial and an introduction to ArcTools to familiarize you with using ARC/INFO.

This workbook assumes that you have some knowledge of your computer's operating system, specifically,

- Directory structure and file management
  Changing directories
  Listing directories and files
  Creating, copying, renaming, and deleting a directory
  Copying, renaming, and deleting files

- Text editor
  Creating a new file and editing an existing file
  Displaying the contents of a file

- Windowing system
  Creating, moving, and resizing windows

- Mouse (if applicable)
  Using the mouse buttons

You should also know who to ask for help if you find you need assistance with these topics. Typically, this is your computer system administrator or an experienced fellow computer user.

estimated times   Although the amount of time needed to finish this training will vary, we estimate that most people can complete it within 40 hours. The estimated time to complete each lesson is listed at its beginning.

required materials   Before you start, make sure you have all the items needed to complete this training. If you aren't sure, check with your computer system administrator.

hardware

- Workstation or minicomputer configured for ARC/INFO
- Digitizing table compatible with and configured for ARC/INFO
- X Windows™ graphics terminal (preferably color) that supports both ARC/INFO graphics and menus
- Plotter configured for use with ARC/INFO (optional)

software

- ARC/INFO Version 7.0 or higher.

(ARC TIN, ARC NETWORK, ARC COGO, and ARC GRID are extensions to ARC/INFO and are not used in this workbook.)

data sets   The data set needed to complete the exercises in the workbook is included on ARC/INFO Version 7.1 software CD with the Samples data. Follow the instructions in Appendix A to determine whether or not the ARC/INFO sample data is loaded on your system. Or, ask your system administrator if the sample data is loaded and where it is located.

If the Samples data is not loaded on your system, you can use the data on the CD attached to the back of this book. Refer to Appendix A for instructions on copying the data from the CD.

You'll find postings of any new information that wasn't available at the time the book was published on our discussion forum at www.esri.com/esribooks. Go to the Understanding GIS (UNIX, Windows NT) conference. You'll also find user discussions relating to the book and CD.

local workspace   You should have a login account and a local workspace on your system in which you can perform the exercises. The pathname to your workspace is indicated by 'yourname' throughout this workbook. You'll need approximately 4 megabytes of disk space to complete all the exercises.

Workbook overview

This training workbook presents basic GIS and ARC/INFO concepts and functions in the context of a sample GIS project. The project solves a problem typical of many GIS applications, combining several layers of data to find relationships between the layers.

In most cases, you'll use only one method or procedure to complete each of the project tasks. There may, however, be alternative methods for completing these tasks. What's more, as you continue to work with ARC/INFO, you can develop procedures that meet the specific requirements of your own projects.

lesson contents
- Lessons 1 and 2 introduce the basic concepts of GIS and ARC/INFO. An online tutorial in Lesson 1 presents some of the functionality of GIS, while a series of exercises in Lesson 2 explains the ARC/INFO data model.

- Lesson 3 provides an overview of the steps involved in a GIS project and presents information about designing a spatial database. It also introduces the details of the sample GIS project.

- Lessons 4 through 9 guide you to project completion and reinforce the concepts introduced in earlier lessons. Each lesson has a similar format emphasizing learning concepts through exercises. More specifically, Lessons 4 through 7 develop the geographic database; Lesson 8 guides you through geographic analysis; and Lesson 9 explores the options for presenting the results of the analysis—specifically, maps and reports.

- Lesson 10 introduces how to customize ARC/INFO using the ARC Macro Language (AML)™. Capabilities include menus, command files, and end user applications.

Each lesson includes a series of exercises using ARC/INFO on an actual database. These exercises build on each other, so that taken together they lead to completion of the project. Most lessons also include optional advanced topics and exercises.

Although the workbook lessons lead you through the sample project from beginning to end, supplementary data sets let you begin any lesson without completing the preceding one.

How to use this workbook

scheduling your sessions

If you are new to GIS and ARC/INFO, you will want to start with Lesson 1 and spend some time becoming familiar with the terms in the Glossary. If familiar with GIS, but new to ARC/INFO, you can start with Lesson 2. Complete Lessons 3 through 9 in series, particularly if your job involves all aspects of GIS production. These lessons provide a complete overview of a GIS project.

Alternatively, if your job involves only certain aspects of GIS production, or if you need to learn about a certain aspect of the GIS process, complete only the applicable lessons, and then complete the remaining lessons when needed. This chart summarizes the lessons appropriate to various GIS tasks.

If you need to...	Complete lesson...
Obtain an overview of GIS capabilities, applications, and terminology	1-2, and review the Glossary and Appendix E
Design a geographic database	3
Build and manage a geographic database	4-7
Perform geographic analysis	8
Create maps and reports	9
Build an end-user application using AML	10

workbook conventions

A number of symbols and other graphic conventions guide you in getting the information you need.

entering commands

As you proceed through the workbook, you will notice different text styles in the sample computer dialog. The bold text signifies items you, the user, must enter. The plain text represents computer responses; for example,

If you type this...
the computer responds with this:

```
Arc: USAGE CLEAN
Usage: CLEAN <in_cover> {out_cover} {dangle_length}
       {fuzzy_tolerance} {POLY | LINE}
```

platform independence

This workbook can be used with any UNIX® or Windows® NT workstation on which ARC/INFO operates. ARC/INFO commands are the same on every platform; however, pathnames vary depending on which operating system you use. For Windows NT, you must substitute PC-style pathnames as you work through the exercises. For example, the following UNIX path:

```
Arc:   &WORKSPACE   $AIDATA/ugis/data
```

is equivalent to the following path on your Windows NT workstation:

```
Arc:   &WORKSPACE   %AIDATA%\ugis\data
```

getting more information

This workbook provides an introduction to the concepts and capabilities of GIS and ARC/INFO. We expect that as you work through the lessons you will want additional information about particular topics. You have several sources.

printed documentation

Refer to the printed software documentation at various points in the workbook for additional information. Every ARC/INFO installation should have the following user's guides available:

Getting Started
ARC/INFO Data Management
Map Projections & Coordinate Management
System Administrator's Guide
What's new in ARC/INFO at Version 7.1
Graphics Device Interface
Supported Graphics Devices
License Management

online documentation

Refer to ArcDoc, ARC/INFO's online help system for additional help with concepts and commands. Typing HELP at any ARC/INFO prompt launches online help and displays its Table of Contents.

Access the help index or search online help by clicking on the Index or Find tabs located to the right of the Contents tab.

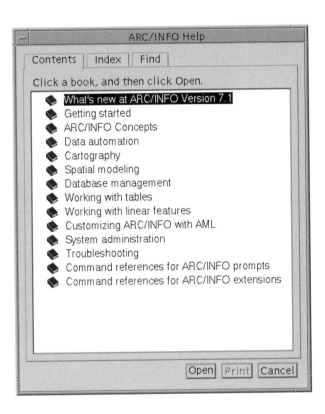

Those running ARC/INFO Version 7.1 on the Windows NT platform should refer to the online book, *Using ARC/INFO on NT*.

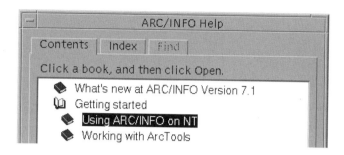

references for further reading   You'll find a list of references for further reading at the end of many of the lessons. These are only some of the available sources for a particular topic but should get you started in your search for additional information. Cited sources range from introductory to advanced discussions of related topics.

additional training   ESRI offers a number of instructor-led courses and workbooks covering various topics in ARC/INFO. The section 'What next?' at the end of this workbook contains more information.

Before you begin

Before beginning the workbook, you must perform two important tasks:

- Create a workspace containing the database used in the workbook
- Create a station file for your graphics terminal

Contact your system administrator if you need help completing either of these tasks. You should also recognize several conventions used for display environments. These are discussed at the end of this section.

setting up a training workspace

Before you begin the workbook lessons, you need to copy the directory called UGIS that was installed on your system from the ARC/INFO CD. The steps to accomplish this in UNIX and Windows NT are provided below. (If you need help creating an ARC/INFO workspace, contact your system administrator.)

UNIX

1. After logging in, move to your local ARC/INFO workspace.

```
%  cd  /<path>/<your_ARC/INFO_workspace>
```

2. Copy the UGIS directory to your workspace. The pathname to the UGIS directory is set with the AIDATA variable. Before you proceed, check with your system administrator to verify that AIDATA has been set.

```
%  cp  -r  $AIDATA/ugis  ugis
```

If the UGIS data is not loaded on your system, you can copy the data from the CD packaged with this book. (Check with your system administrator, if you do not know how to mount a CD drive on your computer.)

```
cp  -r  <cdrom_device>/unix/ugis  ugis
```

Check our discussion forum at www.esri.com\esribooks. Go to the Understanding GIS (UNIX, Windows NT) conference. You'll find postings of any new information that wasn't available at the time the book was published. You'll also find user discussions relating to the book and CD.

3. Now start ARC/INFO.

```
%  arc
```

The ARC/INFO prompt appears:

```
Arc:
```

4. During the exercises, you'll move to various workspaces using the &WORKSPACE command in ARC/NFO. Use &WORKSPACE now to move to the DATA workspace under UGIS.

```
Arc:  &WORKSPACE  ugis/data
```

Windows NT 1. Start ARC/INFO by clicking the Arc icon in your Windows Program Manager.

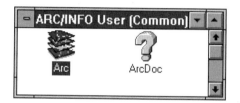

2. At the `Arc:` prompt, move to your local workspace using the &WORKSPACE command in ARC/INFO. Replace "yourname" with the pathname to your local workspace.

```
Arc:  &WORKSPACE  <drive>:\yourname
```

3. Copy the UGIS directory from the sample data to your workspace. The pathname to the sample data is set with the %AIDATA% variable. Before you proceed, check with your system administrator to verify that %AIDATA% has been set.

```
Arc: &sys xcopy %AIDATA%\ugis\*.* UGIS\*.* /s/e/v
```

If the UGIS data is not loaded on your system, you can copy the data from the CD packaged with this book.

Use the Windows NT File Manager to copy all the data from the nt directory on the CD to your local workspace or use the following command from the ARC/NFO command prompt.

```
Arc: &sys xcopy <drive:>\nt\ugis\*.* ugis\*.* /s/e/v
```

4. Move to the DATA workspace under UGIS.

```
Arc:  &WORKSPACE  ugis\data
```

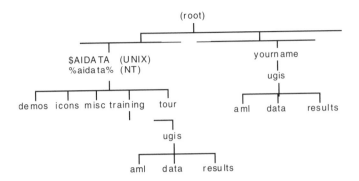

creating and using a station file

Because ARC/INFO is device independent, you must specify which devices you are using. Commands in ARC/INFO that use menus and display graphics on the screen require you to establish the display environment; that is, specify the graphics display device, the AML terminal device, and the method for coordinate input that you will use during the ARC/INFO session. The following table lists the ARC/INFO commands that establish these environments.

Command	Establishes the...
DISPLAY	graphics display environment
&TERMINAL	terminal type for use with menus
COORDINATE	method of coordinate input
DIGITIZER	digitizer type

You must set the display environment before drawing any graphics on the screen. You can issue the commands that set these parameters interactively at the beginning of an ARC/INFO session, or store them in a file called a *station file*. A station file contains the command statements that define the graphics display device, the AML terminal device, and the coordinate input method. A station file can optionally contain other setup commands. We recommend that your station file include &FULLSCREEN &POPUP for displaying dialog listings in a window for easy scrolling. For example, the contents of a station file for a workstation console or supported X Window device might contain the following statements:

```
DISPLAY 9999
&TERMINAL 9999
COORDINATE MOUSE
DIGITIZER 9100 /dev/ttya
&FULLSCREEN &POPUP
```

The contents of a station file for a Windows NT workstation might contain the following statements:

```
DISPLAY 9999
&TERMINAL 9999
COORDINATE MOUSE
DIGITIZER 26500 COM1
&FULLSCREEN &POPUP
```

You need a station file to complete the lessons in this workbook. Lessons 4 and 5 require a digitizer, so make sure your station file includes the DIGITIZER command. See the *Graphics Device Interfaces* guide for recommendations on digitizer communications for your computer. Also, many exercises allow you to use a mouse for interactive graphics. If you have a mouse attached to your terminal, you'll want to change from the default method of interactive coordinate entry, the screen cursor, by including COORDINATE MOUSE in your station file. *Supported Graphics Devices* provides a complete list of display devices and digitizers supported by ARC/INFO. If necessary, have your system administrator create a station file for your particular hardware configuration.

specifying a station file   Station files are created as system text files prefixed with STAT_. ARC/INFO distinguishes station files by the characters following the prefix. The length of the file name and characters that can be used in the name depend on the operating system. Typically, the name serves to identify the type of device being used. For example, the station file that establishes the display environment for a UNIX or Windows NT workstation, might be named stat_9999.

UNIX   stat_9999
Windows NT stat_9999

Notice that the file name is lowercase. The &STATION command is used along with the station file name to execute that file. You can omit the STAT_ prefix when executing station files. For example,

Arc: **&station 9999**

executes the station file named STAT_9999.

For more information, check with your system administrator or read about station files in the online documentation under *Customizing ARC/INFO with AML--> AML(ARC Macro Language)-->AML Basics-->Establishing the display environment.*

a note about windows   ARC/INFO uses the interface tools provided by the window manager installed on your computer. Your display may look slightly different than what is shown in the workbook.

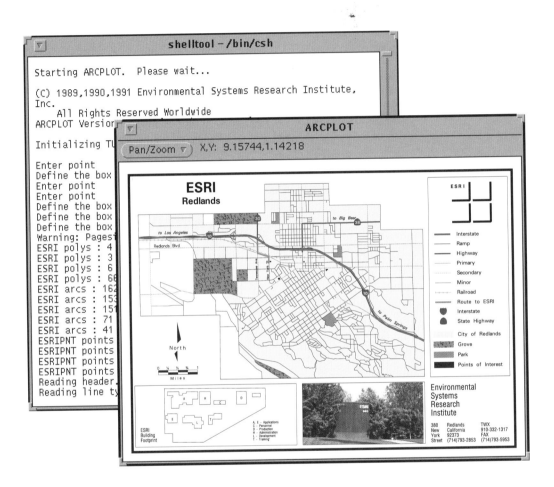

Your station file sets the original size of the graphics window, but you can move and resize it. You can also move graphics and terminal windows to the front or back, just like other windows. The graphics window closes whenever you quit a graphics program.

If you don't know how to use your system's windowing system, be sure to complete the online tutorial introduced in the ARC/INFO user's guide, *Getting Started*.

Lesson 1 Why GIS?

Many organizations now spend large amounts of money on geographic information systems (GIS) and on geographic databases. Predictions suggest billions of dollars will be spent on these items over the next decade. Why should this be true now when only a few years ago GIS was a rarity?

Rapidly declining computer hardware costs have made GIS affordable to an increasingly wider audience. More importantly, we have come to realize that geography (and the data describing it) is part of our everyday world; almost every decision we make is constrained, influenced, or dictated by some fact of geography. We send fire trucks to fires by the fastest available routes. Our central government often awards grants to local governments based on population. We study disease by identifying areas of prevalence and rate of spread. This demand for geographic information parallels the need for GIS, explaining its rapidly growing popularity.

Such generalizations do not, however, explain why and how a GIS can help you. First, you must know what a GIS is and what it can be used for. This lesson addresses topics to help you understand GIS; specifically,

- What is a GIS?
- Questions a GIS can answer
- Some applications of GIS
- The components of a GIS
- Using a GIS

The estimated time needed to complete this lesson is 2 hours.

What is a GIS?

The use of geographic information systems (GIS) grew dramatically in the 1980s. It is now commonplace for business, government, and academia to use GIS for many diverse applications. Consequently, many definitions of GIS have developed. For example, turning to the Glossary of this workbook, you'll find a GIS described as:

> An organized collection of computer hardware, software, geographic data, and personnel designed to efficiently capture, store, update, manipulate, analyze, and display all forms of geographically referenced information.

While accurate, comprehensive, and widely accepted, this definition doesn't help the newcomer to GIS much. Its meaning will become clear as you progress through the workbook, but for the moment, consider a simpler definition:

> A computer system capable of holding and using data describing places on the earth's surface.

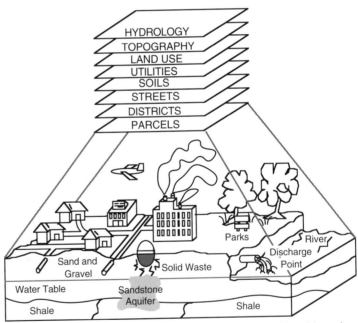

A number of related data layers can represent the many geographies of the real world.

Understanding GIS—The ARC/INFO Method

spatial operations   Many computer programs, such as spreadsheets (e.g., Lotus 1-2-3), statistics packages (e.g., SAS; Minitab), or drafting packages (e.g., AutoCAD) can handle simple geographic or spatial data. Why, then, are they not usually thought of as a GIS? The generally accepted answer is that a GIS is only a GIS if it permits spatial operations on the data. As an example, consider the table below.

Name	Latitude	Longitude	GIS Population
London	51N	0	80
Zurich	47N	8E	25
Utrecht	52N	5E	40
Santa Barbara	34N	119W	50
Orono	45N	69W	30
Buffalo	42N	78W	30

This table shows the approximate number of people working with certain aspects of GIS in selected centers of activity.

aspatial queries   Asking "What's the average number of people working with GIS in each location?" is an aspatial query—the answer doesn't require the stored value of latitude and longitude; nor does it describe where the places are in relation to each other.

spatial queries   "How many people work in GIS in the major centers of Western Europe?" "Which centers lie within 1,000 miles of each other?" "What's the shortest route passing through all these centers?" These are spatial queries that can only be answered using latitude and longitude data and other information, such as the radius of the earth. A geographic information system can readily answer such questions.

data linkage   A GIS typically links data from different sets. As an example, suppose you need to know what percentage of each country's total food production is grown for export. You've located the data you need, but your total food production for each country is stored in one computer file, and the food export data is contained in a separate file. You must combine these files to solve the problem. Once the files are combined, it's a simple process to have the computer perform the arithmetic to produce your answer.

If this seems trivial—hardly needing a GIS—consider the different ways in which data sets may need to be linked.

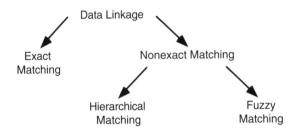

exact matching   *Exact matching* occurs when you have information in one computer file about many geographic features (e.g., counties) and additional information in another file about the same set of features. The operation to bring them together is easy, achieved by using a key common to both files—in this case, the county name. So, the record in each file with the same county name is extracted and the two are joined and stored in another file.

COUNTY	POPULATION
LAKE	108,000
LINCOLN	45,000
MADISON	213,000
ORANGE	1,145,000
PENN	22,000

COUNTY	AVG. HOUSING COST
LAKE	89,000
LINCOLN	77,000
MADISON	104,000
ORANGE	167,000
PENN	75,000

COUNTY	POPULATION	AVG. HOUSING COST
LAKE	108,000	89,000
LINCOLN	45,000	77,000
MADISON	213,000	104,000
ORANGE	1,145,000	167,000
PENN	22,000	75,000

The top two tables can be joined by performing an exact match on the name of the county.

hierarchical matching   Some types of information, however, are collected in more detail or more frequently than other types of information. For example, finance and unemployment data covering large areas is collected frequently. On the other hand, population data is collected for small areas, but at less frequent intervals. If the smaller areas nest (i.e., fit exactly) within the larger ones, then the solution for matching these data is to use *hierarchical matching*. Group the small areas together until they cover the same area as the larger area, total their data, and then perform an exact match.

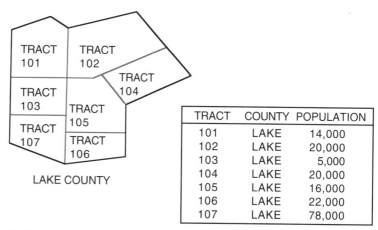

TRACT	COUNTY	POPULATION
101	LAKE	14,000
102	LAKE	20,000
103	LAKE	5,000
104	LAKE	20,000
105	LAKE	16,000
106	LAKE	22,000
107	LAKE	78,000

The hierarchical structure illustrated in this diagram shows that Lake County is composed of several tracts. To obtain meaningful values for the county, the values for each tract must be added.

fuzzy matching   On many occasions, the boundaries of the smaller areas do not match those of the larger ones. This is especially true when dealing with environmental data. For example, crop boundaries, usually defined by field edges, rarely match the boundary between types of soil. If you want to determine the most productive soil for a particular crop, you need to overlay the two data sets and compute crop productivity for each and every soil type. In principle, this is like laying one map over another and noting the combinations of soil and crop productivity. (Lesson 8 describes this overlay process more thoroughly.)

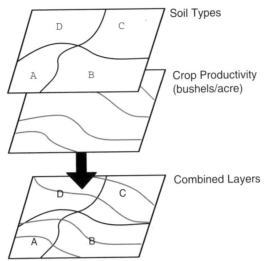

Soil Types

Crop Productivity
(bushels/acre)

Combined Layers

*When data boundaries between layers don't match, the layers can be joined,
creating a new layer containing the characteristics of both.*

A GIS can perform all these operations because it uses geography, or
space, as the common key between the data sets. Information is
linked only if it relates to the same geographic area.

Why is data linkage so important? Consider a situation where you
have two data sets for the same area, such as yearly income by county
and average cost of housing. Each data set might be analyzed and
mapped individually. Alternatively, they can be combined to produce
one valid combination. If, however, you have 20 data sets for the
county, you have over one million possible combinations. Although
not all combinations are meaningful (e.g., unemployment and soil
type), you can answer many more questions than if the data sets are
kept separate. Combining them adds value to the database. To do
this, you need a GIS.

Questions a GIS can answer

So far, a GIS has been described in two ways: 1) through formal definitions, and 2) through its ability to carry out spatial operations, linking data sets using location as the common key. You can, however, also distinguish a GIS by listing the types of questions it can (or should be able to) answer. For any application there are five generic questions that a sophisticated GIS can answer.

location   What is at...?

The first of these questions seeks to find out what exists at a particular location. A location can be described in many ways using, for example, a place name, a post or zip code, or a geographic reference, such as latitude and longitude.

condition   Where is it?

The second question is the converse of the first and requires spatial analysis to answer. Instead of identifying what exists at a given location, you want to find a location where certain conditions are satisfied (e.g., an unforested section of land at least 2,000 square meters in size, within 100 meters of a road, and with soils suitable for supporting buildings).

trends   What has changed since...?

The third question might involve both of the first two and seeks to find the differences within an area over time.

patterns   What spatial patterns exist?

This question is more sophisticated. You might ask this question to determine whether cancer is a major cause of death among residents near a nuclear power station. Just as important, you might want to know how many anomalies there are that don't fit the pattern and where they are located.

modeling   What if...?

"What if..." questions are posed to determine what happens, for example, if a new road is added to a network, or if a toxic substance seeps into the local ground water supply. Answering this type of question requires geographic as well as other information.

Sample GIS applications

Applications for GIS technology developed around the world. Many of the early applications in Europe built land registration systems and environmental databases. However, Britain's largest GIS expenditure in the 1980s was for developing utility systems and creating a comprehensive topographic database for the country.

Canada developed an important forestry application to plan the volume of timber to cut, identify access to the timber, and report the results to the Provincial governments. Applications in China and Japan emphasized monitoring and modeling possible environmental changes.

In the United States, the U.S. Bureau of Census and the U.S. Geological Survey used GIS technology for their Topologically Integrated Geographic Encoding and Referencing (TIGER) project. They produced a computerized description of the U.S. transportation network—at a cost of about $170 million—to facilitate taking and reporting the 1990 census.

Today, the number and variety of applications for GIS are impressive. The amount of geographic data that has been gathered is staggering and includes volumes of satellite imagery collected from space. Local governments use GIS for planning and zoning, property assessment and land records, parcel mapping, public safety, and environmental planning. Resource managers rely on GIS for fish and wildlife planning; management of forested, agricultural, and coastal lands; and energy and mineral resource management.

GIS supports the daily activities of automated mapping and facilities management with applications for electricity, water, sewer, gas, telecommunications, and cable television utilities, using capabilities such as load management, trouble call analysis, voltage drop, basemap generation and maintenance, line system analysis, siting, network pressure and flow analysis, leak detection, and inventory. Demographers use GIS for target market analysis, facility siting, address matching and geocoding, as well as product profiles, forecasting, and planning. GIS also has an increasing role in supporting education and research in the classroom, the computer lab, the research institute, and the public library.

The most important point to note is that these diverse applications are carried out using similar software and techniques—a GIS is truly a general-purpose tool. Appendix E contains several maps illustrating a few of the many GIS applications.

Components of a GIS

Several components constitute a GIS:

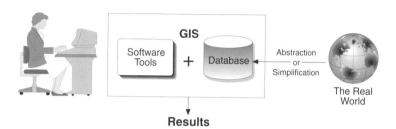

The user becomes part of the GIS whenever complicated analyses, such as spatial analyses and modeling, have to be carried out. These usually require skill in selecting and using tools from the GIS toolbox and intimate knowledge of the data being used. At present and for years to come general-purpose GIS will rely on users to know what they are doing—pressing a button is not enough.

what a GIS is not　　A GIS is not simply a computer system for making maps, although it can create maps at different scales, in different projections, and with different colors. A GIS is an analytical tool. The major advantage of a GIS is that it allows you to identify the spatial relationships between map features.

A GIS does not store a map in any conventional sense; nor does it store a particular image or view of a geographic area. Instead, a GIS stores the data from which you can draw a desired view to suit a particular purpose.

A GIS links spatial data with geographic information about a particular feature on a map. The information is stored as attributes of the graphically represented feature. For example, the centerline that represents a road on a map doesn't tell you much about the road except its location. To find out the road's width or pavement type, you must query the database. Using the information stored in the database, you could create a display symbolizing the roads according to the type of information that needs to be shown.

A GIS also uses the stored feature attributes to compute new information about map features; for example, to calculate the length of a particular road segment or to determine the total area of a particular soil type.

geographic database

In short, a GIS doesn't hold maps or pictures—it holds a database. The database concept is central to a GIS and is the main difference between a GIS and drafting or computer mapping systems, which can only produce good graphic output. All contemporary geographic information systems incorporate a database management system.

If you want to go beyond just making pictures, you need to know three things about every feature stored in the computer: what it is, where it is, and how it relates to other features (e.g., which roads link to form a network). Database systems provide the means of storing a wide range of such information and updating it without the need to rewrite programs. In ARC/INFO, ARC handles where the features are, while the INFO® component handles the feature descriptions and how each feature is related to others.

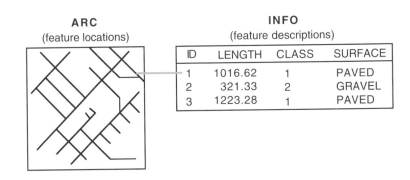

ARC (feature locations)	**INFO** (feature descriptions)			
	ID	LENGTH	CLASS	SURFACE
	1	1016.62	1	PAVED
	2	321.33	2	GRAVEL
	3	1223.28	1	PAVED

Essentially, a GIS gives you the ability to associate information with a feature on a map and to create new relationships that can determine the suitability of various sites for development, evaluate environmental impacts, calculate harvest volumes, identify the best location for a new facility, and so on.

Using a GIS

This section shows how a GIS can solve a spatial analysis problem similar to those described earlier. Throughout the rest of the workbook, you will see how one GIS, ARC/INFO, processes data and generates results that can help solve specific problems.

EXERCISE   **Use ARC/INFO to solve a spatial problem**

In this exercise, you will determine the total area of forested land adjoining existing roads. This information might be needed, for example, to determine the timber revenues lost due to implementing a visual buffer around scenic roads. Given a map of land use and a map of roads, you will first examine the information on each. You will then combine the maps and determine the area of forested land that lies within 100 meters of existing roads. This is what the maps look like:

LANDUSE   ROADS

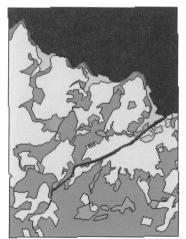

A map of a particular spatial feature (e.g., land use or flood zone boundaries) can be thought of as a layer of data about an area. In ARC/INFO, these layers are called *coverages*. We describe and discuss coverages in more detail in subsequent lessons.

ARC/INFO uses a command language that functions similarly to the way your computer's operating system works: commands entered at a prompt perform specific tasks. ARC/INFO can also be customized to allow users to use menus to point and click on the task they want to perform. This exercise uses such a menu system. Note that only a few of the many options available in ARC/INFO are represented in this particular menu system.

Before you start, you need to make sure the training data has been copied to your local directory. Refer to the Introduction if this has not yet been done.

| HELP |

If you aren't familiar with using a workstation and mouse, be sure to work through the online tutorial referenced in the user's guide, *Getting Started*. This tutorial teaches how to use the ARC/INFO software's menu interfaces within the native window manager environment of your workstation (e.g., CDE or Windows NT).

Once the data has been copied into your local workspace, start ARC/INFO.

UNIX   % **arc**
Windows NT You are already in arc

The `Arc:` prompt appears. If not already there, you can use the ARC/INFO directive &WORKSPACE to move to your local workspace containing the data for *Understanding GIS*. Remember to replace 'yourname' with the pathname of your local workspace.

UNIX   Arc: **&WORKSPACE /yourname/ugis/data**
Windows NT Arc: **&WORKSPACE <drive>:\yourname\ugis\data**

Now you're ready to start.

Step 1

Start the menu system in ARC/INFO

Typing the command shown below displays the usage for starting the menu system.

Arc: **&RUN INTRO**   9999
Usage: &RUN INTRO <station_file>
Arc:

Note that <station_file> refers to the name of a station file set up for your terminal type. Refer to the section 'Creating and using a station file' in the Introduction for more information on station files.

Reissue the command. This time, substitute the name of your station file (e.g., 9999) for <station_file>.

Arc: **&RUN INTRO <station_file>**

The ARCPLOT™ program begins and the main menu of the menu system appears on your screen.

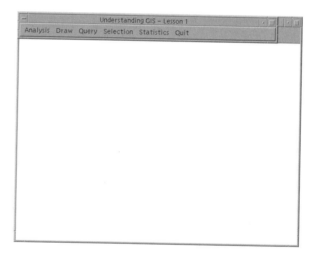

The main menu contains options for displaying and accessing information about the layers in the database. The main menu includes the choices Analysis, Draw, Query, Selection, Statistics, and Quit.

The Draw Tool and the Pan/Zoom Tool automatically open alongside the graphics window when the menu system starts.

The display window and menu configuration on your computer may look slightly different depending on your screen size or window manager.

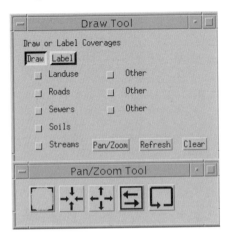

You can reposition these windows just as you would any window on your system. You can also close and reopen them. The Draw option on the main menu opens the Draw Tool. The Pan/Zoom button on the Draw Tool opens the Pan/Zoom Tool. Make menu selections by using your mouse to point to and click on the desired choice.

Step 2

Draw and query the contents of the LANDUSE coverage

Use the Draw Tool to draw the LANDUSE coverage. Under Draw or Label Coverages, choose **Draw**. Then, select the check box next to **LANDUSE**. (Depending on your window manager, a selected box will appear to be pressed inward or have a check mark inside.)

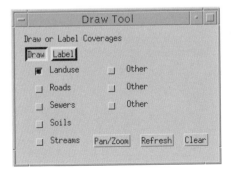

The LANDUSE coverage looks like this.

The boundaries that enclose the land use areas are referred to as *polygons.* Each polygon is shaded according to the type of land use it represents, as follows:

Type	Color
Urban	Light gray
Agriculture	Yellow
Brush land	Orange
Forest	Green
Water	Blue
Barren	Dark gray

To list the attributes of a particular polygon, you can query the coverage. Select **Query** from the main menu, and choose **LANDUSE** by pressing it in the scrolling window of the Query Tool.

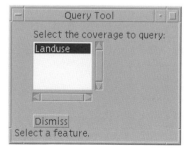

(Notice that this Query Tool only allows queries of coverages that are currently drawn on the screen.)

Move the crosshairs over one of the forest polygons (shaded green) and select it. The area you select is outlined in black and the attributes of this polygon are displayed. You can see that there are several attributes for the polygon including its area, perimeter, land use code (LU-CODE), and cost per hectare (COST/HA). Notice that the value for LU-CODE is 400, the code for forest. Here is a sample listing for one of the forest polygons:

Press the **QUIT** button to close the Text window. Then **Dismiss** the Query Tool.

Here are the codes for all the land use types:

Type	Code
Urban	100
Agriculture	200
Brush land	300
Forest	400
Water	500
Barren	700

Before continuing with the exercise, take a minute to examine the Pan/Zoom Tool included in this menu system. You can use it throughout this exercise to zoom in and out, and to pan across the view shown in your graphics window.

Each icon evokes a different function.

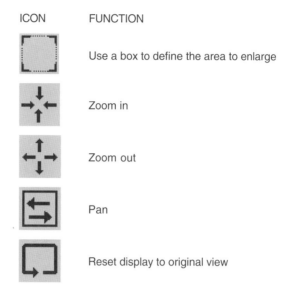

ICON	FUNCTION
	Use a box to define the area to enlarge
	Zoom in
	Zoom out
	Pan
	Reset display to original view

Step 3 **Select and draw the forest polygons from the LANDUSE coverage along with the roads from the ROADS coverage**

Select and draw only the forest polygons. Choose **Selection**, from the main menu. The Selection Tool appears. In this case, the selected coverage is already set to LANDUSE and all its available attributes are selected (i.e., their selection boxes appear with check marks or look pressed inward).

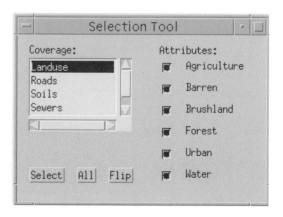

The Flip button toggles attributes from selected to unselected. Because all attributes are currently selected, you can press the **Flip** button to clear the selection (all the checked boxes will become empty, or the pressed boxes will pop up). Then, select the **Forest** check box and press **Select**.

```
LANDUSE polys : 20 of 77 selected.
```

The screen clears and the coverage redraws including only the areas with the selected attribute (Forest).

Close the Selection Tool.

Return to the Draw Tool to draw the ROADS coverage. Under Draw or Label Coverages, make sure Draw is still selected, and activate the ROADS coverage by selecting the check box next to **ROADS**. Be sure to leave the box next to LANDUSE selected.

The roads are added to the display, which now looks like this:

There are two classes of roads. Improved roads are drawn with a thick red line, and semi-improved roads are drawn with a dashed red line. Although you can see that many roads pass through forest, you still cannot tell which parts of the forested land lie within 100 meters of a road. In the next step, you'll create a 100-meter buffer area around the roads.

Step 4

Create a 100-meter buffer area around the roads

From the main menu, select **Analysis**, then **Buffer**.

The Buffer Tool appears. Choose **ROADS** from the scrolling list, then use the slider bar to set the Distance to **100**. Press **OK**.

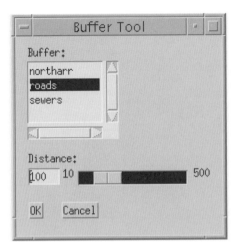

The buffer operation might require a few minutes to complete. ARC/INFO displays a series of messages as the buffer develops:

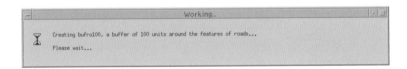

```
Buffering...
Sorting...
Intersecting...
Assembling polygons...
Creating new labels...
Finding inside polygons...
Dissolving...
Building nodes...
Creating bufro100.PAT...
```

When the Working window disappears, a new coverage named
BUFRO100 exists. **Cancel** the Buffer Tool and return to the Draw
Tool. Select **Other**.

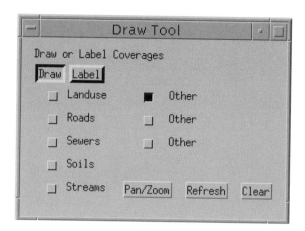

The Draw Other Coverage tool appears. Draw **BUFRO100** with
Default Symbology (a solid black or white line) by making the
appropriate selections from the scrolling lists and pressing **Ok**.

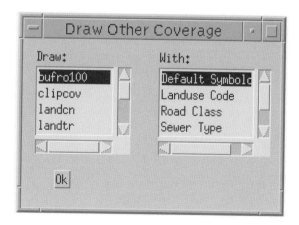

The road buffer coverage BUFRO100 is added to the screen display of forested areas and roads.

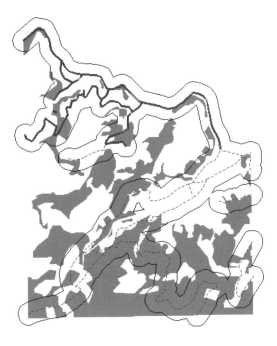

This buffer represents areas within 100 meters of roads. You can now see the forested areas that fall within the 100-meter road buffer. In the next step, you'll combine the LANDUSE coverage with the BUFRO100 coverage to create and display a new coverage that contains only those forested areas that lie within the buffer.

Select **Query** from the main menu. Use the Query Tool to list the attributes of the area inside the buffer. Choose **BUFRO100** as the coverage to query.

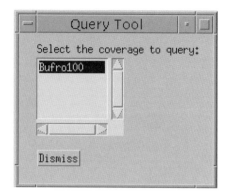

Using the crosshairs in the map graphics window, select a point inside the buffer.

Notice that, in addition to area and perimeter, the buffer polygons have an attribute called INSIDE. A value of 100 represents the area inside the buffer. (Areas outside the buffer are coded 1.) **Quit** from the Text window when you finish viewing attributes for the buffer polygon, and **Dismiss** the Query Tool.

Before proceeding to the next step, go to the Draw Tool and select **Clear** to clear the display.

| Step 5 | **Overlay LANDUSE and BUFRO100 using the intersect operation and display the results** |

In this step, you will overlay the land use and buffered roads coverages to create a new coverage that is the intersection of their features and attributes. This operation enables you to determine precisely which forested areas fall within the buffer and determine their total area.

From the main menu, select **Analysis**, then **Overlay**.

The Analysis Tool appears. Select **Intersect** as the operation to perform, select **LANDUSE** to overlay with **BUFFRO100**, then press **OK**.

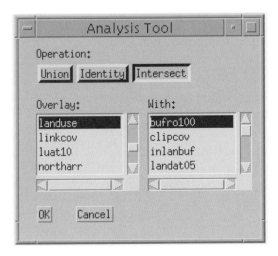

The intersect operation performs a polygon overlay to create a new coverage that contains only those areas occupied by both the input and intersect coverages (i.e., LANDUSE and BUFRO100).

Overlay operations may take several minutes to complete. Again, messages appear in the dialog area describing the overlay steps.

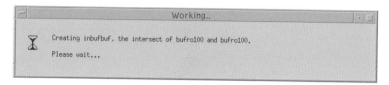

```
Intersecting LANDUSE with BUFRO100 to create INLANBUF (UNIX)
Intersecting c:\...\ugis\data\landuse with
c:\...ugis\data\bufro100 to create Inlanbuf (NT)
Sorting...
Intersecting...
Assembling polygons...
Creating new labels...
Creating INLANBUF.PAT
** Item 'AREA' duplicated, Join File version dropped **
** Item 'PERIMETER' duplicated, Join File version dropped **
** Item 'AREA' duplicated, Join File version dropped **
** Item 'PERIMETER' duplicated, Join File version dropped **
```

When the Working window disappears, the operation is complete. **Cancel** the Analysis Tool. Go to the Draw Tool and select **Other**. From the Draw Other Coverage tool, draw **INLANBUF** with **LANDUSE CODE**, then press **Ok**.

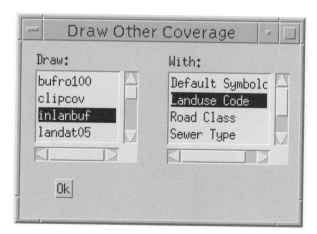

The new coverage INLANBUF draws, symbolized by land use codes. Now it's easy to see exactly which portions of the forested areas lie within 100 meters of the roads. Add the roads to the display by selecting **ROADS** from the Draw Tool.

INLANBUF coverage   INLANBUF and ROADS coverages

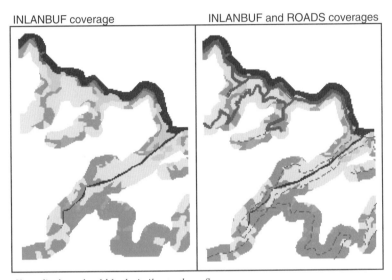

Your displays should look similar to these figures.

Open the Query Tool by selecting the **Query** button on the main menu. Query one of the forested polygons (green) from the **INLANBUF** coverage. Notice that it now contains attributes from both the land use and road buffer coverages (i.e., LANDUSE and BUFRO100). Here is a sample listing for one of the forested polygons:

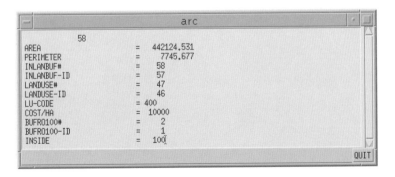

As you would expect, this polygon has an LU-CODE of 400 (i.e., the land use is forest), and the INSIDE value equals 100 (i.e., the area is located inside the buffer). **Quit** from the Text window when you finish viewing the attributes. Then **Dismiss** the Query Tool.

Now, display only the forested areas that lie within 100 meters of roads. The Selection Tool should still be displayed on your screen. If not, open the **Selection** Tool from the main menu. Choose **INLANBUF** as the coverage and **Forest** as the attribute to display, and press **Select**.

```
INLANBUF POLYS : 31 of 93 selected.
```

Your display shows the roads and the forested areas that lie within 100 meters of them.

Close the Selection Tool.

Forested areas from the INLANBUF coverage are displayed with the primary and secondary roads from the ROADS coverage.

Step
6

Generate statistics for the analysis

The final step of this analysis is to calculate the total forested area required to create a scenic buffer around the roads.

To perform the area calculation, select **Statistics** from the main menu. Use the scroll bar in the Statistics Tool to locate **INLANBUF** in the scrolling list of available coverages, then select it.

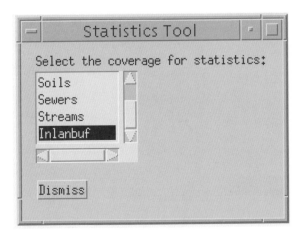

Because only the forested polygons from INLANBUF are currently selected, the statistical report generated includes only information about those polygons. This is the information you want.

Along with the total area (SUM-AREA), the report includes other statistical information about the forested polygons, including average area, maximum area, and minimum area. **Quit** from the Text window, and **Dismiss** the Statistics Tool when you finish viewing the report.

This exercise presented an overview of some typical GIS functions. In subsequent lessons, you'll use ARC/INFO to complete a small GIS project.

Note: Although the streams coverage is a choice on the menu, it does not exist at this time. You will create the streams coverage in a later lesson.

Now that you've finished this exercise, feel free to use the menu system to display and query other coverages in the database. Keep in mind that this menu system was created for this exercise and performs only a tiny fraction of ARC/INFO's capabilities. The final lesson in this workbook guides you through creating a menu-driven application of your own.

When you finish using the menu system, return to the Arc: prompt by selecting **Quit** from the main menu.

Finally, to end the ARC/INFO session, type QUIT at the Arc: prompt.

Arc: **QUIT**

END

Summary

This lesson introduced background information about geographic information systems including:

- The formal definition of a GIS
- The sort of questions a GIS can answer
- Sample applications of GIS
- The components of a GIS
- A sample application written in the ARC Macro Language (AML)

It also introduced some of the underlying concepts of GIS, such as

- Spatial operations
- Data linkage
- The role of maps in a GIS
- The central importance of the database concept

The exercise introduced you to the ARC/INFO database containing spatial and descriptive data. You saw how new information and new data layers could be extracted from existing information and data layers. In this way, a GIS can be used to derive the data required to clarify certain proposals and aid informed decisions.

Now that you know "Why GIS?" it's time to learn how a GIS really functions. Then you'll be ready to apply ARC/INFO to a real-world example.

references for
further reading

Bernhardsen, Tor. *Geographic Information Systems* (Norwegian Mapping Authority, 1992). New York, NY: John Wiley & Sons.

Chrisman, Nicholas. *Exploring Geographic Information Systems.* New York, NY: John Wiley & Sons, 1997.

Chrisman, Nicholas. "The Risks of Software Innovation: A Case Study of the Harvard Lab." *American Cartographer* 15, 3 (1988): 291-300.

Coppock, J. T., and K. E. Anderson (Eds.). *International Journal of Geographical Information Systems (IJGIS).* London: Taylor and Francis, 1987. The IJGIS is published quarterly by Taylor and Francis Ltd., 4 John Street, London, UK WC1N 2ET.

Dangermond, J., and L. K. Smith. "GIS and the Revolution in Cartography: The Nature of the Role Played by a Commercial Organization." *American Cartographer* 15, 3 (1988): 301-10.

ESRI, Inc. *Getting to Know Desktop GIS.* Redlands, CA: 1995.

ESRI, Inc. *Getting Started User's Guide.* Redlands, CA: 1994
——. *ARC/INFO Data Management.* Redlands, CA: 1994.

Maguire, David J., M.F. Goodchild, D.W. Rhind. *Geographical Information Systems: Principles and Applications.* John Wiley & Sons: 1991.

Masser, Ian, and Michael Blakemore (Eds). *Handling Geographical Information and Potential Applications.* John Wiley & Sons: 1991

Rhind, D. "Personality as a Factor in the Development of a Discipline: The Example of Computer-Assisted Cartography." *American Cartographer* 15, 3 (1988): 277-89.

Rhind, D., and H. Mounsey. *Understanding GIS.* London: Taylor and Francis, 1989.

Tomlinson, R. F. "The Impact of the Transition from Analogue to Digital Cartographic Representation." *American Cartographer* 15, 3 (1988): 246-61.
——. "Geographic Information Systems—A New Frontier." Proceedings of the International Symposium on Spatial Data Handling, Zurich, 1984.

Lesson 2 Geographic data concepts

Your first step in a GIS project is to create a digital map database. To
automate maps, you must be explicit about which information to
store, how to structure and record the data, and how you expect to use
the map database. Your GIS has a data model for representing maps
in the computer. Once you understand how digital maps are created
and stored, you can begin building a database to support your project.

Here are the specific topics addressed in this lesson:

- The two basic types of map information: spatial and descriptive

- The major geographic feature types: point, lines, and polygons

- How geographic features are stored in the computer as x,y
  coordinates

- Topology, and why it is important

- How the computer stores descriptive map information in a tabular
  database

- How a common identifier links spatial data and descriptive data

These constitute the basic structure allowing the GIS to perform the
types of problem-solving tasks presented in the previous lesson. By
the end of this lesson, you will complete the background research you
need to begin your project.

The estimated time needed to complete this lesson is 2 hours.

Basic map concepts

There are two basic types of map information:

- Spatial information, which describes the location and shape of geographic features and their spatial relationships to other features

- Descriptive information abut the features

map features   Maps convey information by representing features with graphic map components. Points represent locational information about features such as wells and telephone poles; lines represent linear features such as roads, streams, and pipelines; and areas represent features such as lakes, county boundaries, and census tracts.

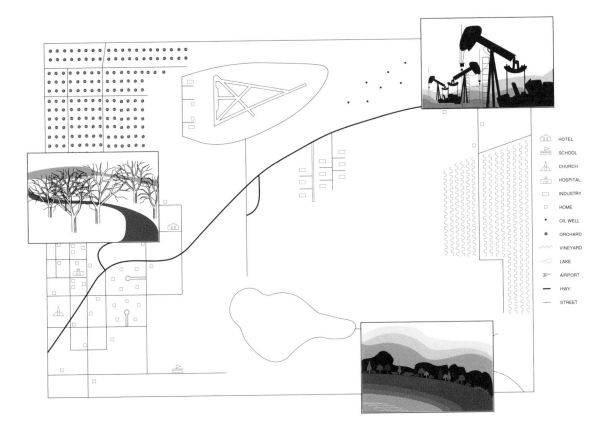

point feature

A discrete location, usually depicted by a special symbol or label, represents a point feature. It defines a map object whose boundary or shape is too small to be shown as a line or area. Points also represent locations that have no area, such as the elevation of mountain peaks.

line feature

A line feature is a set of ordered coordinates that, when connected, represent the linear shape of a map object too narrow to display as an area. Or, it could be a feature that has no width, such as a contour line. In ARC/INFO, lines are referred to as *arcs*.

area feature

An area feature is a closed figure whose boundary encloses a homogeneous area, such as a state, county, or water body.

spatial relationships

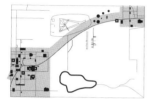

Maps also graphically represent spatial relationships between map features but depend on the map reader to interpret them. For example, you can look at a map and tell whether a city is next to a lake; find the relative distance along roads between two cities (as well as the shortest path to take); identify the nearest hospital and the streets used to drive there; estimate the elevation of a lake from the surrounding contour lines; and so on. The map does not represent this kind of information explicitly. Instead, you must derive or interpret these spatial relationships from the map graphics.

symbols and labels depict descriptive information

As graphic displays, maps represent feature locations and their characteristics meaningfully so that interpretations can be made easily. The characteristics of map features (i.e., their attributes) are represented as graphic symbols. For example, roads are drawn with various line widths, patterns, colors, and labels to represent different types; streams are drawn with blue lines and are labeled with their names; hospital locations are depicted using a special symbol such as ✚; lakes are shaded blue; forested areas, green; and so on. In this way, geographic features can be displayed along with their associated descriptive data. In the next selection, you will see how a digital map database stores such information.

Storing geographic data

A digital map database consists of two types of information: spatial and descriptive. The computer stores a series of files that contain either the spatial or descriptive information about the map features. The power of a GIS lies in its ability to link these two types of data and maintain the spatial relationships between the map features.

Maps
(spatial data)

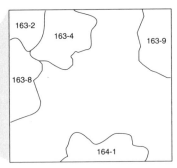

Forest stands have characteristics such as area, type, average height and harvest date.

Descriptive information
(tabular data)

STAND-NO	TYPE	AVE.HEIGHT	HRVST.DATE
163-2	WP	50	1993
163-4	DF	30	1995
163-8	WP	80	1989
163-9	WP	65	1991
164-1	MX	35	1996

Graphic data/Tabular data integration

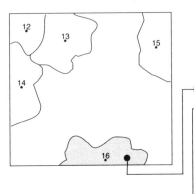

AREA	PERIMETER	STAND#	STAND-ID	STAND-NO
205	1331	2	12	163-2
355	2022	3	13	163-4
320	1931	4	14	163-8
240	1402	5	15	163-9
220	1600	6	16	164-1

STAND-NO	TYPE	AVE.HEIGHT	HRVST.DATE
163-2	PINE	50	1993
163-4	FIR	30	1995
163-8	PINE	80	1989
163-9	PINE	65	1991
164-1	MIXED	35	1996

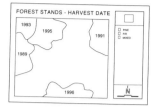

Integrating graphic and tabular data opens the way for powerful new ways of looking at and analyzing data. You can access information in the tabular database through the map, or you can create maps based on the information in the tabular database. In the example on the previous page, for instance, you could use the computer's screen cursor to point to a forest stand on the map and display a list of all relevant descriptive information. Conversely you could create a map of forest stands displaying each according to its harvest date. To access and display this data, the computer must store both the graphic and tabular data in formats it can recognize and retrieve.

representing maps in the computer

Features on the earth's surface are mapped on flat, two-dimensional maps as point, lines, and areas. An x,y (Cartesian) coordinate system is used to reference map locations to ground locations.

In this example, a building location is represented as a single x,y coordinate pair (2,3); a road becomes a line, represented by a series of connected coordinate pairs; and a lake is represented as a series of coordinates defining an enclosed polygon.

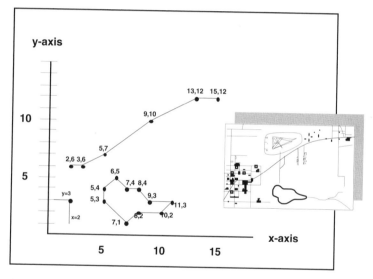

Representing points, lines, and areas on an x,y plane

Each point is recorded as a single x,y location. Lines (arcs) are recorded as a series of ordered x,y coordinates. Areas are recorded as a series of x,y coordinates defining arcs that enclose the area. (This is the origin of the term *polygon*, which means many-sided figure.) By using x,y coordinates, you can represent points, lines, and polygons as a list of coordinates instead of as a picture or graph. In the figure above, for example, the coordinate pair 2,3 represents a point location; the coordinate pairs 2,6 3,6 5,7 9,10 13,12 and 15,12 represent an arc; and the coordinate pairs 6,5 7,4 8,4 9,3 11,3 10,2 8,2 7,1 5,3 5,4 and 6,5 represent a polygon.

Notice how the first and last coordinates of a polygon are the same; a polygon always closes. Conceptually, these coordinate lists represent how map features are stored in a computer as sets of x,y digits (from here comes the term *digitize*, used to refer to automating map data).

The coordinates shown so far represent *page units*, such as inches or centimeters, used to measure a distance on the map or find an x,y location using a ruler. But maps usually represent real-world coordinates that have been projected on a flat surface. These coordinates represent a real location on the earth's surface in one of several coordinate systems.

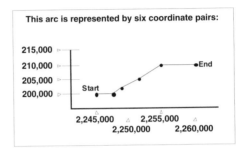

x	y
2,244,674	200,000
2,247,874	200,000
2,248,362	203,118
2,252,932	206,176
2,254,683	209,897
2,261,102	209,897

In this example, the real-world coordinates are projected into a coordinate system called Universal Transverse Mercator (UTM). The units are meters. Other commonly used map projections are Lambert Conic Conformal and Albers Conic Equal-Area with x ,y coordinates measured in feet or meters. Latitude-longitude is a commonly used geographic reference system. It isn't, however, a map projection because it measure angles from the center of the earth (in degrees, minutes, and seconds) rather than distances on the earth's surface. Lesson 7 discusses coordinate systems and map projections in more detail.

representing multiple features

It's easy to see how the computer stores coordinates for one feature. If you have many features, each can be assigned a sequence number or identifier. Then coordinates can be recorded for each feature by keeping a sequence number with the list of coordinates for each feature; for example,

Points

Point number	x,y coordinates
1	2,4
2	3,2
3	5,3
4	6,2

Lines (Arcs)

Line number	x,y coordinates
1	1,5 3,6 6,5 7,6
2	1,1 3,3 6,2 7,3

Polygons

Polygon number	x,y coordinates
1	2,4 2,5 3,6 4,5 3,4
	2,4
2	3,2 3,3 4,3 5,4 6,2
	5,1 4,1 4,2 3,2

Define map features

Connect the dots surrounding each shaded polygon in the diagram below to define the border of the polygon. As you draw to each dot, record the x,y pair for the dot in the table below. Use the graph to determine the x- and y-coordinates. Remember that polygons must close, so you must connect from the last dot back to the first. (See Appendix D for the exercise answers.)

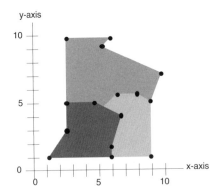

Polygon	x,y pairs
1	
2	
3	

END

what is topology? So far you've learned how points, lines, and polygons can represent map features. However, as you learned at the beginning of this lesson, your mind interprets additional information from maps about the spatial relationships between features. For example, you can trace a route along a street map to find your way from an airport to a hotel; likewise, you can identify two parcels of contiguous land and the street along which they are located.

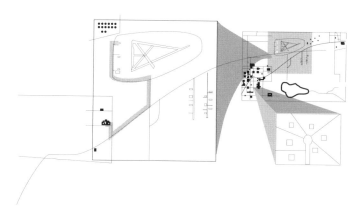

You interpreted these relationships by identifying connecting lines along a path, by defining the areas enclosed within these lines, and by identifying contiguous areas.

In digital maps, such spatial relationships are depicted using topology. Topology is a mathematical procedure for explicitly defining spatial relationships. The principle in practice is simple. Topology expresses different types of spatial relationships as lists of features (e.g., as area is defined by the arcs comprising its border).

The ability to create and store topological relationships has a number of advantages. Topology stores data more efficiently. This allows processing of larger data sets and faster processing. When topological relationships exist, you can perform analyses such as modeling the flow through connecting lines in a network, combining adjacent polygons that have similar characteristics, and overlaying geographic features.

The three major topological concepts of ARC/INFO are:

■ Arcs connect to each other at nodes (connectivity)

■ Arcs that connect to surround an area define a polygon (area definition)

■ Arcs have direction and left and right sides (contiguity)

connectivity

Arc-node topology

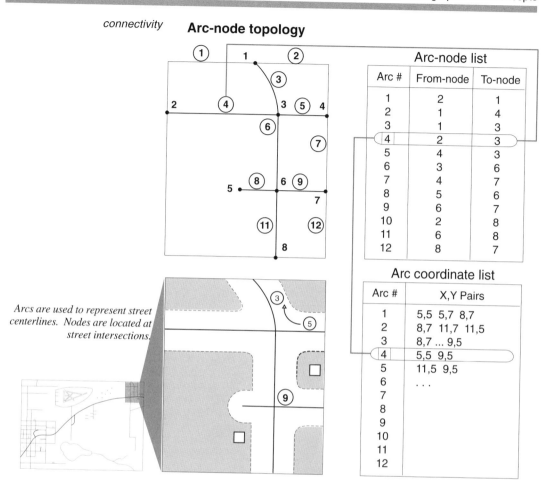

Arc-node list

Arc #	From-node	To-node
1	2	1
2	1	4
3	1	3
4	2	3
5	4	3
6	3	6
7	4	7
8	5	6
9	6	7
10	2	8
11	6	8
12	8	7

Arc coordinate list

Arc #	X,Y Pairs
1	5,5 5,7 8,7
2	8,7 11,7 11,5
3	8,7 ... 9,5
4	5,5 9,5
5	11,5 9,5
6	. . .
7	
8	
9	
10	
11	
12	

Arcs are used to represent street centerlines. Nodes are located at street intersections.

The points (x,y pairs) along the arc, called *vertices*, define the shape of the arc. The endpoints of the arc are called *nodes*. Each arc has two nodes: a from-node and a to-node. Arcs join only at nodes. By tracking all the arcs that meet at any node, ARC/INFO knows which arcs connect. In the illustration above, arcs 3, 4, 5, and 6 all join at node 3. With this information, the computer knows that it is possible to travel along arc 5 and turn onto arc 3 because they share a common node (3), but it's not possible to turn directly from arc 5 onto arc 9 because arc 5 and arc 9 don't share a common node.

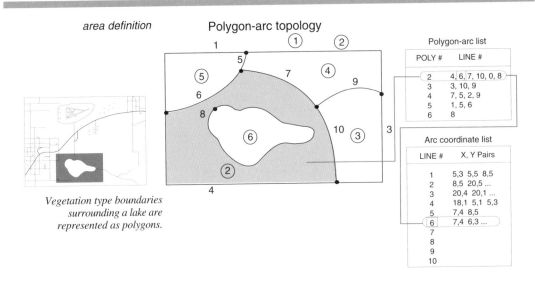

area definition

Polygon-arc topology

Polygon-arc list

POLY #	LINE #
2	4, 6, 7, 10, 0, 8
3	3, 10, 9
4	7, 5, 2, 9
5	1, 5, 6
6	8

Arc coordinate list

LINE #	X, Y Pairs
1	5,3 5,5 8,5
2	8,5 20,5 ...
3	20,4 20,1 ...
4	18,1 5,1 5,3
5	7,4 8,5
6	7,4 6,3 ...
7	
8	
9	
10	

Vegetation type boundaries surrounding a lake are represented as polygons.

Polygons are represented as a series of x,y coordinates that connect to enclose an area. Some systems store polygons in this format. ARC/INFO, however, stores the arcs defining the polygon, rather than a closed set of x,y pairs. A list of the arcs that make up each polygon is also stored and used to construct the polygon when necessary (for example, to draw the polygons). In the illustration above, arcs 4, 6, 7, 10, and 8 comprise polygon 2. (The 0 before the 8 indicates that this arc creates an island inside polygon 2.)

Though an arc may appear in the list of arcs for more than one polygon (in the illustration above, arc 6 appears in the list for polygons 2 and 5), each is stored only once. Storing each arc only once reduces the amount of data in the database and also ensures that the boundaries of adjacent polygons don't overlap.

contiguity

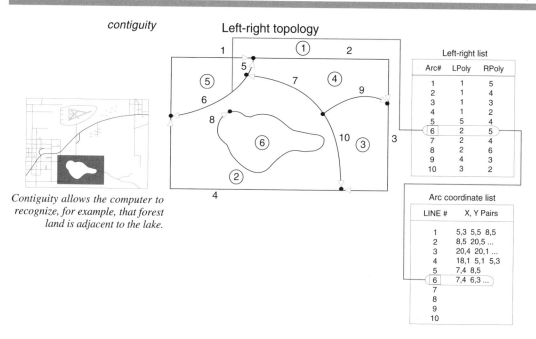

Contiguity allows the computer to recognize, for example, that forest land is adjacent to the lake.

Because every arc has direction (a from-node and a to-node), ARC/INFO maintains a list of the polygons on the left and right sides of each arc. Polygons sharing a common arc are adjacent. In the illustration above, polygon 2 is on the left of arc 6, and polygon 5 is on the right. So, we know that polygons 2 and 5 are adjacent. Notice that the label for polygon 1 is outside the boundary of the area. This polygon is called the *external* or *universe polygon*, and represents the area outside all the polygons in your map.

EXERCISE

Generate topology

The map of roads below shows seven numbered nodes (the circled numbers). Use the table to list the from-node and to-node of each arc. (See Appendix D for the exercise answers.)

Roads map

Arc	From-node	To-node
1		
2		
3		
4		
5		
6		

Note that one or more arcs can share a node; but by definition, a node cannot exist without an arc. Now list the arcs you would traverse to get from node 6 to node 1. Also, indicate your direction of travel across each arc (i.e., beginning at the from-node and traveling to the to-node, or vice versa). This demonstrates arc connectivity.

Path from Node 6 to Node 1

Arc #	5				
Direction	–				

+ = from- to to-node
– = to- to from-node

The next part of this exercise illustrates area definition and contiguity for the polygon map below. Using the first table, define each polygon (circled numbers) by listing the arcs that connect to create it. Record the number of each arc. Then in the second table, for each arc, list the polygons on the left and right sides. Arrows indicate the direction of the arcs.

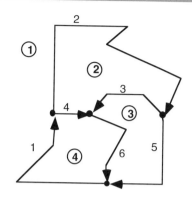

polygon # of arcs   list of arcs

polygon	# of arcs	list of arcs
2		
3		
4		

arc   left polygon   right polygon

arc	left polygon	right polygon
1		
2		
3		
4		
5		
6		

END

organizing map information So far, you have seen how geographic data is stored as a series of x,y coordinate pairs representing points, lines, and polygons. You have also seen how topology makes explicit the relationships between these features. Now, let's take a look at how this information is organized.

Map features are logically organized into sets of layers or *themes* of information. A base map can be organized into layers such as streams, soils, wells, administrative boundaries, and so on. Additionally, smaller areas, commonly corresponding to paper map sheets, can often be spatially combined into larger units called *study areas*.

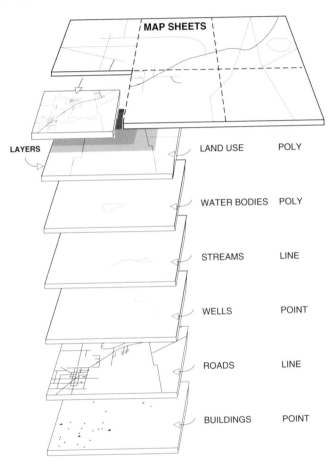

MAP SHEETS

LAYERS

LAND USE   POLY

WATER BODIES POLY

STREAMS   LINE

WELLS   POINT

ROADS   LINE

BUILDINGS   POINT

ARC/INFO coverages Each layer in ARC/INFO is called a *coverage*. A coverage consists of topologically linked geographic features and their associated descriptive data stored as an automated map; for example,

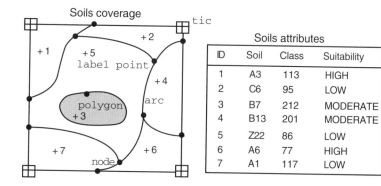

We have already discussed arcs, nodes, and polygons. Additional coverage features include label points and tics.

point features and label points Points serve two functions in ARC/INFO. In a point coverage, they represent point features such as wells, students, or crime incidents. As *label points*, they serve to identify (label) each polygon in a polygon coverage. A label point is the link between a polygon and its associated attributes.

tics *Tics* are points that represent locations on the earth's surface for which real-world coordinates are known. Coverages use a common set of tics so that layers register to each other and to adjacent map sheets.

V FYI   Although arcs, nodes, labels, and polygons appear most
frequently, there are additional feature classes
that can be present in a coverage. The table on the following page
summarizes some of these. Which set of features a coverage contains
depends on the type of geographic phenomena being modeled. The
chart below briefly describes the types of phenomena each feature
class can model.

Feature class	Application and use	Examples
Arcs	Linear features	Streets, contours, streams, sewers, power lines, gas lines
Nodes	Points along linear features	Valves on pipelines, intersections on streets, power poles, manhole covers
Label points	Point locations	Well sites, mountain peaks
Polygons	Area features	Soil units, land use, parcels, building footprints, forest stands, ownership
Regions	Overlapping area features	Parcel histories, wildlife inventories
Tics	Geographic registration and control	Registration for digitizing
Annotation	Feature labels	Street names, place names on road maps
Links	Rubber sheeting and adjustment	Edgematching map sheets, feature snapping, datum adjustments
Routes	Linear features	Streets, contours, streams, sewers, power lines, gas lines, and street addresses
Sections	Define route features	–
Coverage Extent	Defines map extent	–

ARC/INFO Data Management describes coverages in more detail and
provides examples of coverage designs.

Summary table of coverage features

Feature class	Description	Attribute table	Example
Arc	A line defined by an ordered set of x,y coordinates. Represents linear features, polygon boundaries.	AAT	
Node	The endpoints of an arc, or the point where two or more arcs connect.	NAT	
Label point	A point defined by an x,y coordinate—a point features or the User-IDs of a polygon.	PAT	+ 23
Polygon	An area defined by the arcs that make up its boundary, including arcs defining islands inside. A label point is used to assign a User-ID.	PAT	
Region	An area made up of polygon features.	PAT. subclass	Region 1 = Polys 1 & 2 Region 2 = Polys 2 & 3
Tic	A geographic control point used to register and transform the coordinates in a coverage.	TIC	
Annotation	A text string describing a geographic feature. Shape points are used to position and draw annotation.	TAT.subclass	
Route	A linear feature composed of one or more arcs or parts of arcs.	RAT.subclass	
Section	An arc or portion of an arc used to define a route. The building blocks of routes.	SEC.subclass	

EXERCISE

Organize the data

Identify the individual layers in this map and indicate the feature type (point, line, or polygon) for each. For example, one layer is lakes, a polygon feature. Record your answers below the map. (See Appendix D for the exercise answers.)

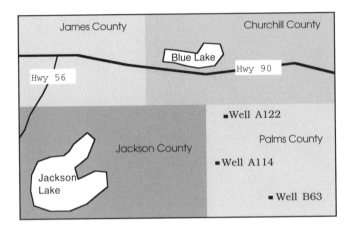

Layer   Feature type

_____   _____

_____   _____

_____   _____

_____   _____

END

Now that you're familiar with how geographic data is stored and organized, let's take a closer look at how the computer handles descriptive data.

*representing descriptive
data in the computer*

The computer stores descriptive *attributes* associated with map features similarly to the way it stores coordinates. Attributes are stored as sets of numbers and characters. For example, the attributes for a set of lines representing roads might include:

Road type -   1 = divided highway
                       2 = arterial or collector roads
                       3 = major roads
                       4 = residential streets
                       5 = unpaved

Surface material -   concrete
                       asphalt
                       gravel

Width -   measured in feet
Number of lanes -   count of lanes
Name -   the name of each road

The computer stores the descriptors for each road segment (arc) as a string of values in a previously defined format, such as

```
2  Asphalt  48  4  N. Main St
```

These might be the attributes of an arterial road (2) paved with asphalt, 48-feet wide, with four lanes, and named N Main St. The name or description of each attribute can also be stored; for example,

ROAD-TYPE	SURFACE	WIDTH	LANES	NAME
2	Asphalt	48	4	N Main St

Given many features, one set of attributes is stored for each.

ROAD-TYPE	SURFACE	WIDTH	LANES	NAME
2	Asphalt	48	4	N Main St
1	Concrete	60	4	Hwy 42
4	Asphalt	32	2	Elm St

feature attribute tables   ARC/INFO stores the descriptive information for a feature in an INFO data file, a tabular data file in which a *record* stores all the information about one occurrence of a feature (in this case, a point, arc, or polygon), and an *item* stores one type of information (i.e., attribute information) for all features in the database. These data files are known as *feature attribute tables*.

Feature attribute table

FEATURE-NO	ROAD-TYPE	SURFACE	WIDTH	LANES	NAME
1	2	Asphalt	48	4	N Main ST
2	2	Asphalt	48	4	N Main ST
3	2	Asphalt	48	4	N Main ST
4	1	Concrete	60	4	Highway 42
5	1	Concrete	60	4	Highway 42
6	4	Asphalt	32	2	Elm ST

Record ◀

Item

FYI   ARC/INFO can also access data stored in such sophisticated relational database management systems as ORACLE, INGRES, SYBASE, and INFORMIX. See the references at the end of this lesson for information on these interfaces.

connecting features and attributes   As we discussed earlier, the power of GIS lies in its link between the graphic (spatial) data and the tabular (descriptive) data. There are three noteworthy characteristics of this connection:

- There is a one-to-one relationship between features on the map and the records in the feature attribute table.

- The link between the feature and its record is maintained through a unique numerical identifier assigned to each feature. (For polygons, the identifier is assigned by the polygon's label point.)

Understanding GIS—The ARC/INFO Method

■ The unique identifier is physically stored in two places: in the files that contain the x,y coordinate pairs and with the corresponding record in the feature attribute table.

ARC/INFO automatically creates and maintains this connection. For example, consider the coordinates and attributes for the following set of features:

Roads map

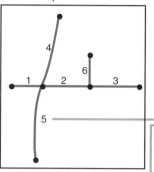

Feature coordinates

FEATURE-NO	X,Y pairs				
1	3,5	5,5			
2	5,5	8,5			
3	8,5	11,5			
4	6,9	5,8	5,7	5,6	5,5
5	5,5	4,4	4,1		
6	8,5	8,7			

Feature attributes

FEATURE-NO	ROAD-TYPE	SURFACE	WIDTH	LANES	NAME
1	2	Asphalt	48	4	N Main ST
2	2	Asphalt	48	4	N Main ST
3	2	Asphalt	48	4	N Main ST
4	1	Concrete	60	4	Highway 42
5	1	Concrete	60	4	Highway 42
6	4	Asphalt	32	2	Elm ST

Notice how both the coordinate records and the attribute records share a common element: the feature number. The feature number associates the attributes with the feature coordinates maintaining a one-to-one correspondence between the coordinate records and the attribute records. Once this connection is established, you can query the map to display attribute information, or create a map based on the attributes stored in the feature attribute table.

the relate and join relational operators

The concept described above applies to more than just keeping track of features and their attributes. You can connect any two tables if they share a common attribute. A *relate* uses a common item to establish temporary connections between corresponding records in two tables. In a relate, each record in one table is connected to a record in another table that shares the same value for a common item. A relate has the effect of making a feature attribute table 'wider' by temporarily adding feature attributes that aren't actually stored in the feature attribute table; for example,

PARCEL-NO	OWNER
11-115-001	BROWN, D.
11-115-002	GREENE, J.
11-115-003	SMITH, L.

PARCEL-NO	ZONING	LEGAL-AREA
11-115-001	R1	12,001
11-115-002	R2	15,775
11-115-003	COMM	19,136

Whereas a relate temporarily connects two attribute tables, a *relational join* relates and merges two attribute tables using their common item.

PARCEL-NO	OWNER	ZONING	LEGAL-AREA
11-115-001	BROWN, D.	R1	12,001
11-115-002	GREENE, J.	R2	15,775
11-115-003	SMITH, L.	COMM	19,136

ARC/INFO can relate or join an INFO data file containing descriptive attributes, as you saw in the previous section. If a relate is used, the related tabular data file can be maintained and updated separately. For example, records in tax assessor files can be related to a map of parcels containing unique numbers for each parcel. For TIGER coverages of streets, census data about tracts can be related to polygons using the tract numbers contained in both.

Although conceptually simple, relate and join operations are fundamental to GIS. They are used often. For example, when a spatial overlay is performed, each new output feature has attributes of both sets of input features used to create it. In essence, polygon overlay is a 'spatial join'. In this case, records are matched based on the location of their associated geographic features, rather than using a common item in two tables.

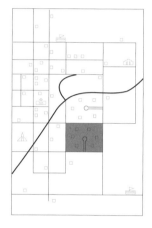

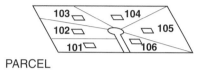

PARCEL

ID	ZONING
101	RES
102	RES
103	RSE
104	COM
105	IND
106	COM

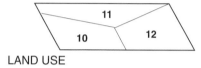

LAND USE

ID	LANDUSE
10	RES
11	COM
12	IND

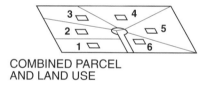

COMBINED PARCEL
AND LAND USE

ID	ZONING RES	LANDUSE
1	RES	RES
2	RES	RES
3	RES	COM
4	COM	COM
5	IND	IND
6	COM	IND

In the illustration above, a parcels layer with a zoning attribute is combined with a land use layer. This creates a new table containing attributes from both layers, which makes it easy to see discrepancies between zoning and use for each parcel.

During map display, features can be drawn using symbols contained in a related file. For example, you could classify the types of land use as residential (100), commercial (200), and industrial (300) with each type having a corresponding symbol number in a related table. Now when the map is drawn, each land use polygon is uniquely shaded based on its type of land use.

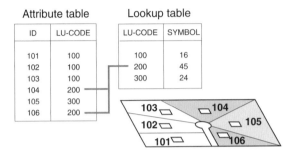

In this type of many-to-one relate, many records in one table might relate to a single record in another table. This reduces the amount of space needed to store data.

Use the identifier to connect features with their attributes and to relate two tables

In the first part of this exercise, you will connect descriptive attributes with their corresponding geographic features. Then you will perform a manual relate between two INFO data files.

Using the PARCEL coverage, complete the descriptive information in the boxes connected to the three parcels. Refer to the Assessor's Parcel List for the attribute information. Notice that, in this case, the PARCEL-ID is used to relate the parcel to the attributes. (See Appendix D for the exercise answers.)

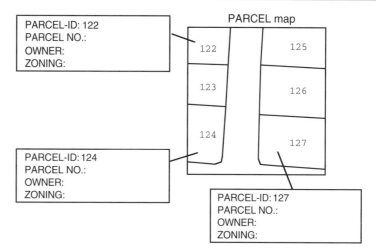

PARCEL map

PARCEL-ID: 122
PARCEL NO.:
OWNER:
ZONING:

PARCEL-ID: 124
PARCEL NO.:
OWNER:
ZONING:

PARCEL-ID: 127
PARCEL NO.:
OWNER:
ZONING:

Assessor's Parcel List

PARCEL-ID	PARCEL NO.	OWNER	ZONING
122	1011-23-446	Jones Title	R-2
123	1011-23-440	Jones Title	R-1
124	1011-23-472	R. Smith	R-2
125	1011-23-547	S. Brown	R-2
126	1011-23-511	J. Stevens	C-1
127	1011-23-455	R. Davies	C-1

Now relate these tables by drawing arrows to connect common parcel numbers; that is, use the parcel number as the relate item.

STREET	VALUE	PARCEL NO.
Orange	101,000	1011-23-547
Lemon	145,000	1011-23-455
Orange	98,500	1011-23-446
Orange	128,000	1011-23-511
Lemon	139,000	1011-23-472
Orange	100,500	1011-23-440

PARCEL NO.	OWNER	ZONING
1011-23-446	Jones Title	R-2
1011-23-440	Jones Title	R-1
1011-23-472	R. Smith	R-2
1011-23-547	S. Brown	R-2
1011-23-511	J. Stevens	C-1
1011-23-455	R.Davies	C-1

This is what the computer does when it performs a relate.

END

FYI

In addition to coverages, ARC/INFO employs a number of geographic data models for representing spatial information. These include grids, TINs, images, and CAD drawings. Each has important strengths for the types of geographic phenomena it can represent and has important utilities for application in a GIS database. The following table summarizes the geographic data models that ARC/INFO supports.

Geographic data set	Structure	Spatial objects	Attribute tables	Uses
Coverages 	vector arc-node topological georelational	label points arcs nodes polygons annotation routes sections tics	PAT AAT NAT PAT TAT RAT SEC TIC	• Cartographic database • Automation and update of spatial data • Linear feature modeling • Base maps for cartography • Spatial database management
Grids 	raster georelational	cells	VAT	• Spatial analysis and modeling • Spatial process modeling (runoff, fire spread, corridor calculation) • Surface representation • Scanning for data automation
Tins 	surface, triangulated irregular network	xyz nodes edges triangles	None	• Surface representation (especially terrain) • Surface modeling and display (e.g., contouring, visibility, 3-D display, profiles)

Geographic data set	Structure	Spatial objects	Attribute tables	Uses
Lattices +	surface, digital elevation model, grid, raster	xyz points	None	• Surface representation • Surface modeling and display (e.g., cut-fill, shaded relief, 3-D display, slope/aspect)
Images 	raster	pixels bands	None	• Images as map pictures • Images as attributes • Data automation • Display • Change detection • Multimedia databases
Drawings 	CAD	entities layers	None	• Drawings as map backdrops • Drawings as attributes

terminology review

arc—string of x,y coordinates; a line feature

attributes—tabular data associated with geographic features

coverage—automated map layer

feature attribute table—INFO data file storing descriptive map data

geographic features—the points, lines, and polygons that make up a map

item—one type of information about all entries in an INFO data file

label point—x,y coordinate used to identify a polygon

node—x,y coordinate; the endpoint of an arc

point—x,y coordinate; a point feature

polygon—area defined by a closed string of x,y coordinates

record—all information about a single entry in an INFO data file

relate—an operation that connects corresponding records of two tables

relational join—an operation that relates and merges two tables

spatial overlay—an operation that merges the features of two coverage layers into a new layer and relationally joins their feature attribute tables

tic—x,y coordinate used for registration

topology—a list of explicit relationships between geographic features (connectivity, contiguity, and definition of area)

vertex—x,y coordinate pair that occurs along an arc between the nodes and helps define the shape of the arc

Summary

In this lesson, you learned some of the major concepts of GIS data storage and, briefly, how ARC/INFO implements them.

GIS Concept	ARC/INFO Implementation
types of map information: spatial descriptive	point, arc, and polygon features character or numeric feature attributes
storing spatial data	points—x,y coordinate pair arcs—series of x,y coordinate pairs polygons—series of arcs enclosing an area
topology	connectivity—list of arcs that connect at each node area definition—list of arcs that define a polygon contiguity—left poly/right poly
storing descriptive data	records and items in a tabular database
associating spatial and descriptive data	unique identifier stored in two places: with the spatial data and with the descriptive data in the tabular database

You also briefly examined the important GIS concepts of relate and join, including the spatial join functionality of spatial overlay.

You'll put your knowledge to work in Lessons 3 through 9. Lesson 3 prepares you with a broad overview of an ARC/INFO project and a discussion of how to design your geographic database.

references for further reading

Aronoff, Stan. *Geographic Information Systems: a Management Perspective.* Ottawa, Canada: WDL Publications, 1989.

Bugayevskiy, Lev and John Synder. *Map Projections: A Reference Manual.* Bristol, PA: Taylor & Francis, 1995.

ESRI, *ARC/INFO Data Management:* Redlands, CA: 1994.
————. *Map Display, Query and Output* (online documentation). Redlands, CA: 1994.

Peucker, T. K., and N. Chrisman. "Cartographic Data Structures." *American Cartographer* 2,1 (1975).

Lesson 3 Starting your ARC/INFO project

In the last lesson, you saw how the computer stores map features as points, lines, and polygons according to an x,y coordinate system. You also learned how a tabular database stores descriptive information as attributes, and how a unique identifier associates these attributes with the map features.

You will now begin to apply these concepts to a GIS project. This lesson begins with an overview of the four major steps in a typical GIS project:

- Determine the objectives
- Build the database
- Perform the analysis
- Present the results of the analysis

The remainder of the lesson deals with the initial step in building the database: the database design. Specifically, you will examine aspects of

- Identifying the required spatial data layers
- Determining the required feature attributes
- Defining each attribute and its codes
- Registering coordinates using a master tic file
- Coding schemes
- Allocating storage

By the end of this lesson, you will be familiar with database design issues and with the data you will use in subsequent lessons to build your project database.

The estimated time needed to complete this lesson is 2 hours.

Project overview

A GIS project can be organized into a series of logical steps. Although many GIS projects you undertake will follow a similar sequence, be aware that many considerations influence the design and implementation of a specific project.

build the database

design the database

input spatial data

edit and create topology

input attribute data

manage and manipulate the data

analyze the data

present the results of the analysis

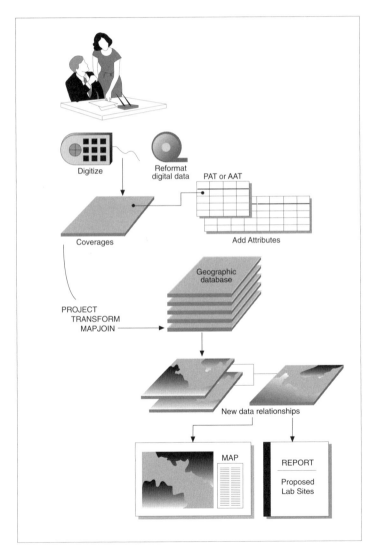

Digitize

Reformat digital data

PAT or AAT

Coverages

Add Attributes

Geographic database

PROJECT
TRANSFORM
MAPJOIN

New data relationships

MAP

REPORT

Proposed Lab Sites

Step 1

Determine the objectives of the project

To begin, determine the objectives of the project. Important issues to consider are:

- What is the problem to solve? How is it solved now? Are there alternative methods for solving the problem using your GIS?

- What are the final products of the project—reports, working maps, presentation quality maps? How frequently might these products be generated?

- Who is the intended audience for the final products—technicians, planners, the general public?

- Are there, or will there be, other uses for this same data? If so, what might the specific requirements be?

These issues affect the scope of the project and its implementation.

Step 2

Build the database

This is the most critical and often the most time-consuming part of the project. The completeness and accuracy of the database determines the quality of the analysis and final products. Here are the steps for developing a digital database:

- Design the database—determine the study area boundary, which coordinate system to use, which data layers (or coverages) you need, what features are in each layer, what attributes each feature type needs, and how to code and organize the attributes. This is the subject of this lesson.

- Automate the data. This, in turn, involves several steps:

    Get the spatial data into the database—digitize and/or convert data from other systems (Lesson 4).

    Make the spatial data usable—verify and edit errors, and then create topology (Lesson 5).

    Get the attribute data into the database—enter the attribute data into the computer, and associate the attributes with the spatial features (Lesson 6).

- Manage the database—put the spatial data into real-world coordinates, join adjacent coverages, and maintain the database (Lesson 7).

Step
3

Analyze the data

Analysis is where the true value of a geographic information system becomes apparent. A GIS efficiently performs analytical tasks that are extremely time-consuming, or even impossible, to do manually. With GIS, you can test alternative scenarios simply by making minor revisions in the analytic method. You can use your GIS in conjunction with your knowledge of the project objectives and the database you develop. We discuss geographic analysis in detail in Lesson 8.

Step
4

Present the results of the analysis

A GIS offers many options for creating customized maps and reports. The final products should relate directly to the objectives of the project and the intended audience. These you determined at the beginning of the project. Your skill at summarizing and presenting graphic and tabular results of your analysis helps determine how your analysis affects the decision-making process. Lesson 9 covers creating maps and reports.

Determining the objectives of the project

Through the rest of this workbook, you'll be working on a small GIS project to learn the functionality of ARC/INFO as well as the flow of a GIS project.

Note: Although the data used in the project represents real-world data, the location of the study area represents a fictitious area.

This is your introduction to the GIS project: A local university plans to construct a small lab and office building for performing research and extension projects in aquaculture. They've narrowed the area down to a coastal farming area near several small towns but need to select a specific site that meets the following requirements:

- At least 2,000 square meters in size.

- Must overlie soils suitable for construction of buildings.

- The site should not be forested (eliminating the cost of clearing land). And, because a regional agricultural preservation plan prohibits converting farmland in this area, the current land use must be brush land.

- A local ordinance designed to prevent rampant development allows new construction only within 300 meters of existing sewer lines.

- A recent national water quality act requires that no construction occur within 20 meters of streams.

Your task is to locate potential sites that meet these requirements. You also need to create a map that shows the potential sites along with the location of improved and semi-improved roads, and a report that lists each site with its area and estimated purchase cost.

Here is a summary of the criteria for the project:

Selection criteria for proposed lab site
☐ Choose soil types suitable for development
☐ Preferred land use is brush land
☐ Site must be beyond 20 meters of existing streams
☐ Site must be within 300 meters of existing sewer lines
☐ Site must contain an area of at least 2,000 square meters

Designing the database

The next step in developing a digital database is to design it. Spending time designing the database before automating it ensures that all the needed coverage features and attributes will be available when it's time to perform analysis and create final products. Modifying a database during analysis or mapping consumes time and money. Additionally, a well-designed database can ensure that the data is usable for future projects.

Many factors influence the design of a database. The process we present here is general and simplified for the purpose of this workbook; however, the issues we discuss here introduce you to more sophisticated database design.

Designing a database consists of three major steps: identify the geographic features, attributes, and data layers the project requires; define the storage parameters for each attribute; and ensure coordinate registration. Keep in mind that the available source data, whether map manuscripts or digital data, play an important part in the design process. You should do preliminary research to determine what source data is available for your study area.

identifying data layers and attributes

The first step of database design is to determine what data to include in the database. This is a three-part process:

- Identify geographic features and their attributes.
- Organize the data layers.
- Identify coverages to be automated.

identify geographic features and their attributes

First, identify the geographic features you need in the database and the attributes associated with each. This is determined by the analysis you wish to perform and the map products you want to create. Based on the criteria for the analysis and subsequent maps, each feature might require several attributes. For example, consider the following criteria:

- Identify soils suitable for development.
- Use land use codes to select brush land for development.
- Estimate a purchase cost based on area and the land use class.

Based on these criteria, you need soils polygons as one geographic feature, with suitability rating as an attribute, and land use polygons as another feature, with land use code and per-unit cost as attributes. The list of features and attributes looks like this:

Geographic feature	Feature class	Feature attributes
Soils	Polygons	Suitability
Land use	Polygons	Land use code
		Cost per hectare

If the map of the results should include land use polygons labeled by land use type, locations of roads drawn with line symbols to indicate their surfacing, and major streams, you would have to expand your list of geographic features and attributes.

Geographic feature	Feature class	Feature attributes
Soils	Polygons	Suitability
Land use	Polygons	Land use code
		Cost per hectare
		Land use type
Roads	Lines	Road code
Streams	Lines	Stream class

organize the data layers

Once you identify the needed features and their attributes, you can start to organize the geographic features into layers of data. A number of factors influence how you should organize layers in a geographic database. These factors differ with each application. Two of the most common considerations for organizing data layers are feature types (point, line, or polygon) and feature themes.

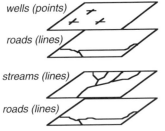

wells (points)

roads (lines)

streams (lines)

roads (lines)

Typically, layers are organized so that feature types (points, lines, and polygons) are stored in separate layers. For example, well sites represented by points might be stored in one layer, while roads represented by lines are organized in another layer.

Features can also be organized thematically by what they represent. For example, streams might be organized in one layer and roads in another. Although streams and roads are both line features, it makes sense to store them separately. For example, the attributes associated with a stream might include its name, stream class, and rate of flow, while attributes for roads might include a name, surface type, and number of lanes. Because their associated attributes differ significantly, the streams and roads should be stored in separate layers that reference the same geographic area.

The layers for the example presented above look like this:

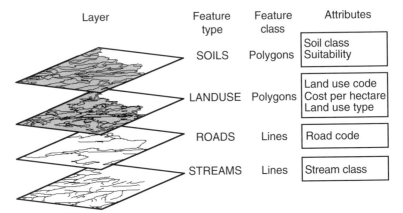

Layer	Feature type	Feature class	Attributes
SOILS	Polygons		Soil class / Suitability
LANDUSE	Polygons		Land use code / Cost per hectare / Land use type
ROADS	Lines		Road code
STREAMS	Lines		Stream class

identify coverages to be automated

The process of identifying the geographic features and their attributes, and organizing this information into layers determines what coverages your digital geographic database will contain. In some cases, the data layers will be available on separate maps (e.g., a map showing only parcel boundaries), or will already be in digital format on the computer. In other cases, you will have to automate layers from a single base map. In these instances, it is often easier to create separate map manuscripts for each layer, because the amount of information on the base map may make data capture more difficult. This is often done by tracing the needed features onto MYLAR® or some other dimensionally stable, transparent material.

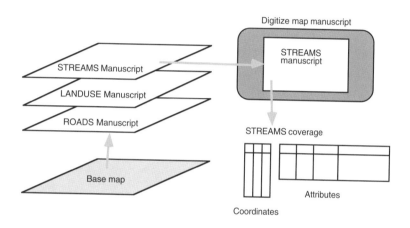

Once each map manuscript has been digitized, you'll have the needed geographic features stored as x,y coordinates in the digital database, along with the attributes in the coverage feature attribute table.

EXERCISE   **Identify the required data layers for the project**

Here again, is the summary of the selection criteria for the project:

Selection criteria for proposed lab site
☐   Choose soil types suitable for development
☐   Preferred land use is brush land
☐   Site must be beyond 20 meters of existing streams
☐   Site must be within 300 meters of existing sewer lines
☐   Site must contain an area of at least 2,000 square meters

You can translate each selection criterion into the need for a specific data layer with specific feature attributes (except for site area requirement—this criterion will be derived from a new layer resulting from the spatial join of the other layers). Based on the list of criteria given above, complete the following table. For example, the first criterion is to find sites with soils suitable for development. So, one of the layers will be SOILS, a POLYGON coverage. Fill in the remaining lines. This illustrates the process of identifying the data layers you need for the project. (See Appendix D for the exercise answers.)

Criterion	Layer	Feature Type	Feature Class

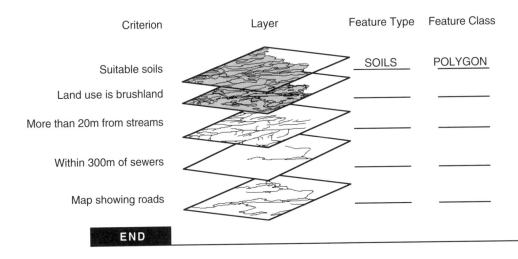

Criterion	Feature Type	Feature Class
Suitable soils	SOILS	POLYGON
Land use is brushland	_____	_____
More than 20m from streams	_____	_____
Within 300m of sewers	_____	_____
Map showing roads	_____	_____

END

defining each attribute

Once you determine the attributes needed by each layer in your database, you'll want to decide the specific parameters for each attribute and the types of values to store. Deciding now makes the task of building the data files to hold the attribute values much easier (as you will see in Lesson 6).

coding

You've seen how the computer stores attributes as numbers and characters. You must decide which attributes to store as numbers and which as characters. For example, if you want to label streets with their names, you must store the name as it should appear (e.g., N. Main St.). Similarly, for attributes representing a numeric value, such as street width or length, the actual value must be stored (e.g., 321.375).

Some attributes described by a character string are better represented as a code in the computer. If the attribute describes a class, it might be easier and more efficient to store a code for the class rather than a lengthy description. For example, you could store the character string 'Urban/Developed' by defining either a character code (UD) or a numeric code (100). Coding attributes makes it easier to select and draw features of a particular class. For example, the code could be used to look up a symbol number in another table, so that each feature having that code will be drawn using the same symbol.

Attribute table

AREA	ID	LU-CODE
4322	10	200
3901	11	300
5200	12	300
1698	13	100
2004	14	200

Lookup table

LU-CODE	SYMBOL	LABEL
100	16	Urban
200	45	Agriculture
300	24	Brushland

Also, attributes that have many repeating values are best represented using code values to reduce the database size.

FYI

As you design a database, remember that while you can group features into fewer classes at a later time, it is difficult to separate too few classes into more if they were not coded that way initially.

Numeric values that represent a range can also be stored as a code. For example, a coverage of polygons that represent slope classes of 0–10%, 11–30%, 31–45%, and over 45% are more easily represented in the computer by codes 1, 2, 3, and 4, respectively.

SLOPE	CODE
0-10	1
11-30	2
31-45	3
45+	4

allocating storage   In addition to deciding how to store each attribute, you must also determine how much storage space each requires. For example, determine the number of characters needed to store the street names by the longest street name. For numeric items, determine the number of required digits and decimal places. The overhead of storing large amounts of data is important. The less space each attribute uses results in smaller data files, less disk storage used on your computer, and faster processing times. We address these issues in more detail in Lesson 6.

building a data dictionary   A data dictionary is a list that maintains, for each coverage, the names of the attributes and a description of the attribute values (including a description of each code, if necessary). Having a data dictionary for your database is invaluable as a reference during the project as well as for transferring information to others.

Here is a sample data dictionary in table form:

Layer	Feature	Class	Attributes	Value	Description
	SOILS	Polygons	Soil-code		Abbreviation for soil type
			Suit	0	Unsuitable
				1	Poor suitability
				2	Moderate suitability
				3	Good suitability
	LANDUSE	Polygons	Lu-code	100	Urban
				200	Agriculture
				300	Brushland
				400	Forest
				500	Water
				600	Wetlands
				700	Barren
			Cost per hectare		Actual monetary value
	STREAMS	Lines	Strm-code	1	Major stream
				2	Minor stream
	SEWERS	Lines	Diameter		Actual diameter is stored
			Symbol	1	60 cm pipe
				77	45 cm pipe
	ROADS	Lines	Rd-code	1	Improved
				2	Semi-improved

coordinate registration

Once you've identified all the coverages your database requires, you should ensure that the coverages register correctly to each other. As you've seen, in most cases, your database consists of a number of coverages representing various features for the same geographic area. When you combine the data from one coverage with another (e.g., when overlaying two coverages to create a new one), the coincident data must match exactly. If the coordinate registration is close, but not exact, you'll experience offset problems: sliver polygons when performing overlays; ragged edges when generating maps; and inaccurate measurements when compiling data for reports.

For example, the LANDUSE and SOILS layers in the figure below represent the same geographic area, but each uses a different set of tics (coordinate registration points). So even minor errors in registration, introduced when the maps were automated, result in an offset between the layers.

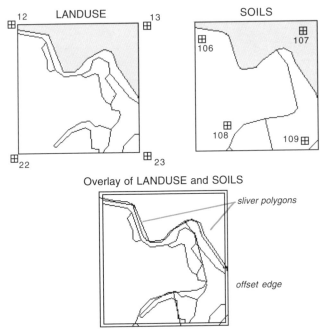

When the SOILS are overlaid on top of the LANDUSE polygons, the edges of the coverages don't match. Notice also the sliver polygons along the shoreline, which appears in both coverages.

FYI

If you have features that appear in more than one coverage (e.g., the study area boundary or a shoreline), it's a good idea to make a template coverage containing those features and create new coverages from the template. Then, you can add the features unique to each coverage.

Registering coordinates is a four-step process. First, you should make sure you have tic locations for which you can obtain accurate real-world coordinates. Second, to ensure accurate registration, make sure that you use the same tics for all coverages in your database when you create coverages. You'll see how to do this in Lesson 4. Next, use the real-world tic coordinates you obtained in the first step to create a coverage that contains only tics. Finally, transform the coverage from digitizer units to real-world coordinates using the tic coverage. This ensures that the coverages are in the same coordinate system and will overlay correctly. You'll do these last two steps in Lesson 7.

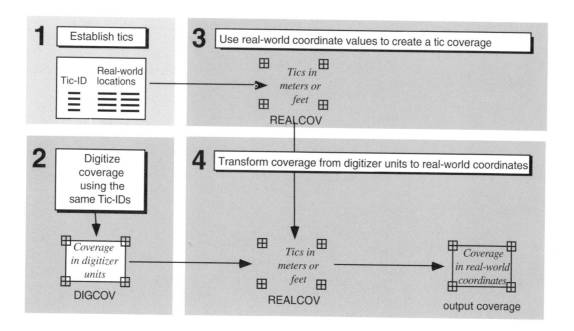

creating a master tic file

The first step in ensuring that coordinates register properly is to obtain valid tic coordinate locations. Although you won't actually use the tic coordinate values you record until you transform your coverages, it's important to identify the tic locations before you create the coverages. Trying to retrofit tics to existing coverages is time-consuming and introduces errors into the data.

One way of establishing the tic locations is to create a master tic file containing the ID, x-coordinate, and y-coordinate for each tic. Because the tics you create will later be used to transform the coverage into real-world coordinates, you'll want to make sure that you can identify tic locations for which real-world coordinates are known or can be determined. Often, the tics are located on a regular grid that is recorded on the base map, such as degrees of latitude and longitude.

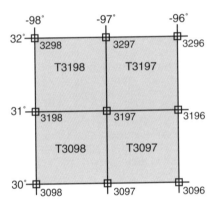

In this diagram, the geographic database spans four map sheets, each measuring 1° x 1°. To create the master tic file, first number each tic with a unique ID and determine its coordinates based on coordinate locations marked on the map. Then create a table with the ID, x-coordinate location, and y-coordinate location for each tic.

ID	x-coordinate	y-coordinate
3298	-98°	32°
3297	-97°	32°
3296	-96°	32°
3198	-98°	31°
.	.	.
.	.	.
.	.	.

If no previously defined tic locations (such as a corner of a grid) exist on the map manuscript, you'll have to create them. Tics should be placed at locations that can be readily identified on each manuscript when it is automated, such as a corner of the study area boundary. You should also make certain that you can obtain accurate real-world coordinate values for these locations. Once you have decided on the tic locations, indicate the location and ID on each manuscript to be automated. Then create the master tic file.

As we discussed in the previous lesson, latitude–longitude values are not measured in a Cartesian coordinate system. However, these are often the most readily available source of accurate measurements on the map manuscript. ARC/INFO lets you convert these measurements into a projection system that uses a Cartesian coordinate system. You'll see how to do this in Lesson 7, where you'll then use the projected tic locations to transform your coverage into real-world coordinates.

FYI

Many maps show coordinates in a projection other than the projection in which the map was created. As the illustration on page 7-11 shows, all map projections distort the Earth in some way such that lines of equal coordinate value can have different curvatures. In contrast to drawing straight lines across a map to connect coordinates on either side, graticule lines may be curved lines. For this reason, it is best to use grid intersections printed on the map when you derive coordinate values for tics in a projection other than the one in which the map was created. Lesson 7 goes into more detail about map projections.

EXERCISE   **Create a master TIC file**

Using the reference grid on page 1 of Appendix C, record the coordinate locations of the tics. Notice that, in this case, the grid is latitude–longitude and the tic locations are measured in degrees, minutes, and seconds. The coordinates for several locations on the edge of the map are indicated. Calculate the coordinates for the tics, remembering that each marker along the side of the map represents a distance of 15 seconds. Notice that some of the coordinates are positive and others are negative. In the table below, write in the x-coordinate value and the y-coordinate value, in degrees, minutes, and seconds, for each Tic-ID. (See Appendix D for the exercise answers.)

Tic-ID	x-coordinate	y-coordinate
12	-74	-41° 04' 30"
13		
14		
22		
23		
24		
32		
33		
34		

END

Starting the data automation project

Once you establish a solid design for the database, you can begin building it by collecting all the data you need for the project (i.e., the layers and attributes you identified in the design stage). You need to collect those layers that already exist in digital format, either as ARC/INFO coverages or in a format that converts to ARC/INFO. For those layers not available in digital format, you should obtain the best possible manuscript maps to automate.

workspace organization and naming conventions

Before you begin the database development, it's a good idea to set up a workspace organization to contain the coverages, files, and maps you will create. Also, now is the time to establish some conventions for naming coverages and files. These steps will help you efficiently manage the data for the project.

Typical workspace organization includes a project directory, under which are workspaces for each layer. For example, you may have a ROADS workspace, a SOILS workspace, a LAND workspace, and so on. Each workspace will contain the coverages and files for the data layer at each stage of the database development process. So you may have the newly created coverage, the coverage with topology created, the edited coverage, and so on.

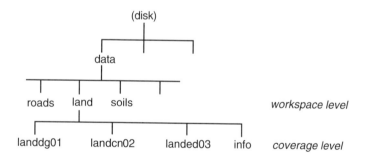

Coverages are accessed from the workspace level. In the illustration above, you would attach to the LAND workspace to display the LANDDG01 coverage.

Your project will proceed more efficiently if you establish, in the beginning, some conventions for naming coverages and files at each stage of the process. A naming convention provides you with an easy way to keep track of just where in the process a coverage is simply by reading its name; for example,

- LANDDG01—the newly digitized coverage
- LANDCN02—the coverage with topology created (i.e., it has been cleaned)
- LANDED03—the edited coverage with errors fixed

The same conventions can be used for each data layer type:

- LANDDG01—the newly digitized LANDUSE coverage
- SOILSDG01—the newly digitized SOILS coverage

backing up your data

You can save a lot of time and frustration by backing up your work daily onto storage media such as magnetic tape or diskettes. Back up final coverages undergoing extensive processing more often. This ensures that data is not lost due to computer malfunction or accidental deletion. Also, you should perform all processing on *copies* of existing coverages. Once a coverage is successfully processed, you can safely delete the original, duplicate coverage. This allows you to return to the previous step and to a usable coverage.

EXERCISE   **Review the available data for the project**

Review the available maps and digital data for your project. Because you only have one week to complete the project, look to existing sources of digital data first. A preliminary investigation of available data turns up the following sources:

- The local public works agency maintains a digital database of roads and sewers, which includes the entire study area and is in ARC/INFO format.

- The regional Parks and Recreation department has digitally mapped all the streams for the entire region. The data is not in ARC/INFO format, but their coordinates and attributes can be converted into an ASCII format and from there into ARC/INFO.

- The state soil conservation agency has recently made available soil maps for the county in ARC/INFO format. The university's Civil Engineering department has just acquired this data for the study area.

■ The university Landscape Architecture department has obtained land use maps of the area from the regional planning agency and previously digitized a portion of the site for an earlier agricultural lands study (which later formed the basis of a regional agricultural preservation plan). Only an area in the southeast portion of the study area, for which data was previously unavailable, was not digitized. Subsequently, a map manuscript was created for this area based on aerial photography.

The chart below shows the current status of each coverage in the project database. Completed processing steps for each coverage have been checked off.

Coverage name	Digitized/ converted	Topology created	Edited	Attributes added	Projected	Transformed to real-world coordinates	Mapjoined
SOILS	√	√	√	√	√	√	√
LANDUSE	☐	☐	☐	☐	☐	☐	☐
STREAMS	☐	☐	☐	☐	√	√	n/a
SEWERS	√	√	√	√	√	√	√
ROADS	√	√	√	√	√	√	√

You can see that you need to process the LANDUSE and STREAMS coverages. The other coverages are already in usable form. (Fortunately, they have all been projected into the same coordinate system, and will overlay correctly.) A copy of the chart is also included in Appendix C. Use it to track the progress of the coverages as you build the database. Simply check off each step you complete.

Before starting the exercise, you must make sure that the existing digital data is installed on your disk. If you have not already done so, refer to Appendix A for verifying data installation.

In addition to your data, you've obtained a prototype menu system developed by the Public Works department to perform display and query for the regional database. The system was developed using the ARC Macro Language (AML), ARC/INFO's programming language. You can use it to view the available digital data for the study area.

First start ARC/INFO. In UNIX, type **arc** at the system prompt. In Windows NT, click the ARC/INFO icon in the window manager.

UNIX   Arc: **% arc**
Windows NT   You are already in Arc

Now use the ARC/INFO &WORKSPACE directive to move to the workspace containing the data.

UNIX
Windows NT

```
Arc: &WORKSPACE /yourname/ugis/data
Arc: &WORKSPACE <drive>:\yourname\ugis\data
```

Copy the menu system from your AML directory to your DATA workspace.

UNIX
Windows NT

```
Arc: &sys cp ../aml/projdb.* .
Arc: &sys copy ..\aml\projdb.*
```

Type the following command to start the menu system, replacing <station_file> with either the name of your station file or (or simply type 9999). {COLOR | BW} refers to the type of shade symbols to use—color or black-and-white. Depending on whether you have a color or monochrome terminal, enter the appropriate choice.

```
Arc: &run projdb <station_file> {COLOR | BW}
```

ARCPLOT is initiated and the Pulldown menu appears. This menu has options for displaying and obtaining information about the individual layers in the database. To draw the LANDUSE coverage,

Select **Draw** and then choose **LANDUSE**.

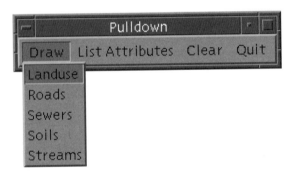

Each polygon is shaded according to the type of land use.

Color	Type
Light gray	Urban
Yellow	Agriculture
Orange	Brush land
Green	Forest
Blue	Water
Dark gray	Barren

Notice that the lower right corner of the study area is not included in this coverage. This is the portion of the LANDUSE coverage that you need to digitize from the map manuscript.

To view the attributes for the LANDUSE coverage,

Select **List Attributes** and choose **LANDUSE**.

All the attributes are listed on the screen. If the list requires more space than the window allows, select the appropriate option at the bottom of the window or use the scroll bar along the right side of the window to scroll the display. When you are done,

Select **Quit**

to close the attribute listing window.

You can display each coverage by making appropriate selections from the Draw column of the menu. You can also view the attributes by selecting the coverage name from the List Attributes column. Refer to Appendix B for a complete description of each coverage. Note that you cannot view the streams at this point because the streams data is not yet in ARC/INFO format.

When you finish viewing the coverages that are currently available in the database,

Select **Quit**

to leave the menu and end the display session.

END

Advanced topic—Building an application system

In this lesson, we described the steps involved in conducting a single GIS project, including developing a database specific to the project. In some cases, there is an economy of scale to be gained by developing an application system. This is a system consisting of a comprehensive database that can meet the needs of a variety of users within a specific geographic area. The database can be used not only for special projects, but for ongoing tasks.

Although activities differ between agencies within a geographic area, they share a common jurisdiction. Problems surface in a manual system when data needed to execute these tasks is located within a single department, making access difficult. Conversely, if each department maintains its own data, it can mean duplicate effort and inconsistent files. A properly planned and implemented application system provides separate users with different views of the same database and eliminates redundancy and inconsistency.

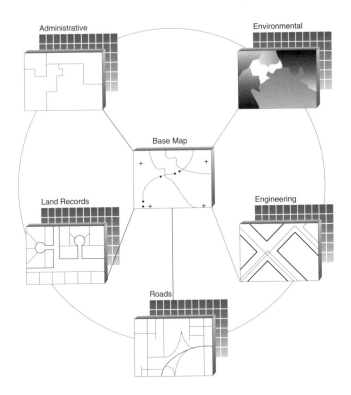

The first step in designing such a system is to thoroughly assess the users' needs. This might consist of interviews with potential users of the system to ensure that the data they require for their tasks is included. Once the needs have been determined, the design phase can proceed. Finally, a pilot project identifies any missing elements in the database design and allows for corrections before major time and resource commitments are made to automating the entire database.

Summary

concept review   You've seen how coverages and their associated feature attribute tables are the basic building blocks of your database. Each requirement of your project, whether for analysis or a specific product (map or report), translates directly into the need for one or more geographic features with specific attributes. The geographic features are created and stored as separate layers based on feature type (point, line, or polygon) and by logical feature groups (streams are separate from roads because they each have attributes specific to that feature class).

lesson summary   This lesson identified some of the general steps involved in performing a GIS project. These include

- Building the database
- Performing the analysis
- Presenting the results of the analysis

It also discussed considerations for developing a solid database design as the first step in the project.

Design step	Task
Define the scope of the project.	Determine the specific criteria for analysis and resulting maps.
Identify the geographic features and attributes.	Translate geographic features into a list of of coverage features and feature types.
Define the data layers and attributes.	Translate the criteria into a list of coverages and items.
Define the individual attributes.	Determine each item type, width, and code values; create data dictionary.
Establish coordinate registration.	Identify tics and create master tic file.
Organize the data automation project.	Create workspaces and coverage naming conventions.

references for further reading

Burrough, P.A. *Principles of Geographical Information Systems for Land Resources Assessment.* Oxford, England: Oxford University Press, 1986.

Date, C. J. *An Introduction to Database Systems,* Third edition. Reading, MA: Addison-Wesley Publishing Company, 1981.

Date, C. J. *Database: A Primer.* Reading, MA: Addison-Wesley Publishing Company, 1983.

DeMeus, Michael. *Fundamentals of Geographic Information Systems.* New York, NY: John Wiley & Sons, 1997.

ESRI, Inc. *ARC/INFO Data Management.* Redlands, CA, 1994.

Howe, D.R. *Data Analysis for Data Base Design.* London: Edward Arnold, Ltd., 1983.

Martin, J. *Managing the Data-Base Environment.* Englewood Cliffs, NJ: Prentice-Hall, 1983.

Robinson, A., J. Morrison, P. Muehrcke, A.J. Kimerling and S. Guptill. *Elements of Cartography*, Sixth edition. New York: John Wiley and Sons, 1995.

project status   At this point, the database design for the project is complete. In the next lesson, you'll begin automating the database.

workspace contents   The following chart shows the coverages and files now available in your DATA workspace.

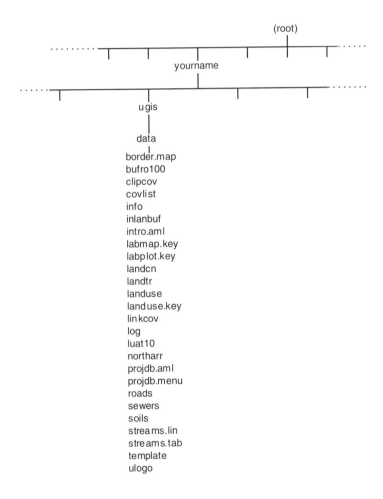

task summary   The following chart summarizes the steps for the project. The shaded lesson box in the left column indicates the portion of the project you've completed so far.

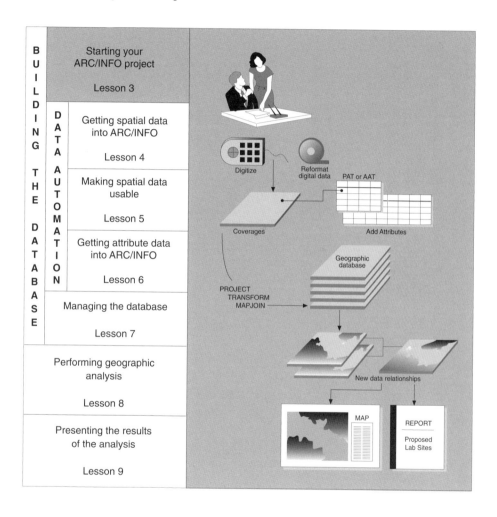

Lesson 4 Getting spatial data into ARC/INFO

The next step in building your database is automating the data; that is, converting features on a map to a digital format on the computer. In ARC/INFO, a digital map is called a *coverage*, and the process of capturing spatial data manually is called *digitizing*. To digitize effectively, you must train your eyes to see the data on a map in a different light. A lake will be digitized as a polygon, and the best place to begin capturing its outline might be an incoming stream.

Automating the spatial data on a map requires that you:

- Prepare manuscripts for automation
- Capture features from a map manuscript
- Visually evaluate the quality of the data captured

During this lesson, you'll create the spatial portion of a new coverage by digitizing it in ARCEDIT™ program. To capture data manually, you'll add the data you see, deleting mistakes as you go. ARCEDIT is an ARC/INFO program that can be used to digitize and edit data.

Coverages must be created for each data layer needed for a particular project. Of course, if this data has already been captured, you need only make sure that it's in the proper format. Previously digitized data, even in another system's format, might be used as an alternative source of data. Near the end of this lesson, you'll investigate some alternative data sources and explore how they can be used to create ARC/INFO coverages without digitizing.

By the end of this lesson, you'll have a digital version of the map manuscript, which you'll later correct and join to the existing land use coverage.

The estimated time needed to complete this lesson is 4 hours.

Data capture

Data on a map can be captured by digitizing each feature, one by one, or by using an electronic scanner to capture an entire sheet of features. Data in the form of known coordinate values can also be captured by typing in the x- and y-coordinates. Both of these options require some preparation of the data before the computer can properly interpret it. As this lesson progresses, you'll prepare a map sheet of data and then capture the coordinates by digitizing.

key terms

Before you begin to digitize, here is a brief introduction to some digitizing terms and the symbols used to represent them.

Terms	Symbol	Description
Arc	——	A line feature or the border of a polygon. An arc is defined by a from-node and a to-node and vertices in between.
Node	●	An arc endpoint. In many cases, the end of one arc marks the beginning of another, so it can be said that nodes also mark intersections.
Vertex	○	A point within an arc that provides its shape.
Pseudo node	◇	The point at which an arc connects to itself (a loop), or to only one other arc.
Dangling node	☐	An arc endpoint not connected to another arc.
Label point	+	Used either to represent a point feature or to identify a polygon.
User-ID	70	A number assigned to each feature. These values should be unique. Once established, the user can alter these values as needed.
Tic	⊞	A registration or geographic control point. These allow all coverage features to be registered to the same coordinate system.
RMS Error	0.004	The calculated difference between recorded and specified tic locations, expressed as a residual of the means squared. Values are usually just slightly greater than 0.000—the higher the value, the greater the error.

digitizing   Digitizing converts the spatial features on a map into digital format. Point, line, and area features that compose a map are converted into x,y coordinates. A single coordinate represents a point and a string of coordinates represents a line. One or more lines that outline an area, with a label point inside, identify the area (or polygon). So digitizing is a procedure for capturing a series of points and lines.

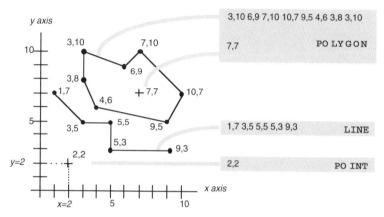

Spatial data can be displayed graphically or listed using x,y coordinates.

FYI   Label points are used for two different purposes: to represent point features and to identify the presence of a polygon. To avoid confusion, do not digitize both kinds of label points in the same coverage.

Digitizing involves manually tracing all features on a map. This can be demonstrated by taking any map manuscript and breaking it into its component parts—a number of points and lines. The spatial data in the mapped regions (polygons) shown below can be captured by digitizing five lines and five label points.

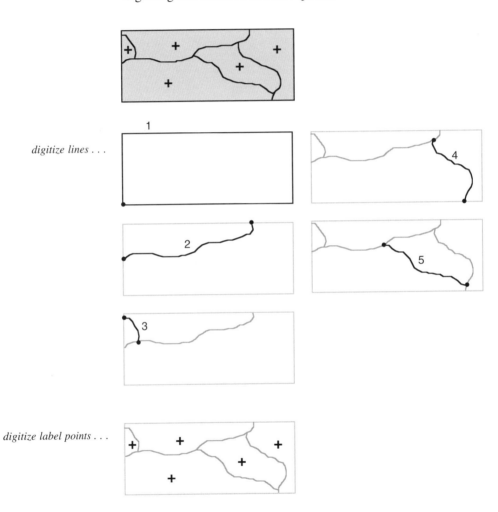

digitize lines . . .

digitize label points . . .

digitizing techniques   The most common digitizer used for mapping consists of a fine wire grid embedded in the surface of a table. Smaller digitizing tables are sometimes referred to as *digitizing tablets*.

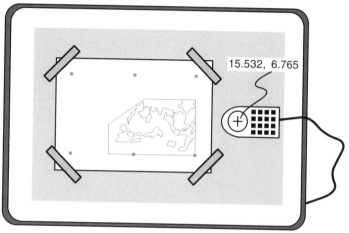

This diagram illustrates a map taped onto the surface of a digitizing tablet. The underlying electronic wire grid records the location of the keypad crosshairs and transmits it to the computer in the form of x,y coordinates.

To digitize, the map must be taped down to a digitizing table and the points and lines traced with a digitizer cursor or *keypad*. The keypad, so called in this workbook to avoid confusion with the screen cursor, records the position at which the crosshairs intersect.

▽FYI◁   The area of electrical sensitivity does not extend all the way to the edge of the digitizing table. No values are returned when you press a button on the keypad unless it is over the active area. So, to determine coordinate values, make sure your map is located within the active area (i.e., not too close to the edge of the table).

The buttons on the keypad perform programmed functions, such as recording a point or beginning a line. When a keypad button is pressed, the computer records the current x,y coordinate location of that position in digitizer units (usually centimeters or inches). This becomes the x,y coordinate of the point feature, or one of the points comprising a line or polygon.

An intersection forms whenever two or more lines meet at the same location. When digitizing, you may choose to input each intersection explicitly with a node, or you may opt to ignore intersections and input a number of longer lines. Either way is acceptable. Consider how you might digitize the outline of this coverage.

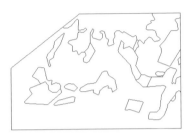

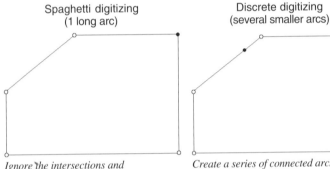

Spaghetti digitizing
(1 long arc)

Discrete digitizing
(several smaller arcs)

*Ignore the intersections and
digitize the outline as one long arc.*

*Create a series of connected arcs by
digitizing each intersection as a node.*

FYI *Spaghetti digitizing* is aptly named because intersections
are not explicitly identified as arcs are digitized. So,
the set of arcs overlap, much like spaghetti. This method is typically
used to define predominantly straight lines, such as outlines, grids,
and land use data. For precise features, or those that curve and twist,
discrete digitizing is preferred. Explicitly marking each intersection
provides greater coordinate accuracy.

Intersections not specifically identified during the digitizing process
are identified later in the automation process. Lesson 5 discusses how
intersections are created automatically.

Steps used to capture data by digitizing

To ensure that your maps are digitized most efficiently and accurately, here are four steps you should follow.

Step 1: Use good base maps
Step 2: Define your procedures
Step 3: Prepare your maps
Step 4: Digitize your maps

Step 1

Use good base maps

The quality of the map manuscripts from which you digitize directly affects the accuracy of your digital data. You should always get the most reliable, most current maps possible. Here are some guidelines:

■ Manuscripts should be in good condition, clean and readable, not torn or folded. This makes the manuscript easier to read, and ensures that feature locations can be digitized as accurately as possible.

■ Map materials such as paper are affected by climatic conditions, which sometimes distort features so much that they may not register between digitizing sessions. To minimize distortion, map manuscripts should be copied onto a stable material, such as MYLAR, that minimizes stretching and shrinking.

Step 2

Define your procedures

Determine how the maps will be digitized. Before starting a large project, you may want to digitize a small portion of one or more of your manuscripts to ensure that your procedures produce the desired result. Here are some guidelines:

■ Establish a standard sequence of procedures. For example, you may want all the arcs digitized before the points. The person digitizing should be familiar with the standard procedures and know where to get information and who to contact if they have a question. You may want to develop a project handbook that lists standard procedures and naming conventions.

■ Establish a sequence for digitizing features and map sheets so you can track which portions of the database have already been digitized. Using a tabular format to monitor the status of the database allows each map sheet to be marked off as the automation process is completed.

■ Establish standard naming conventions. As you saw in the last lesson, a coverage goes through a number of stages before it is complete. It's a good idea to identify each stage using a standard abbreviation. For example, if the first stage is digitizing, DG01 could be the standard suffix for all coverages being digitized.

■ Establish schedules and shifts. Digitizing is tiring work, so scheduling time off for persons digitizing helps ensure accuracy. A schedule such as two hours on, two hours off, for example, might be appropriate.

Step 3

Prepare your maps

Map preparation helps minimize problems at the digitizing stage as well as later, during the editing phase. Overall, the goal is to minimize the number of times the person who digitizes and edits will have to stop work. Here are some guidelines for preparing the map manuscript:

Locate tic registration points and assign them a unique number; these must be known points for which you can obtain real-world coordinates. Once established, the same tic numbers and locations will be recorded and used for each separate manuscript.

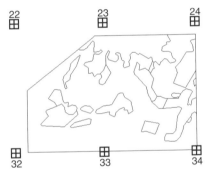

Make a new boundary, slightly larger than the real one by 3 mm or 1/8 inch, and then extend the internal lines just beyond it. This ensures that the data you digitize will completely fill your study area. Later, the real boundary of the study area will be used to clip all the data that extends beyond the edges.

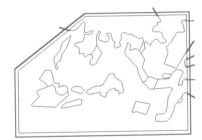

Where lines don't clearly intersect, indicate a definite intersection by marking node points on the manuscript. This helps establish consistent intersections.

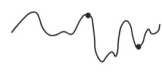

Mark nodes on long arcs (those greater than 10 cm). Accuracy increases when the segments are short enough to keep your attention.

Indicate start nodes for island polygons. This helps ensure that the boundary begins and ends at the same place— producing a closed polygon.

Make sure all polygons close and have a single label point with a unique identifier. Polygons can be made of more than one arc, but should contain only one label point.

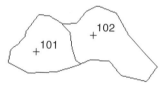

Step 4

Digitize your maps

This step can be accomplished in ARC/INFO using ARCEDIT. ARCEDIT has sophisticated capabilities for feature, attribute, and graphics editing and is the primary program you will use to digitize new coverages and maintain existing coverages in your geographic database. You'll use ARCEDIT in this lesson.

EXERCISE   **Prepare a map manuscript for automation**

As you saw in the last lesson, a portion of the land use map needs to be digitized to complete the land use coverage for the study area.

In this exercise, you'll prepare the land use map for digitizing. First, make a photocopy of the land use map manuscript in Appendix C. This will become your map manuscript. (Using paper copies introduces some distortion and causes an added source of error but allows the provided map to be used more than once.)

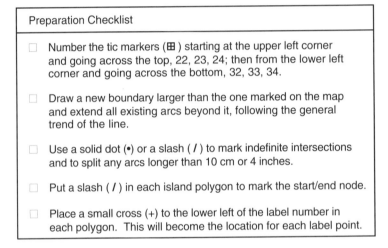

Preparation Checklist

☐   Number the tic markers (⊞) starting at the upper left corner and going across the top, 22, 23, 24; then from the lower left corner and going across the bottom, 32, 33, 34.

☐   Draw a new boundary larger than the one marked on the map and extend all existing arcs beyond it, following the general trend of the line.

☐   Use a solid dot (•) or a slash (/) to mark indefinite intersections and to split any arcs longer than 10 cm or 4 inches.

☐   Put a slash (/) in each island polygon to mark the start/end node.

☐   Place a small cross (+) to the lower left of the label number in each polygon. This will become the location for each label point.

Here is an example of how the lower right corner of the map manuscript should look:

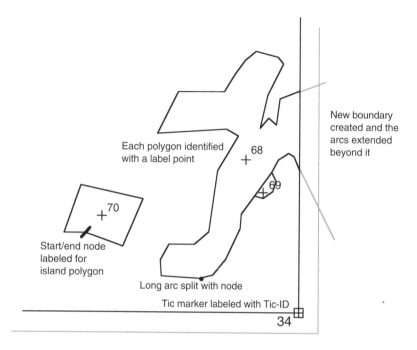

Each polygon identified with a label point

New boundary created and the arcs extended beyond it

Start/end node labeled for island polygon

Long arc split with node

Tic marker labeled with Tic-ID

34

FYI

When you digitize arcs that connect to the outer boundary, extend them a slight distance. This creates *dangles* which are often easier to fix than *undershoots*, as you will discover as you edit errors in Lesson 5.

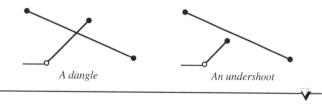

A dangle   *An undershoot*

Compare your prepared manuscript with the completed example in Appendix D.

END

Digitizing maps in ARC/INFO

Now that you've prepared the map manuscript, you're ready to digitize the map. Before you start an ARCEDIT digitizing session, there are some important points about using ARC/INFO that you should know.

command usage

ARC/INFO uses a command language. At the basic level, an operation is performed by typing in a command, along with any command arguments. Command usage refers to a listing of a command name along with its available arguments and options. As you work with ARC/INFO, you'll find that there are many commands that you use frequently enough to become familiar with their usages. Before executing less frequently used commands, you can quickly obtain the usage in one of several ways. The easiest way, when in ARC/INFO, is to type USAGE followed by the command name and press the carriage return. The usage displays on the screen and the prompt reappears so you can enter the correct command line; for example,

```
Arc: USAGE BUILD
Usage: BUILD <cover> {POLY | LINE | POINT | NODE |
ANNO.<subclass>}
Arc:
```

conventions

Here are the conventions used to interpret the command usage:

< >—Arguments appearing in angled brackets are required.

{ }—Arguments appearing in braces are optional.

cover—Arguments appearing in lowercase are replaced by a name that you specify.

POLY—Arguments appearing in uppercase are keywords and must be typed as they are shown, except they can be upper- or lowercase.

|—A bar indicates OR; only one of the available arguments is used.

{POLY | LINE | POINT | NODE | ANNO.<subclass>}—When there is a choice between optional arguments, the first argument is the default.

#—A place holder is used to skip optional arguments.

sample command usage

Knowing these conventions, you'll better understand how to use any available command. For the example listed above, BUILD is the command name, <cover> is a required argument indicating the name of the coverage you want to BUILD, and {POLY | LINE | POINT | ANNO.<subclass>} is an optional argument used to specify the type of feature to be processed. If you don't specify this argument, the first option listed is used as the default—in this case, POLY.

Now look at another example:

Usage: NODEERRORS <cover> {ALL | DANGLES | PSEUDOS}

NODEERRORS is the command, <cover> is a required argument indicating the name of the coverage containing the nodes to list, and {ALL | DANGLES | PSEUDOS} is an optional argument used to specify the type of node errors to list. The default lists ALL node errors.

ARC/INFO provides other ways of getting help at the command line. For example, for a quick list of all the commands available in a particular program, type COMMANDS at any ARC prompt (Arc, Arcedit, Arcplot). If you want to see only the commands beginning with a certain letter, for example, E, type COMMANDS E.

getting help online

ARC/INFO's online help system contains detailed information about using the software. Familiarizing yourself with the online system now will save you valuable time later. To start online help, type HELP from the Arc prompt and press Return.

Online help for ARC/INFO 7.1 does not use hypertext links. The system is self-explanatory, so there is no longer a help topic called *Using online help*. The Master Table of contents looks like this:

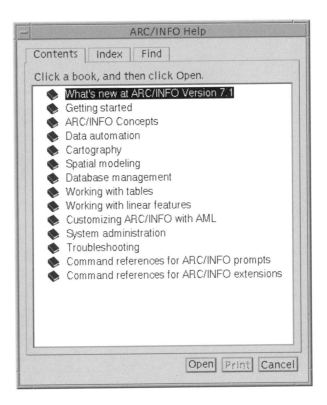

The ARCINFO Command References are accessible through the Master Table of Contents. Command References contain detailed information abut each command and its arguments

Use the functional and alphabetical lists of commands to find a command to perform a specific task.

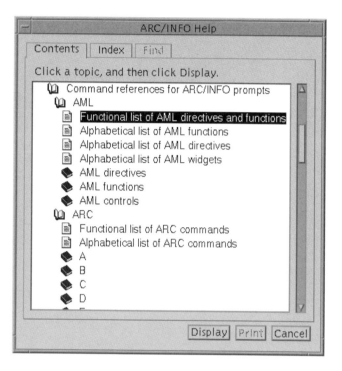

the user's guides The printed documentation that comes with ARC/INFO is another source of help for learning to use the software. *Getting Started* contains an online tutorial and an introduction to ArcTools to familiarize you with using ARC/INFO. *ARC/INFO Data Management* explains ARC/INFO concepts and procedures.

EXERCISE   Use ARCEDIT to digitize the prepared manuscript

Before you start to digitize, make sure the digitizing table is connected to your computer, is configured for ARC/INFO, and is correctly referenced in your station file. Your system administrator can verify this for you.

Next, tape the map manuscript you prepared onto the digitizing table. Here are some guidelines:

■ Place the map in a position comfortable for digitizing.

■ Do not place the map near the extreme edge of the table because points in these areas are often less accurate or inactive.

■ Use only drafting tape on the digitizer table; other adhesive tapes might damage the surface of the table and the map.

■ Make sure that the manuscript is flat and securely mounted to the digitizing table.

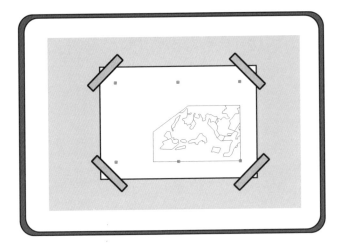

During this exercise, you first create a master tic coverage, then use these tics to create a coverage of land use corresponding to the lower right portion of your study area. Were additional coverages required, they too would receive copies of the master tics. In this way, a series of related coverages all have the same coordinate values for their tic locations.

starting ARC   If you're not currently logged on, log in to your account by entering your user name and password. Make sure that the workbook data is installed and that you have copied the data into your local workspace. The data set needed to complete the exercises in the workbook is included on ARC/INFO Version 7.1 software CD with the sample data. If the Understanding GIS data set is not yet installed on your system, you or your system administrator should install it now. Refer to the ARC/INFO Version 7.1 CD installation booklet for instructions.

UNIX   Start ARC/INFO by typing **arc** at the operating system prompt. The `Arc:` prompt appears.

`Arc:`

Begin all ARC/INFO sessions this way. Non-bold text represents what you see on the screen, bold text indicates what you should type to initiate an action.

Go to the UGIS workspace in your local directory.

`Arc:` **&WORKSPACE /yourname/ugis**

Use the CREATEWORKSPACE command to create a new workspace for your land use coverages. Name it LAND. This is where you will create the new coverages.

`Arc:` **CREATEWORKSPACE LAND**

Finally, move to the LAND workspace.

`Arc:` **&WORKSPACE LAND**

Windows NT   Click on the Arc icon in the program manager to start ARC/INFO. An ARC/INFO window displaying the `Arc:` prompt appears.

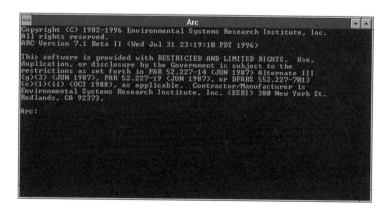

Begin all ARC/INFO sessions this way. Non-bold text represents what you see on the screen, bold text indicates what you should type to initiate an action.

Go to the UGIS workspace in your local directory.

```
Arc: &WORKSPACE  <drive>:\yourname\ugis
```

Use the CREATEWORKSPACE command to create a new workspace for your land use coverages. Name it LAND. This is where you will create the new coverages.

```
Arc: CREATEWORKSPACE  LAND
```

Finally, move to the LAND workspace.

```
Arc: &WORKSPACE  LAND
```

starting **ARCEDIT** Before starting ARCEDIT, use your station configuration file to specify the display device and the digitizer you'll use. You can do this either from ARC, as shown here, or after you start ARCEDIT. If you don't yet have a station file, have your system administrator create one for you. Refer to the Introduction of the workbook for a discussion of station files.

```
Arc: &Station  <name>
```

Now start ARCEDIT by typing

```
Arc: Arcedit
```

The Arcedit prompt and graphics window appear.

You'll digitize during this session, so use the COORDINATE command at the Arcedit: prompt to specify the DIGITIZER as your coordinate input device.

```
Arcedit: COORDINATE DIGITIZER
```

create a new coverage   New coverages are created with the CREATE command. If the new coverage does not copy tics from another coverage, CREATE begins with a dialog to identify the tic locations and the extent of the coverage. Tics are reference points identified by known coordinates on a map and are used to orient the coverage. It's important to digitize tics as accurately as possible. They're used in subsequent editing sessions and to orient the coverage to related coverages captured at other times. Accurately digitized tics also allow you to resume digitizing if you are unable to complete a map in one session or if you need to reposition the map on the digitizing table between sessions. You must digitize at least four tics to register the coverage correctly.

FYI

Using more than four tics increases accuracy. Additional tic locations should be spaced evenly across the map.

Specify the name of the new coverage, TICCOV, with the CREATE command:

```
Arcedit: CREATE TICCOV
Creating <drive>:\yourname\UGIS\LAND\TICCOV
Digitize a minimum of 4 tics  (from digitizer).
Signal end of tic input with Tic-ID = 0
```

TICCOV is an empty coverage. Once created, no other coverage can have the same name. Prompts now ask you to enter the tics. These tics will be used to perform all subsequent transformations.

FYI

While digitizing, responses are entered from the either key*board* attached to the terminal or the key*pad* attached to the digitizing table. When using the keyboard, remember to press a carriage return (<CR>) after entering a response. When using the keypad, note that some responses are made using only the buttons, while others combine a button with a location identified by the keypad crosshairs.

tic entry To establish registration coordinates for the new coverage, you must digitize the Tic-ID values and their corresponding locations using the digitizing table and keypad. You'll use the land use manuscript to create the master tics. Digitizing tics is a two-step process.

1) Enter a Tic-ID value with the numeric buttons on the keypad.

2) Enter the corresponding tic location by positioning the keypad crosshairs and pressing any active button.

HELP
Sometimes, when the button is pressed, no value is received. Remember to keep the keypad in contact with the map on the table. When entering point locations, hold the keypad firmly and always look directly over the crosshairs. Also, make sure your map lies completely within the active area of the digitizing table.

digitize the first Tic-ID Use the keypad to enter tics. Before digitizing the location of tic number 22, enter its Tic-ID value. Press the 2 button on the keypad twice, and then verify that the correct value was received by looking at the screen. If it's correct, press the A or * button to indicate you've finished entering the Tic-ID number. Pressing A or * is like entering a carriage return. (When entering Tic-IDs, the keypad must be on the table, but the crosshairs don't have to be centered on the tic.)

```
Tic-ID: 22*   WARNING, the Map extent is not defined
```

HELP
Don't panic if you enter the wrong Tic-ID. If you make a mistake entering the Tic-ID and haven't yet pressed the A or * button, use the B or # button to backspace over the error. Then enter the correct Tic-ID followed by the A or * button.

digitize the first tic location

Now you're ready to enter the tic location. Position the keypad crosshairs at the location of tic number 22. When you're sure that the position is as accurate as possible, press any button on the keypad.

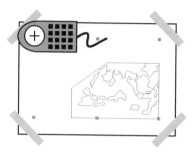

Once you've digitized the first tic, you're prompted for the next Tic-ID.

```
Tic-ID:
```

Enter the remaining tics. Note that these Tic-ID values are 23, 24, 32, 33, and 34. Be careful to digitize each Tic-ID with the correct tic location.

```
Tic-ID: 23*
Tic-ID: 24*
Tic-ID: 32*
Tic-ID: 33*
Tic-ID: 34*
```

To stop digitizing tics, enter a Tic-ID of 0, followed by A or *. (When the zero is entered, the keypad can be positioned anywhere on the table.)

```
Tic-ID: 0*
```

the coverage extent   After tic entry is ended, the following instructions appear:

```
Enter initial boundary
Define the box (from digitizer)
```

Typically, this boundary is slightly larger than the data being digitized. Because your tics mark the boundary of the data, use the keypad and place the crosshairs below and to the left of the lower left corner of the map—beyond the features to be digitized (including the tics)—and press any key.

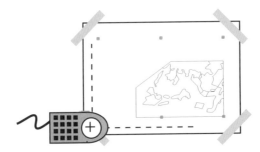

Repeat this for the upper right corner. Position the crosshairs beyond the features and press any button on the keypad.

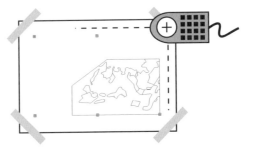

```
The edit coverage is now /yourname/UGIS/LAND/TICCOV
Defaulting the map extent to the BND of
<drive>:\yourname\UGIS\LAND\TICCOV
```

TICCOV is now the coverage being edited. Any features that you add will be added to TICCOV.

boundary file

You've just created the initial boundary file, a coverage INFO file named TICCOV.BND. This boundary, also known as the coverage extent, contains the minimum and maximum coordinates for all coverage features. From now on, it's automatically maintained and updated by ARC/INFO.

> FYI
>
> Entering the boundary doesn't add points to the coverage being digitized—it defines a window containing all the data. The boundary locations entered are used as the minimum and maximum x- and y-coordinates. Note that you could have entered any two diagonally opposing corners to define these extreme values.

save your work

You've just finished creating the master tic coverage. Now save the changes.

```
Arcedit: SAVE
Saving changes for <drive>:\yourname\UGIS\LAND\TICCOV
   BND replaced into <drive>:\yourname\UGIS\LAND\TICCOV
```

Until you save, you are working on a temporary copy of the original coverage. SAVE updates the original coverage with all the changes you have made. It's a good idea to save on a regular basis. Pathnames displayed by the SAVE command depend on your operating system and the location of your data.

> FYI
>
> Unsaved changes can be undone in ARCEDIT using the OOPS command. OOPS restores the coverage to the way it was before the last command was entered. You can enter OOPS any number of times to keep stepping back through each command. Some commands cannot be undone: CREATE is one of these commands.

drawing the coverage

Now draw the tics to check your work so far. Before you issue the DRAW command, you must first tell ARCEDIT which features you want to draw using the DRAWENVIRONMENT command. You can specify features, or features along with options such as their User-ID. The DRAW command clears the graphics window and draws only those features specified with DRAWENVIRONMENT.

```
Arcedit: DRAWENVIRONMENT TIC ID
Arcedit: DRAW
```

Your tic coverage should look like this:

22   23   24
⊞   ⊞   ⊞

32   33   34
⊞   ⊞   ⊞

Make sure the Tic-IDs displayed on your screen match those marked on the map.

Tic-ID: **22*** WARNING, the Map extent is not defined

| **HELP** |

If you do not see all of the tics, then reset the display area by typing the MAPEXTENT command.

Arcedit: **MAPEXTENT TIC TICCOV**
Arcedit: **DRAW**

FYI

The master tic coverage for a study area is typically created and verified before digitizing any of the map sheets. In this case, we demonstrated how to create tics using the digitizer. It's important that these tic locations be as accurate as possible.

Although not shown in this exercise, the next step is to generate a hardcopy plot of the tic locations at the same scale as your map sheet. This plot is laid over the original map sheets to verify that the locations are accurate. Once accurate tic locations are verified, these tics should be used to create every digitized coverage for the study area.

---

digitizing from a map manuscript

At this point, you have a master tic coverage for the area to be digitized. You're now ready to create the missing portion of the land use map by digitizing from the map manuscript. Because you'll be digitizing polygons, do the following:

- Enter the tics
- Digitize arcs
- Digitize label points

Continue by creating a new coverage, LANDDG01. Specify that its
initial tics should be copied from the master tic coverage, TICCOV.

```
Arcedit: CREATE LANDDG01 TICCOV
 Creating <drive>:\yourname\UGIS\LAND\LANDDG01
 The edit coverage is now <drive>:\yourname\UGIS\LAND\LANDDG01
 Use COORDINATE DIGITIZER DEFAULT to orient
<drive>:\yourname\UGIS\LAND\LANDDG01
 if required.
```

tic registration   Orient the map manuscript on the digitizer using the COORDINATE
DIGITIZER command with the DEFAULT option. When ARCEDIT
prompts you, digitize the same Tic-IDs and tic locations you used for
TICCOV. Enter them with the digitizing keypad and crosshairs.

```
Arcedit: COORDINATE DIGITIZER DEFAULT
Defaulting transformation coverage to <drive>:\yourname\UGIS\
LAND\LANDDG01
Digitize a minimum of 4 tics.
Signal end of tic input with Tic-ID = 0
Tic-ID: 22*
Tic-ID: 23*
Tic-ID: 24*
Tic-ID: 32*
Tic-ID: 33*
Tic-ID: 34*
Tic-ID: 0*
Scale  (X,Y)  = (1.000,1.001) Skew (degrees) = (.019)
Rotation (degrees) = (-0.26) Translation = (-.004, -0.007)
RMS error (input, output) = (0.002, 0.002)
```

Notice the RMS error displayed in the dialog area after the tics are
entered. Calculated in both digitizer units and map units, this
value tells you how well you matched the previous set of tics. At
this point in the process, because the digitizer units and the map
units are the same, the error values are the same. In our example,
the RMS is 0.002 and the digitizer units are inches.

▽FYI
         You must set your own value for an acceptable RMS
         error and then match that value to ensure that the quality
of the data entered is maintained at the desired level of accuracy. Perfect
registrations, an RMS of 0.000, are highly improbable. When digitizing
in inches, we usually set the limit at 0.003 or 0.004. Your value
depends on the nature of the data, the scale of the base map, and the
material from which the data is digitized—parcel boundaries are more
precise than soil boundaries; large-scale maps (1:10,000) are more
precise than small-scale maps (1:250,000); and data on MYLAR is more
stable than on paper maps. The more precise the data, the lower the
acceptable RMS. These exercises use paper maps, so you may need to
accept an RMS value as high as 0.005 or 0.006 inches.

HELP   If your RMS is too high, reenter the
COORDINATE command with the name of the coverage whose
tics will be digitized.

Arcedit: **COORDINATE DIGITIZER LANDDG01**

You will again be prompted to enter the Tic-IDs and their locations.
A new RMS error will result, hopefully a value that you can accept.

setting editing environments

ARCEDIT lets you control what happens as you add and edit
coverages. The following sections discuss ARCEDIT commands that
control the editing environment.

setting the node snapping environment

Before adding arcs to the new coverage, it helps to establish a node
snapping environment.

As each new arc is added, the starting node may fall within a given distance (e.g., 0.05 inches) of an existing node.

This new node location will snap to the existing node if it is within the node snap tolerance.

This helps you to ensure that arcs connect correctly to adjoining arcs.
The default node snapping tolerance is quite small. To change this
value, use the NODESNAP command.

Arcedit: **NODESNAP CLOSEST .05**

setting the drawing environment

Previously, you set the drawing environment to include tics and their
IDs. Now that you are about to digitize, you should add arcs, nodes,
and label points to the drawing environment. Also, specify that the
IDs will be displayed for label points.

Arcedit: **DRAWENVIRONMENT ARC NODE LABELS IDS**

adding arcs   ARCEDIT is feature-oriented editing. This means that edits are made to one type of feature at a time. This speeds up editing because editing operations can be executed by a single word command such as ADD, MOVE, SELECT. You must always specify the type of feature before starting to edit.

Specify that arcs will be edited:

```
Arcedit: EDITFEATURE ARC
0 element(s) for edit feature ARCS
```

Now type ADD to open the menu for adding arcs:

```
Arcedit: ADD
- - - - - - - - - - Options - - - - - - - - - - -
1) Vertex          2) Node                  3) Curve
4) Delete vertex   5) Delete arc            6) Spline on/off
7) Square on/off   8) Digitizing Options    9) Quit
(Line) User-ID: 1 Points 0
```

The following examples correspond to the lower right corner of your map sheet. The next several pages show you how to digitize the arcs numbered 1 through 6. After following these instructions, you'll then need to apply these same procedures to the rest of the manuscript.

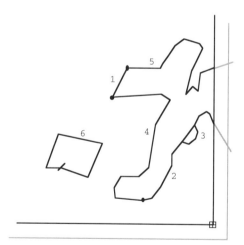

Arc number 1 is a two-point arc. Position the cursor on the node (represented by a solid circle) and enter the button numbers as shown. The 2 button on the keypad tells ARCEDIT that you are beginning or ending an arc.

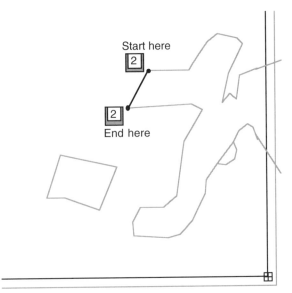

Once digitized, arc number 1 should appear on your graphics display screen.

Arc number 2 is curved. You'll need to enter enough vertices to construct the smooth shape of the curve. Imagine a connect-the-dots drawing; the closer the points are together, the smoother the resulting line. The diagram below shows where the nodes of the arc should be located (solid black circles) using the 2 button. Between the nodes, use the 1 button to enter the vertices (marked with hollow circles). As you digitize the arc, use your best judgment to determine where to place the vertices. Your locations do not have to exactly match the ones in the diagram; these points are only examples.

FYI There are no hard-and-fast rules about how many vertices you should digitize to represent a curve. Generating more vertices is not always better. Too many vertices increase the amount of stored data. Use your judgment. The goal is to digitize enough vertices so that a plot of your coverage will accurately overlay your manuscript.

Position the keypad crosshairs and enter the button numbers as shown. Carefully trace the shape of the arc with the keypad crosshairs, pressing the 1 button repeatedly to enter vertices as you go.

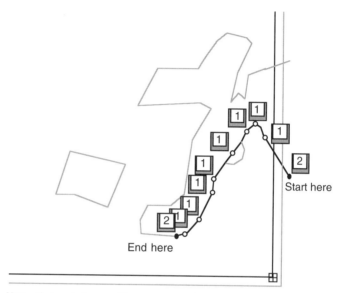

Notice that, as before, nothing appears on the screen until the ending node is entered; then, the entire arc is drawn.

HELP

You might make errors while digitizing an arc. If you digitize an erroneous vertex, use the 4 button on the keypad to remove it (the last vertex entered). If you lose your place along the arc, use the 0 button to display the position of the cursor on the terminal screen. Each time you press the 0 button, a cross appears on the screen showing the position of the keypad crosshairs.

If you want to restart the arc from the beginning, the 5 button will remove the arc currently being digitized. If you have already ended the arc with a node, the 5 button cannot remove it. See the HELP section on page 4-33 for instructions on removing an arc.

FYI

The previous example uses a method call point-mode digitizing. In point-mode digitizing, the arc's shape is defined by pressing the 1 button to add a vertex every time the arc changes direction.

Stream-mode digitizing is an alternative method for entering arcs in ARC/INFO. The following graphics illustrate the two ways to perform stream digitizing.

To add an arc using stream-mode digitizing, hold down the 1 button and trace the line; the software automatically places vertices along a digitized arc at specified intervals.

Optionally, you can press and release the C key, trace the line, and end the digitized arc by pressing the 2 button.

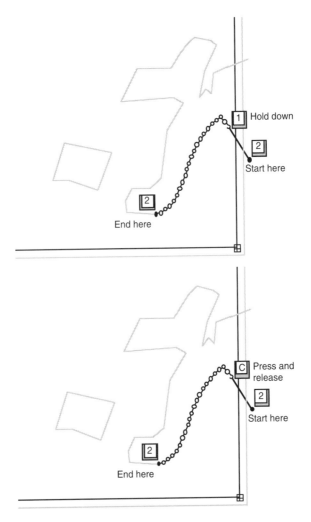

Understanding GIS—The ARC/INFO Method

Point mode is good for entering two-point arcs or arcs needing only a few vertices. Stream mode considerably reduces the time it takes to enter long, sinuous arcs that require large numbers of vertices to define their shapes.

Set your digitizer to stream mode by specifying the STREAM option. If you don't know the argument parameters for your digitizer, ask your system administrator for help.

```
Arcedit:  USAGE  DIGITIZER
Usage: DIGITIZER <digitizer_type>
{<device_port>:{option1}:{option2}:{option3}}
{POINT | STREAM}
```

In this exercise, digitizing is demonstrated using point mode. You can, however, use either mode to digitize arcs.

Be careful when entering arcs in stream mode. Even a slight movement of the cursor will add unwanted vertices, which will have to be deleted. Use WEEDTOLERANCE to control the number of vertices entered while digitizing in either mode.

Now digitize arcs 3, 4, and 5. Start and end each arc with a node (the 2 button) and enter vertices (using the 1 button) according to the shape of the arc.

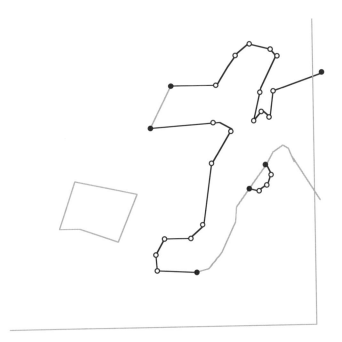

Notice that, even though you're digitizing polygons, you don't have to digitize the entire polygon as a single arc—you can digitize each arc that makes up the polygon. In the case of polygon number 68, its boundary is actually outlined by five different arcs (including the border arc). When you create topology for these polygons in the next lesson, ARC/INFO will determine which arcs make up each polygon and maintain an accurate list of them. This polygon-arc topology, discussed in Lesson 2, is used to calculate the area of each polygon.

Only one arc remains to be digitized from this corner sample of your
map sheet. Locate arc number 6. This arc encloses an island polygon.
Digitize it as you did the previous arcs, starting and stopping at the
slash mark you added when preparing the map. Position the crosshairs
at the slash mark and enter the button numbers shown. (Your starting
point may differ from the one shown.)

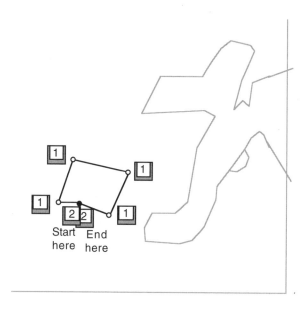

```
┌─────────┐
│  HELP   │
└─────────┘
```

Don't panic if you need to remove an arc. If you make an error while adding the arcs, you can delete it and start over. Before any feature can be deleted, it must first be selected.

Arcedit: **SELECT**

Place the keypad crosshairs over the arc to be removed and press any button. Once the arc is selected, the corresponding Arc #, User-ID, and number of vertices are displayed on the screen and, depending on your hardware, the selected arc either changes color or blinks.

Once you select the correct arc, remove it with the DELETE command.

Arcedit: **DELETE**

You can redigitize deleted arcs using the ADD command as described in the previous section.

digitize remaining arcs

Now that you've digitized six of the arcs, finish digitizing the rest of the arcs on the manuscript. Start by digitizing the outer boundary as a single arc. Be sure to digitize the extended boundary instead of the real one. You'll find it helpful to check off each arc after it's digitized.

When you finish digitizing all the arcs, end the ADD session by pressing the 9 button on the keypad. If you digitized the perimeter as a single arc plus all the interior arcs exactly as shown on the map manuscript, you will have 31 arcs. It is not necessarily a problem if your coverage contains fewer or more arcs than this number. Small digitizing errors, which can be corrected, can make this number vary.

```
(Line) User-ID: 31 Points 0    1 2 3 4 5 6
(Line) User-ID: 32 Points 0  (press 9)
31 arc(s) added to <drive>:\yourname\UGIS\LAND\LANDDG01
```

> **HELP**
>
> Don't panic if your first attempt at digitizing isn't successful—it's easier once you've been through the process. If your first coverage is a mess, it's easy to clean up and start over. One way is to simply select all the arcs, delete them, and then redigitize them.
>
> ```
> Arcedit: SELECT ALL
> 31 element(s) now selected
> : DELETE
> ```
>
> You can also use the KILL command to delete the digitized version of the coverage. KILL is permanent - a coverage can't be recovered once it has been deleted - so be sure to enter the correct coverage name. (You can use KILL in ARC as well as ARCEDIT.)
>
> ```
> Arcedit: KILL LANDGO1
> This will fully delete LADNG01.
> Continue <y/n>: y
> Deleted coverage LANDG01.
> ```
>
> In this case, repeat the process of creating and digitizing LANDG01 using the process explained beginning on page 4-24.

saving the digitized arcs

It's a good idea to periodically save the edits you've made during an ARCEDIT session.

```
Arcedit: SAVE
Saving changes for <drive>:\yourname\UGIS\LAND\LANDDG01
Saving arcs...
31 arc(s) written to <drive>:\yourname\UGIS\LAND\LANDDG01
   from the original 0, 31 added and 0 deleted
Reopening arcs...
   BND replaced into <drive>:\yourname\UGIS\LAND\LANDDG01
Saving set tolerances to TOL file...
Re-establishing edit feature ARC
```

adding labels

To finish digitizing the LANDDG01 map sheet, you must add the label points to the coverage. These points identify the polygons that surround them and are used later to attach attributes to the polygons. To add labels, specify labels as the feature to be edited.

Arcedit: **EDITFEATURE LABEL**
0 element(s) for edit feature LABEL

Type ADD to open the menu for adding labels:

Arcedit: **ADD**

```
- - - - - - - - - Options - - - - - - - - - -
1) Add Label          5) Delete last label
8) Digitizing options  9) Quit
(Label) User-ID: 1 Coordinate =
```

assigning specific User-IDs

Each polygon on the map is labeled with a unique value, ranging from 59 to 77, making a total of 19 labels. These values will be used later to identify each polygon in the feature attribute table. By default, the first label that's digitized is assigned a User-ID of 1. Before adding your first label point, change this value to equal the value of the lowest User-ID you'll enter, in this case, 59.

Press the 8 button to display the submenu:

(Label) User-ID: 1 Coordinate = **(press 8)**

Press the 1 button to choose the New User-ID option. At the prompt, enter the value of the new User-ID. Enter 59 using the keypad; then press A or *.

```
- - - - - - - - - - DIGITIZING OPTIONS - - - - - - - - - -
1) New User-ID           2) New Symbol    3) Autoincrement OFF
4) Autoincrement RESUME  5) New Angle     6) New Scale
9) Quit              - - - - Enter Option
(Label) User-ID: 1 Coordinate = (press 1)
```

New User-ID **59***

You are now ready to add labels. Position the keypad crosshairs over the location of label point 59 on the map sheet; then press the 1 button to enter it.

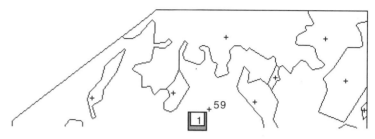

```
(Label) User-ID: 59 Coordinate = 10.432,6.154
(Label) User-ID: 60 Coordinate =
```

The value of the next User-ID is automatically incremented by 1. The prompt tells you that the next label point will receive a User-ID of 60.

You may have already noticed that the User-ID values of the label points on the map sheet also increment by 1. Be sure to match the label point you enter from the map with the User-ID value listed in the dialog area on the screen.

Enter the label points marked 60 and 61 by positioning the keypad crosshairs at the locations indicated and pressing the 1 button.

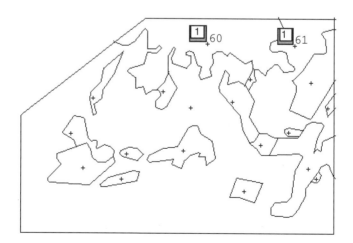

```
(Label) User-ID: 59 Coordinate = 10.432,6.154
(Label) User-ID: 60 Coordinate = 10.752,7.400
(Label) User-ID: 61 Coordinate = 12.410,7.365
```

> **HELP**
>
> If you make an error as you add labels, don't worry—you can delete them. Simply press the 5 button to delete the most recently entered label point.

digitize the remaining labels

Digitize the remaining labels for the LANDDG01 coverage making sure that you assign the correct User-IDs. Then, after all the label points have been entered, end the ADD session by pressing the 9 button on the digitizer keypad.

```
(Label) User-ID: 78 Coordinate =  (press 9)
19 label(s) added to <drive>:\yourname\UGIS\LAND\LANDDG01
```

save the changes

Once again, save your edits. This saves any additions or edits you have made since the last save, including the labels just digitized.

```
Arcedit: SAVE
Saving changes for <drive>:\yourname\UGIS\LAND\LANDDG01
Saving arcs...
** NOTE ** Arc(s) unchanged
Reopening arcs...
Saving labels...
19 label(s) written to <drive>:\yourname\UGIS\LAND\LANDDG01
  from the original 0, 19 added and 0 deleted
    BND replaced into <drive>:\yourname\UGIS\LAND\LANDDG01
Saving set tolerances to TOL file
Re-establishing edit feature POINT
```

drawing the coverage

The digitizing session is now complete. To check your work so far, draw all the coverage features.

```
Arcedit: DRAW
```

Understanding GIS—The ARC/INFO Method

This identifies all the elements of the map you have entered by digitizing. Your screen should look similar to this:

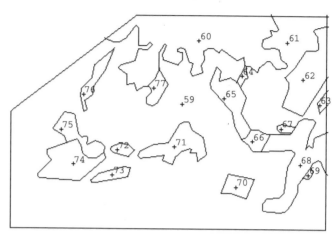

Verify that there is one, and only one, label point in each polygon.

Any obvious errors (e.g., a missing arc or label point), can be corrected now. Next, draw your coverage, highlighting the node errors, but without displaying the labels.

Arcedit: **DRAWENVIRONMENT NODE ERRORS LABEL OFF**
Arcedit: **DRAW**

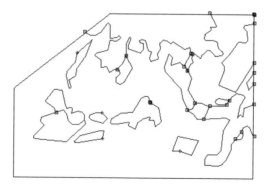

Two kinds of node errors are marked: pseudo nodes, labeled with diamonds, and dangling nodes, labeled with boxes. These errors are explained and corrected in the next lesson.

You may have different errors than the ones shown
above depending on your accuracy.

exiting ARCEDIT

Your digitizing session is now finished. To leave ARCEDIT, type
QUIT. If you've made changes since your last save, a prompt asking
whether you want to save appears. Answer yes (or y) to save the
changes.

```
: QUIT
Keep all edit changes (Y/N) :Y
Leaving ARCEDIT...
```

HELP

If you want to start your ARCEDIT session over,
you can QUIT or RESET without saving your changes. If your
system fails while in ARCEDIT (or any other ARC program) you can
break out by pressing the control <Ctrl> key along with the
appropriate break key for your operating system.

UNIX

```
Arcedit: <ctrl> c
```

Windows NT

```
Arcedit: <Ctrl> c

Arcedit: Are you sure (y/n)? Y
Program interrupted by user
Try RESTOREARCEDT to recover your edit session
Arc:
```

RESTOREARCEDIT restores edits made to a coverage during an
ARCEDIT session that aborts or halts execution due to system
failure. Go to the RESTOREARCEDIT command in the online
Command References for ARC/INFO-->ARC for more information
on restoring your ARCEDIT session.

Note that if you break out of ARC/INFO while graphics are being
drawn on the screen, the drawing is interrupted and you are returned
to the program prompt.

*listing information about
coverages in your workspace*

The current workspace now contains two coverages, TICCOV and
LANDDG01. The LISTCOVERAGES command lists the set of
coverages in your workspace.

```
Arc: LISTCOVERAGES
Listing for: /YOURNAME/UGIS/LAND

Available Coverages
- - - - - - - - - - - - -
LANDDG01          TICCOV
```

Now use the DESCRIBE command to list information about the new
land use coverage, LANDDG01, you just digitized. (Your display
will vary somewhat from the one shown below.)

```
Arc: DESCRIBE LANDDG01
            Description of SINGLE precision coverage landdg01
                           FEATURE CLASSES
                       Number of  Attribute     Spatial
Feature Class Subclass Features   Data (bytes)  Index?   Topology?
------------- -------- --------   ------------  --------  ---------
ARCS                      31
NODES                     47
POINTS                    19

                           SECONDARY FEATURES
Tics                       6
Arc Segments              248
                              TOLERANCES
Fuzzy      =    0.002 N    Dangle     =     0.000 N
                          COVERAGE BOUNDARY
Xmin       =    7.430      Xmax       =    13.268
Ymin       =    3.454      Ymax       =     7.540
```

DESCRIBE is useful because it identifies the contents of coverages,
shows the map projection information, and helps you keep track of
the status of coverages in your GIS database. Remember to use
DESCRIBE later in this workbook as additional processing steps are
performed on the land use coverage.

You may get different values than the ones listed above
depending on your accuracy.

FYI Your computer's disk stores an ARC/INFO coverage as a directory of files. Each file contains specific information for the coverage. For example, the ARC file contains the User-IDs and the coordinates for each arc, the LAB file contains the User-IDs and coordinates for label points, the TIC file contains tics, and so on. To learn more about coverage contents and the set of files used to define a coverage, refer to *ARC/INFO Data Management*.

When you finish using DESCRIBE, QUIT from ARC.

```
Arc: QUIT
Exiting ARC ...
```

END

Advanced topic – Other ways to create coverages

Digittizing from a map manuscript is only one of several procedures that create ARC/INFO coverages. If your data is already in digital format, you may not need to digitize from manuscript maps. You can obtain digital data from government agencies or commercial firms. Some common data formats include the U.S. Census Bureau data in TIGER files, precision drawings in the form of AutoCAD DXF files, rasterized land data as ERDAS data files, and topological maps such as USGS DLG data files, just to name a few.

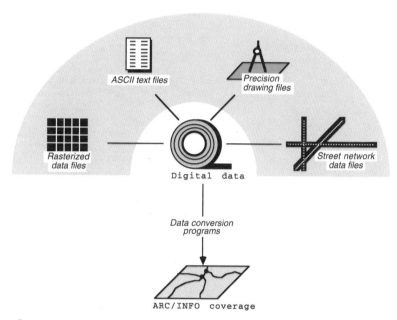

Conversion programs can make use of existing digital data.

The data you need might be in a format that can be converted directly to an ARC/INFO coverage using one of the ARC/INFO software's data conversion commands. These commands provide many tools to transfer data into and out of ARC/INFO between several data sources including other mapping systems, scanned data, satellite images, and other cell-based data.

For example, the ARC command TIGERARC converts U.S. Census Bureau TIGER/Line™ files for street networks into ARC/INFO coverages. Notice that the command names the data formats and the direction of the conversion: TIGERARC—from TIGER formatted data to ARC/INFO formatted data. For more information about data conversion, consult the ARC/INFO user's guide *Data Conversion*.

By formatting data that's already captured, you can create a coverage in a matter of minutes, although large conversions can take hours. The actual process and the amount of time you save depends on the quantity and quality of the data being converted and the compatibility of the different formats.

Not all formats have a specific conversion process. As a generic alternative, ARC/INFO accepts digital data from ASCII text files containing x,y coordinate pairs. (Almost any digital data converts to this format.) The ARC command GENERATE can create a coverage directly from data stored in this format.

Electronic scanners provide an alternative to digitizing map data. Scanning data is faster than digitizing, especially for maps with a lot of lines, but, the map must be carefully prepared because scanners are extremely sensitive. It is important to eliminate any mark, line, or text that should not become part of the coverage. This preparation can provide to be just as time-consuming as digitizing. Also, because nodes are not specifically identified by the scanner, the line intersections that results can require more editing than a digitized version of the same coverage. Processing spatial data to make it usable is the topic of Lesson 5.

When comparing different forms of data capture, keep these factors in mind:

■ How much time is required to prepare the data?

■ How much time is required for data input?

■ How does the accuracy of the captured data affect subsequent editing and processing requirements?

ADVANCED EXERCISE	**Reformat spatial data from an ASCII file to a coverage**

You've been provided with an ASCII text file of x,y coordinates. These coordinates correspond to all of the streams in the study area for your project. Your task is to verify that it is in the proper format, and then, to use the GENERATE command to convert this data into an ARC/INFO coverage.

If necessary, start ARC/INFO; then go to your UGIS workspace.

UNIX   Arc: **&WORKSPACE /yourname/ugis**

Windows NT   Arc: **&WORKSPACE <drive>:\yourname\ugis**

From this level, create a new workspace to contain the streams data named STRM.

Arc: **CREATEWORKSPACE STRM**

Then move to that directory.

Arc: **&WORKSPACE STRM**

Next copy the coordinate data provided in a file named STREAMS.LIN, into this workspace.

UNIX   Arc: **&sys cp ../data/streams.lin streams.lin**

Windows NT   Arc: **&sys copy ..\data\streams.lin streams.lin**

Display the contents of this ASCII data file on your screen using the &POPUP directive. Verify that it contains a list of x,y coordinate pairs for each line, along with a unique identifier to indicate which stream it represents. These will later become the arc User-IDS.

Arc: **&POPUP STREAMS.LIN**

| HELP |

If you didn't specify a station file during the current ARC/INFO session, you got an error message when you issued the &POPUP directive. To continue, specify your station file (e.g., 9999) and repeat &POPUP.

Arc: **&POPUP STREAMS.LIN**
AML ERROR - Terminal type has not been set with the
&TERMINAL directive
Arc: **&STATION <name>** (i.e., 9999)
Arc: **&POPUP STREAMS.LIN**

Notice that the coordinates are already stored in real-world coordinate values.

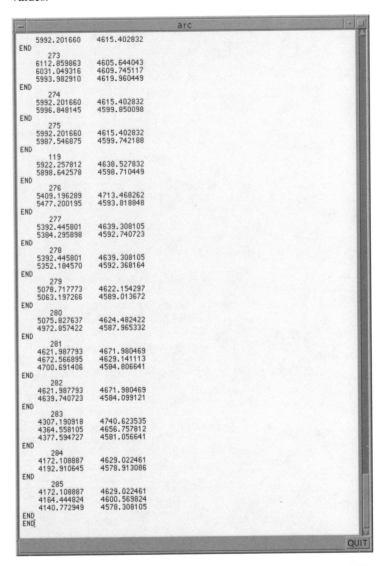

The last arc in this file has a User-ID of 285. Note that a line marking the END separates the coordinates for each arc and an additional END statement marks the end of the file. Go to the GENERATE command in the online Command References ARC for more information on the format that GENERATE requires .

When you finish viewing the contents of the file, close the popup window by pressing the **Quit** button.

starting GENERATE   You're now ready to issue the GENERATE command. Begin by specifying the name of the coverage you want to create, in this case, STRMGN01.

```
Arc: USAGE GENERATE
Usage: GENERATE [cover]
[ARC] GENERATE STRMGN01
```

GENERATE has its own prompt and its own set of subcommands.

```
Generate: COMMANDS
ANNOTATIONS    CIRCLES     COMMANDS    COPYTICS
CURVES         FISHNET     HELP        INPUT
LINES          LINKS       POINTS      POLYGONS
QUIT           ROUTES      TICS        USAGE
```

Similar to the digitizing procedure, create the tics first, and then generate the coverage features. The stream data represents real-world coordinates. Other coverages in your DATA workspace that also contain real-world coordinates are the finished coverages of ROADS, SEWERS, and SOILS. To make the STREAMS coverage register to the ROADS coverage, or any other finished coverage in the database, use the tics from the coverage named TEMPLATE. The GENERATE subcommand COPYTICS allows you to do this.

```
Generate: USAGE COPYTICS
Usage: COPYTICS [cover]
```

UNIX   `Generate: COPYTICS ../data/template`

Windows NT   `Generate: COPYTICS ..\data\template`

Now specify the name of your data source: (i.e., the file that contains the x,y coordinates for the streams) using the INPUT subcommand.

```
Generate: INPUT STREAMS.LIN
```

At this point, GENERATE has not yet read the coordinates from the file. The data cannot be interpreted until you specify the type of feature you are creating. In this case, you will be generating lines. As soon as you specify this, GENERATE reads the line coordinates from the specified input file.

```
Generate: LINES
Creating Lines with coordinates loaded from streams.lin.
```

End the GENERATE session by typing **QUIT**.

```
Generate: QUIT
Externalling BND and TIC...
Arc:
```

GENERATE tells you it's creating the boundary (BND) and tic (TIC) files for the coverage. STRMGN01 is now an ARC/INFO coverage for streams at the same stage as if you had just digitized it.

You'll want to verify that the spatial data was indeed converted. You can do this with any of the several graphic programs within ARC/INFO. We'll use ARCPLOT, which is used whenever you want to query your data or create maps.

Start ARCPLOT.

```
Arc: ARCPLOT
Arcplot:
```

HELP
If you didn't specify a station file during the current ARC/INFO session, you will not see a graphic screen when you start ARCPLOT. To continue, either specify your station file Arcplot: &STATION <name> or specify your display Arcplot: DISPLAY 9999.

We are only interested in displaying the streams (arcs) and the registration points (tics). As you issue the following commands, the specified features will be displayed on your screen.

```
Arcplot: MAPEXTENT TICS STRMGN01
Arcplot: LINECOLOR BLUE
Arcplot: ARCS STRMGN01
Arcplot: TICS STRMGN01
```

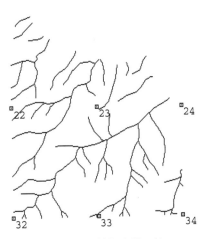

Your display should look like this.

When you finish looking at the stream data, issue the QUIT command twice (once to leave ARCPLOT and again to exit ARC). You'll learn more about ARCPLOT in Lesson 6.

```
Arcplot: QUIT
Leaving ARCPLOT...
Arc:  QUIT
Exiting Arc...
```

END

Summary

concept review   All features on a paper map can be stored digitally once they've been formatted in an x,y coordinate system as either points, lines or polygons.

Spatial data	Digital format
3,10 7,10 6,9 3,8 4,6 +7,7 10,7 9,5	3,10 6,9 7,10 10,7 9,5 4,6 3,8 3,10 7,7
1,7 3,5 5,5 5,3 9,3	1,7 3,5 5,5 5,3 9,3
+2,2	2,2

The x,y coordinate pairs are used to represent points, lines and polygons (areas).

After the spatial features are converted into a digital format, points are represented by a single x,y coordinate pair, lines are represented by a series of x,y coordinate pairs, and polygons are represented by a single label point surrounded by one or more lines (arcs). The computer stores this data in files. When necessary, features are reconstructed and graphically displayed by connecting their coordinate values.

Digitizing is the most common method of capturing data on a map and putting it into a computer file. Digitizing consists of tracing features on a map manuscript which is mounted on a digitizing table. Pressing buttons on a keypad records the x,y coordinate locations of each feature. Other methods of capturing data include reformatting existing digital data and scanning map manuscripts using an electronic scanner.

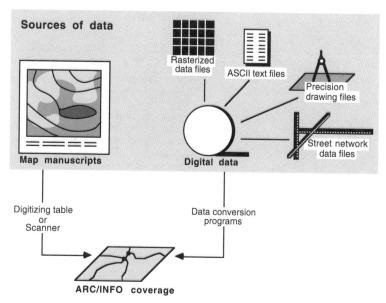

Spatial data can be captured manually from a digitizing table, or automatically by a scanner. Once captured, the data exists in a digital format which can then be reformatted and used by many applications, and even exchanged between different hardware and software systems.

lesson summary

In this lesson, different sources of data were used to create ARC/INFO coverages. One coverage was created by digitizing in ARCEDIT and the other by reformatting stream coordinate data in an ASCII file.

To capture data manually, you must be able to add it from a map manuscript and delete it if you make a mistake. The ARCEDIT commands used for basic digitizing tasks are summarized in the following table:

GIS functionality	ARCEDIT command
Add new features to the current edit coverage.	ADD
Create a new coverage.	CREATE
Delete all currently selected features.	DELETE
Draw, or redraw, the graphics.	DRAW
Specify which features to draw.	DRAWENVIRONMENT
Specify the feature class to edit.	EDITFEATURE
Undo the last transaction.	OOPS
Select features to delete.	SELECT

Spatial data can be obtained without digitizing, by converting data already in a digital format into an ARC/INFO format. You performed this kind of conversion with the GENERATE command if you completed the advanced exercise.

Data	Digital format	Conversion command
Generic coordinates	ASCII text file	GENERATE

references for further reading

For more information on topics related to this lesson, refer to online help under *Data Automation-->Editing coverages and INFO files in ARCEDIT* and under *Data Automation-->Data Conversion*. You will also find the online *Command References* for ARCEDIT helpful.

project status   In this lesson, you created the land use coverage, LNDDG01, and the stream coverage, STRMGN01. In Lesson 5, you'll create topology for these newly created coverages and then edit them until the data is free of errors.

workspace contents   At this point, the directory you created for this workbook should contain several workspaces, ARC/INFO coverages, INFO directories, and some ASCII data files. The following diagram lists what should be in your UGIS directory.

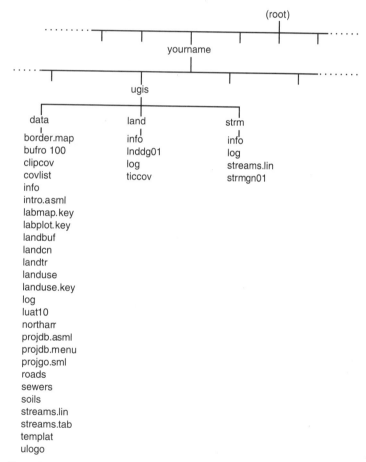

Note: You have the STRM workspace and its contents only if you completed the advanced exercise.

task summary   The shaded lesson boxes indicate the portion of the project completed so far.

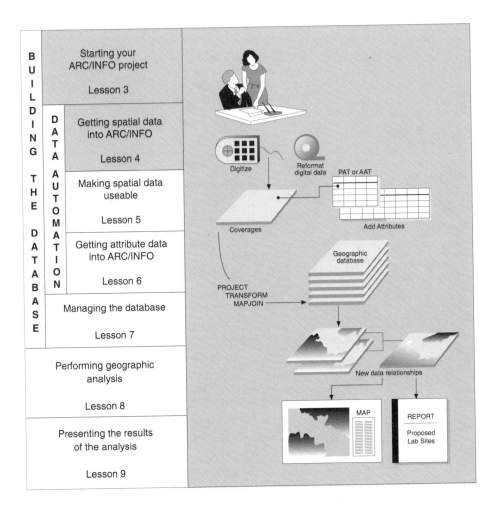

Lesson 5 Making spatial data usable

In the previous lesson, you created a digitized version of your map manuscript. Continuing with the data automation process, you now need to make sure that the data in the newly digitized coverage is free of spatial errors. Specifically, you need to ensure that

- All features that should have been digitized, really were (no missing data)

- All features that are there, should be there (no extra data)

- The features are in the right place and the arcs have the correct shape (data is accurate)

- Features that should connect, actually do

- All polygons have one, and only one, label point

- All features are within the outer boundary

These relationships, which you first encountered in Lesson 2, are known as *topological relationships*. They make digitally explicit the relationships between features that we see when looking at a map. In ARC/INFO, creating topology for a coverage also creates its feature attribute table, which contains the descriptive data for the coverage. Once these relationships are made explicit, you can query, analyze, and display your data.

In this lesson, you will perform the following steps to ensure that the spatial data is correct:

- Construct topology
- Identify errors
- Correct errors
- Reconstruct topology

By the end of this lesson, the land use coverage will be spatially correct and ready to have descriptive information (i.e., attributes) joined to its features.

The estimated time needed to complete this lesson is 4 hours.

Steps for making spatial data usable

Even if you are careful, you cannot digitize every line perfectly. Making spatial data usable requires correcting the coordinate data to make it free of errors and topologically correct. This is accomplished by establishing the existing spatial relationships (constructing topology), identifying errors, correcting errors, and then reconstructing the topology. This section introduces each of these procedures.

automating polygon data

In this lesson, you'll process the land use coverage you just digitized.

The following are the steps for automating polygon data:

Step 1: Construct topology
Step 2: Identify digitizing errors
Step 3: Correct errors
Step 4: Reconstruct topology

Construct topology

As you saw in Lesson 3, topology makes explicit the relationships between the geographic features within a coverage. The process of constructing topology identifies errors that often exist in digitized data, such as

- Arcs that do not connect to other arcs
- Polygons that are not closed
- Polygons that have no label point or too many label points
- Incorrect User-IDs

Constructing topology identifies these errors because it creates arc intersections, identifies arcs that make up each polygon, and associates a label point with each polygon. Until you construct topology, no polygons exist and arcs that cross each other might not connect with a node at their intersection.

In Lesson 2, you manually constructed topology for a small coverage. ARC/INFO provides two commands that create topology for you automatically: BUILD and CLEAN. These are the topics of the next section.

Step
2

Identify digitizing errors

Once you've constructed topology, you can identify most digitizing errors by making a plot of the digitized coverage to overlay and compare with the original source map.

ARC/INFO identifies and marks potential node errors with special symbols. Here is a brief description of the two types of nodes and the potential errors they represent.

 Pseudo nodes, drawn with a diamond symbol, occur where a single line connects with itself (an island) or where only two arcs intersect.

An island pseudo node   Pseudo node marking a two-arc intersection

Pseudo nodes do not necessarily mean that there's an error or a problem. For example, pseudo nodes that represent island polygons (a spatial pseudo node) or the point where a road changes from pavement to gravel (an attribute pseudo node) are acceptable.

A dangling node, represented by a square symbol, connects to only one arc. It is the unconnected node of a dangling arc. Dangling arcs and nodes are created when digitized arcs stop short of, or extend past, an intended intersection point.

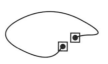

An open polygon   An undershoot   An overshoot

In some cases, dangling nodes are acceptable. For example, dangling nodes can represent cul-de-sacs in a street centerline map.

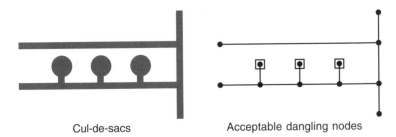

Cul-de-sacs   Acceptable dangling nodes

Common label errors in polygon coverages include having a polygon that contains no label point and having more than one label point in a single polygon. The latter can be a case of too many label points or of not enough polygons. While it can happen that more than one label point is accidentally digitized for a single polygon, it can also be that a polygon contains multiple label points because one or more arcs don't intersect with other arcs as they should (undershoots), resulting in one polygon where there should be more.

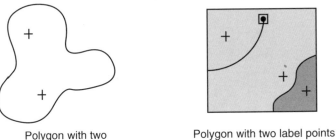

Polygon with two   Polygon with two label points
label points   resulting from a dangling arc

After topology is constructed, the ARC commands NODEERRORS and LABELERRORS automatically identify some of these errors. Other errors must be identified by examining the digitized data and comparing it to the original manuscript.

Here are the node and label errors that are identified automatically:

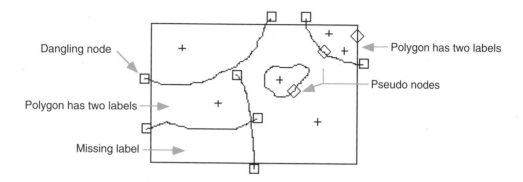

Here are the same errors, as they would be interpreted by you, after comparing them with the source map:

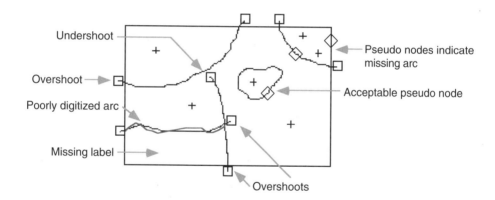

Step
3

Correct the errors

Correcting errors is one of the most important steps in constructing a database. Unless you correct the errors in your data, subsequent calculations, analyses, and maps will not be valid. For example, polygons without label points cannot have descriptive attributes attached to them, and area calculations cannot be accurately computed for unclosed polygons.

Correcting errors simply means adding missing data, and removing and replacing inaccuracies with correct data. You should prepare the verification plot in the same way you prepared the original map for digitizing. The goal is to be consistent and minimize uncertainty for the person making the edits to the coverage. Note the following:

Error	What should be marked
Missing arcs	Draw them in.
Missing label points	Mark position and correct User-ID value.
More than one label point in a polygon	Identify which ones to delete.
A gap between two arcs or an unclosed polygon	Indicate which arc to extend or which node to move.
An overshoot	Indicate whether it should be deleted.
Incorrect User-ID values	Mark the correct value.

For example, this set of errors is marked to be corrected.

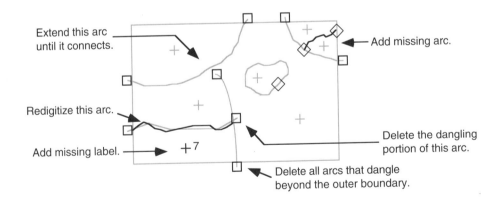

Extend this arc until it connects.

Add missing arc.

Redigitize this arc.

Add missing label.

Delete the dangling portion of this arc.

Delete all arcs that dangle beyond the outer boundary.

Understanding GIS—The ARC/INFO Method

Here is the same set of data after correcting the spatial errors.

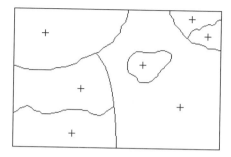

Step 4

Reconstruct topology

Editing the spatial characteristics of a coverage alters its topology. In such cases, you must always reconstruct topology to reestablish the spatial relationships. After you reconstruct the topology, repeat Step 2, checking for any errors that remain. Then, if necessary, repeat Steps 3 and 4. Here is a chart showing the overall process:

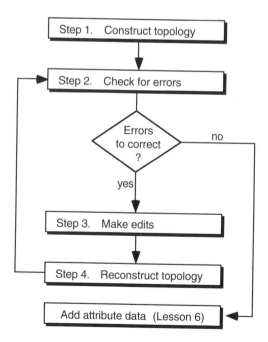

Constructing topology

To create spatial relationships between the features in a coverage, it is necessary to construct topology. ARC/INFO assigns an internal number to each feature. These numbers are then used to determine arc connectivity and polygon contiguity. Once calculated, these values are recorded and stored in a tabular format called a *feature attribute table*.

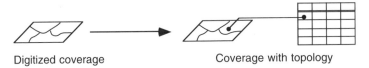

Digitized coverage   Coverage with topology

feature attribute tables

Feature attribute tables are INFO files associated with each feature type. For example, constructing topology for a polygon coverage creates a polygon attribute table (PAT); for a line coverage, an arc attribute table (AAT); and for a point coverage, a point attribute table (PAT). Each table is composed of rows and columns. The columns represent an item, such as the perimeter, whereas the rows represent an individual feature, such as polygon number 2.

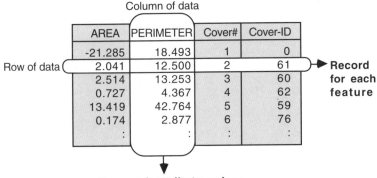

Column of data

AREA	PERIMETER	Cover#	Cover-ID
-21.285	18.493	1	0
2.041	12.500	2	61
2.514	13.253	3	60
0.727	4.367	4	62
13.419	42.764	5	59
0.174	2.877	6	76
:	:	:	:

Row of data   Record for each feature

Item and attribute values

This diagram illustrates how data is stored in a PAT. It highlights the four standard items that are created for every PAT: AREA, PERIMETER, the Cover#, and the Cover-ID. Values for the first six records, which correspond to features in the polygon coverage, are listed.

Feature attribute tables use a template of standard items appropriate for the type of feature. Only point and polygon coverages use the same template, the PAT, which contains the standard items AREA, PERIMETER, Cover#, and Cover-ID. Note that the actual name of the coverage is substituted wherever you see the word 'Cover'.

standard items in an AAT   The AAT contains seven standard items created in the following order:

FNODE#	Internal node number for the beginning of an arc (from-node)
TNODE#	Internal node number for the end of an arc (to-node)
LPOLY#	Internal number for the left polygon (the Cover# in a corresponding PAT)
RPOLY#	Internal number for the right polygon (the Cover# in a corresponding PAT)
LENGTH	Length of each arc, measured in coverage units
Cover#	Internal arc number (values assigned by ARC/INFO)
Cover-ID	User-ID (values assigned by the user)

The values for the left and right polygons in an AAT for a coverage containing only lines always equal zero.

standard items in a PAT   The PAT contains four standard items created in the following order:

AREA	Area of each polygon, measured in coverage units
PERIMETER	Length of each polygon boundary, measured in coverage units
Cover#	Internal polygon number (assigned by ARC/INFO)
Cover-ID	User-ID (assigned by the user)

The PAT for a coverage of points always contains zero values for both AREA and PERIMETER.

BUILD versus CLEAN   The commands BUILD and CLEAN construct topology in ARC/INFO. Although these commands perform similar functions— they both construct topology and create feature attribute tables—there are important differences. BUILD creates or updates a feature attribute table for point, line, polygon, node, or annotation coverages. CLEAN, however, performs coordinate editing and creates feature attribute tables for polygon and line coverages only.

Whether you use BUILD or CLEAN for creating polygon or arc topology depends on how the data was originally digitized; BUILD recognizes only existing intersections (discrete digitizing), whereas CLEAN creates intersections wherever lines cross one another (spaghetti digitizing).

BUILD assumes that the coordinate data is correct, whereas CLEAN finds arcs that cross and places a node at each intersection. In addition, CLEAN corrects undershoots and overshoots within a specified tolerance.

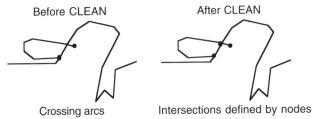

Before CLEAN   After CLEAN

Crossing arcs   Intersections defined by nodes

Intersections, formed by connecting arcs, can be identified by the presence of a node.

Based on these differences, you must choose the appropriate command. To help you decide, these differences are summarized in the table below. For more specific details, see the BUILD and CLEAN commands in the online *Command References* for ARC.

Capabilities	BUILD	CLEAN
Processes:		
Polygons	Yes	Yes
Lines	Yes	Yes
Points	Yes	No
Numbers features	Yes	Yes
Calculates spatial measurements	Yes	Yes
Creates intersections	No	Yes
Processing speed	Faster	Slower

In the upcoming exercise, you'll perform both a BUILD and a CLEAN on your digitized land use coverage.

FYI
    The BUILD and CLEAN commands are also available in ARCEDIT. In ARCEDIT, BUILD and CLEAN offer options for deleting duplicate polygon labels and placing labels in polygons that need them. For more information, see these commands in the online *Command References* for ARC and ARCEDIT.

EXERCISE

Construct topology and examine a PAT

In this exercise, you'll use the CLEAN command to construct topology for your digitized land use coverage. Start ARC, if necessary, and move to the LAND workspace in your UGIS directory.

UNIX   Arc: **&WORKSPACE /yourname/ugis/land**
Windows NT   Arc: **&WORKSPACE <drive>:\yourname\ugis\land**

For this exercise, you'll need the coverage named LANDDG01.

```
Arc: LISTCOVERAGES

Available Coverages
-------------------
  LANDDG01    TICCOV
Arc:
```

HELP

If you did not digitize LANDDG01 in Chapter 4, you will have to create a LAND workspace in your UGIS directory and copy LANDG01.

UNIX   Arc: **&WORKSPACE   /yourname/ugis**
Windows NT   Arc: **&WORKSPACE <drive>:\yourname\ugis**
      Arc: **CREATEWORKSPACE LAND**
      Arc: **W LAND**

UNIX   Arc: **COPY ../RESULTS/LANDDG01 LANDDG01**
Windows NT   Arc: **COPY ..\RESULTS\LANDDG01 LANDDG01**

```
Copied <drive>:\training\ugis\results\landdg01 to landdg01
```

Always use the ARC COPY command to copy coverages. COPY duplicates all information associated with the coverage including its INFO files.

It's easy to determine whether to use BUILD or CLEAN by finding out whether the coverage contains intersecting arcs. If it does, use CLEAN. The INTERSECTERR command identifies any arcs that intersect without a node.

```
Arc: USAGE INTERSECTERR
Usage: INTERSECTERR <cover>
Arc: INTERSECTERR LANDDG01
  Sorting...
  Locating intersections...
```

Internal ID 1	User ID 1	Internal ID 2	User ID 2	Intersection X	Intersection Y
1	1	3	3	12.185	7.500
1	1	1	1	13.228	7.508
20	21	1	1	13.230	7.294
2	2	1	1	9.165	7.039
.	.	.	.	.	.
.	.	.	.	.	.
.	.	.	.	.	.

```
Total number of intersections found:  21
```

INTERSECTERR detected 21 intersections in LANDDG01. Such intersections are usually the result of spaghetti digitizing. Because CLEAN creates intersections wherever the lines overlap, use it instead of BUILD to create the initial topology for your land use coverage.

```
Arc: USAGE CLEAN
Usage: CLEAN <in_cover> {out_cover} {dangle_length}
             {fuzzy_tolerance} {POLY | LINE}
```

Issue the CLEAN command by specifying the name of the new coverage to be created and its feature type. CLEAN processes all the information entered during digitizing and places it in a new, topologically structured coverage that we'll name LANDCN02. The new coverage's suffix is CN for clean and 02 for the second version of the map.

Understanding GIS—The ARC/INFO Method

While cleaning the data, you might as well get rid of all the obvious dangling arcs, including all those arcs that you extended on purpose when digitizing beyond the boundary. This can be done by setting a specific distance as your {dangle_length}. Although the length of the dangles will vary, none of them should be longer than 1/4 of a centimeter, or 1/10 of an inch.

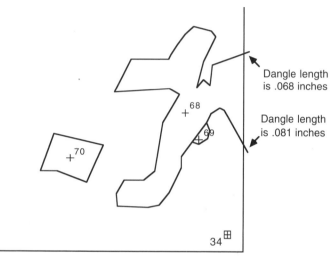

Dangle length is .068 inches

Dangle length is .081 inches

Each dangling arc will be a different length. When you specify a {dangle_length}, only dangling arcs less than that length are removed. Ideally, you want to select a distance that removes as many as possible without affecting any significant dangling arcs located inside the outer boundary.

Specify a dangle distance just slightly longer than your longest dangle; in our case, we use 0.1 inches. Use your judgment to determine whether this value is appropriate for your data.

```
Arc: CLEAN LANDDG01 LANDCN02 0.1
Cleaning <drive>:\yourname\UGIS\LAND\LANDDG01
  Sorting...
  Intersecting...
  Assembling polygons...
Arc:
```

The coverage LANDCN02 now exists as a 'clean' coverage with current topology and a polygon attribute table (PAT) related to the basic coordinate data. To examine the contents of a PAT, use the LIST command.

```
Arc: USAGE LIST
Usage: LIST <info_file> {from} {to} {item...item}
Arc: LIST LANDCN02.PAT
```

The records in your PAT may be in a different order.

Record	AREA	PERIMETER	LANDCN02#	LANDCN02-ID
1	-21.285	18.493	1	0
2	2.041	12.500	2	61
3	2.514	13.253	3	60
4	0.727	4.367	4	62
5	13.419	42.764	5	59
6	0.174	2.877	6	76
7	0.036	0.960	7	64
8	0.399	3.518	8	65
9	0.140	1.727	9	77
10	0.034	0.905	10	63
11	0.296	3.142	11	75
12	0.436	3.839	12	71
13	0.131	1.500	13	66
14	0.548	3.513	14	74
15	0.072	1.078	15	72
16	0.119	1.711	16	73
17	0.016	0.556	17	69
18	0.182	1.788	18	70

```
Arc:
```

The attribute values for each polygon are listed on the screen. This PAT contains its four standard items: AREA, PERIMETER, Cover# and Cover-ID.

Once the standard PAT has been created, additional attribute items can be added as needed (something you will do in the next lesson). For now, you have only the standard items. The listed User-IDs match the User-IDs of the label points you entered during your ARCEDIT session.

Recall that all measurements are recorded in coverage units. The area and perimeter values for each polygon are small because this is the digitized coverage, measured in digitizer units (inches) rather than real-world coordinates (meters or feet).

One record which should have caught your attention is Polygon 1 with a negative area and a User-ID of 0. This is a special polygon referred to as the *external* polygon or the *universe* polygon. It represents the area beyond the outer boundary of the coverage. It's the only polygon that never has a label point, and so has a User-ID value of 0. Its area equals the negative sum of all the polygons in the coverage.

HELP

If your station file includes &FULLSCREEN &POPUP, text, like that generated with the LIST command, displays in a scrolling popup window like the one shown below.

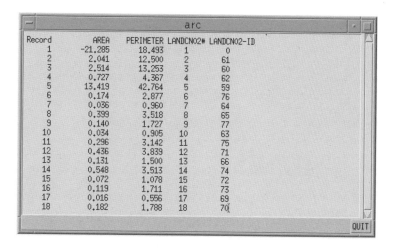

You must always close or **Quit** from the popup window before you can proceed.

If &FULLSCREEN &POPUP is not set in your station file, then text displays in the dialog area of your screen (as shown on the previous page) instead of in a popup window. You will find the two types of text display used interchangeably in this workbook.

END

Identifying digitizing errors

Now that you've created the initial feature topology for your land use coverage, you must check the coverage for any errors that occurred during digitizing. You must confirm the accuracy of arc and label point positions and rectify any mistakes.

Before you can identify digitizing errors, you need to make a map of your data as it exists. ARC/INFO includes a program to create a map of your current data. But first, a few words about maps and plots. You are familiar with what is meant by a map. Now add to this a computer file that describes the same data in a format that can be sent to a plotter—a hardware device that draws coordinates on paper. In ARC/INFO, this kind of file is called a *graphics file*. The computer-generated map is referred to as a *plot*.

In the upcoming exercise, you'll generate a graphics file containing the information you need to identify errors. You can display this graphics file on the screen or send it to a plotter to create a hardcopy plot of your map. This file shows you not only the contents of your coverage, but also highlights any node, label, or arc errors.

EXERCISE   **Use EDITPLOT to create a display of coverage errors**

For this exercise, you'll create a verification plot of a digitized and cleaned land use coverage and check its data against the original map manuscript. You can display this graphics file on your screen and, if your computer is connected to a plotter, use it to make a hardcopy plot of the coverage in its current state.

We provide a test coverage upon which you can practice identifying errors and making edits. After practicing on the provided coverage, repeat the same sequence on your digitized coverage, LANDCN02.

For this exercise, you'll need two coverages: LANDCN and LANDCN02. Copy the test coverage, LANDCN, into your LAND workspace from your DATA workspace. LANDCN02, the coverage you digitized and cleaned, should already exist in your LAND workspace.

UNIX   Arc: **COPY ../data/landcn landcn**
Windows NT   Arc: **COPY ..\data\landcn landcn**
                Copied <drive:>\yourname\ugis\data\landcn to landcn

Now there should be four coverages in your LAND workspace.
From now on, use the abbreviation LC for the LISTCOVERAGES
command.

```
Arc: LC
 Workspace:              <drive>:\yourname\UGIS\LAND

 Available Coverages
 ------------------
  LANDCN    LANDCN02    LANDDG01    TICCOV
Arc:
```

Once you confirm that these coverages are in your LAND workspace,
issue the EDITPLOT command with the name of the coverage you
want to plot. If you're making a hardcopy of your coverage, the plot
should be at the same scale as the original map. Because the coverage
coordinates are in digitizer units, the scale will be 1:1; that is, one unit
on the plot equals one unit on the map manuscript (this is the default
scale). The plot should also show arcs, node errors, and label points
with User-IDs. If you don't specify the {out_graphics_file} name,
the default of <in_cover>.GRA is used.

```
Arc: USAGE EDITPLOT
Usage: EDITPLOT <in_cover> {out_graphics_file} {scale_denominator}
Arc: EDITPLOT LANDCN
```

The EDITPLOT program now asks a series of questions requiring yes
or no responses.

```
Window plot? NO
```

If you respond Yes to the `Window plot?` prompt, EDITPLOT asks
for the x,y coordinates of the lower left and upper right window
corners to zoom in on a specific portion of the coverage. Answering
No tells EDITPLOT that you want to view the entire coverage.

Text for the legend may be up to 70 characters in length.

```
Enter legend text: <CR>
```
Entering a carriage return plots the
default legend: EDITPLOT OF
LANDCN.

```
Plot Tics? YES
```
Responding Yes plots all tics
located inside the coverage
boundary and labels them with
their Tic-ID numbers. This will
help you register the verification
plot to the original map.

Answering Yes plots only polygons with label position errors, and skips the rest of the EDITPLOT questions.

If you entered Yes by mistake, your plot will finish anyway. You'll be returned to the `Arc:` prompt where you can start the EDITPLOT command sequence over again.

`Plot ONLY Polygons with label errors? NO`

Responding No indicates that instead of just some polygons, you want all the polygons to be drawn.

`Plot Arcs? YES`

All arcs are plotted.

`Plot Arc Ids? NO`

Responding No asks that the arc User-IDs not be plotted. Because you're displaying a polygon coverage, not a line coverage, adding this information to your display only makes it more difficult to focus on the polygon data.

`Plot Label Points? YES`

Responding Yes plots all label points along with their User-IDs.

`Plot node errors? YES`

Both pseudo nodes (those shared by only two arcs) and dangling nodes (arc endpoints not shared with any other arc) are plotted.

`Arc:`

The ARC system prompt returns when EDITPLOT finishes. Listing the directory, you'll see a new file named LANDCN.GRA. Note that all commands are first interpreted by ARC; any unrecognized commands are then passed to the operating system.

UNIX `Arc: &sys ls`
Windows NT `Arc: &sys dir /w`

Understanding GIS—The ARC/INFO Method

This file can be drawn on the screen or sent to a plotter. To draw the graphics file on your screen, use your station file to specify the display device. Then issue the DRAW command with the name of the graphics file.

```
Arc: &STATION <name>
Arc: DRAW LANDCN.GRA
WARNING the Map extent is not defined
WARNING: Pagesize exceeds device limits, scaling down
```

Your plot should look something like this...

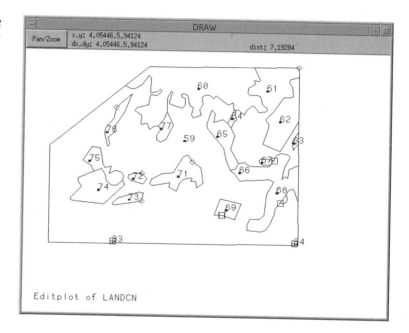

Viewing your plot, you see potential errors flagged in your coverage. You might see errors around nodes that, at first glance, don't appear to be errors (particularly true of dangling nodes). Zooming in to get a close-up look reveals that these nodes really don't connect as they should, creating undershoots and overshoots. In the next section, you'll learn how to zoom in and use ARC/INFO to correct these errors.

Once you finish viewing your plot file and wish to return to the ARC prompt, press the carriage return.

```
Hit <CR> to continue: <CR>
```

▼FYI▼   If you issue a command that initiates a graphic display without first specifying your station file, you will receive an error message and the command will not execute; for example,

```
Arc: DRAW
Device must be graphic.
Arc:
```

To remedy this condition, specify your station file to set the display environment, then reissue the command. You only need to specify your station file one time during each ARC/INFO session.

If your UNIX workstation is attached to a plotter, you should also make a hardcopy plot using the PLOT command available at the Arc: prompt. Check with your system administrator.

If your Windows NT workstation is attached to a plotter, you should also make a hardcopy plot using the Windows NT Print Manager. Check with your system administrator. To print, use the print icon in the ARC/INFO User program group in the Windows Program Manager.

▼FYI▼   A plotter is used to generate a paper plot to overlay directly onto the map manuscript. This allows you to directly compare the data you input to its source. Use a light table to compare the edit plot you create with the map manuscript provided. If a light table isn't available, make the comparison by holding the map and the plot up to any available light source.

You can generate a list of potential errors on the screen using NODEERRORS and LABELERRORS. These commands list the errors marked on your edit plot, allowing you to examine the errors systematically.

A watch file creates a system file of the output displayed on the screen. These files can be spooled to your system printer and checked against your edit plot.

Start a watch file using the &WATCH AML directive and name it
NODE.ERR. Then issue the NODEERRORS command. Most
likely, you're interested in both dangling nodes and pseudo nodes.
To list them both, choose the ALL option.

```
Arc: &WATCH NODE.ERR
Arc: USAGE NODEERRORS
Usage: NODEERRORS <cover> {ALL | DANGLES | PSEUDOS}
Arc: NODEERRORS LANDCN ALL
    Pseudo Node     8 at (    13.22821,    7.50828)
    Pseudo Node    16 at (     8.96204,    6.54644)
  Dangling Node    18 at (    12.68590,    5.39125)
    Pseudo Node    22 at (     9.57501,    5.05692)
    Pseudo Node    23 at (    10.74500,    5.33056)
  Dangling Node    30 at (    12.83447,    4.43760)
    Pseudo Node    25 at (     9.58293,    4.43210)
  Dangling Node    26 at (    11.46413,    4.13696)
  Dangling Node    27 at (    11.47734,    4.13730)
Total number of Pseudo Nodes:    5
Total number of Dangling Nodes: 4
```

Be sure to close the watch file when the listing is complete.

```
Arc: &WATCH &OFF
```

The sample coverage contains five pseudo nodes and four dangling
nodes. Although some may be acceptable (i.e., represent island
polygons, rather than true spatial errors), you must check them all.
To help you further assess which errors must be corrected, create a list
of label errors. Open a watch file to contain label errors named
LABEL.ERR. Then issue the LABELERRORS command.

```
Arc: &WATCH LABEL.ERR
Arc: USAGE LABELERRORS
Usage: LABELERRORS <cover>
Arc: LABELERRORS LANDCN
Polygon          1 has     0 label points.
Polygon         15 has     2 label points.
Label User ID:        69
Label User ID:        59
Polygon         17 has     2 label points.
Label User ID:        68
Label User ID:        66
Arc: &WATCH &OFF
```

The sample land use coverage contains three potential label errors:
Polygon 1 has no label, Polygon 15 has two labels (User-IDs 59 and
69), and Polygon 17 has two labels (User-IDs 66 and 68). Although
some may be acceptable (e.g., because Polygon 1 represents the
external polygon, it does not require a label), you must check them all.

FYI
A spatially correct polygon coverage usually contains pseudo nodes but no dangles. And, the only acceptable label error occurs in Polygon 1 (the universe polygon), which never has a label point.

Whenever you need to, you can display this error information by using the &POPUP directive to display the watch files you just created; for example,

Arc: **&POPUP LABEL.ERR**

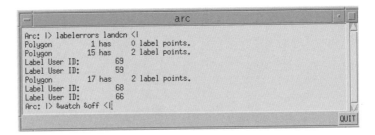

```
arc
Arc: 1> labelerrors landcn <|
Polygon        1 has      0 label points.
Polygon       15 has      2 label points.
Label User ID:        69
Label User ID:        59
Polygon       17 has      2 label points.
Label User ID:        68
Label User ID:        66
Arc: 1> &watch &off <|
                                          QUIT
```

If your computer is attached to a line printer, you can also create a hardcopy of these lists. Check with your system administrator.

END

EXERCISE **Identify necessary edits from a list of node errors, a list of label errors, and an edit plot**

In this exercise, you'll assess the accuracy of the data contained in the LANDCN coverage using data collected in the previous exercise. This done, you can list the errors that need correcting and determine an order in which to correct them.

Although you have an edit plot highlighting potential errors and lists of the node errors and label errors, identifying actual errors is still a manual process. LANDCN contains six errors, listed as 1 through 6 below. Identify these errors on the sample plot by visually comparing the digitized coverage to the original map. Circle the errors on the digitized map and place the correct number next to each one. (See Appendix D for exercise answers.)

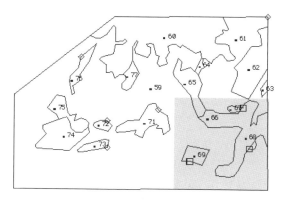

1) Missing label point

2) Polygon with two label points due to a missing arc

3) Dangling node due to an arc overshoot

4) Dangling node due to an arc undershoot

5) Dangling nodes due to an unclosed island polygon

6) Label point with incorrect label User-ID

Data from original map manuscript

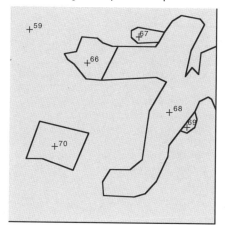

Sample plot from the digitized coverage

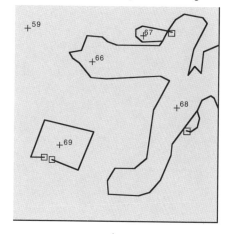

Next compare the errors you marked with the error reports generated by NODEERRORS and LABELERRORS.

NODE.ERR

```
    Pseudo Node      8 at (   13.22821,    7.50828)
    Pseudo Node     16 at (    8.96204,    6.54644)
  Dangling Node     18 at (   12.68590,    5.39125)
    Pseudo Node     22 at (    9.57501,    5.05692)
    Pseudo Node     23 at (   10.74500,    5.33056)
  Dangling Node     30 at (   12.83447,    4.43760)
    Pseudo Node     25 at (    9.58293,    4.43210)
  Dangling Node     26 at (   11.46413,    4.13696)
  Dangling Node     27 at (   11.47734,    4.13730)
  Total number of Pseudo Nodes:    5
  Total number of Dangling Nodes: 4
```

You must be able to account for five pseudo nodes and four dangling nodes. The pseudo nodes are all acceptable; four of them mark island polygons, and one marks the upper-right corner of the coverage where only two lines connect. You must correct all four dangling nodes. One represents an overshoot and one an undershoot. The other two are due to an unclosed polygon, and, when connected, will form another, acceptable, pseudo node. When spatially correct, the node error report should contain six pseudo nodes and zero dangling nodes.

LABEL.ERR

```
  Polygon          1 has      0 label points.
  Polygon         15 has      2 label points.
  Label User ID:        69
  Label User ID:        59
  Polygon         17 has      2 label points.
  Label User ID:        68
  Label User ID:        66
```

You must also be able to account for the label errors listed in LABEL.ERR. Polygon 1, the external polygon, has no label point. This is what you would expect; it's not an error. Next, Polygons 15 and 17 each have two label points. In both cases, the label points correctly mark different polygons. Multiple label points exist because not all polygon boundaries connect properly. Polygon 15 will be corrected when you close the island (User-ID = 69), and Polygon 17, when you add the missing arc. When these corrections are made, the only label error reported should be the missing label for Polygon 1.

FYI

You can use ARCPLOT to create special edit plots. For example, the commands below produce an output file containing label errors, node numbers and node errors. Including the node numbers on the plot makes the errors listed in the NODEERRORS report easy to identify. Because nothing draws on the screen as you create this file, you don't need a graphics terminal to produce it. You can create a hardcopy plot of the output file using the PLOT command at the Arc: prompt. For Windows NT, you can create a hardcopy plot of the output file by selecting the Print Icon in the ARC/INFO program group and selecting the appropriate printer.

```
Arc: ARCPLOT
Arcplot: DISPLAY 1040
ENTER ARC/INFO GRAPHICS FILENAME: MYERRORS
Arcplot: MAPEXTENT LANDCN
Arcplot: MAPSCALE 1
Arcplot: ARCS LANDCN
Arcplot: MARKERCOLOR RED
Arcplot: NODEERRORS LANDCN
Arcplot: TEXTCOLOR GREEN
Arcplot: NODES LANDCN IDSONLY
Arcplot: MARKERCOLOR BLUE
Arcplot: LABELERRORS LANDCN
Arcplot: QUIT
```

END

Correcting spatial data using ARCEDIT

Once identified, you can correct all the spatial errors in ARCEDIT—the graphics and database editor. ARCEDIT performs many functions in addition to digitizing. This section introduces a few of the basic editing commands and explains when to use them.

ARCEDIT employs editing environments and feature-oriented editing. Commands set various editing environments that establish conditions in which the edit session occurs. Environment-setting commands tell ARCEDIT which hardware devices you'll use, the coverages you want to work with, the kinds of features you want to edit, and which features to display. Then, to increase efficiency, ARCEDIT applies feature-oriented editing procedures—essentially a four-stage process:

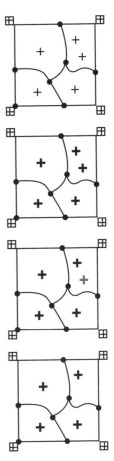

1) Specify the coverage containing features to edit.

2) Specify the feature class to edit. Your choices include tics, arcs, nodes, labels, or any other ARC/INFO feature class.

3) Select specific features within the edit feature class to edit (i.e., exactly which tic, arc, node, or label, etc., is going to be changed).

4) Edit the selected features (e.g., delete, move, or extend).

EXERCISE

Conduct an ARCEDIT session

In this exercise, you'll start ARCEDIT and edit the sample land use coverage. If necessary, move to your LAND workspace. Make sure it contains the LANDCN coverage from the last exercise.

```
Arc: LC

Available Coverages
-------------------

  LANDCN    LANDCN02    LANDDG01    TICCOV
```

You can edit from either a digitizing station or a graphics screen. This exercise uses the screen to introduce the ARCEDIT environment. The following exercise uses the digitizer and screen to correct mistakes.

To maintain database integrity, always edit a *copy* of your most recent coverage. You can copy your current coverage during an ARCEDIT session, but it's safer to copy *before* you begin the session, then work on the copy. For now, copy the sample land use coverage to use as your edit coverage. Then begin the ARCEDIT session.

```
Arc: COPY LANDCN LANDED
Copied landcn to landed
Arc: ARCEDIT
Arcedit:
```

setting the environment

If necessary, use your station file to establish the display environment.

```
Arcedit: &STATION <name>
Warning the Map extent is not defined
```

*edit coverage and
map extent*

Specify the extent of the coverage to display and the name of the coverage to edit; in this case, LANDED.

```
Arcedit: COORDINATE MOUSE
Arcedit: MAPEXTENT LANDED
Arcedit: EDIT LANDED
The edit coverage is now <drive>:\yourname\UGIS\LAND\LANDED
```

The map extent defaults to the BND of the edit coverage if the EDIT command is issued before a map extent is set.

```
Arcedit: EDIT LANDED
The edit coverage is now <drive>:\yourname\UGIS\LAND\LANDED
WARNNG the Map extent is not defined
Defaulting the map extent to the BND of
<drive>:\yourname\UGIS\LAND\LANDED
```

```
┌──────────┐
│  HELP    │
└──────────┘
```

If you misspell a command parameter, the correct usage automatically displays on the screen; for example,

```
Arcedit: EDIT LANDCN.PAT IFNO
Usage: EDIT <cover> {feature_class}
Usage: EDIT <info_file> INFO
Arcedit:
```

Whenever this happens, type the command again correctly.

If you misspell an actual command, rather than one of its parameters, the following message appears:

```
Arcedit: EIDT
Unrecognized command.
Arcedit:
```

When this happens, type it again, spelling it correctly.

drawing environment   As you'll recall from Lesson 4, DRAWENVIRONMENT specifies which features in the edit coverage to draw on the screen when the DRAW command is issued. To display arcs, nodes, and labels, include each in your current drawing environment.

```
Arcedit: DRAWENVIRONMENT ARC NODE LABEL
Arcedit: DRAW
```

```
 ┌──┐
 \FYI/
  \ /
   V
```

The two-letter abbreviation for DRAWENVIRONMENT is DE. Most ARC/INFO commands have similar abbreviations, indicated by uppercase letters when commands are listed on the screen.

```
Arcedit: COMMANDS D
DISPlay   DrawEnvironment   DrawOrder   DrawSelect...
```

As you become more familiar with command names, you'll want to use abbreviations to reduce the amount you type.

enhancing the display   Altering how features are displayed can make features easier to see. For example, if you have a color display, you can change the color used to draw nodes. Using contrasting colors for the arcs and nodes makes them easier for you to differentiate.

Arcedit: **NODECOLOR NODE RED**
Arcedit: **DRAW**

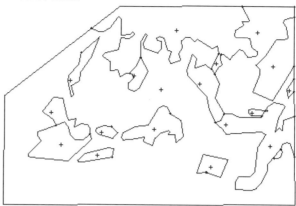

*Whenever the DRAW command is given, the screen clears and
all features in the current drawing environment are redrawn.*

Settings in the drawing environment can be changed or switched off.
For instance, if you're going to begin your session by editing arcs,
you may want to display only the arcs and their node errors. To do
this, leave the arcs as they are, specify that node errors be added, and
turn the labels off.

Arcedit: **DRAWENVIRONMENT NODE ERRORS LABEL OFF**
Arcedit: **DRAW**

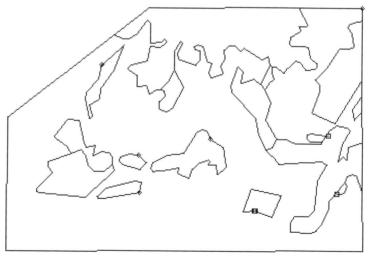

After the drawing environment is changed, the coverage should be redrawn.

edit features

Now specify the type of feature you want to edit; for example, arcs,
nodes, or labels. Once set, no other feature type can be edited until
you reissue the EDITFEATURE command with a new feature type.
This can be done at any time during the ARCEDIT session.

```
Arcedit: EDITFEATURE ARC
39 element(s) for edit feature ARC
```

selecting features

In ARCEDIT, you can only edit selected elements within a feature
class. That is, you have to select a specific arc, or set of arcs, before
you can delete or move them. Before selecting, however, you will
want to zoom in to take a closer look at the error. To do this, open the
Pan/Zoom menu with the button located in the upper left corner of
the graphics display window and select the **Extent** option.

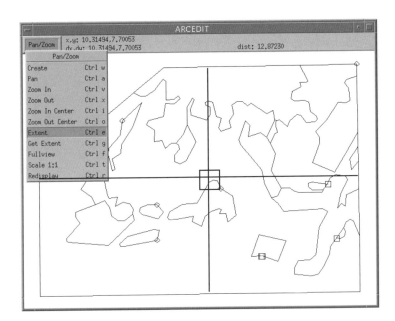

Now when you position the cursor in the graphics display window, the crosshairs appear. To define the area you want to enlarge, first position the cursor crosshairs at any corner of a box that defines the area and enter its location by pressing the appropriate button on your mouse (usually the 1 or 3 button). Next, move the cursor to the opposite corner of the box and finish defining the area by again pressing the appropriate mouse button.

The area you defined is enlarged on the screen.

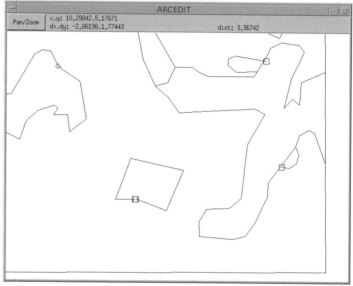

Zooming in on specific portions of a coverage allows you to more easily see and select the features you wish to edit.

You can use this technique whenever the lesson asks you to zoom in on a particular area. You can also use the other options on the Pan/Zoom menu to zoom in, zoom out, and pan to look at different portions of your map. Use the Fullview menu option to return to your original view of the coverage.

The WINDOWS command opens multiple graphics windows on X terminals to provide different views of a coverage. In addition to creating up to 20 graphics windows, the WINDOWS command zooms in and out, changes the map extent, and pans across the display on any type of terminal. The Create option in the Pan/Zoom menu also creates multiple graphics windows.

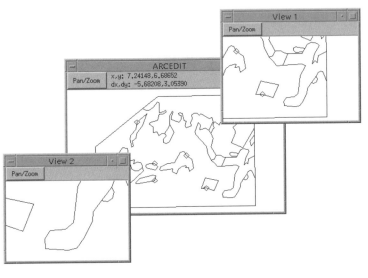

To select a feature or set of features, use the SELECT command.

```
Arcedit: SELECT MANY
1 = Select  2 = Next  3 = Who  9 = Quit
```

The cursor appears on the terminal screen. Position the crosshairs directly over the feature you wish to select, and **press the 1 button** on the mouse or keyboard to select it.

HELP

Windows NT
If you are using a 2-button mouse, usually the left mouse button is 1 and the right mouse button is 3. To access the other button numbers, make the graphic window the active window and use the numbers at the top of the keyboard. If you wish, you can execute 2BUTTON to remap the right mouse button from 3 to 2.

Understanding GIS—The ARC/INFO Method

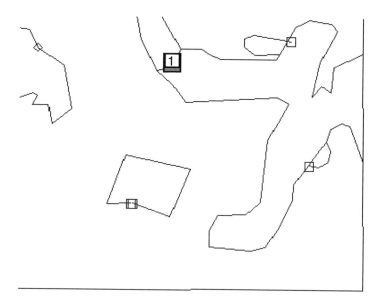

```
Arc 26 User-ID: 25 with 3 points
1 = Select  2 = Next  3 = Who  9 = Quit
```

Every time you select an arc in this manner, the arc is highlighted in yellow and information about it is displayed directly beneath the select menu (i.e., its User-ID and the total number of points or vertices).

HELP

If the edit feature is not set and you try to add or select a feature, ARCEDIT returns the following message:

```
Arcedit: ADD                        Arcedit: SELECT MANY
No edit feature specified           No edit feature selected
```

You must issue the EDITFEATURE command before continuing.

Use numbers 1, 2, 3, or 9 to select the option you want. The selected feature is drawn in yellow. You can add features to the selected set by pointing at them with the cursor and pressing the 1 key. If you select the wrong feature, press the 2 key to select the next nearest feature. Continue pressing the 2 key until the correct feature is selected. You can continue until the correct feature is selected or until the message No more elements within the search radius appears, in which case, the cursor is not within the edit distance of the desired feature.

Note that when you press the 2 key immediately after selecting a feature, that feature becomes unselected and the next feature within the edit distance of the cursor is chosen.

Choose 9 when you've finished selecting features.

```
1 = Select  2 = Next  3 = Who  9 = Quit
1 element(s) now selected.
```

performing edits   You can begin editing once you select the feature, or set of features, to edit. Editing options depend on the feature type you selected.

arcs   Arcs can be deleted, moved, added, or copied using the DELETE, MOVE, ADD, or COPY commands. Delete your selected feature. (It's all right to do this; you can restore it with the OOPS command.)

```
Arcedit: DELETE
1 arc(s) deleted
```

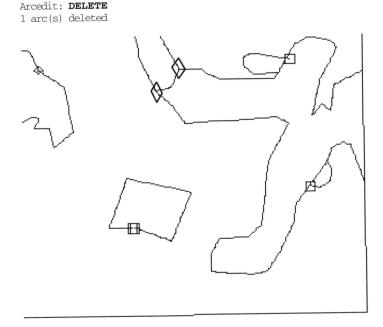

The arc disappears from the screen. To bring it back, type

```
Arcedit: OOPS
0 arc(s) deleted and 1 arc(s) restored
Now at transaction 1
```

Understanding GIS—The ARC/INFO Method

FYI

During ARCEDIT, you can undo the last edit made using the OOPS command. To undo more than one edit, issue the OOPS command as many times as you want. Each time it is issued, OOPS will undo the previous transaction back to the last SAVE.

labels   Labels can also be selected and edited. The only difference is that the current edit feature has to be set to LABEL.

nodes   Although arcs and labels can be deleted, moved, added, or copied using the DELETE, MOVE, ADD, or COPY commands, these same options are not directly available for nodes. Nodes can be deleted, added, or copied only if the arc they are attached to is deleted, added, or copied.

The only command that operates directly on nodes is MOVE. This is because nodes are *always* attached to an arc. So when you move an arc, its nodes move with it; likewise, if you move a node, the arc to which it is attached also moves.

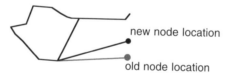

new node location

old node location

Although the edit performed here moved a node, the arc to which it attaches also moved. Notice that the arc's other endpoint stayed in place.

The next exercise requires a digitizer. If your terminal has a digitizer attached, you can stay in ARCEDIT. If you need to move to another terminal to use the digitizer, leave ARCEDIT now.

Arcedit: **QUIT**

You are prompted to keep the changes you made. Answer No.

Keep all edit changes (Y/N): **N**
Leaving ARCEDIT...

END

EXERCISE   ## Correct errors in a digitized coverage

Now that you've been introduced to the basic ARCEDIT environment, you're ready to perform some real edits. The next few pages present procedures for correcting the most common digitizing errors. These correspond to the errors in the sample land use coverage provided.

The first time through this exercise, you will edit LANDED, fixing the errors in the order they are presented. Later, if you choose to edit your own digitized coverage (LANDED03), you can refer to these procedures as needed. Use the following table as a reference.

Digitizing error	Page reference
Add a missing label point	5-45
Add a missing arc	5-47
Correct an overshoot	5-51
Correct an undershoot	5-52
Fix an open polygon	5-53
Change a label User-ID	5-54

Remember to save your edits frequently. When you finish editing, quit ARCEDIT and continue with the next section, 'Using ARC/INFO to reconstruct topology'. The procedures for saving and quitting ARCEDIT are described at the end of this exercise.

Saving your corrections	5-55
Quitting from ARCEDIT	5-56

preparation   Although it's already digitized and cleaned, LANDED still contains six
errors that must be corrected, numbered 1 through 6 below.

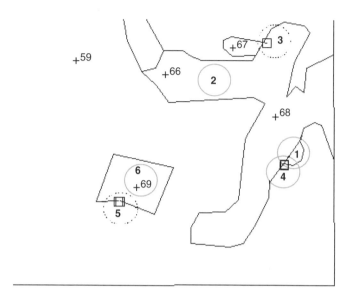

Optimize your editing session by establishing a plan beforehand. An
effective plan considers the editing environments required to perform
the various edits and the location of the edits in the coverage. For
example, missing data should be added from the digitizing table,
whereas data *corrections* can be made more quickly using a graphics
screen. So, make all the edits that require the digitizer at the same
time.

This list was prepared to correct the errors in LANDED.

List of corrections	EDITFEATURE
Data to be added by digitizing:	
1. Add a missing label.	LABEL
2. Add a missing arc.	ARC
Data to be corrected using the graphics screen:	
3. Correct an overshoot.	ARC
4. Correct an undershoot.	ARC
5. Fix an open polygon.	NODE
6. Change a label User-ID.	LABEL

This exercise begins on a digitizing table and ends on a graphics screen. Make sure your workstation has a digitizer available. Before proceeding, tape the original manuscript securely to the digitizer. Then, if not already there, go to your LAND workspace, start ARC, specify your station file, and then start ARCEDIT.

Arc: **ARCEDIT**

To speed the command entry for the environment settings and feature editing, you can use the following abbreviations:

Abbreviation	Command
EF	EDITFEATURE
DE	DRAWENVIRONMENT

Specify LANDED as the edit coverage letting the map extent default to the boundary of LANDED.

Arcedit: **EDIT LANDED**
The edit coverage is now <drive>:\yourname\UGIS
LAND\LANDED.
WARNING, the Map extent is not defined
Defaulting the map extent to the BND of <drive>:\yourname\UGIS
LAND\LANDED.

adding missing data Adding data missed during the original digitizing session should be done directly from the map manuscript. In LANDED, the missing data consist of one label (1) and one arc (2).

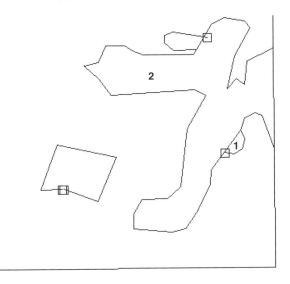

set the editing environment

Because these two features must be added from the digitizer, specify that you'll be entering coordinates from the digitizer, and name the coverage you'll be editing. After doing so, you'll be prompted to enter your tic locations on the digitizer to register your map.

```
Arcedit: COORDINATE DIGITIZER LANDED
Digitize a minimum of 4 tics.
Signal end of tic input with Tic-ID = 0
Tic-ID:
```

HELP

If you receive the message `Digitizer device not specified`, verify that your station file contains the DIGITIZER command and specifies the digitizer you are using. Your system administrator can help you with this.

Enter all six tics just as you did the first time (if you need a refresher, see page 4-19). Because tic locations are used to register the map to the digitizer, be sure to enter the locations as carefully as possible.

Because small differences in digitized tic locations cause the transformation to vary, your scale and RMS values may not be the same as those shown here.

```
Tic-ID: 22*
Tic-ID: 23*
Tic-ID: 24*
Tic-ID: 32*
Tic-ID: 33*
Tic-ID: 33*
Tic-ID: 33*
Tic-ID: 34*
Tic-ID: 0*
Scale (XY) = (0.999,1.001) Skew (degrees) (-.019)
Rotation (degrees) = (-0.052) Translation = (-0.007, -0.007)
RMS Error (input, output) = (0.004, 0.004)
Arcedit:
```

Check your RMS error. If the registration isn't accurate, edits you make will not be in the correct location relative to the features already in the coverage. When entering tics, be consistent and use the same RMS value you previously determined to be both appropriate and acceptable (see page 4-24 for this discussion).

HELP

If your RMS error exceeds your allowable value, you must register the map again. Issue the following command line, and then enter the tic locations again.

```
Arcedit: COORDINATE DIGITIZER LANDED
```

---

set the snapping environment   Before making edits, you can establish a specific *snapping environment* allowing nodes to 'snap' to arcs (ARCSNAP) and nodes to snap to other nodes (NODESNAP). Both commands adjust feature coordinates, but there are differences between them.

ARCSNAP   As you add arcs, ARCSNAP shortens or extends undershoots and overshoots to connect them to an existing arc within a set distance.

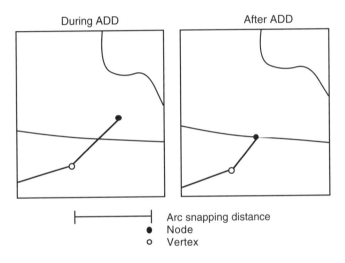

During ADD   After ADD

├─────────────┤   Arc snapping distance
● Node
○ Vertex

NODESNAP   Node snapping ensures that edited arcs connect to nodes of existing arcs in the coverage. This is important for closing polygons and correcting arc overshoots or undershoots.

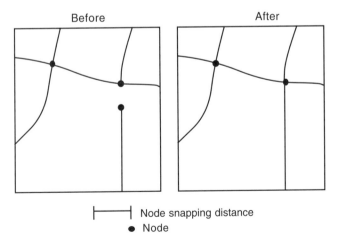

Before   After

├──────┤   Node snapping distance
● Node

The node snapping distance controls how close a node must be to another node before it will snap to it. Specifying a node snapping distance ensures that the *snapping tolerance* will be maintained at a constant value throughout your editing session. Because the coverage units are inches, we'll use a node snapping distance of 0.02.

```
Arcedit: USAGE ARCSNAP
Usage: ARCSNAP ON {* | distance}
Usage: ARCSNAP OFF
Arcedit: ARCSNAP ON .02

Arcedit: USAGE NODESNAP
Usage: NODESNAP <FIRST | CLOSEST | OFF> {DEFAULT | * | distance}
Arcedit: NODESNAP CLOSEST .02
```

INTERSECTARCS

You can also specify that nodes be created automatically wherever an arc crosses an existing arc. The INTERSECTARCS command controls whether arcs will split where they intersect existing arcs.

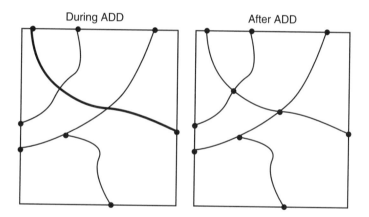

During ADD   After ADD

```
Arcedit: USAGE INTERSECTARCS
Usage: INTERSECTARCS <OFF | ADD | ALL>
Arcedit: INTERSECTARCS ALL
```

Refer to *Data automation-->Editing Coverages & INFO files with ARCEDIT* in the online Help for more information on the snapping environment.

add a missing label point   Adding a missing label is probably the easiest edit to make. Establish LABEL as the feature type to draw and edit.

```
Arcedit: DRAWENV ARC LABEL
Arcedit: EDITF LABEL
18 element(s) for edit feature LABEL
Arcedit: DRAW
```

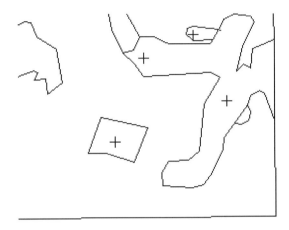

If you haven't already, zoom in on the portion of the coverage shown above using the Extent option on the Pan/Zoom menu.

Now use the ADD command to add the missing label point. The menu that appears on the screen is similar to one you've already seen.

```
Arcedit: ADD
------------------Options------------------
1) Add Label          5) Delete last label
8) Digitizing options  9) Quit
(Label) User-ID: 78 Coordinate =
```

Before adding the label, get the correct value of its User-ID from the original map manuscript you prepared. By default, ARCEDIT will automatically assign a unique User-ID to the new label, determined by increasing the value of the highest unique User-ID in the current edit coverage by one. But, in this case, you want the value to be 69, not 78. To change the current value, choose Digitizing options from the ADD Options menu by pressing the 8 button on the keypad.

```
(Label) User-ID: 78 Coordinate = (press 8)
```

From the Digitizing Options menu, choose the New User-ID option by pressing the 1 button.

```
------------------DIGITIZING OPTIONS------------------
1) New User-ID         2) New Symbol  3) Autoincrement OFF
4) Autoincrement RESUME 5) New Angle  6) New Scale
9) Quit
```

Type the new User-ID value at the prompt. Use the keypad buttons to specify a value of 69, followed by the A or * button to enter its value.

```
New User-ID: 69*
(Label) User-ID: 69 Coordinate =
```

Then, to add the missing label, move the keypad crosshairs over the location where you want to add the label and press the 1 button.

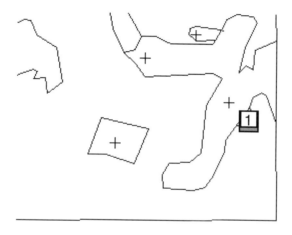

```
(Label) User-ID: 69 Coordinate = 12.904,4.474
(Label) User-ID: 78 Coordinate =
```

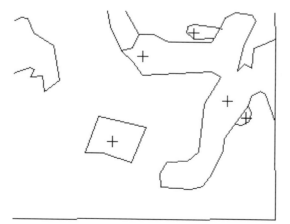

You are adding only one label point, so press the 9 button to return to the ARCEDIT prompt.

```
(Label) User-ID: 78 Coordinate = (press 9)
1 label(s) added to <drive>:\yourname\UGIS\LAND\LANDED
Arcedit:
```

add a missing arc

To add a missing arc, digitize it. First make sure the edit feature is ARC and that the drawing environment includes node errors. (Turn off previously drawn features.)

```
Arcedit: DRAWENV NODE ERRORS LABEL OFF
Arcedit: EDITF ARC
39 element(s) for edit feature ARC
Arcedit: DRAW
```

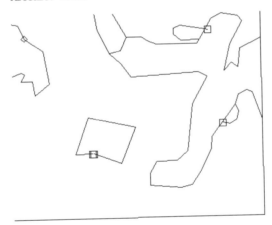

You are now prepared to issue the ADD command.

```
Arcedit: ADD
--------------------Options--------------------
1) Vertex        2) Node           3) Curve
4) Delete vertex 5) Delete arc     6) Spline on/off
7) Square on/off 8) Digitizing Options 9) Quit
(Line) User-ID: 40 Points 0
```

Add the missing arc where indicated below by pressing the 2 button to enter its start and end nodes.

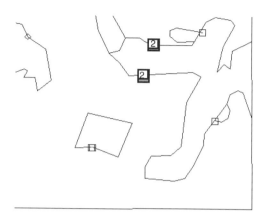

```
(Line) User-ID: 40 Points 2
Snapped both ends to closest arc
(Line) User-ID: 41 Points 0
```

There is only one missing arc, so press the 9 button to quit ADD.

```
(Line) User-ID: 41 Points 0 (press 9)
1 arc(s) added to <drive>:\yourname\UGIS\LAND\LANDED
Arcedit: DRAW
```

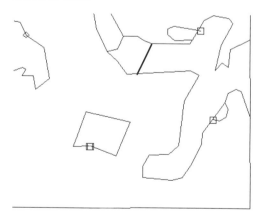

The newly added arc should have snapped into place. If not, you'll see square (dangling node) error symbols around one or both of its nodes.

┌─────────┐
│ HELP   │
└─────────┘

What should you do if the arc you added has
dangling nodes? You can leave it as is and wait until you learn how to
correct undershoots and overshoots later in this lesson, or you can
issue the OOPS command and digitize the arc again.

If you continue to have trouble making it snap into place, you can
increase the snapping tolerance. The current snapping distance, set
using the ARCSNAP command, is 0.02 inches. This distance can be
altered at any time during an ARCEDIT session. To do this, specify
the following:

```
Arcedit: ARCSNAP ON *
Define the tolerance circle (from digitizer)
Enter the center
Enter the edge
```

The * option allows you to enter two points with the crosshairs (by
pressing any button) to indicate a new ARCSNAP distance. Specify a
distance large enough to allow the new arc to snap to the existing arc
when it gets close, but not so large that it might snap to the wrong arc.

---

saving added features   Save your edits frequently. Once satisfied with your edits, issue the
SAVE command. This saves all edits made to the edit coverage
during the session.

```
Arcedit: SAVE
Saving changes for <drive>:\yourname\UGIS\LAND\LANDED
   40 arc(s) written to <drive>:\yourname\UGIS\LAND\LANDED
   from the original 39 arc(s), 5 added and 2 deleted
Reopening arcs...
   19 label attribute record(s) written to
<drive>:\yourname\UGIS\LAND\LANDED
   19 label(s) written to <drive>:\yourname\UGIS\LAND\LANDED
   from the original 18 label(s), 1 added and 0 deleted
Reopening labels...
   BND replaced into <drive>:\yourname\UGIS\LAND\LANDED
   WARNING, topology has been altered please use
   'CLEAN' or 'BUILD'.
Saving set tolerances to TOL file...
Re-establishing edit feature
Arcedit:
```

correcting mistakes graphically

In the sample coverage provided, four mistakes remain: an overshoot (3), an undershoot (4), an open polygon (5), and a label point with an incorrect User-ID (6).

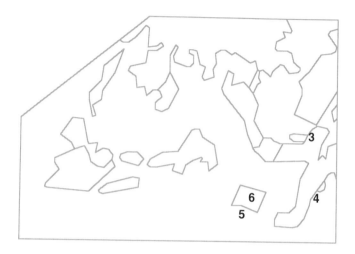

It's often easier to correct these mistakes using a graphics display device instead of a digitizer.

changing from COORDINATE DIGITIZER to coordinate input from your graphics display device

Before correcting the remaining errors, specify that you will use either the graphics display device's mouse (if available) or cursor to enter coordinates with either of the following commands:

Arcedit: **COORDINATE MOUSE**

or

Arcedit: **COORDINATE CURSOR**

correct an overshoot   Set the current edit feature to arcs.

Arcedit: **EDITF ARC**
42 feature(s) for edit feature ARC

If the overshoot (dangling arc, marked by its dangling node) is not easy to see, zoom in on it using either the Zoom in or Extent options on the Pan/Zoom menu.

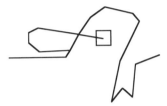

To select the overshoot, use the SELECT command and then position the cursor over the dangling arc and push the 1 button.

Arcedit: **SELECT**
Point to the feature to select

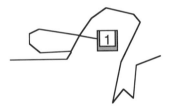

Arc 20 User-ID 19 with 2 points
1 element(s) now selected

Once selected, remove the unwanted arc with the DELETE command.

Arcedit: **DELETE**
1 arc(s) deleted

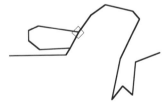

Arcedit: **DRAW**

correct an undershoot   To fix the undershoot in the sample coverage, you'll want to move the node to the point on the neighboring arc where it should connect.

You probably need to change your screen view to see the area where the undershoot occurs. To do this, you can use the Pan option on the Pan/Zoom menu, then move the crosshairs near the bottom of the screen and press any key. Or, you can use the Fullview option to draw the entire coverage, then use either the Extent or Zoom In options to enlarge the area of interest.

The EXTEND command extends the dangling node of the arc to connect to the desired arc. First issue the USAGE command to see how to use EXTEND.

```
Arcedit: USAGE EXTEND
Usage: EXTEND {BOTH | FROM | TO} {* | distance}
```

Select the arc to extend.

```
Arcedit: SELECT
Point to the feature to select.

Arc 33 User-ID: 34 with 5 points
1 element(s) now selected
```

Use your mouse or cursor to select the arc to be corrected. Next, issue EXTEND. You will be prompted to enter the distance used to extend the arc so that it will connect to the desired arc.

```
Arcedit: EXTEND
Enter first point defining the distance
Enter second point defining the distance


1 arc(s) extended
```

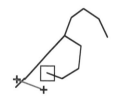

The display is automatically refreshed showing the dangling arc snapped to the adjoining arc to close the polygon.

fix an open polygon   Open polygons have two dangling nodes located very near each other. To correct the error by closing the gap, you must snap the two nodes together. To do this, make sure the edit feature is NODE.

```
Arcedit: EDITF NODE
35 element(s) for edit feature NODE
```

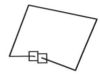

If the gap in the polygon boundary is not easy to see, zoom in.

Before moving two nodes together, you must decide which node you are going to move. In this case, move the node on the left to meet the node on the right. Begin by issuing the MOVE command.

```
Arcedit: MOVE
Point to the node to move <9 to Quit>
Enter point
```

Point to the node to be moved (in this case, the left node) and press the 1 button.

(press 1)

```
Node (11.464, 4.137) selected
1 = Select   2 = Next   3 = Who   4 = Move   9 = Quit
```

Its coordinates appear on the screen. If it's the one you want to move, press the 4 button on the keyboard.

(press 4)

```
Point to where to move the node <4 - Restart, 9 - Quit>
Enter point
```

Specify the node's new location. Position the cursor over the dangling node on the right and press the 1 button.

(press 1)

Your to-coordinate values
may differ slightly.
```
Moved node (11.464, 4.137) to (11.477, 4.138)
Point to the node to move <9 to Quit>
Enter point
```

The node is moved. Press the 9 button on the keyboard to quit the MOVE command.

(press 9)

If the move was successful, a pseudo node (diamond symbol) appears where the two dangling nodes snapped together. This pseudo node is acceptable (not an error) and is what you should have expected.

FYI   You can also use this procedure to correct an undershoot in cases where a node needs to move to snap to a specific point (e.g., the corner of a polygon).

If there isn't a node to which you can snap along the arc, create one using SPLIT or SPLIT VERTEX. See these commands in the online *Command References* for ARCEDIT.

change a label User-ID   There is one label point with an incorrect Label-ID value. To correct it, begin by establishing LABEL as the feature type to edit.

Arcedit: **EDITFEATURE LABEL**
19 element(s) for edit feature LABEL

To view its current value, add labels to the current drawing environment and specify that they be displayed along with their User-IDs.

Arcedit: **DRAWENV LABEL IDS**
Arcedit: **DRAW**

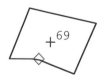

Select the label point with the incorrect id. Use the SELECT command and, while positioning the cursor over the label point, press the 1 button.

```
Arcedit: SELECT
Point to the feature to select

(press 1)
```

```
Label 14 User-ID: 69 (11.565,4.252) Angle 0.000 Scale 1.000
1 element(s) now selected
```

Information about the selected label point appears on the screen. Change its User-ID by *calculating* it equal to another value. In this case, the correct value is 70. Be sure to include one space on each side of the = sign.

```
Arcedit: CALCULATE LANDED-ID = 70
Arcedit: DRAW
```

saving your corrections   You should save changes made to an edit coverage frequently. You can do this at any time during the ARCEDIT session.

```
Arcedit: SAVE
Saving changes for <drive>:\yourname\UGIS\LAND\LANDED
Saving arcs...
    42 arc(s) written to <drive>:\yourname\UGIS\LAND\LANDED
    from the original 42 arc(s), 4 added and 4 deleted
Reopening arcs...
Saving labels...
    **NOTE** Only label attribute(s) updated
Reopening labels...
    BND replaced into <drive>:\yourname\UGIS\LAND\LANDED
Saving set tolerances to TOL file...
Re-establishing edit feature point
Arcedit:
```

⟨FYI⟩

If you forgot to make a copy, or want to create a coverage that contains the intermediate edits you've made since the last time you saved, you can save all your edit changes to a new coverage. To do this, specify the name of the new coverage when you issue the SAVE command; for example,

```
Arcedit: SAVE LANDED02
```

quitting from ARCEDIT

The QUIT command ends the current ARCEDIT session.

```
Arcedit: QUIT
Leaving ARCEDIT ...
Arc:
```

```
HELP
```

If you haven't saved your edits before issuing the QUIT command, you're prompted with the option to do so.

```
Arcedit: QUIT
Keep all edit changes (Y/N): Y
```

If you answer No, the original coverage remains unchanged. If you answer Yes, changes made to the edit coverage overwrite the original coverage. Then you're asked another question:

```
This will replace all changes back into the original coverage
Do you really want to do this (Y/N): Y
```

If you ever accidentally enter QUIT, you can remain in ARCEDIT. Entering Y at the first prompt and N at the second prompt returns you to the ARCEDIT prompt.

more practice

Now that you've edited the sample coverage, you have two options. You can continue to practice correcting errors by editing your own digitized land use coverage, LANDCN02, or you can move on to the next step by renaming the sample coverage, LANDED, to take the place of your own edited land use coverage.

```
Arc: RENAME LANDED LANDED03
```

If you decide that you want more practice, return to page 5-27. Remember to alter the coverage names when you type the command lines provided; that is, whenever you see the sample coverage names LANDCN and LANDED, substitute LANDCN02 and LANDED03, respectively.

Either way, once you have a coverage named LANDED03, you are ready to proceed to the next section, 'Reconstructing topology'.

END

Reconstructing topology

When you saved the changes in ARCEDIT, you probably noticed the message warning that topology had been altered and that BUILD or CLEAN should be used on the coverage.

```
WARNING, topology has been altered.
Please use 'CLEAN' or 'BUILD'.
```

Editing a coverage by moving, adding, or deleting arcs, nodes, and labels alters the previously recorded spatial relationships. To update the relationships recorded for any edited coverage, you must reconstruct its topology.

Topology can be reconstructed by the same commands used to create it: BUILD and CLEAN.

EXERCISE

Use BUILD to reconstruct coverage topology

Because you used the snapping environment during your ARCEDIT session, all the arcs were split at their intersections (marked by nodes). This means that you can reconstruct your land use topology using BUILD.

Before building your edited coverage, copy it as a new coverage.

```
Arc: COPY LANDED03 LANDBD04
Copied landed03 to landed04
Arc: BUILD LANDBD04 POLY
 Building polygons...
Partial processing enabled. 93% of the coverage will be processed.
Arc:
```

Edits were made to only a portion of the coverage, so BUILD uses *partial processing* which recognizes that during any given edit session, some of the previous spatial relationships are not affected. Partial processing only processes the data affected by the edits. In this case, 93 percent of the features in the land use coverage had to be processed to incorporate all the changes that were made. Other features remain unchanged.

After the BUILD command finishes, you'll want to check for any additional errors. The LANDBD04 coverage is spatially correct if your error reports match the following.

```
Arc: NODEERRORS LANDBD04 ALL
    Pseudo Node     8 at (  13.22821,   7.50828)
    Pseudo Node    16 at (   8.96204,   6.54644)
    Pseudo Node    18 at (   9.57501,   5.05692)
    Pseudo Node    19 at (  10.74500,   5.33056)
    Pseudo Node    21 at (   9.58293,   4.43210)
    Pseudo Node    30 at (  11.47694,   4.13798)
Total number of Pseudo Nodes:    6
Total number of Dangling Nodes: 0

Arc: LABELERRORS LANDBD04
Polygon          1 has     0 label points.
Arc:
```

LANDBD04 should have six pseudo nodes (five islands and one acceptable two-arc connection) and one label error (Polygon 1). If it does, you're assured that the coverage is spatially correct and ready to receive descriptive information (to be done in the next lesson).

The node numbers in the error reports for your digitized coverage may differ from those above. If you have additional dangling node errors, you must identify them and return to the previous exercise to correct them.

END

You've just made the spatial data in the land use coverage usable. The steps you performed, summarized in the following flowchart, can be used for any polygon coverage, for any database.

Correcting spatial data for a polygon coverage

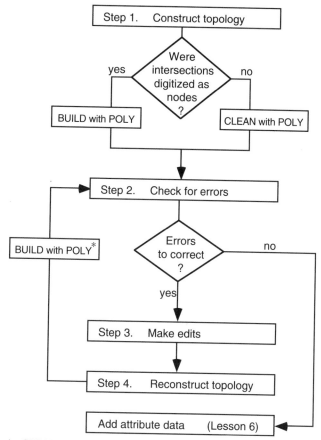

* *CLEAN can also be used to reconstruct topology.*

Advanced topic—Editing a line coverage

So far, you've identified and corrected spatial errors for a polygon coverage only. The steps are similar for an arc coverage, but the criteria used to check for correct topology is slightly different. The advanced exercise for this lesson makes the spatial data in the streams coverage usable.

**ADVANCED
EXERCISE**

Create topology for a line coverage

In your local UGIS directory, move to the STRM workspace. Once there, start ARC and list the coverages.

UNIX   Arc: **&WORKSPACE /yourname/ugis/strm**
Windows NT   Arc: **&WORKSPACE <drive>:\yourname\ugis\strm**

```
Arc: LC
 Workspace: <drive>:\yourname\UGIS\STRM

 Available Coverages
 -------------------
  STRMGN01
```

To complete this exercise, you'll need the streams coverage, STRMGN01.

HELP   If this coverage isn't in your current workspace, copy it from the RESULTS directory.

UNIX   Arc: **copy ../results/strmgn01 strmgn01**
Windows NT   Arc: **copy ..\results\strmgn01 strmgn01**

As with the land use coverage of polygons, make a copy of your most recent coverage before you create topology. The copy is the one that you'll work on.

```
Arc: COPY STRMGN01 STRMBD02
 Copied STRMGN01 to STRMBD02
```

Step 1

Construct topology

After you make a copy of the stream data, use the BUILD command to create topology for the streams coverage. Specify the name of the coverage and the type of feature to build, in this case, LINE.

```
Arc: USAGE BUILD
Usage: BUILD <cover> {POLY | LINE | POINT | NODE | ANNO.<subclass>}
Arc: BUILD STRMBD02 LINE
 Building lines...
Arc:
```

The arc attribute table (AAT) is output by BUILD with the LINE option. Use the LIST command to view the contents of the new AAT.

```
Arc: LIST STRMBD02.AAT
```

Record	FNODE#	TNODE#	LPOLY#	RPOLY#	LENGTH	STRMBD02#	STRMBD02-ID
1	0	0	0	0	224.036	1	200
2	0	0	0	0	301.175	2	201
3	0	0	0	0	195.379	3	202
4	0	0	0	0	357.137	4	203
5	0	0	0	0	155.996	5	204
6	0	0	0	0	126.351	6	205
7	0	0	0	0	54.019	7	206
8	0	0	0	0	21.776	8	207
9	0	0	0	0	41.949	9	208
10	0	0	0	0	295.601	10	209
11	0	0	0	0	168.441	11	210
12	0	0	0	0	300.108	12	211
13	0	0	0	0	282.869	13	212
14	0	0	0	0	547.422	14	213
15	0	0	0	0	323.220	15	214
16	0	0	0	0	380.758	16	215
17	0	0	0	0	580.344	17	216
18	0	0	0	0	199.195	18	217
19	0	0	0	0	260.674	19	218
20	0	0	0	0	172.671	20	219
21	0	0	0	0	344.187	21	220
22	0	0	0	0	538.513	22	221

```
Continue? NO
Arc:
```

Note: If &FULLSCREEN &POPUP is still set, then the results will be displayed in a popup window.

Notice that the AAT contains the seven standard items. The items that record topology, FNODE#, TNODE#, LPOLY#, and RPOLY#, equal 0 for all records. It's no surprise that the left polygon and right polygon numbers equal 0 in this coverage because it does not contain polygon topology. However, we do expect the FNODE# and TNODE# items to contain values other than 0. Usually, the topological connections between arcs (that is, their FNODE# and TNODE# values) are automatically generated as arcs are digitized.

However, recall that you used GENERATE to convert an ASCII text file of coordinates to generate the STRM coverage.

GENERATE does not automatically calculate arc-node topology. So the next step in creating topology for this coverage is to use the RENODE command to number the nodes in this coverage.

```
Arc: USAGE RENODE
Usage: RENODE <cover> {from_node_elev_item} {to_node_elev_item}
Arc: RENODE STRMBD02
119 unique nodes built for STRMBD02
```

Now use LIST again to view STRMBD02.AAT.

```
Arc: LIST STRMBD02.AAT
```

Record	FNODE#	TNODE#	LPOLY#	RPOLY#	LENGTH	STRMBD02#	STRMBD02-ID
1	1	3	0	0	224.036	1	200
2	2	5	0	0	301.175	2	201
3	4	7	0	0	195.379	3	202
4	6	13	0	0	357.137	4	203
5	12	13	0	0	155.996	5	204
6	12	15	0	0	126.351	6	205
7	11	16	0	0	54.019	7	206
8	15	17	0	0	21.776	8	207
9	15	19	0	0	41.949	9	208
10	9	20	0	0	295.601	10	209
11	14	21	0	0	168.441	11	210
12	16	23	0	0	300.108	12	211
13	13	24	0	0	282.869	13	212
14	16	25	0	0	547.422	14	213
15	10	26	0	0	323.220	15	214
16	12	27	0	0	380.758	16	215
17	8	28	0	0	580.344	17	216
18	23	29	0	0	199.195	18	217
19	23	30	0	0	260.674	19	218
20	24	31	0	0	172.671	20	219
21	24	33	0	0	344.187	21	220
22	22	34	0	0	538.513	22	221

```
Continue? NO
```

The nodes are now correctly numbered.

FYI The arc-node topology generated by RENODE is automatically maintained anytime the coverage is edited in ARCEDIT. This means that as new arcs are added, or as existing arcs are edited or deleted, the node numbers are maintained in the coverage AAT.

Understanding GIS—The ARC/INFO Method

Step 2

Identify errors

Check STRMBD02 for errors. Use INTERSECTERR to detect any arcs that intersect without a node.

```
Arc: INTERSECTERR STRMBD02
 Sorting...
 Locating intersections...
Total number of intersections found:    0
```

INTERSECTERR found no arcs that intersect without a node. Next, view the node errors and intersection errors in ARCEDIT.

```
Arc: ARCEDIT
Arcedit: &STATION <name>
Arcedit: EDIT STRMBD02
Arcedit: DRAWENV ARC INTERSECT NODE ERRORS
Arcedit: DRAW
```

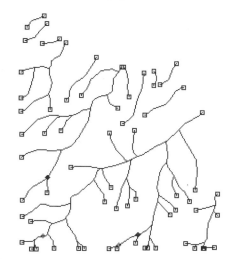

The stream origins are marked with dangling node symbols— examples of acceptable dangling nodes.

To verify that spatial data is truly error free, you would compare a plot or a screen display of the node errors to the list of potential node errors created with INTERSECTERR (here, none were found). You must verify that you were given clean data (i.e., that all the errors listed are acceptable).

When you finish viewing the coverage, leave ARCEDIT.

```
Arcedit: QUIT
Leaving ARCEDIT...
```

END

The following chart summarizes the steps for correcting spatial data for a line coverage.

Correcting spatial data for a line coverage

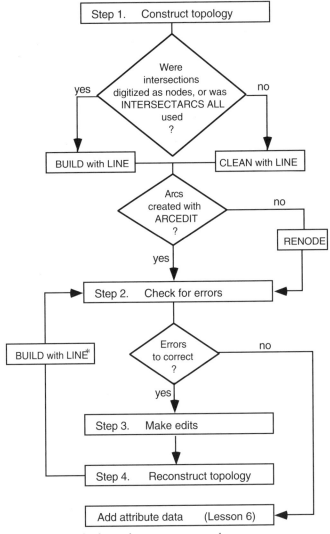

* *CLEAN can also be used to reconstruct topology.*

Summary

concept review — This lesson introduced methods of creating topology for a digitized polygon coverage (LANDDG01) and a generated line coverage (STRMGN01). You learned how both BUILD and CLEAN establish topology and create the standard attribute tables in INFO. And, you learned how to identify and correct errors in the spatial data.

Procedure	Command
1. Construct topology and build a feature attribute table.	BUILD and CLEAN RENODE
2. Identify errors.	EDITPLOT (or ARCEDIT with NODE ERRORS and ARC INTERSECT) NODEERRORS LABELERRORS INTERSECTERR
3. Correct errors.	ARCEDIT (with snapping environments)
4. Reconstruct topology.	BUILD

topology — Topology makes explicit certain relationships between features. ARC/INFO creates and stores three major types of topological relationships: connectivity, area definition, and contiguity. These will prove to be important for analysis and data manipulation.

ARC spatial relationships	INFO attributes
Arcs connect to each other at specific nodes (connectivity).	FNODE#,TNODE# (AAT)
Arcs connect to surround an area defining a polygon (area definition).	FNODE# and TNODE# (AAT) and whether LPOLY# or RPOLY# (AAT) equal the Cover# (PAT)
Arcs have direction and left and right sides (contiguity).	LPOLY#,RPOLY# (AAT)

You saw how CLEAN finds arc intersections and places a node at each so you don't have to explicitly digitize them. If you do digitize each intersection, you can use BUILD to create topology.

You can also set the ARCEDIT command, INTERSECTARCS, to calculate arc intersections and add nodes. In any event, BUILD or CLEAN is used to construct or reconstruct coverage topology. As part of the topology construction process, a coverage attribute table is created—a PAT for polygons and points or an AAT for lines.

spatial data errors   Creating topology helped you identify spatial errors resulting from digitizing. Coordinate data for geographic features is stored as points and arcs. Arcs connect at nodes to define polygons, and each polygon has a label point to identify it. So spatial errors relate to nodes, arcs, and label points.

Nodes with only one arc attached (dangling nodes) and nodes with only two arcs attached (pseudo nodes) are potential node errors.

A label error occurs when a polygon contains no label point, or more than one label point. Polygons with no label point have a record in the PAT, but its User-ID value is 0. As you'll see in the next lesson, polygons with a User-ID of 0 can't have associated attributes. Polygons with more than one label point have more than one record in the PAT, and you can never be sure which one will be used when polygons are processed. Because polygons don't exist until topology is created, you must BUILD or CLEAN polygon coverages before you can identify and correct label errors.

Intersection errors occur where arcs intersect without a node. Avoid these by explicitly digitizing all nodes or using INTERSECTARCS to automatically split arcs where they cross. CLEAN can resolve these errors, but BUILD returns an error message when it encounters them.

Feature	Potential errors		Terminology
Arcs	Only one node at an endpoint		Dangling arc
	Node extends too far		Overshoot
	Node falls short		Undershoot
	No node where arcs intersect		Intersection
Nodes	Only one arc attached		Dangling node
	Only two arcs attached		Pseudo node
	One arc connected to itself		Pseudo node
Labels	None in a polygon		Missing labels
	More than one in a polygon		Too many labels

lesson summary   In this lesson, you recognized why topology is important in helping to identify errors in your digitized data and identified the necessary steps for making your data usable for query, analysis, and display. You used ARC/INFO to:

- Construct topology using the CLEAN command
- Identify errors in your data using the EDITPLOT command
- Edit and correct errors using ARCEDIT
- Reconstruct topology using the BUILD command

You now know that you must be able to edit the data that has been captured manually. The basic errors that were corrected in ARCEDIT have been summarized in the table on this and the following page:

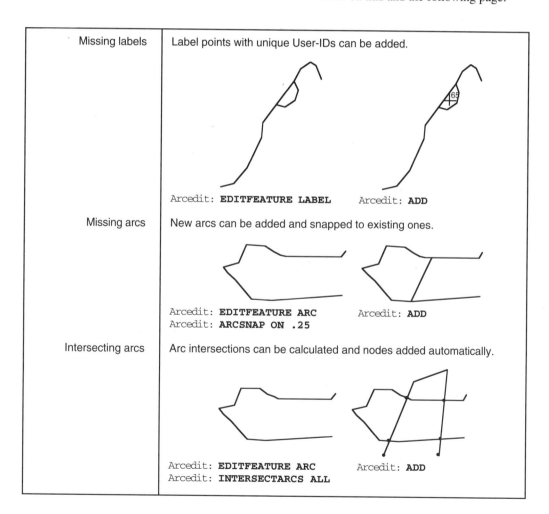

Missing labels	Label points with unique User-IDs can be added.
	Arcedit: **EDITFEATURE LABEL** Arcedit: **ADD**
Missing arcs	New arcs can be added and snapped to existing ones.
	Arcedit: **EDITFEATURE ARC** Arcedit: **ADD** Arcedit: **ARCSNAP ON .25**
Intersecting arcs	Arc intersections can be calculated and nodes added automatically.
	Arcedit: **EDITFEATURE ARC** Arcedit: **ADD** Arcedit: **INTERSECTARCS ALL**

Overshoot	Dangling arcs can be selected and then deleted.

Arcedit: **EDITFEATURE ARC**   Arcedit: **DELETE**
Arcedit: **SELECT**

Undershoot	An arc can be extended to intersect with an existing arc.

Arcedit: **EDITFEATURE ARC**   Arcedit: **EXTEND**
Arcedit: **ARCSNAP ON .25**
Arcedit: **SELECT**

Dangling nodes	A dangling node can be moved to close a polygon.

Arcedit: **EDITFEATURE NODE**   Arcedit: **MOVE**
Arcedit: **NODESNAP CLOSEST .25**

Wrong Label-IDs	Label-IDs can be changed.

Arcedit: **EDITFEATURE LABEL**   Arcedit: **CALCULATE**
Arcedit: **SELECT**   **Cover-ID = 64**

references for further reading

For further information on topics related to this lesson, see online help under *Data Automation-->Editing coverages and INFO files in ARCEDIT.* You will also find the online *Command References* for ARCEDIT helpful.

project status

As a result of the topology construction process, your coverages now have attribute tables (a PAT or an AAT) containing unique values to which other attributes can be added. In the next lesson, you'll use these tables and their User-IDs to add attributes to each coverage—attributes that can be used later to differentiate between areas of different land use and between major and minor streams.

workspace contents   If you've done all the exercises up to this point in the workbook, your directories contain all files listed in the diagram below. As in Lesson 4, the STRM workspace and its contents were created during the advanced exercises. You may or may not have this workspace.

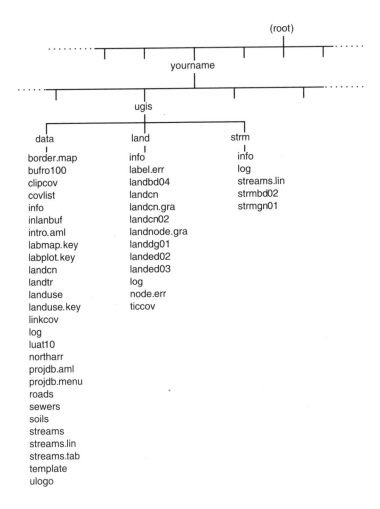

data	land	strm
border.map	info	info
bufro100	label.err	log
clipcov	landbd04	streams.lin
covlist	landcn	strmbd02
info	landcn.gra	strmgn01
inlanbuf	landcn02	
intro.aml	landnode.gra	
labmap.key	landdg01	
labplot.key	landed02	
landcn	landed03	
landtr	log	
landuse	node.err	
landuse.key	ticcov	
linkcov		
log		
luat10		
northarr		
projdb.aml		
projdb.menu		
roads		
sewers		
soils		
streams		
streams.lin		
streams.tab		
template		
ulogo		

task summary   Here is a summary of the tasks completed so far.

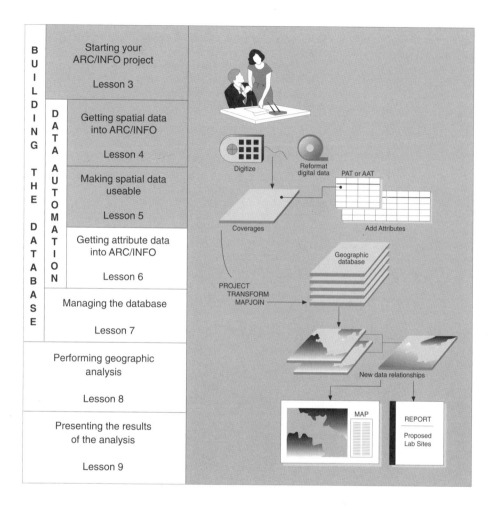

Lesson 6 Getting attribute data into ARC/INFO

In this lesson, you continue to build the database for the project before performing the analysis and creating the final maps.

So far, you've designed the database and automated the necessary maps. You also corrected the errors in the digitized data and created topology for the coverages.

Before you can perform the analysis, you need additional information in the database, for example, which type of land use each polygon represents. To accomplish this, you need to add descriptive attributes to the land use coverage. These attributes include a code indicating the type of land use represented by each polygon (e.g., forest or agriculture) and a cost-per-hectare value so you can calculate the cost of each potential site.

As you saw in the last lesson, creating coverage topology creates a feature attribute table. This tabular data file stores standard attributes about the features. Each geographic feature in the coverage has a corresponding record in the feature attribute table. To add additional attributes for each feature, you will

■ Create a new INFO data file to hold the attributes
■ Add the attribute values to the INFO data file
■ Join the INFO data file to the feature attribute table for the coverage

By the end of this lesson, the land use coverage will contain the descriptive information you need to finish creating the database.

The estimated time needed to complete this lesson is 3 hours.

Steps for getting attribute data into ARC/INFO

Complete the following steps to attach the descriptive data to the land use coverage. These steps can be used for any coverage and any database. Although there are other ways to accomplish this task, this is one of the most common approaches.

Step 1: Create a new INFO data file to hold the attributes.

Step 2: Add the attribute values to the newly created INFO data file.

Step 3: Relate or join the attributes in the INFO data file to the feature attribute table.

Create a new INFO data file to hold the attributes

As you saw in Lesson 2, attribute information is stored in a tabular database file called a feature attribute table. For each geographic feature (point, line, or polygon) there is one entry, or *record*, in the file. For each record, there are various kinds of information, or *items*.

A feature attribute table is an INFO data file containing several standard, previously defined items. ARC/INFO creates and maintains the links between records in the feature attribute table and features on the map.

To add attributes to the feature attribute table, you need another INFO data file. You must create this data file and define the new items before you can add the attribute values to it.

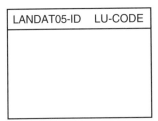

Create an empty INFO data file.

**Step
2**

Add the attribute values to the newly created INFO data file

If the attribute values you are adding are on a list, you can enter them into the data file by typing them on the computer. If the attribute values are already in a file on the computer, you might be able to put them directly into the data file without having to retype them.

LANDAT05-ID	LU-CODE
59	400
60	200
61	400
62	200
.	.
.	.
.	.

Add attribute values to the INFO data file.

<table>
<tr><td>Step
3</td></tr>
</table>

Relate or join the attributes to the feature attribute table

Once the attribute values are added to the INFO data file, you can attach them to the feature attribute table for the coverage using an item common to both as a key. Because the records in the feature attribute table can be linked to corresponding records in the new INFO data file, the new attributes will be associated with the geographic features in the coverage. So, you can perform queries and analyses on the data and create maps using the values in the new attribute table.

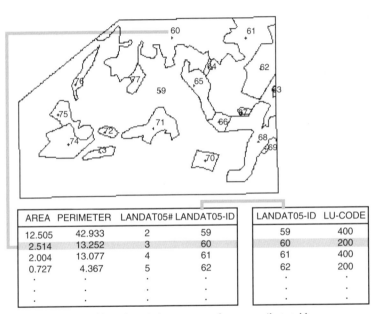

AREA	PERIMETER	LANDAT05#	LANDAT05-ID		LANDAT05-ID	LU-CODE
12.505	42.933	2	59		59	400
2.514	13.252	3	60		60	200
2.004	13.077	4	61		61	400
0.727	4.367	5	62		62	200
.	.	.	.		.	.
.	.	.	.		.	.
.	.	.	.		.	.

Join the INFO data file to the existing coverage feature attribute table.

Using INFO to create a tabular data file

In Lesson 3, you saw that you need to specify specific parameters to hold the descriptive data in each coverage. These include the

- Name of the attribute
- Type of attribute (character or numeric)
- Amount of storage space required for each attribute

In this lesson, you'll use INFO to create a file to contain the attributes for the land use coverage. Here are the specifications for the parameters you must define for your data file:

Parameter	Description	Examples
Item name	Any name (up to 16 alphanumeric characters—names must begin with an alpha character)	LANDDG01-ID ROAD-CODE
Item width	Number of spaces (or bytes) used to store item values	3 bytes for codes ranging from 1 to 500
Item output width	Number of spaces used to display item values	3 spaces for codes ranging from 1 to 500
Item type	Data type of the item. The most common item types are:	
C	Character—any combination of alphanumeric characters	Descriptive string: 'forest' Street address: '224 Elm Street'
I	Integer—any characters that make up a valid integer	Class code: 200 Highway number: 91
B	Binary integer—an integer number stored in binary format	Class code: 200 Unique ID: 11733
N	Number—any characters that make up a valid decimal number	Percent: .10 Monetary value: 101.30
F	Binary floating point—a decimal number stored in binary format	Area: 2344.45 Length: 46.4
D	Date—stored as 8 bytes; displayed as 8 or 10 spaces	12/31/89 12/31/1989
Number of decimals	For N or F, the number of digits to the right of the decimal place.	Two places for monetary values: 4.22

How do you know which item types to specify?

- If the attribute values contain nonnumeric characters, you must specify type C (character).

- If the values are numeric with a decimal place, you must use N or F. Storing numeric values as F (floating point binary) allows you to store large numbers in a small amount of space. If you have many records in your data file, this is a real advantage. For example, the numeric value of 45.3 requires 4 bytes of storage when stored as either N or F; by comparison, 4423378.33 requires 10 bytes of storage as N but still only 4 bytes as F.

- If the values are numeric with no decimal, store them as I or B. Again, using B (binary integer) saves storage space.

- You can store numeric values as character items, but you can't manipulate characters arithmetically. For example, if 213 and 300 are numbers, then, added together, they equal 513. However, the character strings '213' and '300' have no numeric value and cannot be added. ZIP codes are often stored as numbers instead of characters because they're sometimes manipulated as values.

How do you know how much space to specify?

- Define the *item width* for types C, I, or N to accommodate the longest value to be stored (up to 320 for C; up to 16 for I and N). Unnecessarily long widths waste storage space.

- There are specific widths you can specify for types B (binary integer), F (binary floating point), or D (date):

B: 2 bytes (up to 32,767); 4 bytes (up to 2,147,483,647)
F: 4 bytes (up to 7-digit precision); 8 bytes (up to 14-digit precision)
D: 8 bytes (YYYYMMDD)

- *Output width* should be sufficient to display the longest character string or numeric value. Always include one space for the decimal point, if necessary. For item type D, the output width can be either 8 or 10 depending on the format (e.g., 12/31/92 or 12/31/1992).

For more information on INFO data files, refer to online help under *Working with Tables-->Managing Tabular Data.*

defining a relate item   Adding feature attributes to a coverage associates the data already contained in the feature attribute table (e.g., AAT or PAT) with data held in a separate table. A procedure merges the two tables such that records in the two tables can be associated using a common item, often the User-ID. In Lesson 4, unique User-IDs were assigned to each arc and label point as they were digitized.

When defining your data file, you need to make sure it contains one item defined exactly the same as the User-ID in the feature attribute table (specifically, item type = B, item width = 4, output width = 5). This item is the *relate item*.

AREA	PERIMETER	LANDAT05#	LANDAT05-ID
12.505	42.933	2	59
2.514	13.252	3	60
2.004	13.077	4	61
0.727	4.367	5	62
.	.	.	.
.	.	.	.
.	.	.	.

LANDAT05-ID	LU-CODE
59	400
60	200
61	400
62	200
.	.
.	.
.	.

EXERCISE

Use the DEFINE command to create a new INFO data file

If necessary, start ARC and move to the LAND workspace.

UNIX   Arc: **&WORKSPACE /yourname/ugis/land**
Windows NT   Arc: **&WORKSPACE <drive>:\yourname\ugis\land**

In this exercise, you'll use INFO to create and format a new INFO data file to hold the land use attributes.

The last coverage processed in Lesson 5 was the topologically correct coverage, LANDBD04. Before you create and join a new INFO data file to the PAT of LANDBD04, copy it and give it a new name. Because you will add attributes to this coverage, name it LANDAT05.

Arc: **COPY LANDBD04 LANDAT05**
Copied LANDBD04 to LANDAT05

HELP

If LANDBD04 does not exist in your LAND workspace, copy it from the RESULTS workspace:

UNIX   Arc: **copy ../results/landbd04 landat05**
Windows NT   Arc: **copy ..\results\landbd04 landat05**

Now create the new INFO data file. To start INFO, type:

Arc: **INFO**

INFO prompts you for the user name. When in ARC/INFO, the user name is always ARC.

ENTER USER NAME> **ARC**

The ENTER COMMAND> prompt indicates that you have entered INFO.

You could name the file you're creating anything you like, but, for this exercise, use the name LANDUSE.DAT. It's always a good idea to adopt a simple name that reminds you of the contents of the file. The .DAT suffix indicates that this is data for the land use coverage.

HELP
INFO is case sensitive. Be sure you enter all file names in uppercase while in INFO. If you create a file name in lowercase, ARC will not be able to use it.

To create the new file, enter DEFINE followed by the name of the file. The ITEM NAME> prompt then appears.

```
ENTER COMMAND> DEFINE LANDUSE.DAT
ITEM NAME, WIDTH [,OUTPUT WIDTH], TYPE [,DECIMAL PLACES] [,PROT.LEVEL]
    1
ITEM NAME>
```

FYI You can also create and edit INFO data files in ARCEDIT. The items and item definitions are entered at a prompt the same way items are defined with the INFO command, DEFINE.

ARCEDIT command	Purpose
CREATE	Create a new INFO FILE
EDIT	Select an existing INFO file
ADD	Add records
DELETE	Delete records

Refer to *Data Automation-->Editing coverages and INFO files with ARCEDIT* in the online Help.

After specifying the name of the file, you must define the characteristics of its items. The User-ID for the coverage with the attributes attached is named LANDAT05-ID; so this is what to name the relate item in the new data file you're creating. Because this item will be used to join the two files (LANDAT05.PAT and LANDUSE.DAT), you must define the relate item in LANDUSE.DAT exactly the same way it is defined in the coverage PAT.

The User-ID in a feature attribute table is always defined the same.

Substitute the coverage name for 'cover' (e.g., for the LANDAT05 coverage, the item name is LANDAT05-ID).

item name	= cover-ID
item width	= 4
output width	= 5
item type	= B

Type in these values as DEFINE prompts you:

```
ITEM NAME> LANDAT05-ID
ITEM WIDTH> 4
ITEM OUTPUT WIDTH> 5
ITEM TYPE> B
```

Once the first item is fully defined, INFO prompts for the next item definition; in this example, LU-CODE. This item will hold a code describing the type of land use for each polygon in the land use coverage. This will allow you, during the analysis phase, to find those sites that meet the land use requirements for the development site. Here is the list of values for LU-CODE for each land use type:

LU-CODE	Land use type
100	Urban
200	Agriculture
300	Brush land
400	Forest land
500	Water
600	Wetlands
700	Barren

This is a 3-digit numeric code, so we'll define an item type of integer with an item width and an output width of 3.

```
    5
ITEM NAME> LU-CODE
ITEM WIDTH> 3
ITEM OUTPUT WIDTH> 3
ITEM TYPE> I
```

Because only two items are being defined, enter a carriage return in response to the third prompt for an item name.

```
    8
ITEM NAME> <CR>
ODD RECORD LENGTH ROUNDED UP TO EVEN

ENTER COMMAND>
```

HELP
If you type in an incorrect value while defining the file, just use ERASE to delete the file, and then start over.

```
ENTER COMMAND> ERASE LANDUSE.DAT
THIS COMMAND WILL ERASE THE SPECIFIED DF
DO YOU WANT TO CONTINUE ( Y OR N ) Y
ENTER COMMAND>
```

It's a good idea to list the set of data files in the current directory to make sure the data file exists. Use the DIRECTORY command to do this (DIRECTORY can be abbreviated to DIR):

```
ENTER COMMAND> DIR
```

TYPE	NAME	INTERNAL NAME	NO.RECS	LENGTH	EXTERNL
DF	TICCOV.TIC	ARC0000DAT	6	12	XX
DF	TICCOV.BND	ARC0001DAT	1	16	XX
	.				
	.				
	.				
DF	LANDAT05.TIC	ARC0021DAT	6	12	XX
DF	LANDAT05.BND	ARC0022DAT	1	16	XX
DF	LANDAT05.PAT	ARC0023DAT	20	16	XX
DF	LANDUSE.DAT	ARC0024DAT	–	8	

FYI

> The abbreviation DF in the first column of the directory listing stands for *data file*. The last column, EXTERNL, indicates which files are external files (i.e., the data is stored in a system file elsewhere on the disk, not in the current directory). Note that the PAT, TIC, and BND files are external—the coverage directory stores these data. The internal name may be different for your computer.

It's also a good idea to make sure you defined all the items correctly. Use the ITEMS command to review the template of the data file. It displays the data file name, the number of defined items, and the characteristics of each.

```
ENTER COMMAND> ITEMS
DATAFILE NAME: LANDUSE.DAT
    2 ITEMS: STARTING IN POSITION 1
COL ITEM NAME    WDTH    OPUT    TYP  N.DEC  ALTERNATE NAME
    1   LANDAT05-ID   4      5        B      -
    5   LU-CODE       3      3        I      -
```

END

Using INFO to enter descriptive attributes

Now that the data file exists, you can add the values for the attribute data to the file. You will do this by typing the information at the keyboard.

In INFO, the ADD command allows you to enter the attribute information into the data file. ADD prompts you for the value of each item in each record.

EXERCISE **Use ADD to enter attributes into an INFO data file**

Below is a list of the attribute values for each land use polygon. This was compiled for you by listing the User-ID for each polygon on the land use map along with a numeric code corresponding to the land use type.

LANDAT05-ID	LU-CODE
59	400
60	200
61	400
62	200
63	200
64	300
65	200
66	300
67	300
68	200
69	300
70	200
71	300
72	300
73	300
74	300
75	200
76	300
77	300

You can see that the land use polygons in the area you digitized have values of 200, 300, or 400 (you may remember that these values represent agriculture, brush land, and forest, respectively). You'll need to enter these values into the INFO data file you just created.

FYI

Similar to ARCEDIT, where you specify a coverage to edit, in INFO, you need to specify the file with which you'll be working. All subsequent operations are performed on the specified file until you specify another. In INFO, this is done using the SELECT command.

```
ENTER COMMAND> SELECT LANDUSE.DAT
    0 RECORD(S) SELECTED
```

You just created LANDUSE.DAT, so it is currently selected; you don't have to select it again.

Issue the ADD command to begin adding the attribute values to the data file.

```
ENTER COMMAND> ADD
```

ADD prompts you to enter the value for each item you specified when you defined the file. The number preceding the prompt tells you which record you are adding. Type the values for the first three records on the list.

```
   1
LANDAT05-ID> 59
LU-CODE> 400
   2
LANDAT05-ID> 60
LU-CODE> 200
   3
LANDAT05-ID> 61
LU-CODE> 400
```

Now continue adding the rest of the records from the list on the previous page. Don't worry if you enter a value incorrectly; you can correct it later. (See the HELP section below.) When the last record has been added, enter a carriage return in response to the LANDAT05-ID> prompt. The ENTER COMMAND> prompt then reappears.

```
   20
LANDAT05-ID> <CR>
     19 RECORD(S) ADDED
ENTER COMMAND>
```

Use the LIST command to display the values you just typed. INFO lists the item values and the record number ($RECNO) for each line in the LANDUSE.DAT file.

ENTER COMMAND> **LIST**

$RECNO	LANDAT05-ID	LU-CODE
1	59	400
2	60	200
3	61	400
4	62	200
5	63	200
6	64	300
7	65	200
8	66	300
9	67	300
10	68	200
11	69	300
12	70	200
13	71	300
14	72	300
15	73	300
16	74	300
17	75	200
18	76	300
19	77	300

Compare the values on your screen to the original list.

┌─────────────┐
│ **HELP**   │
└─────────────┘
───

If any of the item values are wrong, you can use the UPDATE command to change the value of a particular record.

ENTER COMMAND: **UPDATE**

UPDATE prompts for the record number. Enter the number of the record you want to correct; for example, had you entered an LU-CODE of 300 instead of 400 for record 1,

RECNO?> **1**

The current values are then displayed.

```
           1
LANDAT05-ID      = 59
LU-CODE          = 300
?>
```

To change one of the values, at the ?> prompt, enter the item name followed by = and the new value. Be sure to type one space before and one space after the = sign.

```
?> LU-CODE = 400
?>
```

When you finish correcting that record, enter a carriage return at the ?> prompt. You can either type the number of another record to correct, or enter a carriage return to stop updating.

```
?> <CR>
RECNO?> <CR>
```

ENTER COMMAND> **LIST**

─── ▭─

When you finish adding records and correcting errors, leave INFO by typing Q STOP. Note that INFO saves your work automatically.

ENTER COMMAND> **Q STOP**

The LANDUSE.DAT data file now contains 19 records, one for each polygon in the coverage LANDAT05. In the next section, you'll join this file to the polygon attribute table (PAT) for the coverage.

███ **END** ███ ──

Using ARC/INFO to link attributes to geographic features

Creating topology for the land use coverage in Lesson 5 also created the polygon attribute table (PAT) for the coverage. The link between each geographic feature and a corresponding record in the attribute table was established automatically.

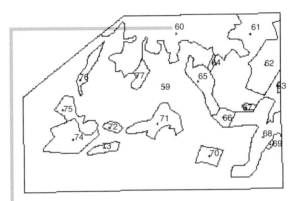

AREA	PERIMETER	LANDAT05#	LANDAT05-ID
12.505	42.933	2	59
2.514	13.252	3	60
2.004	13.077	4	61
0.727	4.367	5	62
.	.	.	.
.	.	.	.
.	.	.	.

LANDAT05-ID	LU-CODE
59	400
60	200
61	400
62	200
.	.
.	.

When the additional attributes contained in the new data file are joined to the PAT, they too are automatically linked to the geographic features.

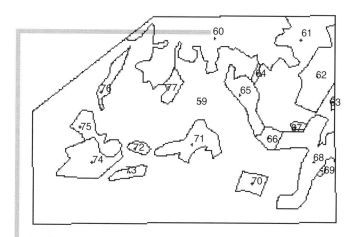

AREA	PERIMETER	LANDAT05#	LANDAT05-ID	LU-CODE
12.505	42.933	2	59	400
2.514	13.252	3	60	200
2.004	13.077	4	61	400
0.727	4.367	5	62	200
.	.	.	.	.
.	.	.	.	.
.	.	.	.	.

The JOINITEM command physically merges a data file with a feature attribute table using an item common to both. The item definitions and the item values from the two files are merged to create an output file. When the value of the relate item is the same in both tables, a record in the data file is matched to a record in the feature attribute table and both records are copied to the output file.

EXERCISE   **Use JOINITEM to join an INFO data file to a polygon attribute table**

JOINITEM is an ARC command, usable only from the `Arc:` prompt. If you're currently in INFO (i.e., at the `ENTER COMMAND>` prompt), type Q STOP to quit.

From the `Arc:` prompt, display the command usage for JOINITEM.

Arc: **USAGE JOINITEM**
Usage: JOINITEM <in_info_file> <join_info_file> <out_info_file>
            <relate_item> <start_item> {LINEAR | ORDERED |
LINK}

The JOINITEM arguments are

Argument	Description
<in_info_file>	Name of the file to which the items will be joined
<join_info_file>	Name of the file containing the additional attributes
<out_info_file>	Name of the file to be created
<relate_item>	Name of the relate item
<start_item>	Name of the item in the <in_info_file> after which the additional items will appear in the table

The optional argument {LINEAR | ORDERED | LINK} indicates the type of relate to be performed. This exercise uses the default, LINEAR. For more information on this option, refer to the JOINITEM command in the online *Command References for ARC/INFO prompts*.

Here are the specific values you should enter:

■ The two data files to be merged are the coverage attribute table, LANDAT05.PAT (<in_info_file>), and the new data file, LANDUSE.DAT (<join_info_file>).

■ You want to update the attribute table so, rather than create a new file, overwrite the existing file giving the <out_info_file> the same name as the <in_info_file>, LANDAT05.PAT.

■ The <relate_item> is LANDAT05-ID because it exists in both files.

■ The <start_item> is the item from the <in_info_file> list after which the <join_info_file> items will be inserted. In this case, specify LANDAT05-ID because the only items in LANDAT05.PAT are the standard items, and these cannot be separated.

Enter the JOINITEM command with its arguments.

```
Arc: JOINITEM LANDAT05.PAT LANDUSE.DAT LANDAT05.PAT ~
Arc: LANDAT05-ID LANDAT05-ID
Joining landat05.pat and landuse.dat to create landat05.pat
```

To check whether the join was successful, you can view the items and records using the LIST command at the Arc: prompt.

```
Arc: LIST LANDAT05.PAT
```

The new polygon attribute table for LANDAT05 should look something like this:

Records in your file may appear in a slightly different order.

Record	AREA	PERIMETER	LANDAT05#	LANDAT05-ID	LU-CODE
1	-21.285	18.493	1	0	0
2	2.514	13.252	2	60	200
3	0.727	4.367	3	62	200
4	0.174	2.877	4	76	300
5	0.036	0.960	5	64	300
6	0.140	1.735	6	77	300
7	0.034	0.905	7	63	200
8	0.296	3.142	8	75	200
9	0.436	3.839	9	71	300
10	0.548	3.513	10	74	300
11	0.072	1.078	11	72	300
12	0.119	1.711	12	73	300
13	2.004	13.077	13	61	400
14	12.505	42.933	14	59	400
15	0.399	3.518	15	65	200
16	0.914	7.451	16	68	200
17	0.037	0.819	17	67	300
18	0.131	1.500	18	66	300
19	0.016	0.556	19	69	300
20	0.182	1.788	20	70	200

Note that the LU-CODE value for the first record is 0. This record is for the external polygon for the coverage. Because there was no matching record in the LANDUSE.DAT file for a LANDAT05-ID of 0, no attributes were attached to this record.

display the results graphically
Another way to display the results of the INFO ADD and ARC JOINITEM operations is to graphically display the coverage features along with the attributes you've added. To do this, use ARCPLOT, the program that lets you display and query coverages as well as create high-quality map products.

You've already displayed the land use coverage several times during the digitizing and editing stages, but now that the attributes are attached you can display each land use polygon and label it with its LU-CODE value. At the `Arc:` prompt, start ARCPLOT. Specify your station file to set the display device, if necessary.

```
Arc: ARCPLOT
Arcplot: &STATION <name>
```

The first ARCPLOT command you need to issue is MAPEXTENT. This tells ARCPLOT the extent of the geographic area you want to display. If you want to look at an entire coverage, the easiest way to specify the map extent is with the name of the coverage to display, in this case, LANDAT05.

```
Arcplot: MAPEXTENT LANDAT05
```

Nothing is drawn on the screen at this point. To draw the polygons for LANDAT05, use the POLYGONS command.

```
Arcplot: POLYGONS LANDAT05
```

The outlines of the polygons are now displayed using the current line symbol (the default, a white line). Now, label each polygon with the LU-CODE values you added to the PAT in the previous exercise. In the POLYGONTEXT command, specify the name of the coverage to label (in this case, LANDAT05), and the item values to use to label each polygon (in this case, LU-CODE).

```
Arcplot: POLYGONTEXT LANDAT05 LU-CODE
```

The POLYGONTEXT command labels each polygon with its land use value. This is possible because you added the LU-CODE attribute to the polygon attribute table of LANDAT05.

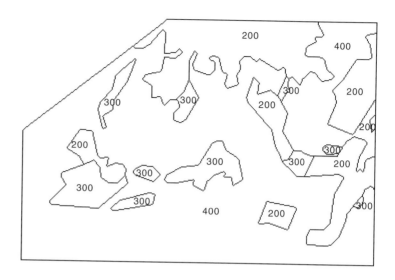

When done viewing the land use polygons, type QUIT to leave
ARCPLOT.

```
Arcplot: QUIT
Arc:
```

END

relate and join   As we've seen, one record in the related file is connected to a
corresponding record in the feature attribute table when their relate
items match. The correspondence is *one-to-one*. You may, however,
have values that repeat, a *many-to-one* correspondence, in the related
data file. You can connect or merge these using a *relate* or join.

In this case, there is an attribute to join to each land use code:
development cost per hectare. To meet this need, you should define a
data file containing LU-CODE and COST/HA as shown here.

AREA	PERIMETER	LANDAT05#	LANDAT05-ID	LU-CODE
2.514	13.252	2	60	200
0.727	4.367	3	62	200
0.174	2.877	4	76	300
0.036	0.960	5	64	300
.	.	.	.	.
.	.	.	.	.
.	.	.	.	.

LU-CODE	COST/HA
200	15000
300	10000
400	10000

EXERCISE

Join one record in an INFO data file to many records in a coverage PAT

The first step in joining the new attribute is to create an INFO data file to contain the cost-per-hectare (COST/HA) values. Because there are only three unique values for LU-CODE in the LANDAT05 coverage (200, 300, and 400), the new file needs only three records and associated COST/HA values. In this portion of the study area, cost-per-hectare values are consistent for each land use type. Here are the COST/HA values for each LU-CODE:

LU-CODE	COST/HA
200	15000
300	10000
400	10000

First start INFO.

```
Arc: INFO
ENTER USER NAME> ARC
```

To create the new file, enter DEFINE followed by the name of the file.

Remember: Define file names using uppercase characters when in INFO.

```
ENTER COMMAND> DEFINE COST.DAT
ITEM NAME, WIDTH [,OUTPUT WIDTH], TYPE [,DECIMAL PLACES]
[,PROT.LEVEL]
    1
ITEM NAME>
```

Again, the relate item must match the definition of the corresponding item in LANDAT05.PAT, in this case, LU-CODE. LU-CODE is defined as

item width   = 3
output width = 3
item type   = I

A shortcut to waiting for each of the DEFINE prompts is to enter all the parameters on one line following the ITEM NAME> prompt. Separate the parameters with commas but no spaces.

```
    1
ITEM NAME> LU-CODE,3,3,I
    4
ITEM NAME>
```

The next item, COST/HA, is defined as:

Item width   = 6
Output width = 6
Item type   = I

```
    4
ITEM NAME> COST/HA,6,6,I
   10
ITEM NAME>
```

Because there are only two items in this file, enter a carriage return at the
ITEM NAME> prompt to stop defining items.

```
ITEM NAME> <CR>
ODD RECORD LENGTH ROUNDED UP TO EVEN
ENTER COMMAND>
```

Now add the values to the new file.

```
ENTER COMMAND> ADD

   1
LU-CODE> 200
COST/HA> 15000
   2
LU-CODE> 300
COST/HA> 10000
   3
LU-CODE> 400
COST/HA> 10000
```

At the next prompt, since you've entered all the values, enter a carriage return. Then list the file to make sure you entered the values correctly.

```
   4
LU-CODE> <CR>
    3 RECORD(S) ADDED

ENTER COMMAND> LIST
$RECNO     LU-CODE      COST/HA
        1    200        15,000
        2    300        10,000
        3    400        10,000
```

If the values are correct, quit INFO. If you need to change any of the values, review the procedure for using UPDATE on page 6-15.

```
ENTER COMMAND> Q STOP
Arc:
```

Finally, you can join the data file to LANDAT05.PAT. Each LU-CODE value in the PAT for which there exists a match in the data file, COST.DAT, will receive the corresponding COST/HA value.

LANDAT05.PAT

AREA	PERIMETER	LANDAT05#	LANDAT05-ID	LU-CODE
2.514	13.252	2	60	200
0.727	4.367	3	62	200
0.174	2.877	4	76	300
0.036	0.960	5	64	300
.	.	.	.	.
.	.	.	.	.
.	.	.	.	.

COST.DAT

LU-CODE	COST/HA
200	15000
300	10000
400	10000

Use the JOINITEM command to complete the attribute join.

```
Arc: JOINITEM LANDAT05.PAT COST.DAT LANDAT05.PAT ~
Arc: LU-CODE LU-CODE
Joining LANDAT05.PAT and COST.DAT to create LANDAT05.PAT
```

To check whether the join was successful, use the LIST command at the Arc: prompt.

```
Arc: LIST LANDAT05.PAT
```

Record	AREA	PERIMETER	LANDAT05#	LANDAT05-ID	LU-CODE	COST/HA
1	-21.285	18.493	1	0	0	0
2	2.514	13.252	2	60	200	15000
3	0.727	4.367	3	62	200	15000
4	0.174	2.877	4	76	300	10000
5	0.036	0.960	5	64	300	10000
.	.	.	.	.	.	.
.	.	.	.	.	.	.
.	.	.	.	.	.	.

Each record now has the correct COST/HA value attached. For large feature attribute tables, this method is much more efficient than entering each value individually.

END

Your land use coverage for the southeast portion of the study area is now complete. In the next lesson, you'll join this coverage to the existing land use coverage, which contains the information for the rest of the study area.

▽FYI⁄

Instead of requiring that all descriptive data be stored in a single feature attribute table, ARC/INFO allows you to relate tabular files temporarily. Tables sharing a common item can be related. Records in one file are temporarily connected to the records in the related file that share the same values for the common item. For example, the lookup table LANDUSE.LUT can be related to LANDAT05.PAT through their common item, LU-CODE.

LANDAT05.PAT

AREA	PERIMETER	LANDAT05#	LANDAT05-ID	LU-CODE
2.514	13.252	2	60	200
0.727	4.367	3	62	200
0.174	2.877	4	76	300
0.036	0.960	5	64	300
0.140	1.735	6	77	300
0.034	0.905	7	63	200

LANDUSE.LUT

LU-CODE	TYPE
100	Urban
200	Agriculture
300	Brushland
400	Forest
500	Water
700	Barren

The values for LU-CODE are used to associate records between the two tables. Relates such as this minimize redundancy and data storage requirements.

Using the RELATE operation instead of JOINITEM offers several advantages for designing and implementing your tabular database.

- Relates reduce redundancy in data storage for items with many repeating values. For example, a descriptor, symbol number, and text label might be associated with each value for LU-CODE. Each of these values can be stored once for each land use type in a related table instead of repeating these values for each land use polygon.

- Such data reduction results in more efficient software performance.

- People in different departments can refer to the same coverage and yet have their own descriptive data available in a separate table which they maintain independently of other departments.

- Many applications operate only on descriptive data—not on locational data (e.g., tax assessor files or permit tracking by parcel). This ability to store attribute data separately from the coverage lets you use tabular data for purposes independent of the coverage information.

- Attribute data can be stored in external relational database management systems.

- While JOINITEM requires that the common items have the same name, RELATE allows items with different names to be used.

For more information, see online help under *Working with Tables -->Managing Tabular Data.*

▽

Advanced topic—Adding attributes from an existing digital file

Earlier, you added attributes to the INFO data file LANDUSE.DAT by entering them at the keyboard, one by one. An alternative to keying in attributes is to load them from an existing text file. The ADD FROM command in INFO can be used to accomplish this if a correctly formatted digital file containing the attributes exists on the computer.

ADVANCED EXERCISE

Use ADD FROM within INFO to add attributes from an existing digital file

In the last lesson, you created an arc attribute table (AAT) for STRMBD02, the streams coverage. Now you need to add an attribute to the coverage that differentiates major and minor streams.

First go to the STRM workspace.

UNIX   Arc: **&WORKSPACE /yourname/ugis/strm**
Windows NT   Arc: **&WORKSPACE <drive>:\yourname\ugis\strm**

Next copy STREAMS.TAB, a text file containing the tabular attribute data for the streams from the DATA workspace. Interrupt ARC temporarily to execute an operating system command by issuing the &SYSTEM directive (abbreviate &SYS) followed by the command.

UNIX   Arc: **&sys cp ../data/streams.tab streams.tab**
Windows NT   Arc: **&sys copy ..\data\streams.tab streams.tab**

Now display the contents of the file on the screen.

Arc: **&POPUP STREAMS.TAB**

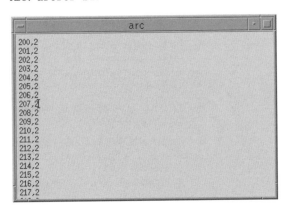

    Understanding GIS—The ARC/INFO Method

Listed are an identifier (the User-ID for each arc) and a code for each record. (In this case, 1 refers to a major stream; 2, minor.)

Before continuing, use the LISTCOVERAGES command to make sure that the STRMBD02 coverage from Lesson 5 exists in the STRM workspace:

Arc: **LISTCOVERAGES**

Available coverages
- - - - - - - - - -

STRMBD02   STRMGN01

```
HELP
```
              If STRMBD02 doesn't exist in your STRM workspace, copy it from the RESULTS workspace.

UNIX   Arc: **copy ../results/strmbd02 strmbd02**
Windows NT Arc: **copy ..\results\strmbd02 strmbd02**

Make a copy of STRMBD02. Name the new coverage STRMAT03 because it will become the coverage with attributes attached.

Arc: **COPY STRMBD02 STRMAT03**
Copied STRMBD02 to STRMAT03

Now enter INFO and create a data file to hold the stream attributes. The identifier (User-ID) will be the relate item, so it must be defined the same as the User-ID in the arc attribute table.

Arc: **INFO**
ENTER USER NAME> **ARC**

ENTER COMMAND> **DEFINE STREAMS.DAT**
ITEM NAME, WIDTH [,OUTPUT WIDTH], TYPE [,DECIMAL PLACES]
[,PROT.LEVEL]
     1
ITEM NAME

ITEM NAME> **STRMAT03-ID**
ITEM WIDTH> **4**
ITEM OUTPUT WIDTH> **5**
ITEM TYPE> **B**

The stream code is only one digit, so its width can be 1.

```
    5
ITEM NAME> STRM-CODE
ITEM WIDTH> 1
ITEM OUTPUT WIDTH> 1
ITEM TYPE> I
```

Only two items are being defined, so enter a carriage return at the third prompt for an item name:

```
    6
ITEM NAME> <CR>
ODD RECORD LENGTH ROUNDED UP TO EVEN
ENTER COMMAND>
```

Display the item definitions on the screen to make sure they are correct.

```
ENTER COMMAND> ITEMS
DATAFILE NAME: STREAMS.DAT
2 ITEMS: STARTING IN POSITION 1
COL ITEM NAME       WDTH  OPUT  TYP  N.DEC  ALTERNATE  NAME
  1 STRMAT03-ID       4    5     B     -
  5 STRM-CODE         1    1     I     -
```

Now you can use the ADD FROM command to read the attribute values directly from the STREAMS.TAB text file. ADD FROM adds values contained in an ASCII text file to records in the currently selected INFO data file; in this case, STREAMS.DAT. INFO requires that you enter the full pathname to the text file.

UNIX   `ENTER COMMAND> ADD FROM ../STREAMS.TAB`
Windows NT `ENTER COMMAND> ADD FROM ..\STREAMS.TAB`
```
106 RECORD(S) ADDED
```

List the records to make sure the attributes were added correctly.

```
ENTER COMMAND> LIST

$RECNO    STRMAT03-ID STRM-CODE
      1   200         2
      2   201         2
      3   202         2
      4   203         2
      5   204         2
      6   205         2
      7   206         2
      8   207         2
      9   208         2
     10   209         2
      .     .         .
      .     .         .
      .     .         .

More? N

ENTER COMMAND>
```

The records were added to STREAMS.DAT in the same order they were listed in the ASCII data file, STREAMS.TAB. Now that the records are in an INFO data file, they can be joined to the AAT for the streams coverage.

Quit from INFO and use the JOINITEM command to join the STREAMS.DAT data file with STRMAT03.AAT.

```
ENTER COMMAND> Q STOP
Arc: JOINITEM STRMAT03.AAT STREAMS.DAT STRMAT03.AAT ~
Arc: STRMAT03-ID STRMAT03-ID
Joining STRMAT03.AAT and STREAMS.DAT to create STRMAT03.AAT
```

Now the streams have the STRM-CODE attribute attached. To see the graphic results, display the STRMAT03 coverage in ARCPLOT. Earlier in this lesson, you labeled the land use polygons with their land use code values. This time, instead of labeling the streams, we'll draw the major and minor streams using different line symbols based on the STRM-CODE values.

First enter ARCPLOT and specify your station file, if necessary, to set the display.

```
Arc: ARCPLOT
Arcplot: &STATION <name>
```

Then set the map extent.

```
Arcplot: MAPEXTENT STRMAT03
```

You can draw the streams by issuing the ARCS command.

Arcplot: **ARCS STRMAT03**

The ARCS command draws all the streams using the current line symbol, in this case, a white line. Now use the STRM-CODE attribute to draw the streams. First, clear the screen.

Arcplot: **CLEAR**

The ARCLINES command draws each arc with the symbol specified by an item value (in this case, STRM-CODE).

Arcplot: **ARCLINES STRMAT03 STRM-CODE**

The major streams have a STRM-CODE value of 1, so they are drawn with the line symbol 1, a white line on a black canvas, which appear here reversed (i.e., as a thick black line). Minor streams are drawn using the line symbol number 2, a red line. This is possible because you added the STRM-CODE attribute to STRMAT03.AAT.

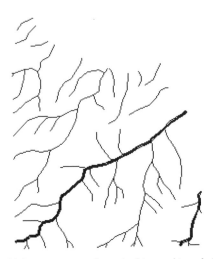

Major streams are shown in this graphic as bold lines.

When you finish viewing the streams, type QUIT to leave ARCPLOT.

Arcplot: **QUIT**
Leaving Arcplot...

END

Summary

concept review
ARC/INFO stores two types of data for coverage features: locational data, maintained by ARC, and attribute data, which you can maintain. Attribute data is stored in INFO data files. These files contain rows (records) and columns (items) in a tabular format. This type of table holds the thematic attribute data related to the spatial information recorded from a map. It can hold any number of records and items, but all records must contain the same items.

feature attribute table
The INFO data file created automatically when topology is established for a coverage is referred to as the feature attribute table (such as a PAT or an AAT). Feature attribute tables are a special kind of INFO data file and always contain certain attribute information about coverage features. These standard items are automatically created in a specific order.

Each record (row) in the feature attribute table contains a description about one map feature. Each record also contains a unique identifier. This same identifier can be found in every record in the locational data file, so records in the two files can be related (matched together). (Note that for polygons, each record in the PAT actually represents the label point of the polygon. This explains the need for only one label point per polygon.)

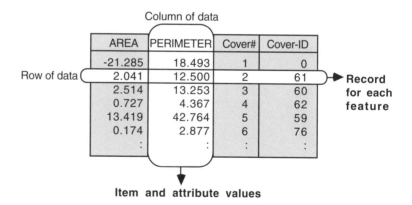

Column of data

AREA	PERIMETER	Cover#	Cover-ID
-21.285	18.493	1	0
2.041	12.500	2	61
2.514	13.253	3	60
0.727	4.367	4	62
13.419	42.764	5	59
0.174	2.877	6	76
:	:	:	:

Row of data

Record for each feature

Item and attribute values

associating and maintaining feature attributes

Adding attributes about features to a coverage involves associating new information about each feature with existing records in the feature attribute table. Records in the two tables can be associated through a common item, often the User-ID. The two tables can be merged using the relational join procedure to match a record in one table to a record in another table when their values for the common item are the same.

In these lessons, additional attribute data is held in INFO data files; however, ARC/INFO can also relate attribute data stored in external relational database management systems.

lesson summary

This lesson introduced several methods for adding attributes to your project coverages. In all cases, the basic procedure was the same: create an empty INFO data file, add attributes to it, and join it to the feature attribute table for the coverage. In one case, you added attributes to the data file by typing them in; in another, the computer read them in from a text file. You also saw how attributes are joined to a feature attribute table by a one-to-one relate or a one-to-many relate. The diagram below summarizes these operations.

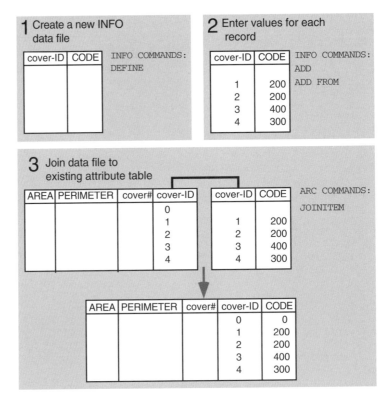

Understanding GIS—The ARC/INFO Method

This lesson also presented six INFO commands for listing and verifying the attribute data in the tabular database.

Database functionality	INFO command
List available data files.	DIR
Specify a data file.	SELECT
Display item definitions.	ITEMS
Display item values for all records.	LIST
Edit item record values.	UPDATE
Delete a data file.	ERASE

The ARCPLOT subsystem was used to produce screen displays to verify the coverage status. Here are the ARCPLOT commands you used:

GIS functionality	ARCPLOT command
Specify geographic extent of area to display.	MAPEXTENT
Draw polygon outlines.	POLYGONS
Label polygons with an item value.	POLYGONTEXT
Draw arcs.	ARCS
Draw arcs symbolized using an item value.	ARCLINES

references for further reading

For more information on topics related to this lesson, see online help under *Data Automation-->Editing coverages and INFO files in ARCEDIT* and *Working with Tables-->Using INFO*. You will also find the online *Command References* for ARC helpful.

project status   In the next lesson, you'll join your newly created land use coverage to the existing land use coverage which contains the information for the rest of the study area. This will create a composite land use coverage that encompasses the entire study area and is the final step in building the database.

workspace contents   Here are the coverages and files you should have in your local UGIS workspaces at this point. STRM is the workspace you created if you completed the advanced exercise in Lesson 4.

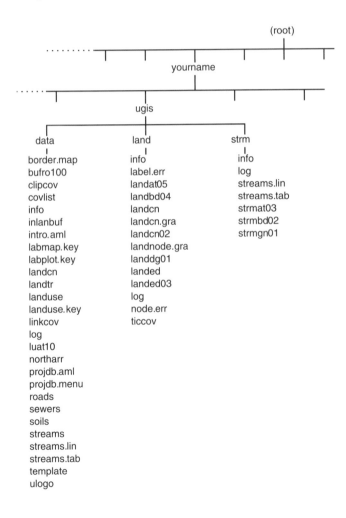

task summary   The shaded lesson boxes indicate the portion of the project completed so far.

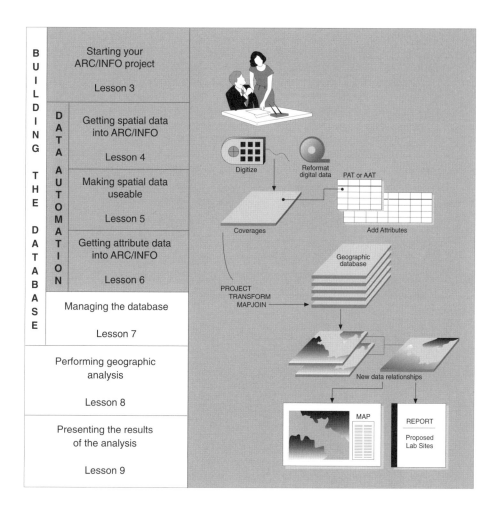

Lesson 7 Managing the database

At this point, you have the beginnings of a geographic database for your GIS project. The aim of this lesson is to finish building your project database, and to ensure its functionality. A functional project database should contain a number of associated coverages with the following characteristics:

- Each coverage contains clean topology.
- The accuracy of all feature locations has been verified.
- Feature attribute tables are present.
- The accuracy of the feature attribute values has been verified.
- A system of tics or ground control points exists.

Exercises in previous lessons have helped you establish these characteristics for your database. Additional criteria for developing a usable geographic database include

- Record all geographic features using real-world coordinates.

- Store all related coverages in one common coordinate system.

- Spatially reference the features of each coverage against features in associated coverages.

Meeting these criteria will ensure that the coverages in your project database are georeferenced.

In this lesson, you'll finish creating the updated land use coverage for the lower right portion of the study area and merge the updated coverage with the existing, adjacent land use coverage named LUAT10. In the upcoming exercises, you'll learn how to:

- Create a tic coverage containing real-world coordinates

- Project latitude-longitude values for tic locations into a UTM coordinate system

- Transform the digitizer coordinates of your land use coverage into real-world coordinates

- Edgematch the two adjacent land use coverages

- Join the two adjacent coverages into one land use coverage for the entire study area

The estimated time needed to complete this lesson is 4 hours.

EXERCISE **Draw coverage layers stored in real-world coordinates**

In the last three lessons, you've been automating the lower right portion of the land use layer in digitizer units (probably in inches or centimeters). Perhaps the best way to illustrate the need to georeference all the coverages in your database is to draw them. First start ARC/INFO.

Now move to the DATA subdirectory under UGIS in your local workspace. Then specify your station file.

UNIX　　　Arc: **&WORKSPACE**　　**/yourname/ugis/data**
Windows NT　Arc: **&WORKSPACE**　　**<drive>:\yourname\ugis\data**

　　　　　　Arc: **&STATION**　　**<name>**

| HELP |

For this exercise, you will need the LANDAT05 coverage from Lesson 6. If this coverage is not in your LAND workspace, copy it from the RESULTS workspace.

UNIX　　　Arc: **&WORKSPACE**　　**../land**
　　　　　　Arc: **copy ../results/landat05　landat05**
　　　　　　Arc: **&WORKSPACE**　　**../data**
Windows NT　Arc: **&WORKSPACE**　　**..\land**
　　　　　　Arc: **copy ..\results\landat05　landat05**
　　　　　　Arc: **&WORKSPACE**　　**..\data**

Start ARCPLOT and set the geographic area to be displayed (the map extent) to the BND of the SOILS coverage.

Arc: **ARCPLOT**
Arcplot: **MAPEXTENT SOILS**

Specify a special set of shade symbols to use.

Arcplot: **SHADESET COLOR**

Now draw features from various coverages in the existing project
database using the following commands:

```
Arcplot: POLYGONSHADES SOILS SUIT SOILS.LUT
Arcplot: LINESYMBOL 46
Arcplot: ARCS ROADS
Arcplot: LINESYMBOL 3
Arcplot: LINECOLOR AQUAMARINE
Arcplot: ARCS ../RESULTS/STREAMS
Arcplot: ARCS ..\RESULTS\STREAMS
Arcplot: LINECOLOR YELLOW
Arcplot: ARCS SEWERS
Arcplot: LINECOLOR GRAY
Arcplot: POLYGONS LUAT10
```

UNIX
Windows NT

All these coverages are layers in your project database. Their features
overplot each other because they're represented in one common
coordinate system. The coordinates are measured in real-world units;
if you list the attributes for a land use polygon in coverage LUAT10,
you'll notice that the AREA and PERIMETER items are measured in
real-world units. Use the IDENTIFY command to do this:

```
Arcplot: LINESIZE .03
Arcplot: LINECOLOR 1
Arcplot: IDENTIFY LUAT10 POLY *
```

When the crosshairs appear on your screen, use your mouse or
cursor-controlling device to position the crosshairs inside any land use
polygon from LUAT10. Then press any numeric key (or any mouse
key) to select that polygon.

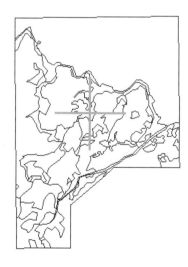

ARCPLOT draws the outline of the selected polygon in red and lists its polygon attributes on your screen. The attribute listing you see will depend on which polygon you select. Here is a sample attribute listing for one of the land use polygons:

```
Record      AREA   PERIMETER  LUAT10#  LUAT10-ID  LU-CODE COST/HA
    21  43202.402  1461.476      21       18        400    20000
```

Notice how the measurements for AREA and PERIMETER are in real-world units.

Remember that at the start of this exercise you established a geographic window large enough to display all the features contained in the SOILS coverage using MAPEXTENT SOILS. Now use the SHOW command to list the coordinate values defining this map extent:

```
Arcplot: SHOW MAPEXTENT
3868.989, 4437.155, 6281.976, 7516.981
```

FYI

You may get different precision reported on your machine depending on the current &FORMAT setting.

The lower left corner of the geographic window is located at 3868.989,4437.155 meters. Now draw the update coverage for land use, LANDAT05, which you've been preparing in the last three lessons. Move to the workspace in which LANDAT05 is located.

UNIX   `Arcplot: &WORKSPACE  /yourname/ugis/land`
Windows NT `Arcplot: &WORKSPACE  <drive>:\yourname\ugis\land`

Draw the LANDAT05 coverage.

```
Arcplot: POLYGONS  LANDAT05
```

Notice that nothing is added to your coverage display. That's because LANDAT05 is still in its original digitizer units. Therefore, at this point, it can't be georeferenced against the other coverages in the project database. You can draw LANDAT05, but first you have to change the current map extent to specify the area in which LANDAT05 can be displayed.

```
Arcplot:  MAPEXTENT  LANDAT0
Arcplot:  CLEAR
Arcplot:  POLYGONS  LANDAT05
```

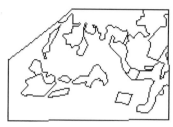

The updated coverage for land use is drawn in red. List its geographic area.

```
Arcplot:  SHOW  MAPEXTENT
7.1388, 3.1627, 13.5511, 7.7997
```

Your values will differ somewhat from the coordinates shown here. Note, however, that LANDAT05 is still in digitizer units (in this case, inches). In subsequent exercises, you'll convert the coordinates of LANDAT05 to match the coordinates within the rest of the project database.

For now quit ARCPLOT and continue with the lesson.

```
Arcplot:  QUIT
```

END

Coordinate systems for a multicoverage database

Coverage data to be automated are organized thematically, as a series of layers (such as soils, land use, streams, and roads), and spatially, by map sheets or *tiles*. Think of tiles as a group of adjacent coverages for a single thematic layer, which spans a number of map sheets. In general, thematic layers refer to the vertical structure and tiles, used as spatial partitions, refer to the horizontal structure.

thematic layers   As presented in Lessons 2 and 3, geographic features representing different thematic data are stored in separate coverages or layers. Thematic layers for the same area represent vertical coverages.

Coverage	Layer name	Attributes
	LANDUSE	Use, development cost
	ROADS	Name, type, width
	STREAMS	Name, class, flow

Layers are useful because they

- Help organize related features
- Minimize the number of attributes associated with each feature
- Facilitate map update and maintenance because there are usually different data sources for each layer
- Simplify map display because related features are easier to draw, label, and symbolize

spatial partitions or tiles   Often, a single layer of thematic data is automated as a set of adjacent coverages—one coverage for each map sheet. These map sheet coverages can subsequently be merged for analysis and display. In contrast, updates are typically performed on a map sheet basis or by some other subunit such as subdivision boundaries, census tracts, forest management units, and so on. By spatially partitioning your data, tiles simplify automation and update. Whenever necessary, tiles can be joined to allow analysis, query, and display operations across the entire database.

The display below illustrates the spatial relationship between the two adjacent coverages making up the land use layer.

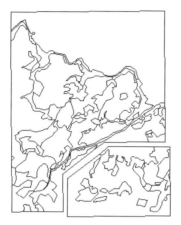 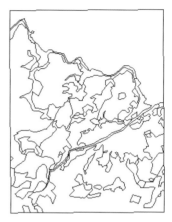

In this lesson, you'll join the spatial partition of the two adjacent land use coverages into a single land use coverage for the entire study area.

Because the update coverage for land use, LANDAT05, is still in digitizer units, the next step is to spatially reference LANDAT05 with the other database coverages in a common, real-world coordinate system. Afterward you will be able to combine the two land use coverages into a single land use layer.

real-world coordinate systems

For any database to be useful for spatial analysis, all parts of the database must be registered to a common coordinate system. A coordinate system is composed of a spheroid (a mathematical description of the earth's shape) and a map projection (a mathematical conversion from spherical to planar coordinates). Most maps display coordinate data by conforming to a recognized global coordinate system. The Universal Transverse Mercator (UTM), State Plane coordinate system, the Albers Conic Equal-Area, and Polar Stereographic projections are examples of systems which use map projections to represent the earth's three-dimensional features on a flat surface. Map projections ensure a known relationship between locations on a map and their true locations on the earth.

latitude-longitude   The most familiar locational reference system is the spherical coordinate system measured in latitude and longitude. This system can be used to identify the locations of points anywhere on the earth's surface.

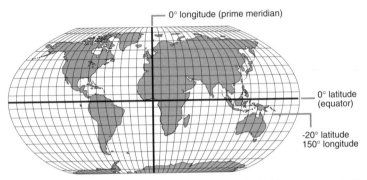

Latitude and longitude reference locations shown on the Robinson map projection.

If we treat the earth as a sphere, a graticule (a reference grid of latitude and longitude lines) can be superimposed on the earth's surface to geographically reference various locations. Longitude and latitude are angles measured from the earth's center to a point on the earth's surface. Longitude is measured East and West, while latitude is measured North and South. Longitude lines, also called *meridians*, stretch between the North and South poles. Latitude lines, also called *parallels*, encircle the globe with parallel rings.

Latitude and longitude are traditionally measured in degrees, minutes, and seconds (DMS). Latitude values range from 0° at the equator to +90° at the North Pole and -90° at the South Pole. Longitude ranges from 0° at the Prime Meridian (the meridian that passes through Greenwich, England) to 180° when traveling east and from 0° to -180° traveling west from the Prime Meridian. For example, Australia, which is south of the equator and east of Greenwich, has positive longitudes and negative latitudes.

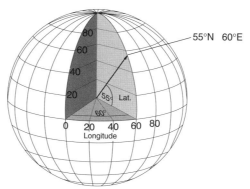

Diagram of latitude and longitude.

Latitude-longitude is a geographic reference system—not a two-dimensional (planar) coordinate system. In the figure above, notice how meridians converge at the poles but separate or diverge as they get closer to the equator. So, the length of one degree of longitude varies depending upon the latitude at which it's measured. For example, one degree of longitude at the equator is 111 kilometers (69 miles) in length, but the length of one degree of longitude converges to zero at the poles.

Because degrees aren't associated with a standard length, they can't be used as an accurate measure of distance or area. And, because this reference system measures angles from the center of the earth, rather than distances on the earth's surface, it's not a planar coordinate system. Similarly, because the global coordinate system is used for the curved surface of the earth, this system cannot be called a map projection.

planar coordinate systems

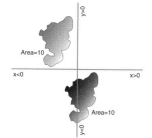

Planar coordinate systems (often called *Cartesian* coordinate systems) have several properties that make them useful for representing real-world coordinates on maps:

- There are two dimensions: x measures distance in a horizontal direction, and y measures distance in a vertical direction.

- Measures of length, angle, and area are constant across the two dimensions.

- Various mathematical formulas exist to *project* the earth's spherical surface onto a flat, two-dimensional surface.

Geographic information systems, like flat maps, use various planar coordinate systems to map the earth's surface. Each coordinate system used is based on a particular map projection.

map projections

Because the earth is a spheroid, the spherical coordinate system has to be modified somewhat. A mathematical conversion must be used to create a flat map sheet from the three-dimensional surface. This transformation is commonly referred to as a *map projection*.

> **FYI**
>
> Because every base map is stored in a projection, you should determine the projection of your base map before automating your map sheet.

Understanding the uses of map projections and latitude-longitude reference points is important as you begin to use ARC/INFO to develop your database. For the moment, please note the following:

- Any representation of the earth's surface in two dimensions *always* distorts shape, area, distance, or direction.

- Different projections produce different distortions.

- The characteristics of each projection make them useful for some applications and not useful for others.

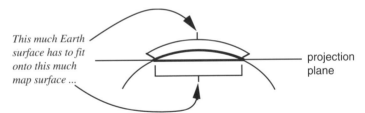

This much Earth surface has to fit onto this much map surface ...

projection plane

therefore, much of the Earth surface has to be represented smaller than nominal scale.

Although you don't need a complete understanding of map projections to ensure that the coordinate values in your database are measured in a real-world coordinate system, it's an important issue when dealing with large amounts of map data whose projection sources may vary. For more about map projections, refer to *Map Projections & Coordinate Management* and consult the references for further reading listed at the end of this lesson.

Some commonly used map projections in the U.S. and North America

Projection	Characteristics	Maps
Mercator	Shape: Preserved Area: Distortion increases toward poles Distance: Distortion increases from Equator or secant latitudes Direction: Straight lines represent constant compass bearing	■ Navigational maps ■ Time zone maps
Transverse Mercator	Shape: Preserved Area: Distortion increases away from Central Meridian Distance: Distortion similar to area Direction: Some distortion	■ 7½' and 15' quadrangle maps for 22 states within the U.S. ■ Maps of North America
Albers Equal-Area Conic	Shape: Some distortion Area: Preserved Distance: Some distortion Direction: Some distortion	■ U.S. maps ■ Some section maps of the U.S.
Lambert Conformal Conic	Shape: Preserved Area: Some distortion Distance: Some distortion Direction: Some distortion	■ 7½' and 15' quad maps for 32 states in the U.S. ■ State base maps
State Plane Coordinate System	Not a map projection—a defined set of coordinate systems which vary from state to state. East-West oriented State Plane Zones use the Lambert Conformal Conic projection while North-South oriented State Plane Zones use Transverse Mercator. Each zone has a set of parameters that define the projection for that zone. Most 7½ and 15' quadrangle maps for the U.S. use State Plane Zones.	
Universal Transverse Mercator *UTM is not used for very large areas.*	Not a map projection—a coordinate system defined by the transverse Mercator projection and a set of zones and offsets. Shape: Preserved Area: Distortion increases away from Central Meridian Distance: Distortion similar to area Direction: Some distortion	■ USGS 1:250,000 scale quadrangle map series (i.e., 1° latitude by 2° longitude)

tic features

Always establish tic points (representing known real-world locations) for a study area before the digitizing stage. Record these common tic locations on each map sheet to provide a common locational reference for each coverage. Once a map is digitized, the tic points become registration or geographic control points for that coverage allowing all coverage features to be registered to a common coordinate system. Additionally, to ensure geographic control, adjacent coverages and other layers of the same area can be spatially registered using the same tics and the same map projection.

transformation

When a map is digitized, the x- and y-coordinates are initially held in digitizer measurements (centimeters or inches). To make this information meaningful, and also to impose a scale factor, you must convert these measurements to the same real-world coordinate system and projection in which the original map was created. This process is known as *transformation*.

Points representing tics can be located on maps by identifying the x- and y-coordinates from a known real-world coordinate system. These are usually given in both the map projection units, usually meters or feet, and degrees of latitude and longitude. Often real-world coordinates for the tics are taken directly from an original map. If these are not available, latitude and longitude values can be used to identify geographic registration points and later converted to real-world coordinates in the same projection used by the base map.

Typically, a tic table is developed manually before any processing takes place. This table contains a list of all the tic numbers and the known locational reference for each tic, read from the original map. If the tic locations are recorded in the projected map coordinates, the transformation process directly converts the existing digitizer measurements to real-world coordinates. If the tic locations are recorded in latitude and longitude, they must be converted (i.e. projected) into the map projection of the base map before performing the transformation.

Before TRANSFORM
(coverage in digitizer units)

(11.75493, 8.7593)

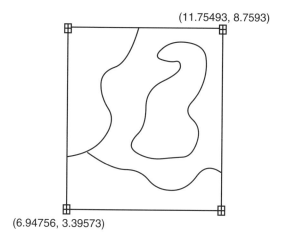

(6.94756, 3.39573)

After TRANSFORM
(coverage in real-world coordinates)

(1393166, 2410436)

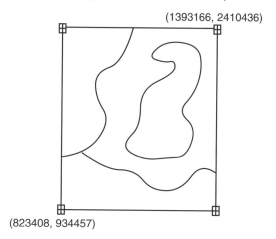

(823408, 934457)

The table on the following page outlines the process used to create a coverage in real-world coordinates. You completed the tasks listed in Part 1 (in Lesson 3) and Part 2 (in Lessons 4 and 5). Now it's time to complete the remaining steps that make up Parts 3 and 4 of the process.

Using ARC/INFO to generate a coverage in real-world coordinates

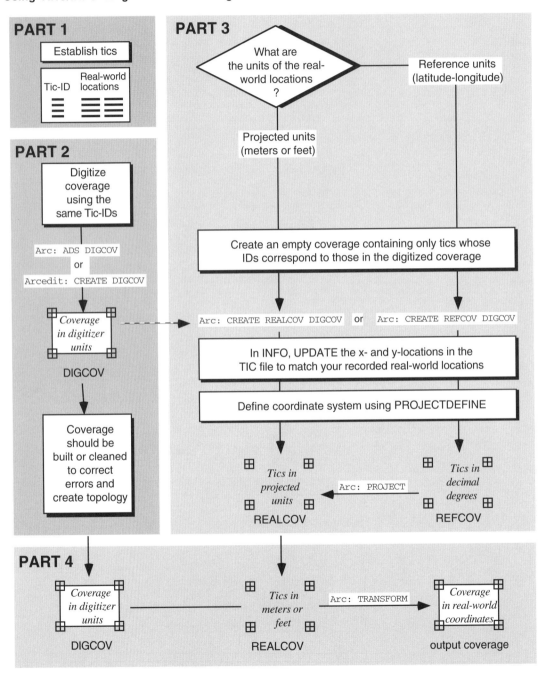

EXERCISE

Convert a coverage from digitizer units to real-world coordinates

In this exercise, you'll convert the updated land use coverage from digitizer units to UTM meters. Recall that the map digitized in Lesson 4 contained six tic locations. Locational references for each tic were marked on the original map manuscript using a latitude-longitude graticule. The table below lists the Tic-IDs and their real-world locations. For each tic location, verify its real-world location in latitude-longitude by referring to page C-1 in Appendix C and reading the latitude-longitude location off the reference grid. You can also refer to the master tic file you created in Lesson 3. Note that the real-world locations are referenced in degrees, minutes, and seconds.

Tic-ID	Real-world locations	
	X (longitude)	Y (latitude)
22	-74° 00 minutes 00 seconds	41° 3 minutes 45 seconds
23	-73 59 15	41 03 45
24	-73 58 30	41 03 45
32	-74 00 00	41 03 00
33	-73 59 15	41 03 00
34	-73 58 30	41 03 00

FYI A common error in reading grid references is to transpose the coordinates (i.e., to record the x-coordinates in the y column and the y-coordinates in the x column). When using latitude and longitude as a reference, longitude provides the x-coordinates and latitude, the y-coordinates. The x-coordinates are recorded along the top or bottom of a map, and the y-coordinates are recorded along the sides.

Before proceeding, these real-world locations must be converted from degrees, minutes, and seconds (DMS) into decimal degrees (DD). Keeping in mind that there are 60 seconds in a minute, and 60 minutes in a degree, decimal degrees can be computed using the following equation:

Decimal Degrees = Degrees + Minutes/60 + Seconds/3600

Here is a table showing both DMS and decimal degrees.

Tic-ID	Real-world locations			
	X (in DMS)	X (in DD)	Y (in DMS)	Y (in DD)
22	-74 00 00	-74.0000	41 03 45	41.0625
23	-73 59 15	-73.9875	41 03 45	41.0625
24	-73 58 30	-73.9750	41 03 45	41.0625
32	-74 00 00	-74.0000	41 03 00	41.0500
33	-73 59 15	-73.9875	41 03 00	41.0500
34	-73 58 30	-73.9750	41 03 00	41.0500

Step 1

Create an empty coverage containing only tics

Start ARC/INFO and attach to your LAND subdirectory under UGIS in your local workspace. Then specify your station file.

```
Arc: &STATION   <name>
```

The ARC command CREATE creates tic and boundary files for a new coverage by copying the TIC and BND files from an existing coverage. You want to use the same Tic-IDs, so use the TIC and BND files from your clean, digitized coverage, LANDAT05, to create an empty coverage called GEOREF01.

```
Arc: USAGE  CREATE
Usage: CREATE <out_cover> {tic_bnd_cover}
Arc: CREATE  GEOREF01  LANDAT05
Creating coverage GEOREF01
Arc:
```

The tic coordinates in LANDAT05 are in digitizer units. In the sample listing below, the digitizer units are recorded in inches. (These values provide a guide only; your values will differ because the tic locations depend on where your map sheet was originally mounted on the digitizer.)

```
Arc:  LIST  LANDAT05.TIC

Record   IDTIC        XTIC         YTIC
     1     22         4.614        9.125
     2     23         8.886        9.146
     3     24        13.150        9.180
     4     32         4.640        3.483
     5     33         8.917        3.512
     6     34        13.176        3.523
```

Because GEOREF01 was created from LANDAT05, both coverages have the same tics.

```
Arc:  LIST  GEOREF01.TIC

Record   IDTIC        XTIC         YTIC
     1     22         4.614        9.125
     2     23         8.886        9.146
     3     24        13.150        9.180
     4     32         4.640        3.483
     5     33         8.917        3.512
     6     34        13.176        3.523
```

Step 2

Update tic coordinates to latitude-longitude locations

Once generated, the TIC file can be updated in INFO with the real-world coordinates recorded from the original map. This lets you convert digitizer values to their corresponding real-world locations. When tic locations are measured in meters or feet, they represent the projected coordinate system of the base map. If, as in our case, these locations are from a graticule measuring degrees of latitude and longitude, they are reference locations only, and haven't yet been projected.

The easiest way to edit coordinate values is in INFO using the UPDATE command with the PROMPT option. Refer to the TIC table on the previous page for the new tic values. Be sure to

- Match the Tic-IDs correctly.
- Enter the coordinates in decimal degree values.
- Record each XTIC value (i.e., longitude) as a negative number.

```
Arc: INFO
ENTER USER NAME> ARC
ENTER COMMAND>
            SELECT  GEOREF01.TIC
         6 RECORD(S) SELECTED
ENTER COMMAND>
            UPDATE   PROMPT
$RECNO> 1
                1
IDTIC           =          22
XTIC            =                  4.614
YTIC            =                  9.125
IDTIC> <CR>
XTIC> -74.0
YTIC> 41.0625
$RECNO> 2
                2
IDTIC           =          23
XTIC            =                  8.886
YTIC            =                  9.146
IDTIC> <CR>
XTIC> -73.9875
YTIC> 41.0625
```

Continue until you've updated the sixth tic. Then, at the last $RECNO>
prompt, enter a carriage return to indicate that you're finished.

```
$RECNO> <CR>
```

To check that you've entered the correct values, issue the INFO
command LIST.

```
ENTER COMMAND> LIST
$RECNO                   IDTIC        XTIC
      YTIC
    1          22        -74.000      41.063
    2          23        -73.988      41.063
    3          24        -73.975      41.063
    4          32        -74.000      41.050
    5          33        -73.988      41.050
    6          34        -73.975      41.050
```

FYI

Notice that the display of XTIC and YTIC values includes only three significant digits (the XTIC and YTIC items are always floating-point binary with three decimal places used for display). The values are rounded off for display only. The stored tic values retain the precision with which they were entered.

HELP

Don't panic if your tic values are incorrect. After examining the list, use the same command—UPDATE PROMPT. At the $RECNO> prompt, enter the record number you wish to change and then update the incorrect values using the same procedure as shown above. When you finish making corrections, leave the UPDATE session by pressing <CR> at the final $RECNO> prompt. List the file again to check the current values.

If you're satisfied that the TIC file is correct, leave INFO.

```
ENTER COMMAND> Q STOP
```

Step 3

Define the coordinate system of the coverage

The tics are now in a real-world coordinate system. At this point, it's a good idea to record the coordinate system with the coverage. This is accomplished using the PROJECTDEFINE command.

```
Arc: USAGE PROJECTDEFINE
Usage: PROJECTDEFINE <COVER | GRID | FILE | TIN>
<target>
Arc: PROJECTDEFINE COVER GEOREF01
Define Projection
Project: PROJECTION GEOGRAPHIC
Project: UNITS DD
Project: PARAMETERS
Arc:
```

Using the DESCRIBE command, notice how the description of the coordinate system is now stored with the coverage. Once defined, this information is always carried with a coverage.

Arc: **DESCRIBE   GEOREF01**

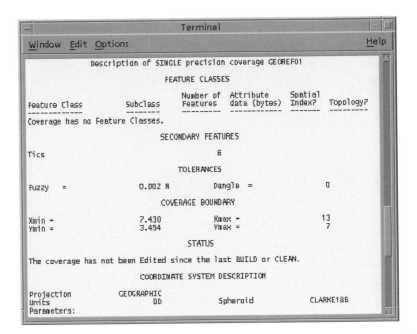

<table>
<tr><td>

**Step
4**

</td><td>

Project the tics from reference units to projected units

</td></tr>
</table>

If the current real-world tic locations are referenced by latitude and longitude, then they are said to be in reference units (degrees) rather than projected units (meters or feet). Before you can perform the transformation, these locations must be projected into the projection of the base map.

The original base map from which the land use update coverage was generated is in the Universal Transverse Mercator (UTM) coordinate system, which employs the Transverse Mercator projection. Therefore, we'll project the tic coordinates recorded in decimal degrees of latitude-longitude into UTM meters. These will form the basis for the real-world coordinates into which the land use update coverage will ultimately be transformed.

Projections can be performed either interactively at the keyboard or automatically read from a text file containing the parameters. To specify the sequence of responses required to project from degrees of latitude and longitude to UTM meters, use the interactive method. The output projection definition corresponds to the projection of the base map as well as to the other coverages in the study area database. Note that the x- and y-shift options have been used to shift significant digits from the left to the right. (For more information, refer to the PROJECT command in the online *Command References* for ARC.)

```
Arc: USAGE PROJECT
Usage: PROJECT
       <COVER | GRID | FILE> <input> <output>
               {projection_file} {NEAREST | BILINEAR |
CUBIC}
               {out_cellsize}
Arc: PROJECT COVER GEOREF01 GEOUTM02

*****************************************************
*       The INPUT projection has been defined....*
*****************************************************
Use OUTPUT to define the output projection and END
to finish.
```

PROJECT prompts for the parameters that define the map projections. The INPUT coordinate system is read from the input coverage. The OUTPUT coordinate system is defined interactively as UTM. Refer to Map Projections & Coordinate Management *for more information about defining input and output projections.*

```
Project: OUTPUT
Project: PROJECTION UTM
Project: UNITS METERS
Project: ZONE 18
Project: XSHIFT -580000
Project: YSHIFT -4540000
Project: PARAMETERS
Project: END
Arc:
```

Now use the LIST command to list the newly projected UTM coordinates (in meters) for the output coverage GEOUTM02.

```
Arc: LIST GEOUTM02.TIC
Record  IDTIC      XTIC         YTIC
       1    22    4024.895     5964.872
       2    23    5074.965     5976.987
       3    24    6125.677     5989.261
       4    32    4040.805     4577.147
       5    33    5091.074     4589.262
       6    34    6141.984     4601.535
```

The coordinate system information stored with the coverage has been automatically updated to reflect the new coordinate system.

Coordinate system information can also be copied from one data set to another using the PROJECTCOPY command. This is useful when many data sets are stored in a common coordinate system because the coordinate information needs to be defined interactively only once, then copied to all other data sets. Coordinate information can also enforce coordinate compatibility during analysis operations such as CLIP and INTERSECT using the PROJECTCOMPARE command.

| Step 5 | **Transform the coverage from digitizer units to real-world coordinates** |

The ARC command TRANSFORM converts coverage coordinates using either a projective or an affine transformation. The affine transformation function, which is based on three or more control points (tics), calculates change in scale, shift in the x-direction, shift in the y-direction, and any rotation for the output coverage. The transformation scale describes the difference in the scale from the input coverage to output coverage coordinates. This scale factor is shown in the report generated as part of the TRANSFORM command processing.

Before using TRANSFORM, create an output coverage containing only the projected tics. Create the output coverage named LANDTR06 using the projected tic locations from GEOUTM02.

```
Arc: USAGE CREATE
Usage: CREATE <out_cover> <tic_bnd_cover>
Arc: CREATE LANDTR06 GEOUTM02
Creating coverage LANDTR06
```

When using TRANSFORM, the input coverage, LANDAT05, is the coverage in digitizer units. The output coverage, LANDTR06, is the coverage containing tics measured in real-world coordinates.

TRANSFORM uses corresponding Tic-IDs to compare the input coverage tics to those of the output coverage. The calculated transformation is applied to all feature coordinates in the input coverage as they are copied to the output coverage. So, all feature coordinates are transformed to UTM meters for the output coverage. TRANSFORM does not alter the original coverage, LANDAT05.

```
Arc:  USAGE  TRANSFORM
Usage: TRANSFORM <in_cover> <out_cover>
           {AFFINE | PROJECTIVE | SIMILARITY}
Arc:  TRANSFORM  LANDAT05  LANDTR06
Transforming coordinates for coverage LANDAT05
```

TRANSFORM generates and displays a report on the screen that compares input and output coverage tics, the parameters used for the transformation, and measures of how accurately the two coverages fit together.

```
┌─                               Terminal                        · ─┐
│  Window  Edit  Options                                    Help     │
├───────────────────────────────────────────────────────────────────┤
│ Scale (X,Y) = (246.145,245.874)  Skew (degrees) = (-0.037)        │
│ Rotation (degrees) = (0.347)  Translation = (2903.706,3714.036)   │
│ RMS Error (input,output) = (0.006,1.522)                          │
│                                                                    │
│ Affine   X = Ax + By + C                                          │
│          Y = Dx + Ey + F                                          │
│     A =      246.141    B =      -1.648   C =      2903.706       │
│     D =        1.489    E =     245.868   F =      3714.036       │
│                                                                    │
│ tic id        input  x        input  y                            │
│               output x        output y      x error      y error  │
│ ------    ---------------    ---------------  ---------   -------  │
│   22            4.614           9.125                              │
│              4024.895        5964.872       -0.531       -0.419    │
│   23            8.886           9.146                              │
│              5074.965        5976.987        0.877       -1.011    │
│   24           13.150           9.180                              │
│              6125.677        5989.261       -0.347        1.423    │
│   32            4.640           3.483                              │
│              4040.805        4577.147       -0.745        0.156    │
│   33            8.917           3.512                              │
│              5091.074        4589.262        1.681        1.539    │
│   34           13.176           3.523                              │
│              6141.984        4601.535       -0.934       -1.688    │
└───────────────────────────────────────────────────────────────────┘
```

As part of the report, TRANSFORM calculates and displays a Root Mean Square (RMS) error. The RMS error describes the deviation between the tic locations in the input coverage and those in the output coverage. Although it never occurs with real-world data, a perfect transformation would produce an RMS error of 0.000. The RMS error is displayed in both digitizer units and in map units (i.e., real-world coordinates). Notice that the error displayed above is about 1.5 meters, acceptable for this exercise.

FYI

Determine an acceptable RMS value by examining your data and the scale at which it is represented. For actual geographic data, keep the RMS error as low as possible. (If digitizer units are inches, the RMS should usually be less than 0.005.)

High RMS errors indicate that the input and output coverage tics don't match well enough to properly register output coverage features to the original source map. This happens for a number of reasons, such as

- Original coverage tics were not digitized accurately

- There is map sheet distortion such as stretching or shrinking

- The real-world coordinate values for tics were not recorded correctly; for example, the x- and y-coordinate values might be transposed for one of your tics

See *Map Projections & Coordinate Management* for more information on map accuracy and RMS error.

Now look at the coordinate information stored with LANDTR06.

Arc: **DESCRIBE   LANDTR06**

```
┌─────────────────────────────────────────────────────────────────────────┐
│ ─                            Terminal                                . □  │
├─────────────────────────────────────────────────────────────────────────┤
│  Window  Edit  Options                                            Help    │
├─────────────────────────────────────────────────────────────────────────┤
│          Description of SINGLE precision coverage LANDTR06          ▲     │
│                          FEATURE CLASSES                                  │
│                                                                          │
│                                  Number of  Attribute     Spatial        │
│    Feature Class        Subclass  Features  data (bytes)  Index?  Topolo  │
│    gy?                                                                    │
│    -------------        --------  --------- ------------  ------- ------  │
│    ---                                                                    │
│    ARCS                               42                                  │
│    POLYGONS                           20          26                Yes   │
│    NODES                              30                                  │
│                                                                          │
│                         SECONDARY FEATURES                                │
│                                                                          │
│    Tics                                6                                  │
│    Arc Segments                      270                                  │
│    Polygon Labels                     19                                  │
│                                                                          │
│                            TOLERANCES                                     │
│                                                                          │
│    Fuzzy   =            0.492 N        Dangle  =            24.587 N      │
│                         COVERAGE BOUNDARY                                 │
│                                                                          │
│    Xmin =               4723.835       Xmax =              6161.713       │
│    Ymin =               4574.391       Ymax =              5579.779       │
│                                                                          │
│                             STATUS                                        │
│                                                                          │
│    The coverage has not been Edited since the last BUILD or CLEAN.        │
│                                                                          │
│                    COORDINATE SYSTEM DESCRIPTION                          │
│                                                                          │
│    Projection          UTM                                               │
│    Zone                 18                                                │
│    Units              METERS           Spheroid           CLARKE1866      │
│    Xshift       -580000.00000          Yshift      -4540000.00           │
│    Parameters:                                                     ▼      │
└─────────────────────────────────────────────────────────────────────────┘
```

HELP Don't panic if your RMS is too high. Check
that the real-world coordinates you recorded in your TIC file are
correct. If you discover an error, start the transformation process
again. But now delete the coverage containing UTM tics and the
newly transformed coverage using the ARC command KILL. Be
careful. KILL executes *immediately* after the command is entered, so
make sure you enter the correct coverage name. A coverage can't be
recovered once it's been killed.

```
Arc:  KILL  GEOUTM02
Arc:  KILL  LANDTR06
```

Once you've deleted these coverages, return to Step 2 on page 7-17
and complete the transformation process again.

ARC/INFO applies the transformation function uniformly to all
coordinates, scaling, rotating, and shifting all features in the output
coverage. Straight lines remain straight after TRANSFORM (i.e.,
TRANSFORM will not add additional vertices to two-point arcs).

END

Joining adjacent maps

Typically, each geographic layer of thematic data is automated as a set of adjacent coverages—one for each map sheet covering the entire region. Coverage boundaries (coverage extents) are usually held initially as direct representations of the map sheet boundaries. However, once all map sheets are converted to digital form and a single coordinate system is adopted through the tic (control) points, the adjacent coverages can be merged into a single coverage and the arcs representing map sheet borders can be removed.

The first step in joining adjacent coverages is to visually compare them to determine whether coverage features match along adjacent borders. Generally, this process is performed by creating verification plots at the original map scale and placing them side by side. Another useful exercise is creating various map displays in ARCPLOT to compare adjacent map edges interactively.

Process used to join adjacent coverages

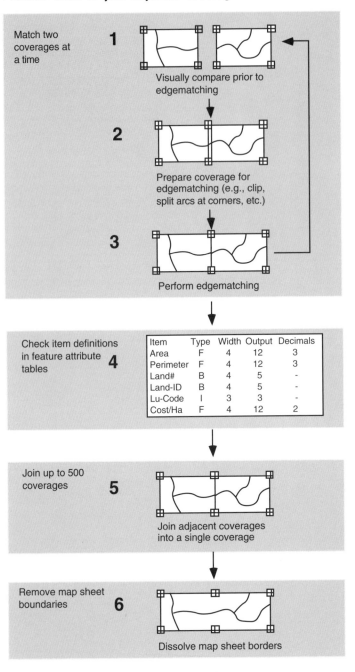

1 Match two coverages at a time

Visually compare prior to edgematching

2

Prepare coverage for edgematching (e.g., clip, split arcs at corners, etc.)

3

Perform edgematching

4 Check item definitions in feature attribute tables

Item	Type	Width	Output	Decimals
Area	F	4	12	3
Perimeter	F	4	12	3
Land#	B	4	5	-
Land-ID	B	4	5	-
Lu-Code	I	3	3	-
Cost/Ha	F	4	12	2

5 Join up to 500 coverages

Join adjacent coverages into a single coverage

6 Remove map sheet boundaries

Dissolve map sheet borders

Understanding GIS—The ARC/INFO Method

EXERCISE

Join two coverages

The following exercises guide you through the operations used to
edgematch and join coverages. You'll perform these operations using
coverages provided for you. These coverages are located in your
DATA subdirectory under UGIS. To complete this exercise, you
need to copy LANDTR, LUAT10, and two other coverages, named
CLIPCOV and LINKCOV. After you complete this edgematching
exercise on LANDTR, you may want to repeat the edgematch and
mapjoin procedures on your own LANDTR06 coverage.

Make sure that you are located in the LAND subdirectory under the
UGIS directory in your local workspace.

Be sure to copy into your local LAND subdirectory the LANDTR,
LUAT10, and CLIPCOV coverages provided as part of the
Understanding GIS database.

UNIX
```
Arc: copy ../data/landtr landtr
Arc: copy ../data/luat10 luat10
Arc: copy ../data/clipcov clipcov
Arc: copy ../data/linkcov linkcov
```
Windows NT
```
Arc: copy ..\data\landtr landtr
Arc: copy ..\data\luat10 luat10
Arc: copy ..\data\clipcov clipcov
Arc: copy ..\data\linkcov linkcov
```

Specify your station file if you haven't already during this session.

```
Arc: &STATION <name>
```

**Step
1**

Compare adjacent coverages to check for matching errors

Before performing a mapjoin, make sure that all the coverage features
that should fit together really do, that item names and definitions for
all attributes following the Cover-ID match, and that attributes for
continuous features are consistent across the map sheet borders.

Points to check before using mapjoin:

☐ Do all features match along the border?
☐ Do the item definitions match?
☐ Are feature attributes consistent across the map sheet borders?

Use ARCPLOT to visually compare the coverages before joining
them.

```
Arc: ARCPLOT
Arcplot:
```

Once the `Arcplot:` prompt appears, specify the map extent of the coverage you want to view.

`Arcplot:` **`MAPEXTENT LANDTR`**

Now draw both of the land use coverages. First draw LUAT10.

`Arcplot:` **`ARCS LUAT10`**

Change the line symbol and draw the arcs in LANDTR.

`Arcplot:` **`LINESYMBOL 2`**
`Arcplot:` **`ARCS LANDTR`**

Notice how LANDTR slightly overlaps the LUAT10 coverage on the display. Remember that when you digitized the LANDTR coverage, you extended it slightly beyond its real border.

A coverage of the boundary of the update area (or map sheet) can be used to clip each coverage layer in the database before joining adjacent map sheet coverages. In this case, a special coverage, CLIPCOV, defines the boundaries of the update area. Change the current line symbol and draw CLIPCOV to see how it overlaps LANDTR.

`Arcplot:` **`LINESYMBOL 3`**
`Arcplot:` **`ARCS CLIPCOV`**

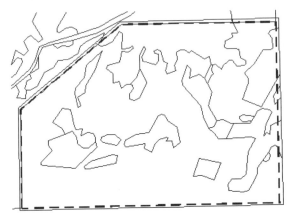

CLIPCOV (dashed line) shows how LANDTR extends slightly beyond the update area boundary. This is the intentional result of digitizing outside the boundary (Lesson 4). When many layers are automated simultaneously, you can use one clip coverage to ensure that each coverage layer has the same map sheet boundary.

Quit ARCPLOT and perform the clip operation on LANDTR.

`Arcplot:` **`Q`**
`Leaving ARCPLOT...`

| Step 2 | **Prepare the adjacent coverages for edgematching** |

The LANDTR coverage overlaps both LUAT10 and the lower right corner of the entire study area boundary. Erase the part of LANDTR that overlaps by using a topological overlay operation named CLIP.

```
Arc: USAGE CLIP
Usage: CLIP
        <in_cover> <clip_cover> <out_cover>
            {POLY | LINE | POINT | NET | LINK | RAW}
            {fuzzy_tolerance}
Arc: CLIP LANDTR CLIPCOV LANDCP07 POLY
Clipping landtr with clipcov to create landcp07.
Sorting...
Intersecting...
Assembling polygons...
Creating new labels...
Creating drive>:\yourname\UGIS\LAND\LANDP07.PAT...
Arc:
```

Before viewing the results of the CLIP operation and performing the edgematch exercise in ARCEDIT, make a copy of your current update coverage for land use (LANDCP07). Name the copy of the coverage LANDEM08 to indicate that this is the coverage to be edgematched.

```
Arc: COPY LANDCP07 LANDEM08
Copied landcp07 to landem08
```

Now before edgematching, start ARCEDIT to look at the results of the CLIP operation in the output coverage, LANDEM08.

```
Arc: ARCEDIT
Arcedit: EDIT LANDEM08
The edit coverage is now
<drive>:\yourname\UGIS\LAND\LANDEM08
Defaulting the map extent to the BND of
<drive>:\yourname\UGIS\LAND\LANDEM08
```

Set the drawing environment to include arcs and nodes, then draw the coverage.

```
Arcedit: DRAWENVIRONMENT ARC NODE
Arcedit: DRAW
```

You also need to draw LUAT10 just to see how well LANDEM08 fits along its borders. Coverages that are not going to be edited can be displayed as background coverages in ARCEDIT. Use the BACKCOVERAGE command to specify LUAT10 as the background coverage and the symbol number to use to draw its features.

```
Arcedit: USAGE BACKCOVERAGE
Usage: BACKCOVERAGE <cover> {symbol}
Arcedit: BACKCOVERAGE LUAT10 4
LUAT10 is now background coverage 1 with draw symbol 4
```

Use the BACKENVIRONMENT command to draw arcs and nodes, from the background coverage. Issue the DRAW command to draw both the edit coverage and the background coverage.

```
Arcedit:  BACKENVIRONMENT  ARC  NODE
Arcedit:  DRAW
```

Notice how LANDEM08 has been clipped along its borders to fit along LUAT10. Now use the **Extent** option in the Pan/Zoom menu to change the map extent to zoom in on the LANDEM08 coverage.

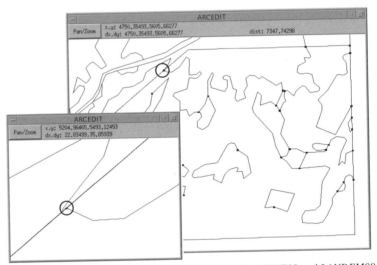

A quick visual comparison on your screen suggests that LUAT10 and LANDEM08 match along their edges. However, as you zoom in, it becomes clear that some nodes do not match precisely.

Step 3

Edgematch the adjacent coverages to be joined

The edgematch operation is used to match border coordinates between coverages that will later be joined.

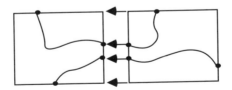

link features   The edgematching process assures that arcs and polygon boundaries match across borders and that map sheet corners match. A feature type called a *link* connects the locations in one coverage to the locations of the matching features in the adjacent coverage. A rubber-sheeting operation then adjusts the linked features of one coverage to precisely match those of the adjacent coverage. Edgematching and rubber sheeting are described in *Data automation-->Editing coverages and tables with ARCEDIT* in the ARC/INFO online Help.

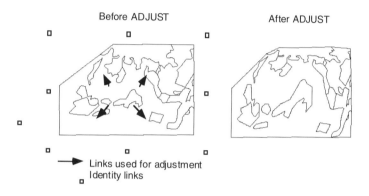

Before ADJUST   After ADJUST

→ Links used for adjustment
▫ Identity links

To illustrate how links are used, here's a quick exercise to illustrate adjustment. Now specify LINK as the edit feature and add links to the drawing environment.

```
Arcedit:  EDITFEATURE  LINK
Adding the extreme boundary points as hull points
8 element(s) for edit feature LINK
Arcedit:  DRAWENV  LINK
Arcedit:  DRAW
```

FYI   Using the Pan/Zoom button on the graphic screen, select Zoom Out Center from the pulldown menu. Notice that green boxes are drawn along the boundary of the edit coverage when you initially specify LINK as the feature class to edit. Whenever the edit feature specifies links for a coverage that doesn't have link features, eight identity links are created around its outer edge. Identity links have the same from- and to-locations. They control adjustment in ARCEDIT by acting as 'nails' to hold the surface down at each location during adjustment. Look for these green boxes along the outer boundary of LANDEM08 as you zoom in and out of the coverage during the next set of operations.

For this exercise, copy some links from a coverage named LINKCOV to the current edit coverage (LANDEM08) using the GET command.

```
Arcedit: GET LINKCOV
Copying the links from
<drive>:\yourname\ugis\land\linkov into
<drive>:\yourname\ugis\land\landemp08
5 link(s) copied
```

Four links are drawn with yellow arrows as they are added to LANDEM08. The fifth one, an identity link (yellow box), appears to the left (within the extent of the LUAT10 coverage) when you zoom out. During adjustment, the from-point on each link moves to the top point. Other portions of the coverage are adjusted according to the influence of the links at that location. The closer a coordinate is to a link, the greater its adjustment. Now you're ready to perform a sample adjustment. Issue the ADJUST command.

```
Arcedit: ADJUST

Adjusting coverage
<drive>:\yourname\ugis\land\landemp08
Building the adjustment structure from the links for the
first pass...
Proximal tolerance set to 0.141...
Removing duplicate points within tolerance...
Within tolerance 0. Remaining 13...
Proximal tolerance set to 0.000...
     adjusting ARCs...
     adjusting LABELs...
Updating the adjustment structure for the second
pass...
     adjusting ARCs...
     adjusting LABELs...
Arcedit:
```

Notice how LANDEM08 is adjusted based on the links, which appear as identity links (green boxes). This demonstrates the effect of rubber sheeting on a coverage; typically, adjustments are not this extreme. Adjustment is used to edgematch one coverage to another. The adjustment for edgematching is performed along the edges of a coverage and is not as dramatic because the links are much shorter, connecting features across boundaries in the adjacent coverages.

Remove LANDEM08 as the current edit coverage. This cancels the adjustment and removes links that were added during this example.

```
Arcedit: REMOVEEDIT LANDEM08
All changes since last SAVE will be lost!
Continue? <Y/N>: Y
Removing <drive>:\yourname\ugis\land\landem08
Arcedit: DRAW
```

edgematching menu

Now that you understand how links are used in adjustment, it's time to perform edgematching. The most common method specifies links that connect nodes in the coverage to be adjusted (i.e., the edit coverage named LANDEM08) to nodes in the snap coverage (i.e., the coverage you're adjusting to, named LUAT10).

The first step is to start the edgematch session, which employs menus that you'll use to specify the parameters needed to make the adjustments.

```
Arcedit: EDGEMATCH
Starting the Edgematch macros...
```

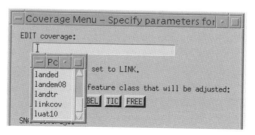

The Coverage Menu appears. Specify **LANDEM08** as the EDIT coverage by typing it at the menu prompt, or pick it from a popup scrolling list opened by pressing the appropriate mouse button on your system. (Probably the right mouse button.)

Notice that EDGEMATCH automatically sets the edit feature to link.

For this exercise, the EDIT coverage feature class to adjust is NODE, the menu default.

Specify **LUAT10** as the SNAP coverage the same way you specified the EDIT coverage (type it at the menu prompt, or choose it from the popup scrolling list).

Next specify the type of feature that will be linked in the snap coverage, in this case NODE, which is again the menu default.

So far, you've specified that links will begin at a node in LANDEM08 and connect to a node in LUAT10. The snap coverage automatically displays as the background coverage, which is all that is needed for this exercise. Notice the place on the menu where you could specify other background coverages if desired.

Now that you've specified all the coverages and features to link, press the **APPLY** button at the bottom of the menu.

```
The edit coverage is now
<drive>:\yourname\ugis\land\landemp08
The snap coverage is now
<drive>:\yourname\ugis\land\luat10
Adding the extreme boundary points as hull points
8 element(s) for edit feature LINK
31 element(s) for edit feature NODE
222 element(s) selected for link feature NODE
<drive>:\yourname\ugis\land\luat10   is now background
coverage 1 with draw symbol 2
```

Two things happen when you press APPLY. The edit coverage and
snap coverage (and any other background coverages) appear in the
graphics display window and in a smaller window named Index,
which you can use as an overview as you zoom in and out during the
edgematching session. At the same time the coverages are drawn, the
Edgematching Menu opens.

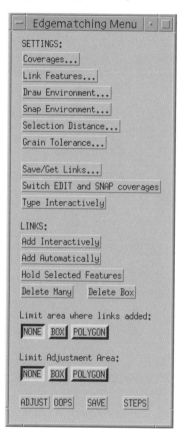

This menu has buttons for setting the environment (e.g., changing the
link features and drawing environment), adding and deleting link
features, defining a limited area within which links will be added,
performing the adjustment, undoing changes (OOPS), and saving the
changes.

Specify a snapping tolerance for adding links between nodes. The snapping tolerance allows you to automatically add links between the nodes in LANDEM08 and LUAT10 that are within a given distance of each other. Specify a snapping distance of 10 meters (remembering that our coverage is now in UTM meters).

Press the **Snap Environment...** button. Backspace to erase the current snapping distance, type **10**, and press **APPLY**.

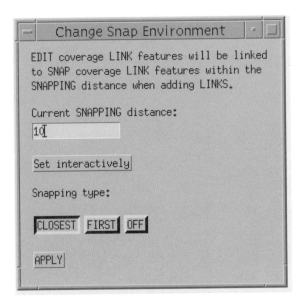

Now add some links to perform the edgematch operation. Press the **Add Automatically** button on the Edgematching Menu to automatically add links between nodes that are within 10 meters of each other.

```
4 link(s) added to LANDEM08
```

Some square boxes and small lines are added to the display. These represent two kinds of links. The boxes represent *identity links;* that is, links with the same location for the from- and to-point. Identity links act as nails to hold the surface down at that location during adjustment. Notice the identity link at the lower left corner of LANDEM08. This link was created at the corner node of LANDEM08 where it connects to the corner node of LUAT10.

The small lines represent adjustment links like those used earlier in the example. These links connect nodes in LANDEM08 with nodes in LUAT10. Using the **Extent** option in the Pan/Zoom menu, zoom in on one to take a closer look. Continue to zoom in until you can see the link connecting the nodes in LANDEM08 and LUAT10.

HELP

You can use the Index window to zoom in to the working window as follows:

Select **Extent** from the Pan/Zoom menu in the working window. Move your mouse inside the Index window to create a box that defines the area to enlarge.

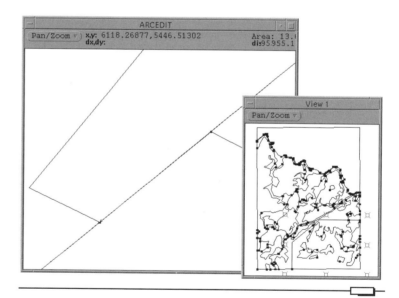

add identity links   Two more links need to be added before performing the adjustment. These occur at the two corners in the upper left portion of LANDEM08 as shown here.

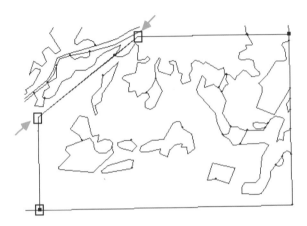

The arcs in LANDEM08 and LUAT10 are coincident along this edge, so you should add one identity link at each corner to nail down these arcs in LANDEM08 during the adjustment. The best way to do this is to zoom in on each corner to add the link. Zoom in to the left-most corner identified below:

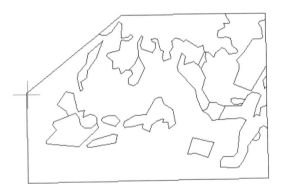

Next change the link feature class. Currently, only links that connect nodes can be added. Select **Link Features...** under SETTINGS: on the Edgematching Menu to display the Set LINK features menu.

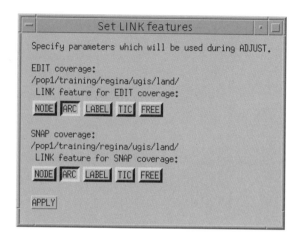

Specify that links connecting individual vertices on arcs will be added by pressing **ARC** in the choice field for both the EDIT coverage and SNAP coverage. Press **APPLY**.

```
43 element(s) for edit feature ARC
281 element(s) for link feature ARC
```

Now add an identity link at the first corner. Press the **Add Interactively** button on the Edgematching Menu. The following menu appears in the dialog area of the screen:

```
- - - - - - - - - - - Options - - - - - - - - - -
1) Free point     2) Snap point     3) Set symbol
5) Delete link    9) Quit
```

The cursor appears on the graphics display screen. Because you're adding identity links, the cursor position must be at the same location for the from- and to-point of the link. (For more information on the process used to add links, see the discussion on link features in online help under *Data Automation-->Editing coverages and INFO files with ARCEDIT-->Rubber sheeting and edgematching-->Link features.*)

```
Position the cursor over the corner
where
the identity link is to be added.
```

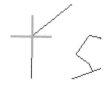

Hold your cursor as steadily as possible and

press the **2** key

to enter the from-point of the link. Without moving the crosshairs,

press the **2** key

again to enter the to-point of the link at the same location. If you correctly entered the identity link, a box will be added at the corner and the coordinate values listed in the dialog area will be the same for both the from- and to-points.

```
Link #13  :(4735.561,5109.521),(4735.561,5109.521)
```

Now using this same procedure, add the second identity link. First reset the map extent to the entire coverage, zoom in on the other corner, and then add the identity link.

```
Press the 2 key to add the from- location
Press the 2 key to add the to- location
```

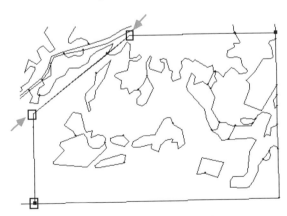

```
Link #14:  (5289.935,5554.647),(5289.935,5554.647)
Press 9 to quit adding links
2 link(s) added to LANDEM08
```

HELP

        Don't worry if you added the links incorrectly. Link features can be deleted using the same process you use to delete other features. If you notice that you've added a bad link, first

```
Press 9 to quit adding links
```

Then press the **Delete Many** button on the Edgematching Menu to point to and select those links that you want to delete. For example,

```
1 = Select      2 = Next      3 = Who      9 = Quit
Enter point
```

```
Press 1—to select links
   1 element(s) now selected
```

```
Press 9—to quit selecting links
   1 link(s) deleted
```

After you delete the incorrect links, select the **Add Interactively** button on the Edgematching Menu to continue adding links.

When you finish adding links, reset the map extent by selecting the **Fullview** option from the Pan/Zoom menu.

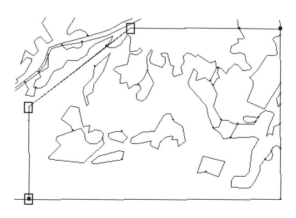

perform the adjustment

The coverage display shows identity links at three of the four corners of LANDEM08 where it matches LUAT10, as well as three smaller links where arcs are supposed to connect across the adjacent coverage borders. Now your coverage is ready to adjust.

Press the **ADJUST** button located at the bottom of the Edgematching Menu.

```
Adjusting coverage LANDEM08
Building the adjustment structure from the links for the
first pass...
Proximal tolerance set to 1.000...
Generating convex hull...
Building Triangular Irregular Network...
      adjusting ARCs...
      adjusting LABELs...
Updating the adjustment structure for the second pass...
      adjusting ARCs...
      adjusting LABELs...
```

If necessary, clean up the graphics display using either the **Fullview** or **Redisplay** options in the Pan/Zoom menu.

Notice how all the links are now drawn as identity links (green boxes). This means that the from-points adjusted to the to-points on each link.

verify the adjustment

The adjustment should have matched features between the two coverages. Check the adjustment by zooming in on each place where the two coverages connect to view the effect of ADJUST on that location.

> **FYI** Each adjustment process will differ somewhat based on how connections are made between nodes in adjacent coverages. For more information about adding links, refer to online help under *Data Automation-->Editing coverages and INFO files in ARCEDIT-->Rubber sheeting and edgematching.*

save the adjusted coverage

Once you're finished checking the effects of your edgematch operation, you can save your results. Press the **SAVE** button located near the bottom of the Edgematching Menu.

```
Saving changes for LANDEM08
43 arc(s) written to LANDEM08
  from the original 43 arc(s), 43 added and 43 deleted
Reopening arcs...
Saving labels...
19 label attribute record(s) written to LANDEM08
19 label(s) written to LANDEM08
  from the original 19 label(s), 19 added and 19
deleted
Reopening labels...
Saving links...
14 link records(s) written to LANDEM08
  from the original 0 link, 14 added and 0 deleted
Reopening links...
  BND replaced into LANDEM08
  WARNING, topology has been altered please use 'CLEAN'
or 'BUILD'.
Saving tolerances to TOL file...
Re-establishing edit feature
Re-establishing link feature
```

Finally, close the Edgematching Menu and return to the Arcedit prompt.

```
Resetting parameters to original settings...
Arcedit:
```

quit ARCEDIT

Now you're ready to exit ARCEDIT and join LANDEM08 and LUAT10 into a single land use coverage.

```
Arcedit: QUIT
Leaving ARCEDIT...
```

rebuild coverage topology

After completing an ARCEDIT session during which arcs were edited (e.g., moved, deleted, added, adjusted, and so on), regenerate polygon topology before performing any other operation. Because arc-polygon topology is implemented as a list of the arcs defining each polygon, this arc list must be updated. You must recreate polygon topology for LANDEM08 using BUILD.

```
Arc: USAGE BUILD
Usage: BUILD <cover> {POLY | LINE | POINT | NODE |
ANNO.<subclass>}
Arc: BUILD LANDEM08 POLY
Building polygons...
Arc:
```

Now that the coverage has polygon topology, it's ready for the one remaining step before the actual mapjoin.

HELP

If BUILD encounters intersections you will need to check the coverage links for erors in ARCEDIT and execute EDGEMTCH again.

Check PAT item definitions between LUAT10 and LANDEM08

The last step before joining coverages is to verify that all coverages to be joined have the same item definitions for items past the cover-ID in the PAT. This is verified using the ITEMS command.

```
Arc:  ITEMS  LUAT10.PAT
COLUMN          ITEM NAME    WIDTH OUTPUT   TYPE N.DEC   ALT
NAME
     1          AREA             4     12      F     3      -
     5          PERIMETER        4     12      F     3      -
     9          LUAT10#          4      5      B     -      -
    13          LUAT10-ID        4      5      B     -      -
    17          LU-CODE          3      3      I     -      -
    20          COST/HA          6      6      I     -      -

Arc:  ITEMS  LANDEM08.PAT
COLUMN          ITEM NAME    WIDTH OUTPUT   TYPE N.DEC   ALT
NAME
     1          AREA             4     12      F     3      -
     5          PERIMETER        4     12      F     3      -
     9          LANDEM08#        4      5      B     -      -
    13          LANDEM08-ID      4      5      B     -      -
    17          LU-CODE          3      3      I     -      -
    20          COST/HA          6      6      I     -      -
```

Notice the two items past the Cover-ID: LU-CODE and COST/HA. Each has the same item definition in both files, so these coverages are ready to be joined.

Understanding GIS—The ARC/INFO Method

FYI

In our example, all the item definitions match correctly. However, this is not always the case. Here is a list of common item matching errors to look for:

Error	What to do
Missing items	Use ADDITEM at the Arc: prompt.
Item widths vary	Use ADDITEM with the correct definition, except specify a new item name; then update values of the new item in INFO using CALCULATE or MOVE; then use DROPITEM to drop the old item; finally, use ALTER in INFO to change the item name.
Output widths vary	Use ALTER in INFO to change the output width.
Items in different order	Use PULLITEMS at the Arc: prompt to alter the order of items in incorrect files.

Step 5

MAPJOIN adjacent coverages

The MAPJOIN operation can append up to 500 adjacent coverages. Once MAPJOIN is invoked, you'll be prompted to enter the names of the coverages to be joined. In this case, there are two coverages, LUAT10 and LANDEM08. MAPJOIN creates a new coverage containing all the features and attributes from both input coverages.

```
Arc: USAGE MAPJOIN
Usage: MAPJOIN
          <out_cover>
          {feature class...feature_class |
template_cover}
          {NONE | FEATURES | TICS | ALL}
{clip_cover}
```

It's a good idea to maintain unique User-IDs for all coverage features that will exist after MAPJOIN. The ID offset argument, {NONE | FEATURES | TICS | ALL}, is used to specify the features that will be assigned User-IDs in the output coverage. Polygons in LUAT10 and LANDEM08 already have unique User-IDs. That is, each land use polygon in the study area already has a unique User-ID (polygons that span both coverages have the same User-ID).

There is one master tic file for both coverages, so you also won't want to offset the Tic-IDs. To retain unique User-IDs for each feature and retain one common set of tic locations use the default option, NONE.

Now execute MAPJOIN. Name the output coverage LANDMJ09.

```
Arc: MAPJOIN LANDMJ09 POLY
Enter Coverages to be MAPJOINed (Type END or a blank line
when done):
= = = = = = = = = = = = = = = = = = = = = = = = = = = = = =

Enter the 1st coverage: LUAT10
Enter the 2nd coverage: LANDEM08
Enter the 3rd coverage: END

  Appending coverages...
  Sorting...
Partial process enabled.  43% of the coverage will be
processed.
  Intersecting...
  Assembling polygons...
  Creating PAT...
Arc:
```

view the results of MAPJOIN

In ARCPLOT, you can see the coverage created by MAPJOIN. Start ARCPLOT and set the map extent to LANDMJ09.

```
Arc: ARCPLOT
Arcplot: MAPEXTENT LANDMJ09
Arcplot: ARCS LANDMJ09
```

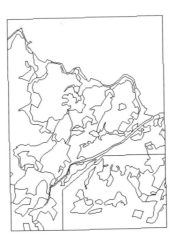

Notice that the map sheet borders still appear in LANDMJ09. These need to be removed for the final land use coverage.

You can use the DROPLINE command in ARCPLOT to visualize the effect of removing the map borders. First set a new line color and text size.

```
Arcplot:  CLEAR
Arcplot:  LINECOLOR 6
Arcplot:  TEXTSIZE .075
Arcplot:  USAGE DROPLINE
Usage: DROPLINE <cover> <item> {lookup_table} {NOTEXT}
```

Specify LU-CODE as the item on which border arcs will be dropped
from the display.

```
Arcplot:  DROPLINE LANDMJ09 LU-CODE
```

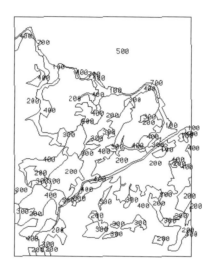

The arcs are drawn and each polygon is labeled with its LU-CODE
value. Notice how the border arcs are dropped between adjacent
polygons that have the same LU-CODE values across the map sheet
boundaries. This indicates a successful MAPJOIN operation.

DROPLINE only visually drops the boundary between adjacent
polygons. The DISSOLVE command, available at the Arc: prompt,
actually merges adjacent polygons and saves the result as a new
coverage.

Step 6

Remove map sheet borders using DISSOLVE

Removing borders between adjacent polygons containing the same
feature attribute values for all items is one of the most common uses of
the DISSOLVE command. While still in ARCPLOT, use the ARC
DISSOLVE command to dissolve on the PAT items in LANDMJ09.

```
Arcplot:  Arc USAGE DISSOLVE
Usage: DISSOLVE <in_cover> <out_cover>
                <dissolve_item | #ALL> {POLY | LINE |
NET | REGION.subclass}
```

```
Arcplot:  Arc DISSOLVE LANDMJ09 LANDDS10 #ALL
 Dissolving  landmj09 by #ALL to create landds10
 Creating landds10.PAT format...
 Creating dissolve table...
 Dissolving...
Number of Polygons (Input,Output) =  81    77
Number of Arcs     (Input,Output) = 321   207
 Creating landds10.pat...
```

verify the final coverage   Verify your DISSOLVE results. CLEAR, set the map extent, and
draw the final land use coverage named LANDDS10.

```
Arcplot:  CLEAR
Arcplot:  MAPEXTENT  LANDDS10
Arcplot:  ARCS  LANDDS10
```

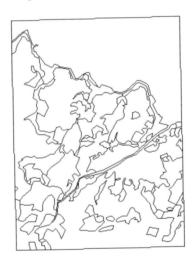

HELP   A display appears similar to that drawn earlier
with DROPLINE; in this case, however, you are viewing a coverage
in which arcs representing the map sheet borders are no longer
included. There is one other important difference in LANDDS10—
DISSOLVE with the #ALL option generates a new set of unique User-
IDs for each polygon in LANDDS10.

Quit ARCPLOT and wrap up this session.

```
Arcplot: Q
Leaving ARCPLOT...
```

END

whew!   Congratulations! You've created a final land use coverage named
LANDDS10. This coverage contains the land use features for the
entire study area in the same UTM coordinate system as the other
coverages in your project database.

Database management

Your project database is now complete. In the lessons that follow, you'll use this data to learn analysis and mapping. But now you need to create a workspace containing all the coverage layers.

Normally, at this point in your project, you would back up your coverage automation directories such as LAND and STRM (STRM is the directory created and used in the advanced exercises in earlier lessons). However, before backing up these directories, you should copy the final land use coverage, LANDDS10, and the final streams coverage, STRMAT03, to your database directory. Assign them names that will make them easy to identify later. In the DATA directory provided with this workbook, these coverages are named LANDUSE and STREAMS.

EXERCISE   **Set up a workspace for geographic analysis**

If desired, you can use your own copies of LANDUSE and STREAMS coverages (named LANDDS10 and STRMAT03) in the next two lessons. Here is the process you would use to copy these coverages to your local DATA subdirectory under UGIS.

Before making copies of the LANDDS10 and STRMAT03 coverages in your local DATA subdirectory, you should change workspaces to that location.

UNIX   `Arc:  &WORKSPACE  /yourname/ugis/data`
Windows NT `Arc:  &WORKSPACE  <drive>:\yourname\ugis\data`

The LANDDS10 coverage is located in the LAND subdirectory, and STRMAT03 is located in the STRM subdirectory, both under UGIS in your local workspace. Copy these to the DATA subdirectory under your local version of UGIS.

UNIX   `Arc:  copy  ../land/landds10  landds10`
Windows NT `Arc:  copy  ..\land\landds10  landds10`

Copy the STRMAT03 coverage to DATA.

UNIX
Windows NT

```
Arc: copy ../strm/strmat03 strmat03
Arc: copy ..\strm\strmat03 strmat03
```

(If you did not create STRMAT 03, copy the STREAMS coverage from the RESULTS directory.)

Now you have a choice. Do you want to continue using the land use and streams coverages that you've created so far, or would you rather use those provided as part of the workbook data set? The coverages provided are named LANDUSE and STREAMS. If you wish to use these, *do not* perform the remaining steps in this exercise. If you wish to use your versions, however, then you will need to complete these steps.

Assuming that you wish to use the LANDDS10 and STRMAT03 coverages you created, you can remove LANDUSE and STREAMS using the ARC command KILL as follows:

```
Arc: USAGE KILL
Usage: KILL <geo_dataset> {ARC | INFO | ALL}
Arc: KILL LANDUSE
```

Rename LANDDS10 and STRMAT03 to LANDUSE and STREAMS, respectively.

```
Arc: USAGE RENAME
Usage: RENAME <old_geo_dataset> <new_geo_dataset>
Arc: RENAME LANDDS10 LANDUSE
```

If you have a copy of STRMAT03 in your local DATA workspace, rename it also.

```
Arc: RENAME STRMAT03 STREAMS
```

This completes the creation of a DATA workspace to be used for analysis and mapping in the following lessons.

END

Summary

concept review   In this lesson, you completed two of the key processes used to create a GIS database. First you converted a coverage to real-world coordinates so it could be georeferenced to other coverages in your project database. Then you used the edgematch-mapjoin process to combine adjacent coverages into one comprehensive coverage for the project area. This *layer* can now be overlaid on other coverage layers—each depicting a different theme, such as SOILS, STREAMS, and ROADS.

You learned about real-world coordinate systems, map projections, and transformed digitizer units into real-world coordinates. You also used the Edgematching Menu to edgematch adjacent coverages and learned the commands that merge them. Now you have all the ingredients of a comprehensive project database.

the master tic file   To accurately register all layers in your database to your base map, before you automate your maps, you should create a master tic file and record tic locations and Tic-IDs on each manuscript you'll digitize.

The following diagram outlines a possible tic numbering system for a geographic database spanning four map sheets. This system consists of several grid cells (map sheets) which measure 1° x 1°. Tic-IDs correspond to their latitude-longitude locations, and the name of each coverage matches its lower left tic.

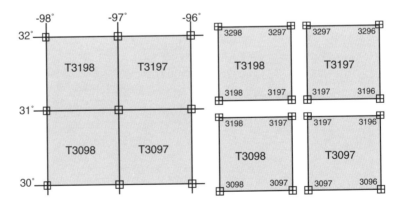

Understanding GIS—The ARC/INFO Method

map sheet templates

Map sheet automation typically involves digitizing beyond the map sheet border. In the final step, one common map sheet border can be used to *clip* each coverage layer to obtain a more accurate and consistent outline for each coverage layer before it is edgematched and joined with adjacent coverages.

In the exercises in this lesson, you clipped the land use coverage with an outline for the update coverage area. Suppose you were to automate a number of layers for the same area and join each with its adjacent layer coverage. Creating and using one common map sheet template as a clipping boundary would make this process easier and more accurate. It is useful to generate map sheet borders at the same time you create the master tic file—especially if standard map sheets, whose corner locations are recorded in real-world coordinates, are used.

lesson summary

The two major tasks performed in this lesson were transforming the digitized coverage into real-world coordinates and joining the transformed coverage to the existing land use coverage for the study area. The charts on the following pages summarize these procedures.

Capturing coverages in real-world coordinates

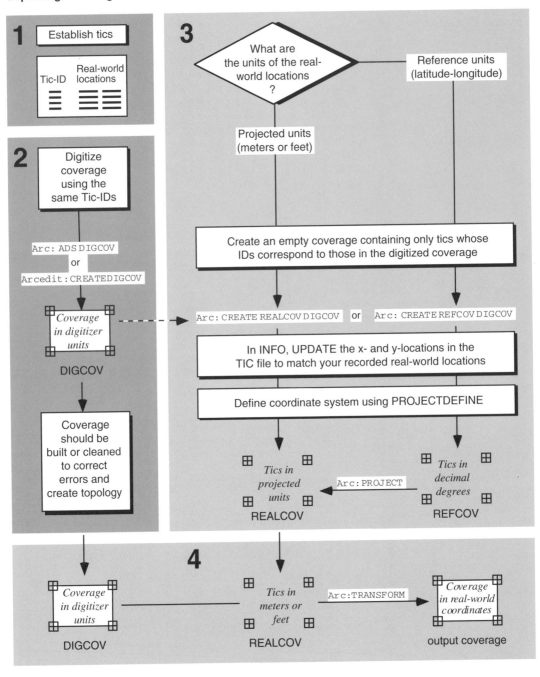

Understanding GIS—The ARC/INFO Method

The edgematch-mapjoin process

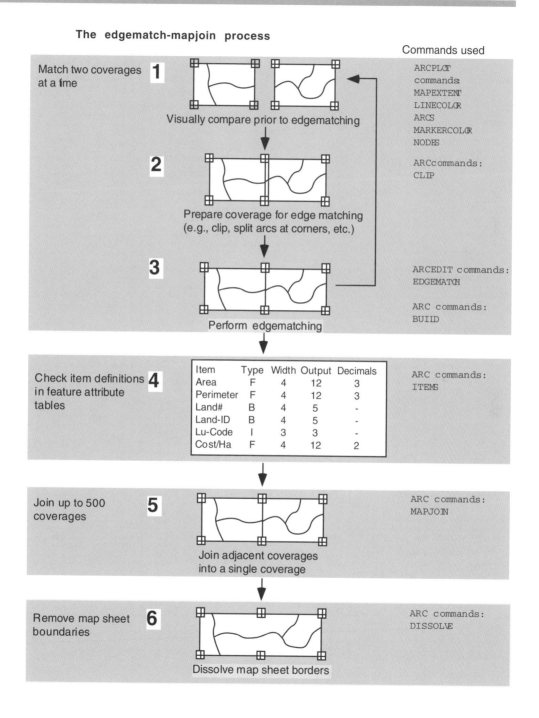

Commands used

1 Match two coverages at a time

Visually compare prior to edgematching

ARCPLOT commands:
MAPEXTENT
LINECOLOR
ARCS
MARKERCOLOR
NODES

2

Prepare coverage for edge matching
(e.g., clip, split arcs at corners, etc.)

ARC commands:
CLIP

3

Perform edgematching

ARCEDIT commands:
EDGEMATCH

ARC commands:
BUILD

4 Check item definitions in feature attribute tables

Item	Type	Width	Output	Decimals
Area	F	4	12	3
Perimeter	F	4	12	3
Land#	B	4	5	-
Land-ID	B	4	5	-
Lu-Code	I	3	3	-
Cost/Ha	F	4	12	2

ARC commands:
ITEMS

5 Join up to 500 coverages

Join adjacent coverages
into a single coverage

ARC commands:
MAPJOIN

6 Remove map sheet boundaries

Dissolve map sheet borders

ARC commands:
DISSOLVE

references for
further reading

Maling, D.H. *Coordinate Systems and Map Projections.*
  George Phillip and Son, Limited: 1973.

Snyder, John P. *Map Projections—A working manual.*
  U.S. Geological Survey Professional Paper 1395. Supt. of Docs
  No. I19.16:1395, Washington: Government Printing Office,
  1987. This document supersedes USGS Bulletin 1532.

Also refer to online help under *Data Automation--> Editing coverages*
and tables in ARCEDIT, Cartography-->Map display and query, and
the online *Command References* for ARC and ARCEDIT.

project status   The database is now complete and available for geographic analysis.

workspace contents   The LAND directory you have used so far to create a complete land
use coverage for your study area will contain a number of coverages
and data files. The following diagram lists what should be in your
UGIS workspace at this time:

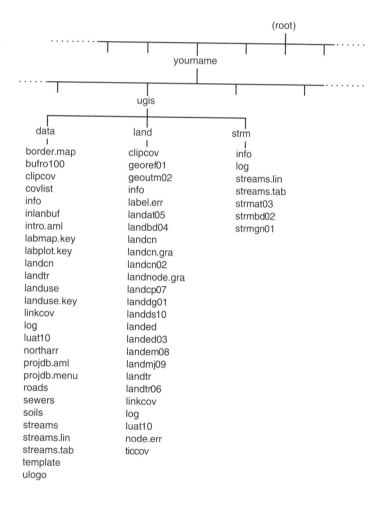

data	**land**	**strm**
border.map	clipcov	info
bufro100	georef01	log
clipcov	geoutm02	streams.lin
covlist	info	streams.tab
info	label.err	strmat03
inlanbuf	landat05	strmbd02
intro.aml	landbd04	strmgn01
labmap.key	landcn	
labplot.key	landcn.gra	
landcn	landcn02	
landtr	landnode.gra	
landuse	landcp07	
landuse.key	landdg01	
linkcov	landds10	
log	landed	
luat10	landed03	
northarr	landem08	
projdb.aml	landmj09	
projdb.menu	landtr	
roads	landtr06	
sewers	linkcov	
soils	log	
streams	luat10	
streams.lin	node.err	
streams.tab	ticcov	
template		
ulogo		

task summary The shaded lesson boxes indicate the portion of the project completed so far.

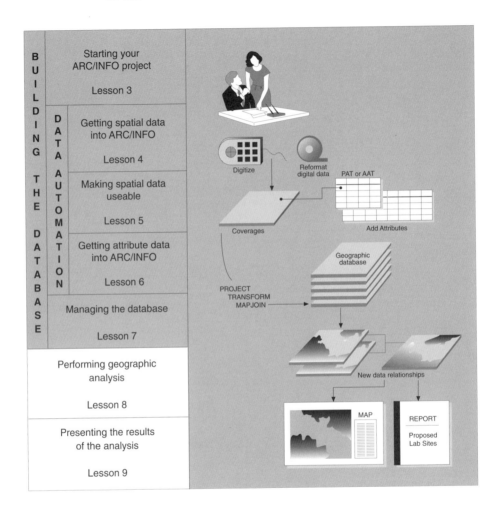

Lesson 8 Performing geographic analysis

Now that the geographic database is complete, the analysis phase of the project can begin. Recall that you've been asked to identify potential sites for locating a new research facility within the study area. Each layer in the database contains specific information the siting analysis will require. To identify new associations between the data layers, it's necessary to further manipulate the data.

In this lesson, spatial analysis will identify sites suitable for locating the proposed lab, and tabular analysis will provide an estimated cost to acquire the land. A committee will use this information to select, and then propose, a suitable lab site for the university.

This lesson introduces concepts of geographic analysis. It describes some of the methods used to identify and apply spatial analysis operations that produce meaningful results. Specifically

■ Preparing the data for analysis
■ Creating buffer zones
■ Using boundary operations
■ Performing polygon overlay
■ Manipulating tabular data

ARC and ARCPLOT commands are used to view the intermediate and final results.

By the end of this lesson, you will have identified the potential sites for the university lab, and the data will be ready to produce a final map and tabular report.

The estimated time needed to complete this lesson is 3 hours.

Introduction to geographic analysis

Geographic analysis allows you to study real-world processes by developing and applying models. Such models illuminate underlying trends in the geographic data, making new information available. A GIS enhances this process by providing tools which can be combined in meaningful sequences to develop new models. These models may reveal new or previously unidentified relationships within and between data sets, increasing our understanding of the real world.

The results of geographic analysis can be communicated by maps, reports, or both. A map is best used to display geographic relationships, whereas a report is most appropriate for summarizing the tabular data and documenting any calculated values. Maps and reports allow you to share with others the data contained in your geographic database.

steps for performing geographic analysis

Before starting any analysis, you need to assess the problem at hand and establish an objective. Think through the process before making judgments about the data or reaching any decisions. Ask questions about the data and the model. Generate a step-by-step procedure to monitor the development and outline the overall objective. The steps below outline the basic procedure for geographic analysis this lesson follows.

Step 1: Establish the objectives and criteria for the analysis.
Step 2: Prepare the data for spatial operations.
Step 3: Perform the spatial operations.
Step 4: Prepare the derived data for tabular analysis.
Step 5: Perform the tabular analysis.
Step 6: Evaluate and interpret the results.
Step 7: Refine the analysis as needed.

Establish the objectives and criteria for the analysis

Before you can perform geographic analysis, you must define your problem and identify a sequence of operations to produce meaningful results. In this workbook, the analysis problem involves finding a suitable site for a new university aquaculture lab.

To review the problem, a local university is planning to construct a small lab and office building to perform research and extension projects in aquaculture. They've narrowed the location down to a coastal farming area near several small towns. They need to select a site that meets the following requirements:

Selection criteria for proposed lab site
☐ Preferred land use is brush land
☐ Choose soil types that are suitable for development
☐ Site must lie within 300 meters of existing sewer lines
☐ Site must lie 20 meters beyond existing streams
☐ Site must contain at least 2,000 square meters

To better understand the kind of spatial operations required to generate results for each of these stated criteria, consider each one individually.

Selection criteria for proposed lab site
√   Preferred land use is brush land
☐   Choose soil types suitable for development
☐   Site must lie within 300 meters of existing sewer lines
☐   Site must lie 20 meters beyond existing streams
☐   Site must contain at least 2,000 square meters

First think about the land use coverage. It contains 76 polygons, all coded for a particular land use. Of these, 26 polygons represent a land use of brush land. These polygons have an LU-CODE value of 300.

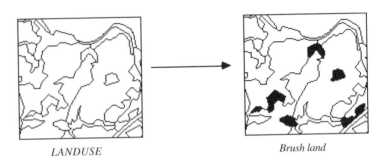

LANDUSE   *Brush land*

Selection criteria for proposed lab site
√ Preferred land use is brush land
√ <u>Choose soil types suitable for development</u>
☐ Site must lie within 300 meters of existing sewer lines
☐ Site must lie 20 meters beyond existing streams
☐ Site must contain at least 2,000 square meters

Next consider the soils coverage. It contains 43 polygons which have
already been coded for suitability based on the underlying soil type
and its stability. Moderately suitable and very suitable soils have code
values of 2 and 3, respectively. So, the equation 'SUIT greater than
or equal to 2' can identify soils suitable for development.
Twenty-eight polygons contain soils suitable for development.

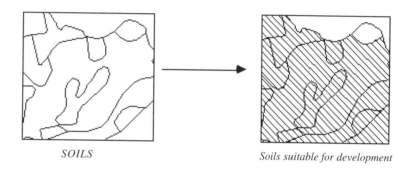

SOILS   *Soils suitable for development*

Selection criteria for proposed lab site
√ Preferred land use is brush land
√ Choose soil types suitable for development
√ <u>Site must lie within 300 meters of existing sewer lines</u>
☐ Site must lie 20 meters beyond existing streams
☐ Site must contain at least 2,000 square meters

For this criterion, you must identify regions that lie near the sewer lines (i.e., within 300 meters). Because buffer zones around sewers are not currently contained in the sewers coverage, they must be derived from the existing sewer lines. Areas near sewer lines are identified using a spatial analysis command called BUFFER. BUFFER generates zones within a given distance of a specified set of coverage features.

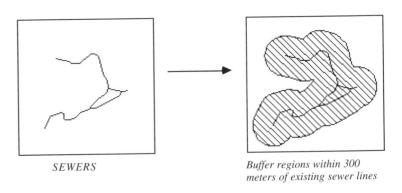

SEWERS

Buffer regions within 300 meters of existing sewer lines

Selection criteria for proposed lab site
√ Preferred land use is brush land
√ Choose soil types suitable for development
√ Site must lie within 300 meters of existing sewer lines
√ <u>Site must lie 20 meters beyond existing streams</u>
☐ Site must contain at least 2,000 square meters

To meet strict environmental guidelines, new development must be recessed at least 20 meters from streams and other water bodies. As with the region around the sewers, buffering the lines in the STREAMS coverage determines the region around the streams to exclude.

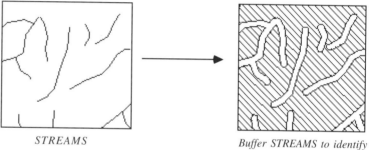

STREAMS

Buffer STREAMS to identify the region 20 meters beyond existing streams

Selection criteria for proposed lab site
√ Preferred land use is brush land
√ Choose soil types suitable for development
√ Site must lie within 300 meters of existing sewer lines
√ Site must lie 20 meters beyond existing streams
√ <u>Site must contain at least 2,000 square meters</u>

To meet the final criterion, you must combine all the previous data in a new coverage and identify all polygons that meet the first four criteria. You can then use the calculated area to generate a list of individual or adjacent polygons containing at least 2,000 square meters (0.2 hectares).

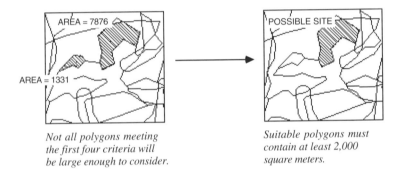

Not all polygons meeting the first four criteria will be large enough to consider.

Suitable polygons must contain at least 2,000 square meters.

Prepare the data for spatial operations

If you successfully designed and implemented your geographic database, all the necessary coverages should be ready for analysis. It could be, however, that these coverages need additional processing. Or it might be that, after reviewing the criteria for the analysis, you discover the need to add one or more attributes to coverages in your database to complete the analysis. Were this the case for your geographic database, you would complete the additional processing now.

Up to this point, you processed the coverages in separate workspaces (e.g., LAND or STRM). Because you'll combine several coverages, it's much more efficient to have them all in one place. Before performing the analysis, establish a workspace and copy into it the coverages you'll need for your analysis.

EXERCISE

Set up your workspace for performing geographic analysis

Perform the geographic analysis in the DATA workspace under your local UGIS workspace.

In Lesson 7, you had the option to copy your version of LANDUSE and STREAMS to your local DATA workspace. If you wish to use the LANDUSE and STREAMS coverages you created in earlier lessons, see the section 'Database management' near the end of Lesson 7. If not, begin this exercise by starting ARC/INFO and use the &WORKSPACE directive to attach to your local DATA workspace.

UNIX
Windows NT

```
Arc: &WORKSPACE /yourname/ugis/data
Arc: &WORKSPACE <drive>:\yourname\ugis\data
```

You'll display coverages on the screen during this lesson, so specify your station file.

```
Arc: &STATION <name>
```

All the coverages needed to perform the upcoming analysis are provided in the DATA workspace. To make sure that you have what you need, use the LISTCOVERAGES (LC) command to list the available coverages now.

```
Arc: LC

Available Coverages
_____

BUFRO100    CLIPCOV     INLANBUF    LANDCN
LANDTR      LANDUSE     LINKCOV     LUAT10
NORTHARR    ROADS       SEWERS      SOILS
STREAMS     TEMPLATE    ULOGO
```

You need the following coverages to perform the exercises in this lesson. Verify their existence in your local DATA workspace.

```
LANDUSE     ROADS       SEWERS      SOILS
STREAMS     TEMPLATE
```

END

Perform the spatial operations

With the data prepared, you can begin performing the spatial operations to combine the coverages. Specifically, you'll look at creating buffer zones around features, manipulating spatial features, and performing polygon overlay.

generating buffers

Generating a buffer is the operation to perform when the analysis requires identifying areas surrounding geographic features. The BUFFER command generates one or more polygons surrounding existing geographic features. This kind of polygon, called a *buffer* or *buffer zone*, is used to determine spatial proximity.

You can buffer any type of feature: point, line, or polygon.

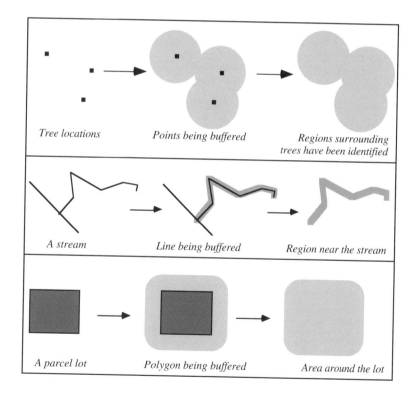

| *Tree locations* | *Points being buffered* | *Regions surrounding trees have been identified* |

| *A stream* | *Line being buffered* | *Region near the stream* |

| *A parcel lot* | *Polygon being buffered* | *Area around the lot* |

Regardless of which feature class is buffered, the output result is a polygon coverage and a PAT.

Generate a 300-meter buffer around sewers

In this exercise, you'll define the area within 300 meters of the existing sewer lines. Display the command usage for BUFFER:

```
Arc: USAGE BUFFER
Usage: BUFFER <in_cover> <out_cover> {buffer_item} {buffer_table}
              {buffer_distance} {fuzzy_tolerance}
              {LINE | POLY | POINT | NODE}
              {ROUND | FLAT} {FULL | LEFT | RIGHT}
```

To generate a buffer around the lines in the SEWERS input coverage, specify that all lines be buffered by a distance of 300. Name the output coverage SEWERBUF. Because you'll specify a specific buffer distance in this case, skip the {buffer_item} and {buffer_table} arguments by typing a # sign (# acts as a place holder for skipping optional arguments in ARC/INFO). The default feature type is LINE, so it doesn't have to be specified.

```
Arc: BUFFER SEWERS SEWERBUF # # 300
 Buffering...
 Sorting...
 Intersecting...
 Assembling polygons...
 Creating new labels...
 Finding inside polygons...
 Dissolving...
 Building nodes...
 Creating sewerbuf.PAT...
Arc:
```

Once you create the buffer output coverage, you can view it on the screen along with the original SEWERS coverage.

```
Arc: ARCPLOT
Arcplot: MAPEXTENT SEWERBUF
Arcplot: ARCS SEWERS
Arcplot: LINECOLOR RED
Arcplot: POLYGONS SEWERBUF
```

The BUFFER command creates a polygon coverage. In addition to the four standard PAT items, each polygon has an item named INSIDE. Display the contents of SEWERBUF.PAT.

Arcplot: **ITEMS SEWERBUF POLY**

COLUMN	ITEM NAME	WIDTH	OUTPUT	TYPE	N.DEC
1	AREA	4	12	F	3
5	PERIMETER	4	12	F	3
9	SEWERBUF#	4	5	B	–
13	SEWERBUF-ID	4	5	B	–
17	INSIDE	4	5	B	–

The INSIDE item contains a code that separates all polygons created by the BUFFER command into two categories: the area inside the buffer zones (INSIDE = 100), and those regions outside the buffer zones (INSIDE = 1).

Arcplot: **LIST SEWERBUF POLY**

Record	AREA	PERIMETER	SEWERBUF#	SEWERBUF-ID	INSIDE
1	-1907939.375	6836.023	1	0	1
2	1907939.375	6836.023	2	1	100

Do not leave ARCPLOT as you will be doing more operations on the following pages.

END

EXERCISE Create a 20-meter buffer around streams

The analysis also specifies that only those areas that lie more than 20 meters from streams can be considered as potential sites for the lab. So, you need to create a 20-meter buffer zone around the streams. To do this, and while still in ARCPLOT, buffer the arcs in the STREAMS coverage by a distance of 20 meters, creating a new coverage called STRMBUF.

```
Arcplot: Arc BUFFER STREAMS STRMBUF # # 20
 Buffering...
 Sorting...
 Intersecting...
 Assembling polygons...
 Creating new labels...
 Finding inside polygons...
 Building nodes...
 Creating strmbuf.PAT...
Arcplot:
```

Now RESET your ARCPLOT session and display the results—both spatial features and their tabular attributes—on your screen.

```
Arcplot: RESET
Arcplot: MAPEXTENT STRMBUF
Arcplot: POLYGONS STRMBUF
Arcplot: LIST STRMBUF POLY
```

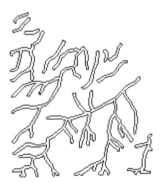

Record	AREA	PERIMETER	STRMBUF#	STRMBUF-ID	INSIDE
1	-863036.188	43206.375	1	0	1
2	10209.157	573.345	2	1	100
3	13292.029	727.386	3	2	100
4	9064.179	516.198	4	3	100
5	75679.875	3812.026	5	4	100
6	24455.156	1285.740	6	5	100
7	13067.740	716.109	7	6	100
8	193251.141	9578.739	8	7	100
9	7983.858	462.056	9	8	100
10	25995.371	1362.663	10	9	100
11	22784.822	1202.056	11	10	100
12	416895.812	20464.326	12	11	100
13	50357.031	2505.731	13	12	100

END

using coverages to manipulate spatial features

Lesson 5 introduced some of the commands and procedures for selecting, erasing, and adding features to a coverage. Lesson 7 introduced the methods for clipping coverages and joining adjacent coverages. These operations create new coverages by either removing features or adding them; that is, they manipulate spatial features.

Geographic features can be identified and selected based on whether they are inside or outside the boundary of other coverages. This allows existing coverages to be overlaid or combined to remove, replace, cut out, or merge geographic features. CLIP, introduced in Lesson 7, and ERASE, the command you'll use next, are two spatial manipulation commands used for feature extraction.

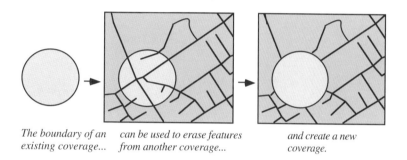

The boundary of an existing coverage...   *can be used to erase features from another coverage...*   *and create a new coverage.*

The ERASE command erases features from one coverage that overlap another. Several other commands, including UPDATE, CLIP, and SPLIT, also manipulate spatial features based on coverage boundaries.

Coverage updating	Merge new features using a cut-and-paste operation.	UPDATE	
Feature extraction (subset a coverage or reduce it)	Cut out a piece of a coverage using a 'cookie cutter'.	CLIP	
	Split a coverage into a number of smaller coverages.	SPLIT	
	Remove part of the inside of a coverage.	ERASE	

Use ERASE to find the area more than 20 meters from streams but less than 300 meters from existing sewers

In the previous exercises, you generated two buffers: one around sewer lines and one around streams. To meet the stated criteria of being within the sewer buffer but beyond the stream buffer, you'll need to combine the two.

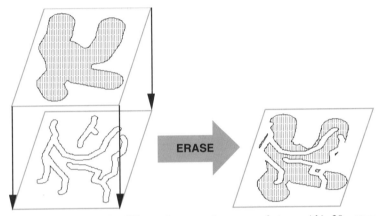

In the next step, ERASE will be used to erase those areas that are within 20 meters of streams from those areas that are part of the sewer buffer. The erased areas will be excluded from further consideration as potential lab sites.

The ARC command that you'll use to create the new coverage is ERASE. You can use this command while still in ARCPLOT.

```
Arcplot: Arc USAGE ERASE
Usage: ERASE <in_cover> <erase_cover> <out_cover>
             {POLY | LINE | POINT | NET | LINK | RAW}
             {fuzzy_tolerance}
```

This command erases features of the input coverage (SEWERBUF) that overlap the erase coverage (STRMBUF). The two sets of features are overlaid and the polygons of the erase coverage define the region to be erased in the output coverage. Name the output coverage created by this command BUFFCOV.

```
Arcplot: Arc ERASE SEWERBUF STRMBUF BUFFCOV
 Erasing sewerbuf with strmbuf to create buffcov
 Sorting...
 Intersecting...
 Assembling polygons...
 Creating new labels...
 Creating buffocv.PAT...
Arcplot:
```

Now display the two coverages that were input to the ERASE command and the resulting output coverage, BUFFCOV, on your screen. The RESELECT command, underlined below, may be new to you. It's used to select a specified subset of coverage features; in this case, using a logical expression (INSIDE = 100). Once polygons from BUFFCOV are selected, they can be shaded using POLYGONSHADES.

```
Arcplot: CLEAR
Arcplot: MAPEXTENT SEWERBUF
Arcplot: POLYGONS SEWERBUF
Arcplot: LINECOLOR RED
Arcplot: POLYGONS STRMBUF
Arcplot: RESELECT BUFFCOV POLY INSIDE = 100
BUFFCOV polys : 8 of 11 selected
Arcplot: POLYGONSHADES BUFFCOV 7
```

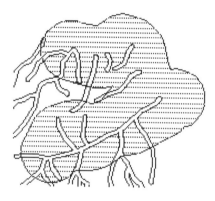

Note that now the INSIDE item indicates those areas within 300 meters of existing sewers, but more than 20 meters from streams.

When you finish viewing the buffers, quit ARCPLOT.

```
Arcplot: QUIT
```

END

performing a polygon overlay

Polygon overlay is a spatial operation that overlays one polygon coverage on another to create a new polygon coverage. The spatial locations of each set of polygons, and their polygon attributes, are joined to derive new data relationships in the output coverage. Joining polygons enables you to perform operations requiring new polygon combinations. The overlay operation illustrated below lets you identify all parcels located on unstable soil types.

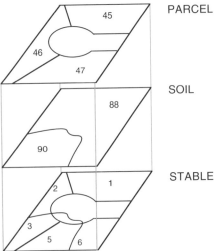

This topological overlay joins polygons from two coverages to establish the spatial relationship between parcels and soil types. The result contains both sets of polygons.

PARCEL.PAT

PARCEL-ID	PARCEL_NO
45	121-99-501
46	121-99-502
47	121-99-503

SOIL.PAT

SOIL-ID	STABILITY
88	STABLE
90	UNSTABLE

STABLE.PAT

STABLE-ID	PARCEL-ID	PARCEL_NO	SOIL-ID	STABILITY
1	45	121-99-501	88	STABLE
2	46	121-99-502	88	STABLE
3	46	121-99-502	90	UNSTABLE
4	–	–	90	UNSTABLE
5	47	121-99-503	90	UNSTABLE
6	47	121-99-503	88	STABLE
7	–	–	88	STABLE

The polygon-on-polygon overlay joins polygon attribute tables from two coverages into one. All combinations are listed in the new polygon attribute table (PAT).

Other overlay operations include line-in-polygon overlay, where line features assume the attributes of the polygon in which they lie, and point-in-polygon overlay, where point features assume polygon attributes.

Three ARC/INFO commands perform polygon overlay: UNION, INTERSECT, and IDENTITY. These commands are similar, differing only in the spatial features that remain in the output coverage. The illustration below shows the result of these commands.

Spatial join
(merging feature attributes)

UNION
Overlay polygons and keep all areas from both coverages

Input coverage   Union coverage   Output coverage

IDENTITY
Overlay points, lines, or polygons on polygons and keep all input coverage features

Input coverage   Identity coverage   Output coverage

INTERSECT
Overlay points, lines, or polygons on polygons but keep only those portions of the input coverage features falling within the overlay coverage features

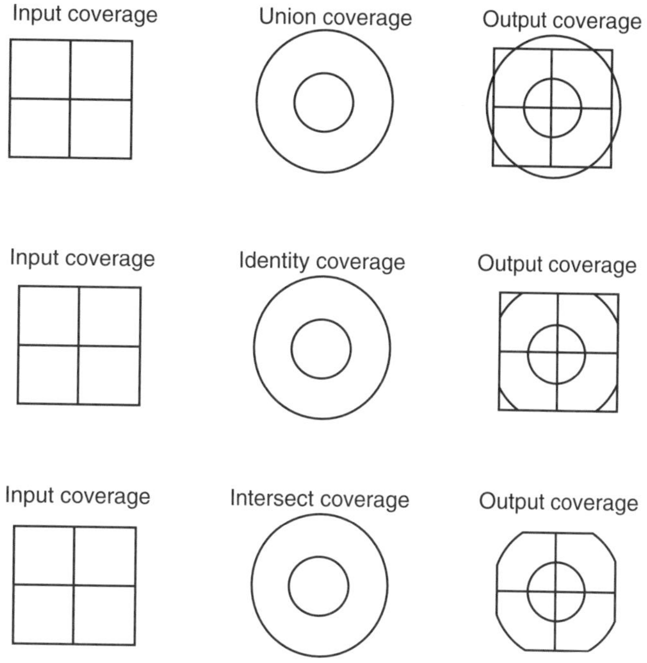

Input coverage   Intersect coverage   Output coverage

tabular results   For all three commands, the attribute tables are joined. This means that the attribute table for the output coverage contains items from both the input and the overlay coverage attribute tables. The following table lists the items saved in the feature attribute table for the output coverage.

out_cover items	AREA PERIMETER out_cover internal number out_cover User-ID
in_cover items	in_cover internal number in_cover User-ID all subsequent in_cover PAT items . .
overlay_cover items	overlay_cover internal number overlay_cover User-ID all subsequent overlay_cover PAT items

For example:

```
Arc: USAGE IDENTITY
Usage IDENTITY <in_cover> <identity_cover> <out_cover>
              {POLY | LINE | POINT} {fuzzy_tolerance}
              {JOIN | NOJOIN}
Arc: IDENTITY PARCEL SOIL STABLE
```

PARCEL.PAT	SOIL.PAT	STABLE.PAT
AREA	AREA	AREA
PERIMETER	PERIMETER	PERIMETER
PARCEL#	SOIL#	STABLE#
PARCEL-ID	SOIL-ID	STABLE-ID
PARCEL_NO	STABILITY	PARCEL#
		PARCEL-ID
		PARCEL_NO
		SOIL#
		SOIL-ID
		STABILITY

EXERCISE

Use IDENTITY to overlay the LANDUSE and SOILS coverages

To identify the polygons suitable for development using their land use codes and the underlying soil stability, you must perform a polygon overlay. Because you're only interested in the soil type as it relates to the polygons contained in the coverage of land use, choose the IDENTITY overlay command. By specifying LANDUSE as the input coverage and SOILS as the identity coverage, the geographic extent of the output coverage will be identical to that of LANDUSE.

Use the IDENTITY command to create a new coverage named LANDSOIL to combine the land use information (LU-CODE) from the LANDUSE.PAT and the soil stability codes (SUIT) from the SOILS.PAT.

```
Arc: USAGE IDENTITY
Usage IDENTITY <in_cover> <identity_cover> <out_cover>
               {POLY | LINE | POINT} {fuzzy_tolerance}
               {JOIN | NOJOIN}
Arc: IDENTITY LANDUSE SOILS LANDSOIL
 Producing identity of landuse with soils to create landsoil
 Sorting...
 Intersecting...
 Assembling polygons...
 Creating new labels...
 Creating landsoil.PAT...
** Item 'AREA' duplicated, Join File version dropped **

** Item 'PERIMETER' duplicated, Join File version dropped **

** Item 'AREA' duplicated, Join File version dropped **

** Item 'PERIMETER' duplicated, Join File version dropped **
Arc:
```

▽FYI

The messages regarding duplicate items indicate that because the AREA and PERIMETER items exist in both LANDUSE.PAT and SOILS.PAT, they are not carried over to the new PAT. Instead, LANDSOIL.PAT will contain new AREA and PERIMETER values calculated for each newly created polygon.

▽

Use ARCPLOT to display the results on your screen. (To be able to do the steps under the FYI heading on the next page, you'll need to start a map composition.) The new coverage, LANDSOIL, shows where the areas of suitable soil coexist with brush land. Issue the RESELECT command again using a more sophisticated logical expression to select all LANDSOIL polygons whose land use is brush land (LU-CODE = 300) *and* whose soil is suitable for development (SUIT $\geq$ 2).

Arc: **ARCPLOT**

Store the screen graphics in a map composition. This will let you use the window pan/zoom capabilities.

Arcplot: **MAP LES08MAP**
Arcplot: **MAPEXTENT LANDSOIL**
Arcplot: **POLYGONS LANDSOIL**
Arcplot: **RESELECT LANDSOIL POLY**
LU-CODE = 300 AND SUIT GE 2
LANDSOIL polys : 40 of 446 selected
Arcplot: **POLYGONSHADES LANDSOIL 3**

FYI The resulting coverage created by the overlay of LANDUSE and SOILS contains a number of *sliver polygons*. Slivers are created during overlay when the two coverages contain different digitized versions of the same feature. In our database, the coastline was digitized twice: once as part of the LANDUSE coverage and again as part of the SOILS coverage. So, slivers were created when the two coverages were overlaid.

In ARCPLOT, you can create another window to zoom in and view the slivers.

Select the **Create** option from the Pan/Zoom menu.

Position the crosshairs at the lower left corner of a box that defines the area you want to enlarge, and

Press **any mouse key**

Finish defining the area to enlarge by dragging the box that appears on the screen until it captures the desired area, and

Press **any mouse key**

A new view window appears. (You can move this window to any place on the screen and can resize it.)

Now redraw LANDSOIL.

Arcplot: **POLYGONS LANDSOIL**

You should be able to see a closeup of the slivers along the coastline displayed in the new view window.

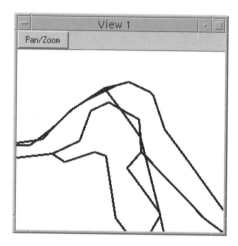

Such slivers point to some important guidelines regarding GIS analysis.

■ When using data from differing sources, it's likely that some common borders will be represented differently.

■ In cases where you automate coverage layers that contain common features, it's best to use a template that contains the most accurate version of the common features. Digitize new features into a copy of this template for each layer.

■ When performing spatial analysis, it's important to determine whether the database you will use can accurately generate the kinds of answers you're looking for. Be aware of data limitations in relation to your model and the decisions to be made from the results. For this project, you can assume that your database is acceptable for the purpose.

Arcplot: **MAP END**
Arcplot: **KILLMAP LES08MAP**
Arcplot: **QUIT**

END

EXERCISE	Use IDENTITY to overlay LANDSOIL and BUFFCOV

One spatial operation remains to be performed: a polygon overlay between the two derived coverages, LANDSOIL and BUFFCOV. This will identify the areas lying within the sewer buffer, outside the stream buffer, having a land use of brush land, and having a soil type suitable for development.

Use the IDENTITY command to perform the polygon overlay, and call the output coverage FINALCOV.

```
Arcplot: Arc IDENTITY LANDSOIL BUFFCOV FINALCOV
  Producing identity of landsoil with buffcov to create finalcov
  Sorting...
  Intersecting...
  Assembling polygons...
  Creating new labels...
  Creating finalcov.PAT...
  ** Item 'AREA' duplicated, Join File version dropped **

  ** Item 'PERIMETER' duplicated, Join File version dropped **

  ** Item 'AREA' duplicated, Join File version dropped **

  ** Item 'PERIMETER' duplicated, Join File version dropped **
Arcplot:
```

Display the final overlay on your screen. The polygons in FINALCOV have all the attributes you need to determine those suitable for the proposed lab site: INSIDE, LU-CODE, SUIT, and AREA.

```
Arcplot: CLEAR
Arcplot: MAPEXTENT FINALCOV
Arcplot: POLYGONS FINALCOV
Arcplot: ITEMS FINALCOV POLY
```

Understanding GIS—The ARC/INFO Method

COLUMN	ITEM NAME	WIDTH	OUTPUT	TYPE	N.DEC
1	AREA	4	12	F	3
5	PERIMETER	4	12	F	3
9	FINALCOV#	4	5	B	–
13	FINALCOV-ID	4	5	B	–
17	LANDSOIL#	4	5	B	–
21	LANDSOIL-ID	4	5	B	–
25	LANDUSE#	4	5	B	–
29	LANDUSE-ID	4	5	B	–
33	LU-CODE	3	3	I	–
36	COST/HA	6	6	I	–
42	SOILS#	4	5	B	–
46	SOILS-ID	4	5	B	–
50	SOIL-CODE	3	3	C	–
53	SUIT	1	1	I	–
54	BUFFCOV#	4	5	B	–
58	BUFFCOV-ID	4	5	B	–
62	INSIDE	4	5	B	–

Quit from ARCPLOT when you finish viewing the attributes.

Arcplot: **QUIT**

END

**performing a sequence
of spatial operations**

Now that the spatial operations have been performed, consider what you've accomplished so far as a continuous sequence of operations.

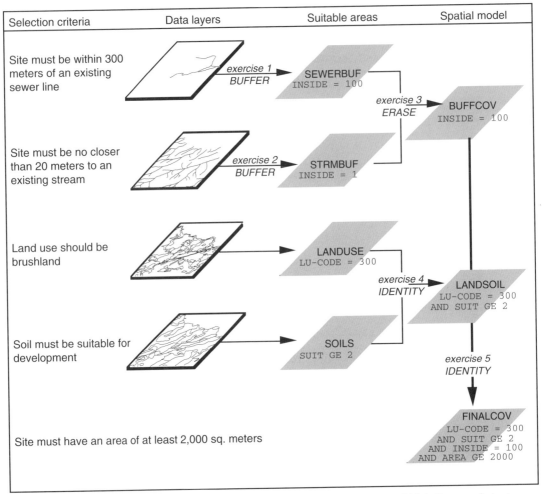

Selection criteria	Data layers	Suitable areas	Spatial model

Site must be within 300 meters of an existing sewer line

exercise 1
BUFFER

SEWERBUF
INSIDE = 100

exercise 3
ERASE

BUFFCOV
INSIDE = 100

Site must be no closer than 20 meters to an existing stream

exercise 2
BUFFER

STRMBUF
INSIDE = 1

Land use should be brushland

LANDUSE
LU-CODE = 300

exercise 4
IDENTITY

LANDSOIL
LU-CODE = 300
AND SUIT GE 2

Soil must be suitable for development

SOILS
SUIT GE 2

exercise 5
IDENTITY

FINALCOV
LU-CODE = 300
AND SUIT GE 2
AND INSIDE = 100
AND AREA GE 2000

Site must have an area of at least 2,000 sq. meters

The spatial analysis commands used so far in this lesson are shown along the arrows, which indicate analysis steps. The next series of exercises apply the logical criteria that define suitable areas in each resulting coverage (shown above within the shaded boxes).

Understanding GIS—The ARC/INFO Method

Prepare the derived data for tabular analysis

The next part of this lesson addresses how to perform tabular operations on items in the feature attribute table using logical and arithmetic equations. Before performing tabular analysis, you need to make sure the feature attribute table contains all the items (columns) it needs to hold the new values you will create.

The ADDITEM command adds items to an existing feature attribute table (or any other INFO data file). The arguments you specify for ADDITEM are similar to the parameters you specify when defining a new data file in INFO: item name, width, output width, type, and number of decimals.

Other ARC/INFO commands that manipulate existing feature attribute tables include DROPITEM, which removes an item from an INFO data file, and PULLITEMS, which selects specified items from an INFO data file and copies them to a new file. For more information on these commands, refer to online help under *Working with Tables -->Managing Tabular Data-->Managing attribute tables*.

EXERCISE

Add the necessary attribute items to FINALCOV.PAT

Your tabular analysis must calculate an approximate purchase cost based on the size of each potential site and its per-hectare cost. Doing this necessitates adding two items to contain the results of these calculations. You will add the item HA to contain a hectare calculation that will be used to simplify the process of calculating a land cost value for each suitable polygon. You will also add the item COST to contain a purchase cost calculation for each suitable polygon. In addition, you'll need to add an item to use for flagging those polygons that meet the requirements for potential sites. You'll add SUITABLE to indicate those sites.

Use the ADDITEM command to add each item to FINALCOV.PAT.

```
Arc: USAGE ADDITEM
Usage: ADDITEM  <in_info_file> <out_info_file> <item_name>
                <item_width> <output_width> <item_type>
                {decimal_places} {start_item}
```

You must issue the ADDITEM command once for each item you add. The input file name in all cases is FINALCOV.PAT. The output file name will also be FINALCOV.PAT because, rather than creating a new coverage, you want to add the items directly to this file. If you don't specify a {start_item}, each new item will be inserted after the last item in the input file.

Arc: **ADDITEM FINALCOV.PAT FINALCOV.PAT HA 4 6 F 2**
Adding HA to FINALCOV.PAT to produce FINALCOV.PAT

Arc: **ADDITEM FINALCOV.PAT FINALCOV.PAT COST 4 7 B**
Adding COST to FINALCOV.PAT to produce FINALCOV.PAT

Arc: **ADDITEM FINALCOV.PAT FINALCOV.PAT SUITABLE 1 1 I**
Adding SUITABLE to FINALCOV.PAT to produce FINALCOV.PAT

Now check the results.

Arc: **ITEMS FINALCOV.PAT**

COLUMN	ITEM NAME	WIDTH	OUTPUT	TYPE	N.DEC
1	AREA	4	12	F	3
5	PERIMETER	4	12	F	3
9	FINALCOV#	4	5	B	–
13	FINALCOV-ID	4	5	B	–
17	LANDSOIL#	4	5	B	–
21	LANDSOIL-ID	4	5	B	–
25	LANDUSE#	4	5	B	–
29	LANDUSE-ID	4	5	B	–
33	LU-CODE	3	3	I	–
36	COST/HA	6	6	I	–
42	SOILS#	4	5	B	–
46	SOILS-ID	4	5	B	–
50	SOIL-CODE	3	3	C	–
53	SUIT	1	1	I	–
54	BUFFCOV#	4	5	B	–
58	BUFFCOV-ID	4	5	B	–
62	INSIDE	4	5	B	–
66	HA	4	6	F	2
70	COST	4	7	B	–
74	SUITABLE	1	1	I	–

Notice that HA, COST, and SUITABLE are the last three items in the file.

Arc: **LIST FINALCOV.PAT HA,COST,SUITABLE**

```
Record        HA      COST SUITABLE
     1       0.00       0 0
     2       0.00       0 0
     3       0.00       0 0
     4       0.00       0 0
     5       0.00       0 0
     6       0.00       0 0
     7       0.00       0 0
     8       0.00       0 0
     9       0.00       0 0
     .        .         . .
     .        .         . .
     .        .         . .
```
Continue? **NO**
Arc:

There are no values for the new items yet. In Lesson 6, you added values to an INFO data file by entering them directly from the keyboard or a file. In the next section, you'll calculate item values using the existing items in the PAT.

END

Perform the tabular analysis

Now that you've created the new items, calculations for the site selection model can be made.

First you must select the subset of features in FINALCOV whose

- LU-CODE equals 300
- SUIT value for SOILS is greater than or equal to 2
- INSIDE code for the buffer zones equals 100
- AREA is greater than or equal to 2,000 square meters

This can be done using several tabular analysis operations available in ARCPLOT. Following are three of the most commonly used operations.

RESELECT   RESELECT (i.e., REduce SELECT) selects a subset of the currently selected set of records based on a given logical expression. For example, the expression

```
Arcplot: RESELECT...AREA > 2000
```

selects all polygons with AREA greater than 2000.

ASELECT   ASELECT (i.e., ADD SELECT) adds records to the currently selected set based on specified criteria. For example, the expression

```
Arcplot: ASELECT...SUIT = 3 AND LU-CODE = 300
```

adds records to the currently selected set that have a SUIT value equal to 3 and an LU-CODE equal to 300. ASELECT can also be used without a logical expression.

```
Arcplot: ASELECT
```

selects all records in the INFO data file. ASELECT without a logical expression is useful for selecting all records after you make a selection error or to reset the selection environment.

logical expressions Logical expressions are used with ASELECT and RESELECT to specify which records to select. Here is the general form of a logical expression:

```
<item> <logical_operator> <expression> {AND | OR | XOR}
{<item> <logical_operator> <expression>} ...
```

Some of the available logical operators include:

EQ or = equal
NE or <> not equal
LT or < less than
GT or > greater than
GE or >= greater than or equal
LE or <= less than or equal
CN contains the specified characters
IN is contained in the set of values or value ranges (e.g., COST is greater than or equal to 10,000 and less than or equal to 20,000)

Examples:

```
LU-CODE = 300
SUIT GE 2
LABEL CN 'MODERATE' OR LABEL CN 'HIGH'
AREA / 10000 GE 2000 AND INSIDE = 100
COST IN {10000->20000}
```

Expressions can use a value, an item, or an arithmetic expression (e.g., `COST/HA * AREA / 10000`). For more help with using logical expressions in ARC/INFO, see online help under *Working with Tables-->Managing Tabular Data-->Attribute query and logical selection*.

CALCULATE The CALCULATE command calculates and assigns values to an item for all currently selected records. For example, once the appropriate records are selected using the RESELECT and ASELECT commands, you can CALCULATE a value for an item named SUITABLE. Using these operations, you can edit attribute items in the feature attribute tables and related data files. The general form of a CALCULATE expression is

```
CALCULATE  <cover> <feature_class>
           <target_item> = <arithmetic expression>
```

Here are some sample CALCULATE expressions:

```
CALCULATE...COST = VALUE * HA
CALCULATE...SUITABLE = 1
CALCULATE...ACRES = AREA / 43560
```

The computation is performed for every selected record, and the result of the arithmetic expression is then assigned to the target item.

Several arithmetic operators are available:

** Exponentiation
* Multiplication
/ Division
+ Addition
- Subtraction

For more help with using arithmetic expressions in ARC/INFO, see online help under *Working with Tables-->Managing Tabular Data -->Attribute query and logical selection.*

EXERCISE

Calculate the potential purchase cost for each site and assign the suitability code

First identify all the polygons that meet the selection criteria.

Criteria	Description
LU-CODE = 300	brush land
SUIT ≥ 2	SUIT values of 2 are moderately suitable. Values of 3 are very suitable soils.
INSIDE = 100	Areas inside the buffer area are more than 20 meters from streams and less than 300 meters from existing sewers.
AREA ≥ 2000	sites at least 2000 meters in size

If you aren't currently there, enter ARCPLOT.

Arc: **ARCPLOT**

Previously in ARCPLOT, you used a logical expression to select a subset of polygons from a PAT. You can also combine logical expressions in one command. Use the RESELECT command to string together the appropriate logical expressions using the logical connector AND. Be sure to include a space between each object in your expression (e.g., LU-CODE *space* = *space*).

Don't worry if this command line wraps around to the next line on the screen. ARC/INFO will still accept it.

Arcplot: **RESELECT FINALCOV POLY LU-CODE = 300 AND SUIT GE 2 AND INSIDE = 100 AND AREA GE 2000**
FINALCOV polys : 8 of 628 selected.

Eight polygons meet the criteria needed to be considered for the lab site. Assign them a SUITABLE value of 1 using CALCULATE.

```
Arcplot: USAGE CALCULATE
Usage: CALCULATE   <cover> <feature_class>
                   <target_item> = <arithmetic_expression>
Usage: CALCULATE   <info_file> INFO
                   <target_item> = <arithmetic_expression>
Arcplot: CALCULATE FINALCOV POLY SUITABLE = 1
```

Now the next time you want to select the suitable sites, to create a map or report, you can just give one logical expression (SUITABLE = 1), rather than the entire string you used in the RESELECT operation earlier.

Use LIST to check the results of the selection process.

```
Arcplot: LIST FINALCOV POLY LU-CODE,SUIT,INSIDE,AREA,  ~
Arcplot: SUITABLE
```

Record	LU-CODE	SUIT	INSIDE	AREA	SUITABLE
173	300	2	100	5640.191	1
228	300	2	100	5495.015	1
286	300	2	100	7125.877	1
309	300	3	100	7546.493	1
323	300	2	100	2653.453	1
333	300	2	100	3087.506	1
347	300	2	100	2701.034	1
473	300	2	100	2573.669	1

The item values should all match the siting criteria for the new lab.

Now perform the calculations to determine an estimated purchase cost for each suitable polygon in FINALCOV. The process shown below involves two steps: (1) convert the calculated area values into hectares; (2) calculate a total cost for each polygon. (Note that one hectare equals 10,000 square meters.)

```
Arcplot: CALCULATE FINALCOV POLY HA = AREA / 10000
```

With the areas converted into hectares, you can calculate an approximate cost for each land parcel using the estimated cost per hectare (COST/HA).

```
Arcplot: CALCULATE FINALCOV POLY COST = HA * COST/HA
```

List the pertinent items to see the results of your calculations.

Arcplot: **LIST FINALCOV POLY AREA,HA,COST/HA,COST**

Record	AREA	HA	COST/HA	COST
173	5640.191	0.56	20000	11280
228	5495.015	0.55	20000	10990
286	7125.877	0.71	10000	7125
309	7546.493	0.75	15000	11319
323	2653.453	0.27	10000	2653
333	3087.506	0.31	10000	3087
347	2701.034	0.27	10000	2701
473	2573.669	0.26	10000	2573

The tabular analysis is now complete. All the attributes needed to generate a final report have been created and are located in FINALCOV.PAT. In the next step, you'll evaluate the results you've obtained so far.

END

Evaluate and interpret the results

Now that the initial analysis has produced some results, it's time to examine them and determine whether these answers are valid. Map displays and reports can help you make this evaluation.

One goal of this step is to determine a set of acceptance criteria for your assessment. Then you can compare your results against these criteria. For example, you may want to visit some of the potential sites identified by the analysis to determine whether they match your expectations. If these sites match, it may be easier to assume that other sites have been correctly identified. Such acceptance criteria help you know when you have reached an acceptable answer instead of continuing to refine your analysis until you run out of time, money, or other resources.

Here are some questions to ask:

- Do the results seem reasonable?

- Would a resource expert come to the same conclusions?

- Were the criteria valid?

- Are there other criteria or data that need to be factored into the analysis?

- Have I made any errors in my assessment?

Once you decide that you've completed the analysis correctly and that your criteria are reasonable, you can visit the sites or apply other acceptance criteria.

If you decide that you can't accept the results, you can use this step to identify the modifications and enhancements that should be performed to improve your analysis. Then you can perform the steps necessary to redo the analysis.

In the following exercises, you'll investigate the results you obtained in the lab siting analysis and suggest some improvements you might make as part of a real project.

EXERCISE   **Display the results of the analysis**

You can graphically display the eight possible sites for the lab using ARCPLOT. You can also perform interactive query to obtain the attributes of the sites, including the purchase cost.

First draw the sites shaded in white, along with the study area boundary and roads.

Arcplot: **MAPEXTENT FINALCOV**
Arcplot: **POLYGONSHADES FINALCOV SUITABLE**
Arcplot: **LINECOLOR GREEN**
Arcplot: **ARCS TEMPLATE**
Arcplot: **LINECOLOR RED**
Arcplot: **ARCS ROADS**

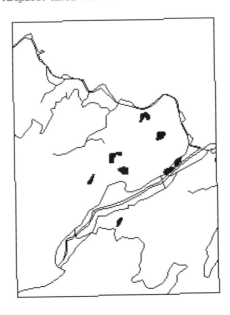

Now use the IDENTIFY command to list the attributes for one of the sites. The * indicates that you'll point to the site using the screen cursor or mouse.

Arcplot: **IDENTIFY FINALCOV POLY ***
Enter point

When prompted, move the cursor inside one of the suitable sites shaded in white on your screen, and

Press **any mouse key** within the polygon

The attributes for that site are displayed; for example,

```
                228
AREA         =      5495.015
PERIMETER    =       303.874
FINALCOV#    =   228
FINALCOV-ID  =   227
LANDSOIL#    =   158
LANDSOIL-ID  =   157
LANDUSE#     =    23
LANDUSE-ID   =    22
LU-CODE      = 300
COST/HA      = 20000
SOILS#       =    12
SOILS-ID     =    10
SOIL-CODE    = Tn4
SUIT         = 2
BUFFCOV#     =     2
BUFFCOV-ID   =     1
INSIDE       =   100
HA           =     0.55
COST         =   10990
SUITABLE     = 1
```

You can continue querying the sites by reissuing the IDENTIFY
command. Next select the eight potential lab sites using the
RESELECT command.

Arcplot: **RESELECT FINALCOV POLY SUITABLE = 1**
FINALCOV polys : 8 of 628 selected.

List the item values of selected polygons.

Arcplot: **TEXTCOLOR DODGERBLUE**
Arcplot: **POLYGONTEXT FINALCOV FINALCOV#**
Arcplot: **LIST FINALCOV POLY SUITABLE,COST,COST/HA,HA**

Record	SUITABLE	COST	COST/HA	HA
173	1	11280	20000	0.56
228	1	10990	20000	0.55
286	1	7125	10000	0.71
309	1	11319	15000	0.75
323	1	2653	10000	0.27
333	1	3087	10000	0.31
347	1	2701	10000	0.27
473	1	2573	10000	0.26

▽FYI▽

These two commands, IDENTIFY and LIST, are useful for investigating the results of your model. In the next section, you may want to use these commands to investigate each site more closely and evaluate the model applied in this exercise.

model evaluation

Using the screen display and the attribute listing, identify some potential problems in the current model and record them, along with your ideas for solutions, in the table provided.

Problem	Solution
Example: There are two adjacent polygons identified as potential sites. Each is greater than 0.2 hectares in size.	Treat these areas as one unit for development, if desired. However, note that each has a different soil type.

The following are assessments that we made about the analysis. They indicate judgments about the limitations of the model and the results.

Evaluating the model results involves making assessments about the quality of the results as shown in the map display and attribute reports, as well as assessing the criteria used in the siting model.

■ Large sites have a high purchase cost because of their size. Some of the smaller sites near the coast are also expensive because the COST/HA value is higher there. Large sites near the coast are especially expensive.

■ Some of the larger sites appear to be more expensive because their COST value is higher. But because only 0.2 hectares needs to be purchased, the cost for development in these areas could be less than shown.

■ Some sites are close to existing roads, making the cost to develop them less than that to develop sites farther away.

■ The overlay process generated many small polygons. Some adjacent polygons, when combined, might meet the analysis criteria, but individually are too small to consider suitable for the lab site. These areas may require further analysis to produce a complete list of potentially suitable lab sites.

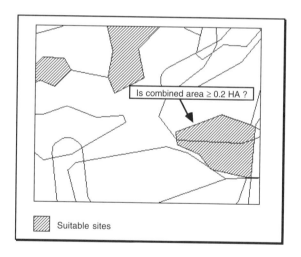

Is combined area ≥ 0.2 HA ?

Suitable sites

■ Using the model results, we visited a few of the potential sites identified by the model and have determined that the analysis produced reasonable answers about potential sites for siting the new laboratory.

In the next analysis step, you'll investigate a few of these limitations and take steps to improve the siting model.

END

Advanced topic—Refine the analysis as necessary

Now that you've assessed the model limitations and results, you need to decide whether or not to further refine the analysis. A GIS is useful at this step because it allows you to easily adjust and repeat appropriate analysis steps to refine the analysis process. You can evaluate alternative approaches to the analysis to see whether one method is better than another or to determine whether other approaches produce differing results. If you wish to further refine your analysis, complete the following advanced exercise.

ADVANCED EXERCISE

Refine the analysis with additional criteria

To ensure that all potential sites for the new laboratory are identified, you should determine whether there are any adjacent areas that, when combined, would meet the area criteria (i.e., the minimum site size of 0.2 hectares). First you'll identify all the polygons that meet the following criteria:

- LU-CODE = 300
- SUIT ≥ 2
- INSIDE = 100

Then determine which, if any, of these sites are adjacent. Adjacent sites can be combined to determine whether their area exceeds 0.2 hectares. If their combined area does exceed 0.2 hectares, they can be added to the list of potential sites.

The steps to complete this query are performed in ARCPLOT. If necessary, specify your station file and start ARCPLOT.

```
Arc: &STATION <name>
Arc: ARCPLOT
```

HELP

If you are still in the ARCPLOT session from the previous exercise, clear the selected set of coverage features and clear the graphics display. (If you do not clear the selected set your next reselect command will give you an erroneous result.)

```
Arcplot: CLEARSELECT
Arcplot: CLEAR
```

Now select those features that meet all the siting criteria except for the 0.2 hectare minimum size. Use the RESELECT command.

```
Arcplot: RESELECT FINALCOV POLY LU-CODE = 300 AND SUIT ~
Arcplot: GE 2 AND INSIDE = 100
FINALCOV polys : 15 of 628 selected.
```

List the item values for the selected records for AREA, HA, COST, and SUITABLE.

```
Arcplot: LIST FINALCOV POLY AREA,HA,COST,SUITABLE
```

Record	AREA	HA	COST	SUITABLE
173	5640.191	0.56	11280	1
184	48.577	0.00	0	0
193	14.432	0.00	0	0
206	37.532	0.00	0	0
228	5495.015	0.55	10990	1
286	7125.877	0.71	7125	1
309	7546.493	0.75	11319	1
313	1721.481	0.00	0	0
323	2653.453	0.27	2653	1
327	580.889	0.00	0	0
333	3087.506	0.31	3087	1
347	2701.034	0.27	2701	1
349	3.948	0.00	0	0
473	2573.669	0.26	2573	1
513	646.508	0.06	0	0

You'll notice that some of the selected polygons are quite small (e.g., AREA values less than 50 square meters). These are polygon slivers created by the overlay process used to create FINALCOV. We'll discuss slivers later in this lesson. For now, however, consider only those polygons whose SUITABLE value is 0 and whose AREA is greater than 500 square meters. These may represent adjacent areas that are suitable as candidate sites.

Now set the map extent to the currently selected polygons and draw their outlines.

Arcplot: **MAPEXTENT POLY FINALCOV**
Arcplot: **POLYGONS FINALCOV**

Notice two adjacent polygons just left of the center of the display screen. Both polygons, however, already meet the 0.2 minimum hectare size criterion. These are the two adjacent polygons described in the assessment table on page 8-38. If desired, use IDENTIFY FINALCOV POLY * to list the attributes of each.

Use the RESELECT command to select those polygons not currently considered to be potential sites (i.e., SUITABLE = 0).

Arcplot: **RESELECT FINALCOV POLY SUITABLE = 0**
FINALCOV polys : 7 of 628 selected.

Next calculate the value for HA as follows:

Arcplot: **CALCULATE FINALCOV POLY HA = AREA / 10000**

Then list the item values as shown here:

Arcplot: **LIST FINALCOV POLY AREA,HA,COST/HA,SUITABLE**

Record	AREA	HA	COST/HA	SUITABLE
184	48.577	0.00	20000	0
193	14.432	0.00	20000	0
206	37.532	0.00	20000	0
313	1721.481	0.17	10000	0
327	580.889	0.06	15000	0
349	3.948	0.00	10000	0
513	646.508	0.06	15000	0

A list of polygons meeting all siting criteria except size appears. Notice the three polygons with HA values greater than 0. (The other polygons with HA values displayed as 0.00 are so small that their AREA values divided by 10,000 round off to 0.00 in the items list. The display width for HA contains only two decimal places.)

Select the subset of polygons with AREA greater than 500 square meters and list their item values.

Arcplot: **RESELECT FINALCOV POLY AREA GT 500**
FINALCOV polys : 3 of 628 selected.
Arcplot: **LIST FINALCOV POLY AREA,HA,COST/HA,SUITABLE**

Record	AREA	HA	COST/HA	SUITABLE
313	1721.481	0.17	10000	0
327	580.889	0.06	15000	0
513	646.508	0.06	15000	0

Are any of these areas located next to another potentially suitable site? Let's find out. Shade the selected polygons. This enables you to determine whether they lie adjacent to other potentially suitable sites.

Arcplot: **POLYGONSHADES FINALCOV 1**

Notice that one of the shaded sites increases the size of an existing candidate site. The other shaded polygons, however, are not immediately adjacent to other suitable sites.

Now that you've investigated the model results, suppose you've determined that you'd like to remove some of the polygon slivers from FINALCOV and add the small area that is adjacent to a potential site to the list of potential areas for a lab site. The following criteria can be used to perform these tasks:

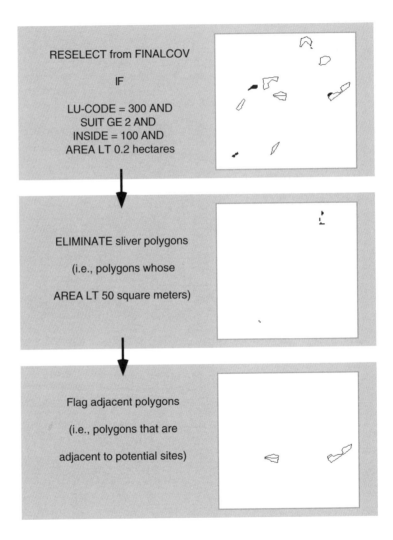

RESELECT from FINALCOV

IF

LU-CODE = 300 AND
SUIT GE 2 AND
INSIDE = 100 AND
AREA LT 0.2 hectares

ELIMINATE sliver polygons

(i.e., polygons whose

AREA LT 50 square meters)

Flag adjacent polygons

(i.e., polygons that are

adjacent to potential sites)

eliminating slivers   Eliminate polygon slivers using the ELIMINATE command at the Arc: prompt. ELIMINATE allows you to identify the polygons to eliminate by specifying a set of criteria. You'll eliminate the sliver polygons by selecting those polygons with AREA LT 50. These are considered slivers because their area is so small. Each will automatically dissolve into the neighboring polygon with which it shares the longest border.

```
Arcplot: Arc USAGE ELIMINATE
Usage: ELIMINATE  <in_cover> <out_cover> {NOKEEPEDGE | KEEPEDGE}
                  {POLY | LINE} {selection_file} {BORDER | AREA}
```

Specify FINALCOV as the input coverage and ELIMCOV as the output coverage. Once invoked, ELIMINATE prompts you for the selection criteria to identify the polygons to be eliminated.

```
Arcplot: Arc ELIMINATE FINALCOV ELIMCOV
Eliminating polygons in finalcov to create elimcov
Enter a logical expression. (Enter a blank line when finished)
>: RES AREA LT 50 <CR>
>: <CR>
Do you wish to re-enter expression (Y/N)? N
Do you wish to enter another expression (Y/N)? N
 125 features out of 628 selected.
Number of Polygons (Input,Output) =      628     504
Number of Arcs      (Input,Output) =     1388    1262
 Creating elimcov.PAT...
Arc:
```

The new output coverage, ELIMCOV, contains 124 fewer polygons than FINALCOV. Now try starting ARCPLOT on your own to RESELECT the set of polygons from ELIMCOV that have

- LU-CODE = 300
- SUIT GE 2
- INSIDE = 100

You should have selected eleven polygons. Start ARCPLOT, set the map extent, and draw the outlines of the polygons. As a final step, shade the selected polygons based on their value for SUITABLE. Here are the ARCPLOT commands used to perform these operations.

```
Arcplot: CLEARSELECT
Arcplot: RESELECT ELIMCOV POLY LU-CODE = 300 AND SUIT ~
Arcplot: GE 2 AND INSIDE = 100
ELIMCOV polys : 11 of 504 selected
Arcplot: MAPEXTENT POLY ELIMCOV
Arcplot: POLYGONS ELIMCOV
Arcplot: POLYGONSHADES ELIMCOV SUITABLE
```

flag adjacent polygons

On your screen, you can identify the adjacent polygon that's not currently rated as suitable for development even though it meets all the model criteria except size. This polygon should be flagged as suitable because it's next to another suitable area. One easy way to do this is to select the polygon and change its value for SUITABLE to 1. You can select the polygon spatially by specifying a selection box that touches part of the polygon.

```
Arcplot: SEARCHTOLERANCE 1
Arcplot: RESELECT ELIMCOV POLY ONE *
Enter point
```

Position the cursor inside the desired polygon as shown, and

Press **any mouse button**

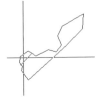

```
ELIMCOV polys : 1 of 504 selected.
```

Shade this polygon using shade symbol 2.

```
Arcplot: POLYGONSHADES ELIMCOV 2
```

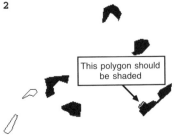

This polygon should be shaded

Understanding GIS—The ARC/INFO Method

```
HELP
```
Don't panic if you made a mistake and selected the wrong polygon. Restore the set of currently selected features for ELIMCOV with ASELECT and RESELECT, then start again.

```
Arcplot: ASELECT ELIMCOV POLY
ELIMCOV polys: 504 of 504 selected.
Arcplot: RESELECT ELIMCOV POLY LU-CODE = 300 AND SUIT GE
        2 AND INSIDE = 100
ELIMCOV polys : 11 of 504 selected.
```

Then refresh the ELIMCOV display on your screen.

```
Arcplot: CLEAR
Arcplot: POLYGONSHADES ELIMCOV SUITABLE
Arcplot: POLYGONS ELIMCOV
```

Now you're ready to select the adjacent polygon again using RESELECT with the ONE option.

Once you select the correct polygon, use CALCULATE to update the polygon's value for the SUITABLE item.

```
Arcplot: CALCULATE ELIMCOV POLY SUITABLE = 1
```

Verify your results by selecting all ELIMCOV polygons whose SUITABLE value is 1. Shade these polygons using shade symbol 2.

```
Arcplot: CLEAR
Arcplot: ASELECT ELIMCOV POLY SUITABLE = 1
ELIMCOV polys : 9 of 504 selected.
Arcplot: POLYGONSHADES ELIMCOV 2
```

Now draw the outlines of the selected polygons.

```
Arcplot: LINESYMBOL 1
Arcplot: POLYGONS ELIMCOV
```

One final step must be completed to update the values for HA and COST within each suitable polygon. Slivers were removed, so the area of some of the potential sites have changed. In addition, you need to calculate COST for the newly added adjacent polygon. The CALCULATE command can be used for this step.

```
Arcplot: CALCULATE ELIMCOV POLY HA = AREA / 10000
Arcplot: CALCULATE ELIMCOV POLY COST = HA * COST/HA
```

FYI The step to refine your analysis often generates few changes to the model results. In these cases, the refinement process actually helps verify that the original criteria you applied produced a reliable answer. In other words, further refinement did not significantly change the model results. One of the major advantages of analysis using a GIS is the ability to readily change your model and to investigate alternatives.

List the results.

Arcplot: **LIST ELIMCOV POLY AREA,HA,COST/HA,COST,SUITABLE**

Record	AREA	HA	COST/HA	COST	SUITABLE
112	5688.768	0.57	20000	11377	1
154	5495.015	0.55	20000	10990	1
196	7125.877	0.71	10000	7125	1
218	7546.493	0.75	15000	11319	1
231	2653.453	0.27	10000	2653	1
235	580.889	0.06	15000	871	1
240	3087.506	0.31	10000	3087	1
254	2701.034	0.27	10000	2701	1
369	2573.669	0.26	10000	2573	1

This completes the advanced exercise. Exit ARCPLOT whenever you desire.

Arcplot: **QUIT**

END

In the next lesson, you'll complete the final analysis step to generate map displays and tabular reports to present the results of your analysis.

Summary

concept review   Geographic analysis is what separates geographic information systems (GIS) from digital mapping systems. This lesson demonstrated four important geographic analysis concepts:

- Coverage registration. Without the accurate registration of the LANDUSE and SOILS coverages, the accuracy of the results of the polygon overlays could not be assured.

- Spatial join of geographic features. Joining features from the various data layers used the topological relationships inherent in the data model: the arcs comprising polygons in two data layers are known; the new arc intersections can be calculated when the layers are overlaid; and the list of arcs comprising each new, resulting polygon can be identified.

- Attribute join through coverage overlay. Joining attributes from the various data layers (LANDUSE, SOILS, STRMBUF, SEWERBUF) used overlapping coverage features to join feature attributes from multiple coverages.

- Attribute manipulation (feature selection, adding items and values). The tabular database structure allowed for logical record selection and calculation of new item values based on the values of attributes from the coverage feature attribute tables.

lesson summary   This lesson outlined some of the techniques available for performing geographic analysis. You now see how to take advantage of ARC/INFO's ability to interpret and display geographic information by generating geographic models and performing geographic analysis. Remember that, to produce meaningful results, you must define your problem and identify a sequence of spatial and attribute manipulation operations before you perform an analysis.

The purpose of this lesson was to identify meaningful analysis operations and help you convert them into command sequences. Here is a summary of these operations.

spatial analysis

GIS Functionality	ARC/INFO Command
Create a buffer zone around features	BUFFER
Perform boundary operations on coverages	ERASE UPDATE SPLIT
Polygon overlay	IDENTITY UNION INTERSECT

tabular analysis

GIS Functionality	ARC/INFO Command
Select features based on attribute values	RESELECT ASELECT
Calculate new attribute values	CALCULATE

references for further reading

Goodchild, Michael F. and David Brusegard. "Spatial Analysis Using GIS: Seminar Workbook." Presented at AM/FM Conference XII, April 1989. (Contact National Center for Geographic Information and Analysis, University of California, Santa Barbara, California 93106.)

For more information on topics related to this lesson, refer to ARC/INFO's online help under *Working with Tables-->Managing Tabular Data*. Also see the online *Command References* for ARC and ARCPLOT.

project status   The analysis phase of the project is complete. The results of spatial analysis can be summarized with a map, a report, or both. This is the topic of the next lesson, 'Presenting the results of the analysis'.

workspace contents   The DATA directory was used in this lesson to perform spatial analysis. A number of new coverages were generated as part of the exercises in this lesson. Here is the current status of DATA:

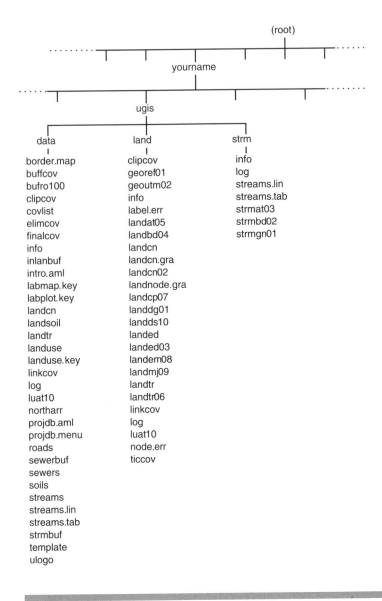

task summary   The chart below indicates the status of the project. The shaded lesson boxes show the steps completed so far.

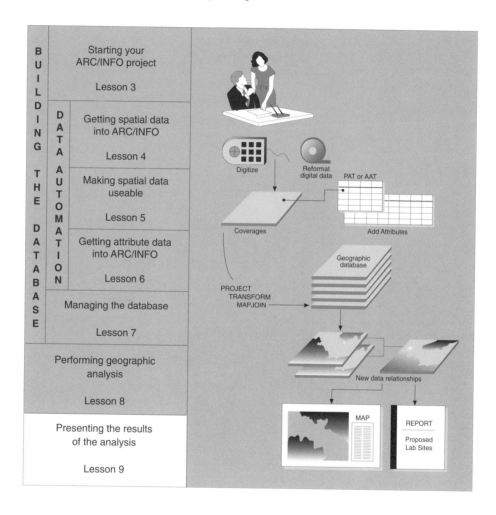

B		Starting your ARC/INFO project Lesson 3
U **I** **L** **D** **I** **N** **G**	**D** **A** **T** **A**	Getting spatial data into ARC/INFO Lesson 4
T **H** **E**	**A** **U** **T** **O**	Making spatial data useable Lesson 5
D **A** **T** **A**	**M** **A** **T** **I**	Getting attribute data into ARC/INFO Lesson 6
B **A** **S** **E**	**O** **N**	Managing the database Lesson 7

Performing geographic analysis

Lesson 8

Presenting the results of the analysis

Lesson 9

Digitize

Reformat digital data

PAT or AAT

Coverages

Add Attributes

Geographic database

PROJECT
TRANSFORM
MAPJOIN

New data relationships

MAP

REPORT

Proposed Lab Sites

Lesson 9 Presenting the results of the analysis

The project is now in its final stages. Initially, you designed and built a digital database for the study area. You then performed a series of tasks to complete the analysis portion of the project. From the analysis, you identified several sites that meet the criteria for suitable locations for the university's research lab.

The analysis now needs to be recorded. Usually this is done by compiling a graphic representation of data (a map) and a written description of the results (a report).

Design and layout must be considered when producing output. A beautiful map and well organized report will help convey your intended message with greater impact, and are likely to improve the credibility of your results, as well as their acceptance.

This lesson examines some of the components of good design for maps and reports.

- Designing the components of a map
- Using symbols effectively
- Determining the purpose of a map
- Defining the map parameters (size and scale)
- Designing the map layout
- Preparing symbol data
- Creating a final map
- Generating a tabular report

You'll use ARCPLOT for your mapping needs, and INFO to generate a final report. You have already used ARCPLOT in previous lessons to display coverages. In this lesson, you'll see some of the cartographic capabilities of ARCPLOT. By the end of this lesson, you'll have a final map and report showing the location, size, and approximate cost of each of the potential lab sites.

The estimated time needed to complete this lesson is 4 hours.

What is a map?

A map is a graphic representation of some part of the earth's surface. Cartographic design uses symbology (the art of representing geographic features with symbols) and typography (the art of arranging printed matter) to convey information that is both easily understood and visually appealing to the map reader.

A map contains a series of themes or coverages that are often combined to form the final product. A map also includes descriptive information which helps the reader interpret the information on the map. Here are some of the primary components of a map:

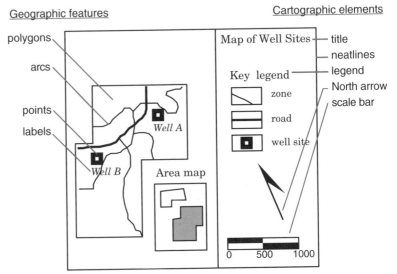

Map components can generally be divided into two types: geographic features and cartographic elements.

geographic features   Geographic map features include areas, lines, and points drawn from various coverages in the geographic database.

- Area features, such as land use areas, are represented by polygons. Polygon boundaries are drawn using line symbols and can be shaded based on attributes using colors, patterns, or both. Polygons can also be labeled with attributes using text symbols.

- Linear features, such as roads and streams, are represented by arcs. Arcs are drawn using line symbols and labeled with attributes using text symbols.

■ Point features (single x,y locations) are represented by point elements. In addition to representing point features, point elements are used as label points which identify polygons. Points are drawn with marker symbols and labeled with attributes using text symbols.

cartographic elements Cartographic elements help make the map easier to read and interpret.

■ Titles and explanatory text describe the purpose of the map and are drawn using text symbols.

■ Neatlines create borders and visual partitions within a map and are drawn using line symbols.

■ Legends describe the symbols used to represent the geographic elements and are drawn using line, shade, marker, and text symbols.

■ North arrows and scale bars describe the orientation and scale of the map. They are drawn using line, shade, and text symbols.

Using symbols

Both the geographic features and cartographic elements on a map are drawn using various symbols. This section briefly describes the characteristics of the symbols you'll use to create maps.

types of symbols There are four types of symbols: shade, lines, marker, and text. The chart on the opposite page shows an example of each and lists the geographic features and cartographic elements for which each is used.

Symbol type		Geographic features	Cartographic elements
Shades		Shaded polygons	Background display windows Legends North arrows Scale bars Shade keys Logos
Lines		Arcs and polygon boundaries	Neatlines Title blocks Underlines Line keys Logos North arrows Scale bars
Markers		Point features and label points	Point keys
Text	Map of land use 	Annotation	Titles Legends Explanatory text

symbol definitions   A set of parameters defines each symbol. The parameters common to most types of symbols are color, pattern, and size.

color   In ARC/INFO, you can specify color three ways: by color name, by color model and component color values, and by hardware device index. The use of color is limited by the device on which you display or plot the symbols. A pen plotter may allow only four or eight pens (specific colors depend on which pens you insert). In contrast, a graphics terminal displays sixteen or more colors at once and a color electrostatic plotter can apply hundreds of colors to your map.

pattern   Pattern refers to the repetition and rhythm of elements in the symbol. For example, a dotted line can be composed of evenly spaced dots,

• • • • • • • • • • • • • • • • • • •

or two dots together, followed by a gap:

•• •• •• •• •• •• •• •• ••

Pattern also provides what we perceive as texture in shade symbols.

size   Size determines the width and height of text and marker symbols,

6 pt   ☆   9 pt   ☆   14 pt   ☆

or the width of line symbols,

or the grain of shade patterns:

These are just some of the parameters that define symbols. Other parameters apply to specific symbol types. For example, in addition to color, pattern, and size, text symbols are defined by

quality: c o n s t a n t or proportional

            KERN or TIGHTKERN

font: Times   Courier   Helvetica

and style: underlined, *italic,* **bold**, etc.

For a complete discussion of symbol definitions and uses, refer to online help under *Cartography-->Map display and query using ARCPLOT-->Specifying symbols.*

symbol files

ARC/INFO stores symbol definitions in symbol files. Each stored symbol has a unique number referencing its own set of definitions. For example, in the default symbol file (PLOTTER.LIN), line symbol 31 is a green, dashed line 0.05 inches wide. ARC/INFO provides several sets of symbol files. To use a symbol, you specify the symbol set and the number of the symbol in the file you want to use.

You can also create your own symbol files. The available symbolset files and options for creating customized symbols are described in online help under *Cartography-->Map display and query using ARCPLOT.*

the current symbols

The current symbols are those defined by the current setting of the symbol characteristics. You can modify the characteristics of the current symbol, or change the current symbol, or choose from a different set of symbols, any number of times during an ARCPLOT session. One way to modify the characteristics of the current symbol is to interactively specify some of its parameters. For example, you might specify that text be drawn in red italic letters, 0.2 centimeters tall.

There is only one current symbol for each of the four symbol groups (line, marker, shade, and text). When you start ARCPLOT, the current symbols are the default symbol from the default symbolset files. These files, called PLOTTER.LIN, PLOTTER.MRK, PLOTTER.SHD, and PLOTTER.TXT, each feature 100 symbols, composed of 25 patterns in four different colors (device index colors 1 to 4). These default sets are especially useful for maps that will be drawn on a four-color plotter.

symbol editors

Four symbol editors provide a graphic interface that allows you to quickly choose and modify a current symbol, edit an existing symbol, or create new symbols and symbolsets. The ARCPLOT commands LINEEDIT, MARKEREDIT, SHADEEDIT, and TEXTEDIT access each editor. For more information about how to use the symbol editors, see each of these commands in the online *Command References* for ARCPLOT.

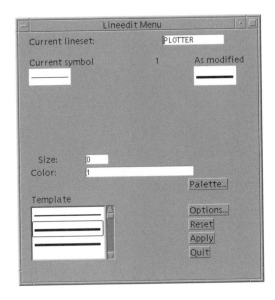

using symbols effectively

How you use symbols directly influences how effectively your map communicates the desired information to the reader. A look at the sample maps in Appendix E will illustrate some of various uses of symbols. Consider the following when you create a display:

using color

Different colors imply the *qualitative* differences between features, but gray tones, or varying shades of a single color, are used to denote a *quantitative* difference between features. Color used qualitatively shows kind, or quality. Color used quantitatively shows amount. For instance, State A could be blue and State B, yellow to show that they are different states (a qualitative difference). But, if you want to show that the unemployment rate is higher in State A than in State B (a quantitative difference), making State A a darker shade of gray than State B will show the higher unemployment rate.

Qualitative differences between features, as well as the overall look of the map, are enhanced by the right color choices, but colors that are too intense can distort the apparent value of the data and make a map difficult to read. Color also connotes cultural meaning and can elicit positive or negative reactions.

Great care must be taken when choosing colors or gray tones. Colors that look good on a display screen may become too dark and obscure text on a hardcopy plot. Also, solid-fill colors that draw instantly on the screen take a long time to plot with a pen plotter. Solid-fill colors cause no problems for electrostatic plotters. Even though an 8-bit device can display a maximum of 256 colors at one time, some electrostatic plotters can plot over 4,000 colors on a single plot.

using patterns

Choose patterns that enhance the reader's ability to discriminate between respective areas both on the map and in the key. Keep in mind that some patterns are harder to distinguish than others.

Take care when choosing line or dot patterns. Contrasts that appear striking when viewed side by side are likely to be less clear as they appear randomly across the map.

Avoid using dense patterns on pen plotters. Like solid-fill colors, dense patterns take longer to draw, causing wear on both the pens and the plotting media. Also, it's easier for a pen plotter to construct line patterns than dot patterns. The pen moves side to side for the lines, while the pen must be continually picked up and put down to create the dots—sometimes causing the pens to clog because the ink cannot flow freely.

using text

Typically, text appears in the title and key, and labels features in the main body of the map. Text also often references the cartographer, data source, and date the map was created.

Character size and the text font (typeface) affect the visual prominence of the data. A large text size is usually adopted for the title, while a small size is used for references and sources. Simple text fonts enhance map readability—elaborate fonts should only be used for specialty maps. Finally, keep in mind that too many fonts will distract the map reader.

Steps for creating your map

Now that you're familiar with the elements of a map, and some of the symbols available to draw them, you can create your own map. Here are the major steps to follow:

Step 1: Define the purpose and requirements of the map
Step 2: Determine the size and scale of the map
Step 3: Design the layout of the map
Step 4: Prepare additional data
Step 5: Create the final map

Define the purpose and requirements of the map

You need to answer three questions before creating a map. First, Why is the map being constructed?; second, Who is the map for?; and third, How will the map be presented? The overall aim is to define the scope of the map, establish a list of objectives, and thereby develop a plan to create the map.

the map message

A map is meant to communicate. It can be packed with detail or be simple in content and yet still convey its overall message. Maps are usually designed for a specific purpose. For example, a road map emphasizes transportation networks, a demographic map highlights centers of population, and a soils map indicates the location of various soil types.

intended audience

You must always consider the intended reader's ability to interpret the information presented on your map. Our powers of recognition depend on personal knowledge and experience. Successful map reading and interpretation requires skill. Proficiency varies between different groups of people. Some people have less experience in map reading than others, in which case, the theme must be clear and the content limited to relevant information. So, the content of a map is determined not only by why it's being produced, but also by who will use it.

EXERCISE

List the required information to display on the map

The first step in creating the final map for the university lab project is to determine which information to include. The audience for the map in this project is a faculty committee representing several departments within the university.

The map should highlight the potential sites and should also include the study area boundary to locate the sites within the study area. The streams, sewers, and soils that are factors in the analysis do not need to be displayed on the map. However, the committee will want to see where the sites are in relation to existing roads.

Here is the project database:

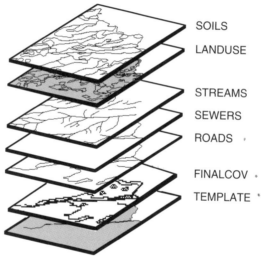

SOILS

LANDUSE

STREAMS

SEWERS

ROADS

FINALCOV

TEMPLATE

List here the three prominent coverages to be included in the map:

_____

_____

_____

(See Appendix D for the answers to this exercise.)

END

| Step |
| 2 |

Determine the size and scale of the map

Size and scale depend on the map's purpose and intended audience determined in Step 1.

output size and medium

Research to find an optimum size or aspect ratio for maps (Robinson, et al.) indicates that maps look better with a width-to-height ratio of 4:3 (e.g., 16 cm x 12 cm, or 32 in x 24 in). Map size must vary depending on its purpose. A map required for display, for example, would need to be large, while a map for a committee report might be limited to the size of the paper used in the final document.

In addition to a map's purpose and intended use, the kind of map you produce will depend on the various output devices available to you. The most common output devices are graphics screens, plotters (pen, ink-jet, or electrostatic), and PostScript™ devices. The type of material used in the plotter (paper or film) is also important. Based on your needs, you must weigh the merits of each output method. What looks good on a graphics screen will not necessarily reproduce effectively on paper or film.

Output media can be categorized by function and quality. The screen environment is often used for development work and as a test area for layout. Screen displays also provide quick views of small areas (as you have already seen in previous lessons), maps, and for showing the graphic results of interactive query. A screen display can be output as is directly to an ink-jet plotter or PostScript printer. This process is sometimes referred to as a *screen dump*.

Alternatively, after the final map design is complete, it can be captured as a graphics file. This file can be output to a plotting device or back to the display screen. A pen plotter, as the name suggests, is a device that uses colored pens to plot good-quality graphics and text. Electrostatic plotters use small electrical charges to hold colors or tones on paper to produce high-quality output.

If a map is to be duplicated, or appear in print, there are other options for output display. For example, PostScript or Scitex™ system output can generate color separations for printing high-quality maps. For more information on output display options, refer to online help under *Cartography-->Map output and plotting*.

scale For practical reasons, maps are scaled representations. The scale of a map is devised such that the important data is retained and presented in a map of a particular size. Size requirements for the finished product limit your choices of map scale.

The best scale for your map depends on the resolution of the original data, as well as the level of detail you want your map to include. For example, a $^{1}/_{4}$-inch square on a 1:250000-scale map represents approximately one square mile (640 acres) on the ground. But, a $^{1}/_{4}$-inch square on a 1:63360-scale map represents $^{1}/_{4}$ square mile (160 acres).

A map may contain many geographic representations at different scales (e.g., a location map at a different scale can be included for reference). It's important to show all map scales on the drawing.

Step 3

Design the layout of the map

Once you know what information your map will contain and the physical parameters of the map, it's time to consider the layout of the information.

visual balance Map components can be arranged in many ways to achieve a visual balance. Correct use of color, patterns, and symbols can help accomplish the outcome you desire. In the final layout of any graphic design, remember where you want the reader's eye to focus.

Sketch several layout designs. Move the main elements around—the map, the title, the scale bar, and the key—until a good balance is achieved. There's no single correct answer to arranging map elements. Often, trial and error is the only way to assess the overall balance.

For many, it's tempting to skimp on the effort given to map design. However, time spent at this task is rewarded by a final product that's easier to read and interpret, and which, in turn, increases the impact of your analysis.

The maps in Appendix E illustrate various approaches to map layout.

EXERCISE   **Lay out the final map**

A map template has already been created for the study area during a previous agricultural lands project. The template contains a neatline around the map, a title block, a North arrow and a scale statement. To save time and money, you'll reuse the template for this project. All you need to do is add a new title and legend, and draw the coverage features.

It's a good idea to lay out the map on graph paper so you can obtain the actual locations (in page units) for each element. You'll specify these locations when you issue the commands to draw your map. The template, coverage, title, and legend have already been sketched for you. Appendix C contains this sketch of the layout. Refer to it now and note the following page coordinates:

The coordinates of the area where the coverage features will be drawn
minimum x-coordinate: .25
minimum y-coordinate: .25
maximum x-coordinate: 6.75
maximum y-coordinate: 7.75

Map element	x-coordinate	y-coordinate
The upper-left corner of the top legend box	7.0	7.2
The lower-left corner of the first title line	0.8	7.4

(See Appendix D for exercise answers.)

END

Step
4

Prepare additional data

Before creating your map, you need to prepare any other files or data, in addition to the coverages, that you will need. Most of this preparatory work relates to the symbols you choose to represent the various map features. For example, for this map, you may want to draw streams using a blue line and roads using a red line. These symbols are not stored as part of the streams or roads coverages; you specify them when you create your map. This way, you can draw these same features in a different map using different symbols. You may also want to create custom symbols at this point.

This step commonly includes these two tasks:

- Specifying the symbol value used to symbolize each feature in a coverage (e.g., shades based on soil type for shading soils polygons, line symbols based on road type for drawing roads, and so on).

- Creating key files that define the symbols and text to appear in a symbol key legend.

symbolizing features using their attribute values

The simplest way to draw coverage features is to use one symbol to draw all the features of the same feature type. For example, you can specify that all road features be drawn with a red line symbol. This uniform symbolization is acceptable if your only intent is to show the location of the roads on your map. But, if you've classified the roads as improved (paved) and semi-improved (gravel), you might want to differentiate the two on the map by using a different symbol for each. To do this, you can use an attribute of a feature to indicate which symbol to use to draw that feature.

There are several ways to use attributes to symbolize features. One is to use an attribute value stored in the feature attribute table for the coverage. So, for example, using the feature attribute table below where 1 indicates improved and 2 indicates semi-improved roads, you could use the values stored for the RD-CODE item as the line symbol number.

ROADS#	ROADS-ID	RD-CODE
1	1	1
2	2	2
3	3	2
4	4	1
5	5	2
6	6	1

Usage: ARCLINES <cover> {item | symbol} {lookup_table}
Example: ARCLINES ROADS RD-CODE

Given this example, each road would be drawn with the symbol indicated by its RD-CODE value:

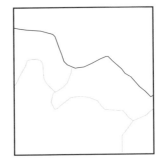

Alternatively, you could add an item in the feature attribute table to store a symbol for each record (e.g., SYMBOL). In this example, improved roads would be drawn using line symbol 6, and semi-improved roads, with line symbol 78.

ROADS#	ROADS-ID	RD-CODE	SYMBOL
1	1	1	6
2	2	2	78
3	3	2	78
4	4	1	6
5	5	2	78

```
Usage:   ARCLINES <cover> {item | symbol} {lookup_table}
Example: ARCLINES ROADS SYMBOL
```

lookup tables   Another way to use attributes to specify symbols is to access a *lookup table*. A lookup table is an INFO data file that contains two items. One item is defined and named the same as an item in the feature attribute table, and the other item is named SYMBOL. For each *unique* attribute value, there is a corresponding record in the lookup table associated with a specific symbol number.

ROADS.LUT

RD-CODE	SYMBOL
1	6
2	78

```
Usage:   ARCLINES <cover> {item | symbol} {lookup_table}
Example: ARCLINES ROADS RD-CODE ROADS.LUT
```

When you draw the map, specify the name of the item in the feature attribute table to reference the symbol. To obtain the correct symbol number for each feature, ARCPLOT looks up the value of this item.

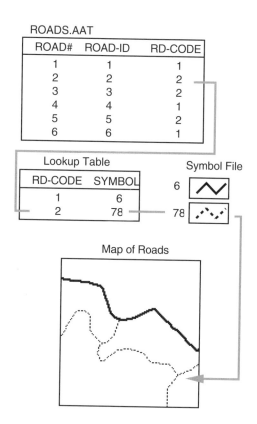

Using a lookup table allows you to assign specific symbols to feature attributes. This provides more flexibility than using item values directly as symbol numbers because the values of your attribute items are not necessarily desirable symbol patterns. Lookup tables also reduce data storage because multiple records in the feature attribute table access the same symbol number in the lookup table.

In our example, all the roads with RD-CODE = 2 use symbol number 78. Even if there are hundreds of roads with this code, the symbol number still only needs to be stored once. And, because they are stored only once, symbols are easy to change if you want to alter how your map looks.

FYI

Any table with related items can be used like a lookup table. See online help under *Working with Tables--> Managing Tabular Data-->The relate environment.*

EXERCISE

Create a lookup table to draw features symbolized by class

The faculty site selection committee wants to know which potential sites are near roads, and whether each road is improved or semi-improved. To do this, you will draw each road with a symbol indicating improved or semi-improved. These symbols have already been chosen and are indicated on the map layout sheet, so all you have to do now is create the lookup table.

First start ARC. Then specify the name of your station file.

```
Arc: &STATION <name>
```

Attach to the DATA workspace if you are not already there.

UNIX   `Arc: &WORKSPACE /yourname/ugis/data`
Windows NT   `Arc: &WORKSPACE <drive>:\yourname\ugis\data`

Before you can create the lookup table for ROADS, you need the item definition values for the road classification item named RD-CODE.

Enter INFO and select the ROADS.AAT file.

```
Arc: INFO
ENTER USER NAME> ARC
ENTER COMMAND> SELECT ROADS.AAT
45 RECORD(S) SELECTED
```

The ITEMS command displays the definition of the RD-CODE item.

```
ENTER COMMAND> ITEMS
DATAFILE NAME: ROADS.AAT
COL  ITEM NAME      WDTH OPUT TYP N.DEC
  1  FNODE#            4    5   B    -
  5  TNODE#            4    5   B    -
  9  LPOLY#            4    5   B    -
 13  RPOLY#            4    5   B    -
 17  LENGTH            4   12   F    3
 21  ROADS#            4    5   B    -
 25  ROADS-ID          4    5   B    -
 29  RD-CODE           1    1   I    -
```

RD-CODE is defined as 1,1,I.

Understanding GIS—The ARC/INFO Method

creating a lookup table in INFO

Now create the lookup table. It should contain two items: an item defined the same as the lookup item (RD-CODE) in the AAT, and another called SYMBOL. You can define SYMBOL any way you like, as long as it's numeric. In this case, use 2,2,I because the symbol number is a two-digit integer.

```
ENTER COMMAND> DEFINE RD.LUT
ITEM NAME,WIDTH[,OUTPUT WIDTH],TYPE[,DECIMAL PLACES][,PROT.LEVEL]
     1
ITEM NAME> RD-CODE
ITEM WIDTH> 1
ITEM OUTPUT WIDTH> 1
ITEM TYPE> I
     2
ITEM NAME> SYMBOL
ITEM WIDTH> 2
ITEM OUTPUT WIDTH> 2
ITEM TYPE> I
```

You're only defining two items, so enter a carriage return at the third prompt.

```
     4
ITEM NAME> <CR>
ODD RECORD LENGTH ROUNDED UP TO EVEN
ENTER COMMAND>
```

Display the item definitions on the screen to make sure they're correct.

```
ENTER COMMAND> ITEMS
DATAFILE NAME: RD>LUT
     2 ITEMS: STARTING IN POSITION  1
COL: ITEM NAME  WIDTH  OUTPUT  TYPE  N.DEC  ALTERNATE NAME
  1  RD-CODE      1      1      I     -
  2  SYMBOL       2      2      I     -
```

Now use the ADD command to enter the values for each code. Remember that 1 represents an improved road and 2 represents a semi-improved road. Use line symbol 6, a thick red line, for improved roads, and line symbol 78, a thin red dashed line, for semi-improved roads.

```
ENTER COMMAND> ADD
```

ADD prompts you to enter a value for each item you specified when you defined the file.

```
     1
RD-CODE> 1
SYMBOL> 6
     2
RD-CODE> 2
SYMBOL> 78
```

When prompted to add the third record, enter a carriage return.

```
3
RD-CODE> <CR>
     2 RECORD(S) ADDED
ENTER COMMAND>
```

Use the LIST command to make sure your lookup table is correct.

```
ENTER COMMAND> LIST
$RECNO    RD-CODE SYMBOL
     1    1         6
     2    2        78
```

Leave INFO by typing Q STOP.

```
ENTER COMMAND> Q STOP
```

You can use this lookup table in ARCPLOT to draw the roads.

END

FYI

Successive records in a lookup table define ranges of values for the lookup item. This makes it easy to assign symbols to features based on classification. When ARCPLOT reads a value for the lookup item in a feature attribute table, it looks for a match in the lookup table. If it doesn't find an exact match, it uses the record with the next greater value for the lookup item. For example, this lookup table assigns symbols to features based on their value for a lookup item named LENGTH:

LENGTH	SYMBOL
10	17
25	3
100	26

LENGTH values ≤ 10 are assigned symbol 17. LENGTH values > 10 and ≤ 25 are assigned symbol 3. LENGTH values > 25 and ≤ 100 are assigned symbol 26. Features with item values greater than the largest value in the lookup table use the value in the last record, so features with LENGTH values > 100 are also assigned symbol 26.

Records in a lookup table must be sorted in ascending order on the lookup item, in this case, LENGTH. For a more complete discussion of lookup tables, refer to online help under *Cartography-->Map display and query using ARCPLOT-->Drawing coverage features.*

key legends

Always use a legend to explain your map symbols. To do this, create a key legend file that defines what to display in the legend. A key legend file is a text file created using the text editor of your operating system. In it, you specify each legend symbol, by number, along with its descriptive text. ARCPLOT reads the text file and creates the legend. Here is an example of a key legend file for roads:

The first line specifies line symbol number 6 as the first symbol in the legend. Always precede the symbol number by a period (.). The next line specifies 'Improved' as the descriptive text for the first symbol in the legend.

```
.6
Improved
.78
Semi-improved
```

Here is what this legend looks like when drawn in ARCPLOT:

     Improved

     Semi-improved

∇ FYI

You can also define legends using items in the feature attribute table or items in an INFO data file. The lookup table (INFO data file) you created to draw the roads, ROADS.LUT, can be used to create a legend by adding an item named DESCRIPTION and listing the descriptive text for each symbol.

ROADS.LUT

RD-CODE	SYMBOL	DESCRIPTION
1	6	Improved
2	78	Semi-improved

This same information can appear and be accessed in the feature attribute table of the coverage.

ROADS.AAT

ROADS#	ROADS-ID	RD-CODE	SYMBOL	DESCRIPTION
1	1	1	6	Improved
2	2	2	78	Semi-improved
3	3	2	78	Semi-improved
4	4	1	6	Improved

∇

EXERCISE   **Create and draw a key legend file for a line coverage**

To put a legend on your map that explains the symbols used to indicate the improved and semi-improved roads, you need to create a key legend file. Using your operating system's text editor, create a new text file named RD.KEY in the data workspace. (If you're using a UNIX workstation, use lowercase letters when naming your files.) Check with your system administrator if you aren't sure how to create a new text file. Then add the following lines exactly as shown:

```
.6
Improved Road
.78
Semi-improved Road
```

Save the file and exit the text editor. You may want to display the file on the computer screen to make sure it's correct. If you quit from ARC/INFO to create your text file (not necessary) be sure to specify your station file when you start ARC again. Then use the &POPUP directive to display your newly created text file on the screen.

```
Arc: &STATION <name>
Arc: &POPUP RD.KEY
```

After you finish viewing the file, close the popup window by selecting the Quit button in its lower right corner. If you see errors in your file, you must return to the operating system's text editor to correct them.

When your key legend file is correct, use it in ARCPLOT to create the key legend.

```
Arc: ARCPLOT
```

Use the KEYBOX command to specify the dimensions of the symbol in the key. For this example, specify 0.5 inches wide with no height to produce straight lines in the key legend.

```
Arcplot: USAGE KEYBOX
Usage: KEYBOX <width> <height>
Arcplot: KEYBOX 0.5 0
```

Next, use KEYPOSITION to specify the location at which to draw the key legend.

```
Arcplot: USAGE KEYPOSITION
Usage: KEYPOSITION <* | xy>
Arcplot: KEYPOSITION *
```

Position the cursor near the upper left corner of your graphic window, and press the left mouse button to enter the location of the upper left corner of the first box.

Draw the line symbol key using the KEYLINE command with the key_file option.

```
Arcplot: USAGE KEYLINE
Usage: KEYLINE <key_file | CLASS> {NOBOX} {NOTEXT}
Usage: KEYLINE <cover> <feature_class> <symbol_item>
              {text_item} {NOBOX}
Usage: KEYLINE <layer> LAYER <symbol _column>
              {text_column} {NOBOX}
Usage: KEYLINE <info_file> INFO <symbol_item> {text_item}
              {NOBOX}
Arcplot: KEYLINE RD.KEY NOBOX
```

The NOBOX option for KEYLINE is used to draw the symbol key without boxes surrounding each symbol.

———————   Improved Road

— — —   Semi-improved Road

Now that you know how to create a symbol key in ARCPLOT using a key legend file, move on to the next step.

END

FYI
Key legends that describe coverage features represented by line symbols are drawn using the KEYLINE command, marker symbols using KEYMARKER, and shade symbols using KEYSHADE.

Step 5

Create the final map

Once all the preparatory work is done, you can begin creating your map on the computer. In ARC/INFO, this is done using the ARCPLOT program and the ARC/INFO Plot System.

Using ARC/INFO to create your map

Once you've established your map design, size, and scale, it's time to translate this layout into ARC/INFO commands. You'll use ARCPLOT to generate a map composition and a graphics file from which hardcopy plots can be generated.

This section introduces a number of ARCPLOT commands. These are only a few of the many commands available in ARCPLOT, but are sufficient to create a simple, yet effective, map of the study area and the analysis results. For now, understanding the command sequences and how they affect each other is more important than creating an elaborate map.

There are five basic steps for creating your map using ARCPLOT.

- Indicate the display method for the map—on the computer's screen or on a graphics plotter.

- Specify the portion of the earth's surface to include in your map based on a coverage, a portion of a coverage, or several adjacent coverages (i.e., specify the map extent).

- Specify certain parameters about the size and layout of your map to translate coverage features from the computer to the display surface. These include the final size of the map page, the position of the geographic features on the map, and the scale of the map. This series of operations is known as the *map-to-page transformation*.

- Draw the geographic features you want on your map, such as land use areas, roads, and streams, and specify which symbols to use for drawing and labeling them.

- Add additional cartographic elements to make your map easier to read and understand. These include neatlines, titles, legends, a scale bar, a North arrow, and so on.

EXERCISE

Create your final map in ARCPLOT

If you are not in the data workspace, then go to the DATA workspace, which contains the coverages you'll use in your map.

UNIX   Arcplot: **&WORKSPACE /yourname/ugis/data**
Windows NT   Arcplot: **&WORKSPACE <drive>:\yourname\ugis\data**

You need the following coverages and files to complete this exercise. They serve as the primary data sources for your map.

- TEMPLATE coverage contained in the DATA directory
- FINALCOV coverage created in Lesson 8
- ROADS coverage contained in the DATA directory

HELP

If FINALCOV is not in your DATA workspace, copy it from the RESULTS workspace now.

UNIX   Arc: **copy ../results/finalcov finalcov**
Windows NT   Arc: **copy ..\results\finalcov finalcov**

If you quit ARCPLOT, then start ARCPLOT now.

Arc: **ARCPLOT**

indicate the display   In ARCPLOT, you can create your map as a display on the computer screen, or you can create a digital file of the map, known as a *graphics file*, which can then be sent to a plotter to create a hardcopy version of the map. In addition to the default ARC/INFO graphics file, optional output file formats include PostScript, Adobe Illustrator™, and CGM.

▽FYI▽

What is a graphics file? A graphics file is a digital file containing drawing instructions for a display device (plotter, printer, or screen) to generate a map. This file contains device-independent vector data, color definitions, font metrics, and raster image data.

Your graphics terminal is the output display device for this exercise. This is the device specified in your station file so, if you haven't already done so in this session, issue the &STATION directive.

Arcplot: **&STATION <name>**

specify the
geographic area

Use the MAPEXTENT command to specify the geographic area you want to show on your map. You can think of the map extent as a window defining the portion of the total area covered by your database available to ARCPLOT. Coverage features, or portions of coverage features, falling outside this window are not drawn.

After the display device is set, MAPEXTENT is usually the first command issued in an ARCPLOT session. There is no default map extent. There are many ways to specify the map extent. The easiest way is to name a coverage. The boundary (BND) file of the coverage you specify defines the map extent window. Now specify the area covered by the final analysis coverage from the last lesson.

Arcplot: **MAPEXTENT FINALCOV**

specify the map parameters (size, position, and scale)

Factors influencing the final map layout include the map's size, the location where the coverage features will be drawn, and the scale at which the features will be drawn. These parameters result from the map design decisions you made earlier and affect how the map reader will interpret your map. These terms are used in the next few pages:

- *physical page* —the actual surface on which the map is displayed; for example, the computer terminal's screen or the plotter sheet.

- *graphics page* —the area on the physical page where map graphics are drawn.

- *map limits* —the area on the graphics page where coverage features are drawn.

- *map extent* —the rectangular limits (xmin, ymin, xmax, ymax), in real-world coordinates, that define the area of the earth's surface you are going to display.

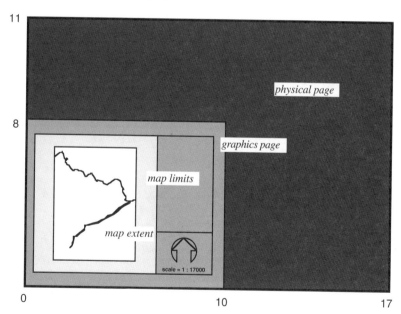

page size   The map is displayed on a physical page. This can be a piece of plotter paper or the screen of your computer terminal. The area on the physical page where the map elements can be drawn is known as the *graphics page*. In ARC/INFO, the graphics page is defined by the PAGESIZE command.

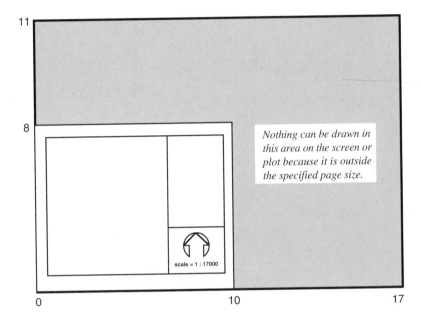

In this illustration, the physical page measures 17 by 11 inches. The graphics page measures 10 by 8 inches and is specified as follows:

Arcplot: **PAGESIZE 10 8**

Page size dimensions are specified in page (or device) units, usually centimeters or inches, rather than real-world map units.

map limits   As discussed at the beginning of this lesson, map elements can be divided into two types: those elements that represent coverage features (points, lines, and polygons), and other cartographic elements that make the map easier to read and understand (titles, legends, etc.). You can reserve an area on the graphics page for displaying coverage features. Limiting where the coverage features can be drawn allows you to designate other space on the page for other map elements. The MAPLIMITS command specifies the coverage drawing area.

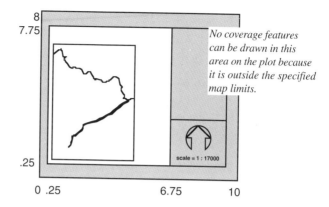

No coverage features can be drawn in this area on the plot because it is outside the specified map limits.

Arcplot: **MAPLIMITS .25 .25 6.75 7.75**

map position

You can also position the coverage features within the map limits. The following illustration shows the results after using the MAPPOSITION command to center the coverage features within the map limits by placing the center of the map *extent* at the center of the map *limits*.

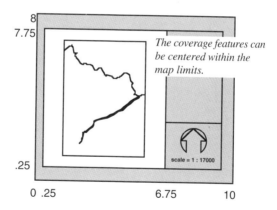

The coverage features can be centered within the map limits.

Usage: **MAPPOSITION**
Usage: MAPPOSITION <*|LL|LR|UL|UR|CEN|xy>
                   <*|LL|LR|UL|UR|CEN|xy>
Arcplot: **MAPPOSITION CEN CEN**

map scale

Finally, you'll want to specify a scale at which to draw the coverage features. ARC/INFO doesn't store a coverage at a specific scale. Rather, it only stores coordinates in real-world units. You can display the coverage at any size by specifying a scale when you draw it.

Scale is specified as a representative fraction; for example, 1:17000, where one unit of measure on the map represents 17,000 of the same units of measure on the earth's surface. In this example, one centimeter on the map will equal 17,000 centimeters on the earth's surface or 1 cm = 170 m.

Specify the denominator of the fraction using the MAPSCALE command. But before you do this, you must tell ARCPLOT what units your coverage is stored in (usually feet or meters), so it can perform the correct scaling. The MAPUNITS command does this.

```
Arcplot: MAPUNITS METERS
Arcplot: MAPSCALE 17000
```

FYI

We've explicitly set the parameters for our map. But if you don't do this, ARCPLOT uses default parameters for you. The default map parameters are

- PAGESIZE—the entire physical page.
- MAPLIMITS—the entire graphics page specified by PAGESIZE.
- MAPPOSITION—the lower-left corner of the map extent at the lower-left corner of the map limits.
- MAPSCALE—the coverage features are drawn as large as possible within the map limits.
- MAPEXTENT—no default; must always be specified.

Here is how using the default settings for our map would look:

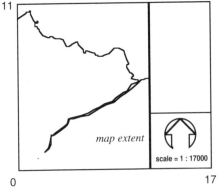

physical page =
graphics page =
map limits

map extent

scale = 1 : 17000

draw the coverage features

Now that you've set all the map parameters, it's time to draw the map. By default, ARCPLOT draws every line using the definitions of the current line symbol. When ARCPLOT starts, line symbol 1 is the current line symbol (a solid white line on the computer screen, black on the plotted page). But suppose you want to draw the outline of the study area with a red line. First change the line symbol. Symbol 2 is a red line.

Arcplot: **LINESYMBOL 2**

To draw the lines making up the outline of the study area with the TEMPLATE coverage containing these arcs, type

Arcplot: **ARCS TEMPLATE**

The arcs are drawn using the current symbol parameters of line symbol 2. Until the current line symbol is changed, any subsequent arcs will also be drawn with line symbol 2. To change the current symbol, issue the LINESYMBOL command again.

Arcplot: **LINESYMBOL 1**

Notice that the arcs from the TEMPLATE coverage did not change color even though you changed the line symbol. Changing the symbol only sets the characteristics of lines drawn *after* the command is given, not lines already drawn on the screen. Now draw the arcs for the TEMPLATE coverage again.

Arcplot: **ARCS TEMPLATE**

As you'd expect, they're drawn in white if your graphic window is black or black if your graphic window is white. You have other map features to draw before the study area outline, so clear the screen.

Arcplot: **CLEAR**

open a map composition

Creating a *map composition* in ARCPLOT allows you to store a map as a graphics file at the same time it draws on the screen. The graphics are recorded as a series of instructions and are written and saved to a graphics file. You can use this map composition to redisplay the map on the screen or send it to a plotting device.

Map elements are the basic components of a map composition. Typically, a map composition has one map element for each feature drawn, for example, one element for the map title, one map element for the North arrow, another for the scale bar, and so on. Each map composition can hold up to 999 map elements. You can position and reposition map elements any number of times. Map elements can also be enlarged or reduced, scaled, shifted, or deleted and can be manipulated individually or as a grouped unit.

Start your map composition by naming the map you want to create, in this case, SITES.MAP.

Arcplot: **MAP SITES.MAP**

This opens a new map composition. All graphic elements drawn on the screen are also stored in a graphics file which you will use later to redisplay your map.

FYI
When you create a map composition for subsequent hardcopy output, specify the desired resolution of the hardcopy device using DISPLAY RESOLUTION.

Arcplot: DISPLAY RESOLUTION <dots_per_inch>

Setting the resolution of the output file enhances, or decreases, the graphic quality of your hardcopy map. <dots_per_inch> is the number of dots-per-inch (dpi) in device pixels to rasterize the graphics in the output file. (This measure is the same in x and y dimensions.) If you know the resolution of the output device you intend to use, you may want to match that resolution. For example, by default ARCPLOT captures graphics at 500 dpi resolution. If you'll be sending the output to a 300 dpi device, you can set the resolution to 300 to compress the size of the output file. On the other hand, if you'll be sending the output to a high-end imagesetter capable of 2000 dpi, you should increase the resolution to 2000. For this project, you can use the default setting.

Now you're ready to begin creating your map. The first element to add to the map composition is the existing map template containing the neatlines, North arrow, and scale. These are stored in a previously created map composition named BORDER.MAP. Use the PLOT command to draw the template.

Arcplot: **PLOT BORDER.MAP**

The template appears on the screen. The map template contains the common cartographic elements found in most maps, including neatlines, North arrow, and scale statement. Notice that the layout contains an area where cartographic features can be drawn.

Now you can include the coverage features on the map. The three coverages you want to draw are the potential sites, the roads, and the study area boundary. Because graphics are drawn on top of, and may partially obscure, any previously drawn graphics, it's a good idea to give some thought to the order in which the features will be drawn. In a map composition, elements can be deleted and redrawn, or even reordered, but it's more efficient to get it right the first time. In this case, we want the roads to be drawn on top of the site locations and the study area boundary to be drawn last to make a clean border. So we'll draw the coverages in this order:

- FINALCOV
- ROADS
- TEMPLATE

Because the potential sites are polygons, you could draw the outlines of the sites. But you can also fill the polygons with a shade pattern. Shading the potential sites with a solid green pattern will make them easy to see. Before you do, you must tell ARCPLOT which ones are the potential sites. RESELECT those polygons in FINALCOV for which the value of SUITABLE is equal to 1.

Arcplot: **RESELECT FINALCOV POLY SUITABLE = 1**
FINALCOV polys: 8 of 628 selected.

Use the POLYGONSHADES command to shade the selected polygons in FINALCOV. Specify the shade symbol on the command line using symbol 3, a solid green pattern.

Arcplot: **POLYGONSHADES FINALCOV 3**

Only the currently selected polygons (i.e., those for which SUITABLE = 1) are shaded.

Draw the polygons using line symbol 1, the current line symbol.

Arcplot: **POLYGONS FINALCOV**

Next draw the roads using a red line (line symbol 2).

Arcplot: **ARCLINES ROADS 2**

ARCLINES drew all the arcs from the ROADS coverage with a red line (line symbol 2). But the site selection committee needs to distinguish between improved and semi-improved roads. Earlier, you created a lookup table specifying symbols to use for these two classes, so drawing them with different symbols should be easy.

First delete the roads you just drew. The MDELETE command deletes selected map elements from the current map composition. Because the last map element drawn is automatically selected, issue MDELETE to delete the roads from your map composition.

Arcplot: **MDELETE**

The roads disappear from the screen. The MFRESH command can be used to refresh the screen display while the map composition is open.

Arcplot: **MFRESH**

Give the ARCLINES command again, this time specifying the name of the item that indicates the class of road, and the name of the lookup table. ARCPLOT will automatically use the RD-CODE ite m value for each road to find the correct symbol number in the lookup table.

Arcplot: **ARCLINES ROADS RD-CODE RD.LUT**

The improved roads are drawn with a thick red line and the semi-improved roads, with a dashed red line.

Next, draw the boundary of the study area using line symbol 1 (still the current line symbol).

Arcplot: **ARCS TEMPLATE**

Finally, you'll want to label each site so it can be cross-referenced with the written report. Use the User-ID as the label, because it's a unique identifier. (You can use any item in the PAT, but this is the easiest for cross-referencing.) Because you've already selected those polygons from FINALCOV for which SUITABLE = 1 (the potential sites), only those polygons will be labeled. Make sure the text is large enough to read, but not so big that it obscures other features. An 8-point text height will be okay.

```
Arcplot: TEXTSIZE 8 PT
Arcplot: TEXTCOLOR PLUM
Arcplot: LABELTEXT FINALCOV FINALCOV-ID
```

Each polygon's User-ID appears next to its respective label point. Now you're ready to add additional descriptive data to the map.

▽ FYI

You can specify TEXTSIZE in inches (default), or by point size. If you are unfamiliar with sizing text using points and picas, you will find the following conversions helpful:

1 pica = 12 points   72 points = 1 inch

For more about text parameters, refer to online help under *Cartography-->Map display and query using ARCPLOT.*

add the additional cartographic elements

The final step uses cartographic elements to add additional explanatory information to the map.

key legend

To add the legend, you first need to specify where it will be located. On the layout in Appendix C, notice that the upper left corner of the key legend is located at 7.0, 7.2 on the page. Specify these coordinates using the KEYPOSITION command.

```
Arcplot: KEYPOSITION 7.0 7.2
```

You can now use the KEYLINE command to draw the key legend using the current text size. Select an attractive cartographic text font (e.g., Univers Medium) and specify professional typographic kerning (character spacing). And, because you'll want a larger text size than was used to label the polygons, reissue the TEXTSIZE command.

```
Arcplot: TEXTFONT 'UNIVERS MEDIUM'
Arcplot: TEXTQUALITY KERN
Arcplot: TEXTSIZE 14 PT
Arcplot: TEXTCOLOR 1
```

To have the roads symbols appear as straight lines, specify a KEYBOX .5 inches wide and with no height, but don't draw the box. When issuing KEYLINE, specify the name of the file containing the parameters for the legend. You created this file earlier.

```
Arcplot: KEYBOX .5 0
Arcplot: KEYLINE RD.KEY NOBOX
```

Add the title to finish the map. Specify a relatively large text size of 24-points (larger than other text on the map) and choose a bold font.

```
Arcplot: TEXTSIZE 24 PT
Arcplot: TEXTFONT 'UNIVERS BOLD'
```

Position the title at 0.8, 7.4 on the page. Unless you specify otherwise, text is always positioned by placing the lower left corner of the first character at the current screen cursor location. Before the text can be drawn you need to use the MOVE command to specify the text position.

```
Arcplot: MOVE 0.8 7.4
```

Use the TEXT command to draw the title on the map. It contains blank spaces, so the title must be placed inside single quotes, as follows:

```
Arcplot: TEXT 'Potential Sites for Aquaculture Lab'
```

You have finished adding elements to the map. To close the map composition and save it, type

```
Arcplot: MAP END
```

Now clear the screen and redraw the map to make sure it's correct.

```
Arcplot: CLEAR
Arcplot: PLOT SITES.MAP
```

Your map should look something like this:

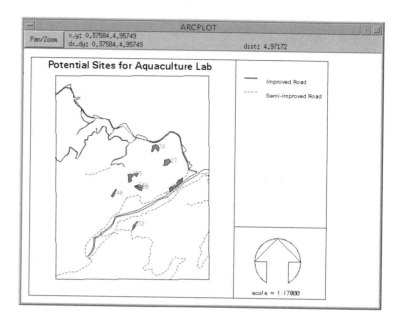

A map composition can be sent directly to a plotter to produce a hardcopy map. You can also edit map compositions to add new map elements or to manipulate existing map elements. Most ARC/INFO plotting and conversion commands that accept graphics files as input will accept map compositions as well.

If you want to save your final map composition as a graphics file, type

Arcplot: **DISPLAY 1040**

ARCPLOT clears the screen and prompts for the name of the graphics file to create.

Enter ARC/INFO Graphics filename: **SITES.GRA**

The .GRA extension is a convention used to distinguish a graphics file. Now use the PLOT command again just as you did above when you drew the map composition SITES.MAP.

Arcplot: **PLOT SITES.MAP**

This time, instead of drawing on the screen, the map composition is sent to the graphics file. This file can now be sent to a plotter (see the HELP section below). To leave ARCPLOT, type QUIT.

```
Arcplot: QUIT
```

You can draw the plot file using the Arc DRAW command.

```
Arc: Usage DRAW
Usage: DRAW <in_meta_file> {device} {options} {tty}
Arc: DRAW SITES.GRA 9999
```

HELP

If your computer has a plotter attached, you can create a hardcopy version of your map using the PLOT command at the ARC prompt. Check with your systems administrator for your specific plot device.

For Windows NT you can select the print icon in the ARC/INFO program group to select a plot device.

END

Designing and generating reports

A report can consist of a number of elements. It usually includes a title or standard heading and a series of columns. The standard heading may include the date, page number, column headings, and the title. Each line in the report contains one entry in each column. All the data on each line are drawn from the same record. Here is a sample report:

title	POTENTIAL SITES	
column headings SITE#	AREA	COST
detail lines 172	5,640.191	11,280
227	5,495.015	10,990
285	7,125.877	7,125
308	7,546.493	11,319
322	2,653.453	2,653
332	3,087.506	3,087
346	2,701.034	2,701
477	2,573.669	2,573

There are many ways to produce reports. In this lesson, you'll generate a text file that can be sent to a line printer.

EXERCISE

Create a tabular report as a text file

The report describing the result of your lab suitability analysis should include the following:

- User-ID (to cross-reference with the map)
- Size of each site
- Cost to purchase the land

The first step in creating a new report such as this is to select the INFO data file from which the report will draw its data. The data file in this case is FINALCOV.PAT, and the items to list are: FINALCOV-ID, AREA, and COST. Including the User-ID allows each record in the report to reference one of the sites on the map.

First start INFO and select the data file to use to create the report.

```
Arc: INFO
ENTER USER NAME> ARC
ENTER COMMAND> SELECT FINALCOV.PAT
      628 RECORD(S) SELECTED
```

Now select the records to be included in the report. These are the sites for which the SUITABLE value is equal to 1.

```
ENTER COMMAND> RESELECT SUITABLE = 1
      8 RECORD(S) SELECTED
```

Now create the report file. The OUTPUT command specifies a system text file to hold the contents of the report, in this case, FINAL.REP. The INIT parameter indicates that the new file will automatically replace an existing file of the same name. INIT allows you to replace temporary versions of a report file while you design your report. INFO requires that you specify the pathname of the file.

UNIX
Windows NT

```
ENTER COMMAND> OUTPUT ../FINAL.REP INIT
ENTER COMMAND> OUTPUT ..\FINAL.REP INIT
```

Now issue the REPORT command to start creating the report.

```
ENTER COMMAND> REPORT
```

REPORT prompts you to define each column in the report, including the name of the item for the column, formatting options, and a text heading for the column. COLUMN CONTENT is the first prompt (i.e., an item name). Specify FINALCOV-ID as the first column.

```
  2 ENTER COLUMN CONTENT> FINALCOV-ID
```

At the next prompt, enter a carriage return because we are using the default option to list the item value of FINALCOV-ID for each record.

```
ENTER REPORT OPTIONS> <CR>
```

Then enter the heading for the first column, in this case, SITE#.

```
ENTER COLUMN HEADINGS> SITE#
```

INFO prompts for the second line in the heading. Enter a carriage return because there is only one line in the column heading.

```
ENTER COLUMN HEADINGS> <CR>
```

Now enter the information for the remaining two columns:

```
7 ENTER COLUMN CONTENT> AREA
ENTER REPORT OPTIONS> <CR>
ENTER COLUMN HEADINGS> AREA
ENTER COLUMN HEADINGS> <CR>

20 ENTER COLUMN CONTENT> COST
ENTER REPORT OPTIONS> <CR>
ENTER COLUMN HEADINGS> COST
ENTER COLUMN HEADINGS> <CR>
```

Enter a carriage return at the next prompt because there are only three columns in this report.

```
28 ENTER COLUMN CONTENT> <CR>
```

Now enter the title for the report.

```
ENTER REPORT TITLE> 'Potential Sites'
```

You're ready to send it to the print (output) file specified earlier, so enter Yes to the next two prompts. Entering Y at the OUTPUT TO PRINTER prompt will save the information to your file, not the printer.

```
DO YOU WISH TO EXECUTE THIS FORM( Y OR N )> Y
OUTPUT TO PRINTER (Y OR N?> Y
```

Use the default at the next two prompts; enter a carriage return at each.

```
LINES PER PAGE?> <CR>
ENTER REPORT OPTIONS> <CR>
```

Nothing appears on your computer screen because you're sending the report to the output text file named FINAL.REP. When the report is finished, the INFO prompt reappears. Enter Q STOP to leave INFO.

```
ENTER COMMAND> Q STOP
```

Use the following command to list your report on the screen.

ARC: **&POPUP FINAL.REP**

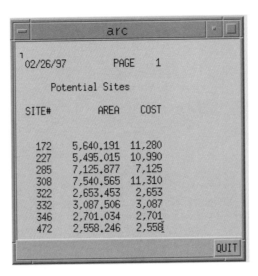

You can edit this file with your system's text editor. If you have a printer connected to your system, you can now print your report (check with your system administrator if you need help).

END

Advanced topic—Creating a map for display

You can use ARCPLOT to create maps showing coverage features. You can also use ARCPLOT to create quality cartographic products by adding graphic elements such as boxes and neatlines, descriptive information such as titles, legends, and reports, and custom elements such as logos.

ADVANCED EXERCISE

Create a cartographic-quality product in ARCPLOT

The university has requested that you create another map to display at a public meeting to discuss the lab site selection process. The map must show the location of each potential site and its surrounding land use, as well as improved roads and major and minor streams. It need only show the portion of the study area containing the sites, but should include a reference map showing the entire area. The final report should also be included on the map.

The new map will look like this:

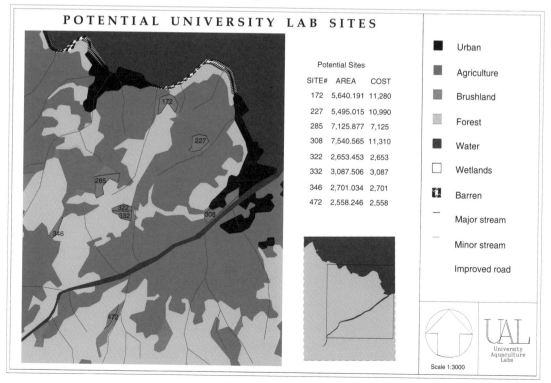

Before starting ARCPLOT, you should edit the text file containing the report, FINAL.REP, because it will be displayed on the map. Using your operating system's text editor, remove the first two lines which contain the date and page number. You may also want to delete one of the blank lines between the title and the column headings. Check with your computer system administrator if you aren't sure how to do this.

HELP

In Lesson 8, did you perform the advanced exercise to create ELIMCOV? If you did, you can use ELIMCOV here, instead of FINALCOV. First repeat the instructions for creating your report on page 9-39, substituting ELIMCOV for FINALCOV. Then substitute ELIMCOV for FINALCOV in the following exercise.

---

specify map parameters

After starting ARCPLOT and setting the display environment (if necessary), open a new map composition.

```
Arc: ARCPLOT
Arcplot: &STATION <name>
Arcplot: MAP LAB.MAP
```

Now specify the map parameters. The map will display only a portion of the study area, so use the MAPEXTENT command to specify the minimum and maximum coordinates of this geographic window in map units (in this case, meters).

```
Arcplot: MAPEXTENT 4550 5090 6090 6740
```

Because the map will be displayed on the wall, it needs to be large enough for easy reading, at least 36 by 24 inches. Specify the MAPLIMITS and MAPPOSITION to center the coverage features on the left side of the page.

```
Arcplot: PAGESIZE 36 24
Warning: Pagesize exceeds device limits, scaling down
Arcplot: MAPLIMITS 1.0 0 18.5 23.0
Arcplot: MAPPOSITION CEN CEN
```

At this size, you can specify a scale of 1:3000 for the coverage features.

```
Arcplot: MAPUNITS METERS
Arcplot: MAPSCALE 3000
```

FYI

Even though you set the PAGESIZE to be 36 inches wide and 24 inches high, ARCPLOT automatically scales the map composition to fit on the graphics screen on your terminal. This allows you to compose a large map on your graphics screen.

draw coverage features

Now you can draw the coverage features using the same commands you used to create the map earlier. The drawing order has already been designed such that each coverage display is drawn on top of previous displays in an order that will create a higher quality map display.

First shade the polygons in LANDUSE based on their LU-CODE values. Before issuing the POLYGONSHADES command, however, consider which set of shade symbols to use.

▽FYI/ ARC/INFO supplies numerous special-purpose shadesets to create attractive cartographic displays. Here is a list of some of those sets:

Shadeset file	Purpose
PLOTTER.SHD	Default shade symbolset for pen plotters containing default hardware colors
BW.SHD	Monochrome display terminals and consoles
CALCOMP.SHD	CalComp™ color electrostatic plotters
CARTO.SHD	High-quality shade symbols for use on pen plotters
COLOR.SHD	Device-independent color display terminals and color workstation consoles
COLORNAMES.SHD	Device-independent shadeset of named colors
COLORRANGE.SHD	Device-independent colorramp of 225 shades of gray
CONTRAST.SHD	Device-independent shadeset colorramp of random colors
RAINBOW.SHD	Device-independent shadeset colorramp of analogous colors

The SHADESET command in ARCPLOT allows you to specify a shadeset file. It can be any symbolset distributed with the software, including those listed above, or one created or customized for use by your organization. For example, users often specify

Arcplot: **SHADESET COLOR**

for color display terminals because it contains sixteen solid-fill colors that make nice screen displays. For more information on using special symbolsets, as well as examples of the colors and patterns contained in each, refer to online help under *Cartography-->Map display and query using ARCPLOT-->Specifying symbols.*

▽

Now shade each land use polygon according to its LU-CODE. First specify the CARTO.SHD symbolset when you issue the SHADESET command.

Arcplot: **SHADESET CARTO**

An INFO lookup table, named LABPLOT.LUT, for the land use polygons specifies symbols from the CARTO shadeset. Use this lookup table to shade the polygons.

Arcplot: **POLYGONSHADES LANDUSE LU-CODE LABPLOT.LUT**

Draw the outline of each potential site using line symbol 5, a thick white line. First you'll have to reselect the suitable sites from FINALCOV.

Arcplot: **RESELECT FINALCOV POLY SUITABLE = 1**
FINALCOV polys: 8 of 628 selected
Arcplot: **LINESYMBOL 5**
Arcplot: **POLYGONS FINALCOV**

Now use the ARCLINES command to draw the streams symbolized by major and minor code (the lookup table is STREAMS.LUT and the lookup item is STRM-CODE).

Arcplot: **ARCLINES STREAMS STRM-CODE STREAMS.LUT**

Next draw the improved roads using a red line, line symbol 2. The attribute for class is RD-CODE, and the value for improved is 1. Because you want to draw only improved roads, you will have to reselect them before drawing.

Arcplot: **RESELECT ROADS ARCS RD-CODE = 1**
ROADS arcs : 18 of 45 selected
Arcplot: **LINESYMBOL 2**
Arcplot: **ARCS ROADS**

Finally, label each suitable site with its User-ID centered in the polygon. The POLYGONTEXT command will do this. First specify an appropriate TEXTSIZE, and a constrasting TEXTCOLOR.

Arcplot: **TEXTSIZE 14 PT**
Arcplot: **TEXTCOLOR YELLOW**
Arcplot: **POLYGONTEXT FINALCOV FINALCOV-ID**

*draw a reference map
and add the report*

The reference map will represent a larger geographic extent and be drawn at a smaller size than the map of sites, so a new set of page parameters needs to be specified. First use the TEMPLATE coverage to change the new map extent to the entire study area.

Arcplot: **MAPEXTENT TEMPLATE**

Use automatic scaling to draw the coverage features as large as possible within the map limits.

Arcplot: **MAPSCALE AUTOMATIC**

Specify new map limits to position the reference map on the page. (You don't need to specify MAPPOSITION again, because it's still set to CEN CEN.)

Arcplot: **MAPLIMITS 19.5 0.25 26.5 10.0**

Shade the TEMPLATE coverage polygons to indicate land and water. There are only two polygons in this coverage (besides the external polygon). Use RESELECT to select the land polygon (LU-CODE NE 500), and then shade the polygon using shade symbol 329.

Arcplot: **RESELECT TEMPLATE POLY LU-CODE NE 500**
TEMPLATE polys: 2 of 3 selected
Arcplot: **POLYGONSHADES TEMPLATE 329**

Now use the NSELECT command to select the water polygon from TEMPLATE. NSELECT switches the selected and unselected sets of features. There is only one other polygon in this coverage, so it will unselect the land polygon and select the water polygon.

Arcplot: **NSELECT TEMPLATE POLY**
TEMPLATE polys: 1 of 3 selected

Now shade this polygon using shade symbol 431.

Arcplot: **POLYGONSHADES TEMPLATE 431**

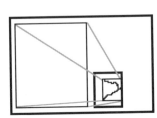

Finally, draw a thick box on the reference map showing the area represented by the map of the sites. An easy way to do this is to use the BOX command and specify the same geographic coordinates that you specified for the map extent of the larger scale map display of suitable sites. Before doing this, you must use the UNITS command to tell ARCPLOT that the coordinates will be in map units (meters) instead of page units (centimeters or inches).

Arcplot: **UNITS MAP**

Then set the line symbol to be a thick white line, and issue the BOX command to specify the lower left and upper right corners of the box.

Arcplot: **LINESYMBOL 5**
Arcplot: **BOX 4550 5090 6090 6740**

Now draw the arcs in TEMPLATE to outline all the polygons. First set the line symbol to 1; then draw the arcs.

Notice that the ARCS command can be used to draw all the arcs in TEMPLATE even though a subset of polygons has been reselected. This is because no arcs have been reselected from TEMPLATE.

Arcplot: **LINESYMBOL 1**
Arcplot: **ARCS TEMPLATE**

The rest of the cartographic elements will be specified in page units, so set the units back to page.

Arcplot: **UNITS PAGE**

Add the report to the map. Specify the text font, quality, and size for the report as well as the position on the page where the lower left corner of the first character will appear.

Arcplot: **TEXTFONT TRIUMVIRATE**
Arcplot: **TEXTQUALITY PROPORTIONAL**
Arcplot: **TEXTSIZE 36 PT**
Arcplot: **TEXTCOLOR 1**
Arcplot: **MOVE 19.8 21**

Next, use the TEXTFILE command to draw the report. TEXTFILE allows you to display the contents of any text file on your map; in this case, FINAL.REP.

Arcplot: **TEXTFILE FINAL.REP**

draw a border, North arrow, scale, and logo

The map will be for public display, so you need to create a new template to include the university's logo and a more authoritative border. It's been decided to adopt line symbol 5 for the border and line symbol 1 for all other neatlines. Line symbol 5 is a wide line and will emphasize the outer border of the map area. Two boxes will be drawn, one for the outer border and one for the inner border. The BOX command can be used to draw the borders. (Note that the coordinates are specified in page units.)

Arcplot: **LINESYMBOL 5**
Arcplot: **BOX 0 0 36 24**
Arcplot: **LINESYMBOL 1**
Arcplot: **BOX .25 .25 35.75 23.75**

Now create lines to separate the different parts of the map. The LINE command draws a line between two or more pairs of x,y coordinates.

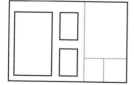

Arcplot: **LINE 27.75 23.75 27.75 .25**
Arcplot: **LINE 27.75 5 35.75 5**
Arcplot: **LINE 31.75 5 31.75 .25**

Include a North arrow. The North arrow has been created and stored as a coverage (NORTHARR); so, it can be manipulated as part of the map. Because it is stored as a geographic feature, specify a new map extent and map limits, just as with the reference map.

Arcplot: **MAPEXTENT NORTHARR**
Arcplot: **MAPLIMITS 28 1 31.5 5**
Arcplot: **ARCS NORTHARR**

Add the university's logo. The logo has also been previously created and stored as a coverage, ULOGO, so you need to specify a map extent.

Arcplot: **MAPEXTENT ANNO ULOGO**

The logo has been created as annotation, a feature type that stores text as a coverage feature in map units. The command used to draw annotation on a map is ANNOTEXT.

Arcplot: **ANNOTEXT ULOGO**

The logo is drawn too small within the last specified map limits, which is the same location as the North arrow. Move the logo to the proper location using MFIT, a map composition command. MFIT lets you interactively specify a box within which to draw currently selected map elements.

Arcplot: **MFIT ***

When prompted, position the cursor over the lower left corner of the box to the right of the North arrow, and press the appropriate button on the mouse or the 1 key on the keyboard. Then move the cursor to the upper-right corner of the box and enter the position. The logo is redrawn within the box. You can repeat the MFIT * command as many times as needed to place the logo exactly where you want it.

Now draw the scale statement beneath the North arrow. Scale can be shown as a representative fraction or graphically. In this example, show the scale as a representative fraction. The text symbol will remain the same as before (i.e., text symbol 1), and the text size should be specified as .40 inches. Use the MOVE command to specify where the scale will be drawn, and then use TEXT to draw it.

Arcplot: **TEXTSIZE .40**
Arcplot: **MOVE 28.5 0.5**
Arcplot: **TEXT 'Scale 1:3000'**

draw the legend and title   For this map, the legend includes two key files: LABPLOT.KEY for the land use polygons, and LABMAP.KEY for the linear features (roads and streams).

First use KEYAREA to designate the area on the map where both keys should appear. For the land use key, construct .6-inch square key boxes, separated by a distance of one inch, and place the text 1 inch to the right of each box.

```
Arcplot: KEYAREA 28.5 22 35 5.5
Arcplot: KEYBOX 0.6 0.6
Arcplot: KEYSEPARATION 1.0 1.0
```

There's plenty of room in the key area, so increase the text size to make it easy to read. Then draw the key using KEYSHADE.

```
Arcplot: TEXTSIZE .6
Arcplot: KEYSHADE LABPLOT.KEY
```

Now specify the size of the key boxes and draw the key legend for the line features. It will automatically follow the land use key in the key area you specified.

```
Arcplot: KEYBOX 0.6 0
Arcplot: KEYLINE LABMAP.KEY NOBOX
```

Finally, place the title on the map. Select a new font, Times Bold, and specify a new text size of 0.8 inches.

```
Arcplot: TEXTFONT 'TIMES BOLD'
Arcplot: TEXTSIZE 0.8
```

Draw the title. Make it fit in the space above the map of the sites.

```
Arcplot: TEXTFIT 'POTENTIAL UNIVERSITY LAB SITES' 2 22.75
25.75 22.75
```

The map is complete, so close the map composition. You can use the PLOT command to redisplay it at anytime.

```
Arcplot: MAP END
Arcplot: CLEAR
Arcplot: PLOT LAB.MAP
```

To leave ARCPLOT, type QUIT.

```
Arcplot: QUIT
```

Use the PLOT command available at the Arc: prompt to send your map composition to a plotter. You can use the DRAW command to view your map composition before plotting it.

Arc: **DRAW LAB.MAP**

Your ARC/INFO system administrator can help you submit your map composition to your plotter.

END

Summary

concept review   Geographic features are displayed on a map in the same form in which they are created and stored in the computer: as points, lines, and polygons. You specify which features you want to display by specifying the feature type and the name of the coverage to draw. Each feature type is typically stored in a separate coverage and is in real-world coordinates. Because each coverage is projected into the same coordinate system, when you draw coverages for the same area, they are drawn on top of each other.

The coverage features are translated from the computer to the display surface through a series of operations known as map-to-page transformation. This includes positioning and scaling the map on the graphics page. Storing coverage features in real-world coordinates allows maps to be correctly scaled, and ensures that measurements such as area and length are accurate.

Associating attributes in the tabular database with the map features allows the features to be drawn and labeled based on their attribute values.

Additional graphics can be added to the map to make it easier to read. These are graphic primitives, such as lines and boxes, and are only stored as part of the map, not as geographic features in the coverage.

lesson summary   This lesson discussed the components of a map and the nature and use of symbols. It also presented a step-by-step approach for creating a map using ARCPLOT. Here is a summary of the ARCPLOT commands you used:

specifying map parameters

GIS Functionality	ARCPLOT Command
Specify geographic extent of area to display.	MAPEXTENT
Specify the size of the physical page.	PAGESIZE
Open a map composition.	MAP
Close a map composition.	MAP END
Specify where on the page coverage features are drawn.	MAPLIMITS
Position coverage features within the map limits.	MAPPOSITION
Specify the units of measure for map features.	MAPUNITS
Specify the scale of the map.	MAPSCALE

drawing coverage features

Cartographic Function	ARCPLOT Command
Draw coverage annotation.	ANNOTEXT
Draw arcs.	ARCS
Draw line features based on attribute values.	ARCLINES
Label polygons with values at label point.	LABELTEXT
Draw polygon outlines.	POLYGONS
Shade polygons based on attribute values.	POLYGONSHADES
Label polygons with attribute values centered in the polygon.	POLYGONTEXT

drawing cartographic elements and manipulating map composition elements

Cartographic Function	ARCPLOT Command
Draw a box.	BOX
Draw a line between two coordinates.	LINE
Specify the area within which to draw a key legend.	KEYAREA
Specify symbol size in a key legend.	KEYBOX
Draw key legend for line features.	KEYLINE
Specify the starting point of a key legend within the key area.	KEYPOSITION
Specify distances between key boxes and text.	KEYSEPARATION
Draw key legend for shaded polygons.	KEYSHADE
Reduces or enlarges selected map elements into a specified box.	MFIT
Moves selected map elements to a new position.	MMOVE
Scales selected map elements by a specified factor.	MSCALE
Specify location to start drawing.	MOVE
Draw descriptive text on map.	TEXT
Draw contents of an ASCII text file on a map.	TEXTFILE
Draw text between two points and adjust spacing.	TEXTFIT
Specify coordinates to be given as map or page.	UNITS

specifying symbols

Cartographic Function	ARCPLOT Command
Specify how much information will be captured in the output file to be sent to the display device.	DISPLAY RESOLUTION
Specify the current symbol to draw line features.	LINESYMBOL
Specify the current shade symbolset file.	SHADESET
Specify the font of the current text symbol.	TEXTFONT
Set the character spacing of current text symbol.	TEXTQUALITY
Specify the size of the current text symbol.	TEXTSIZE

This map shows the application of some of these commands:

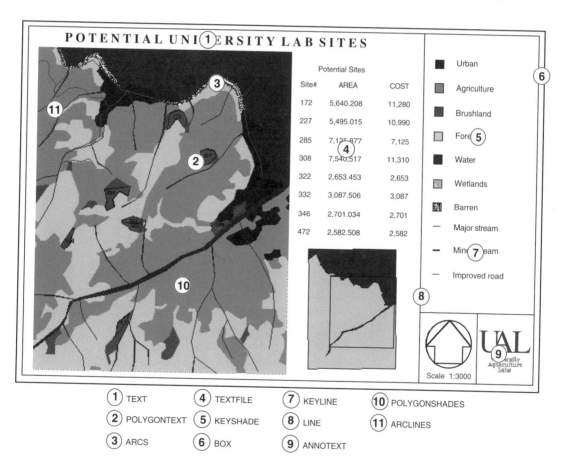

①	TEXT	④	TEXTFILE	⑦	KEYLINE	⑩	POLYGONSHADES
②	POLYGONTEXT	⑤	KEYSHADE	⑧	LINE	⑪	ARCLINES
③	ARCS	⑥	BOX	⑨	ANNOTEXT		

You also used a few basic commands for creating and editing a map composition in ARCPLOT, including MAP to start and end a map composition, MDELETE to delete a map element, MFIT to move and resize an element, and TEXTFIT to space characters.

You should note that these are just a few of the ARCPLOT commands available. Refer to the online *Command References* for ARCPLOT for a full description of available ARCPLOT commands.

Finally, you used the INFO REPORT command to create a report. For a complete discussion of all the REPORT command options, refer to the online *Command References* for INFO.

references for further reading

Clarke, Keith. *Analytical and Computer Cartography*. Prentice Hall, 1990.

Dent, Borden D. *Principles of Thematic Map Design*. Addison-Wesley Publishing Company, 1985.

Greenhood, David. Chapter 6 in *Mapping*. Chicago: University of Chicago Press, 1951.

Keates, J.S. *Cartographic design and production*. London: Longman Group, Limited, 1973. (Out of print.)

Monmonier, Mark. *How to Lie with Maps*. Chicago and London: University of Chicago Press, 1991.

Robinson, Arthur H., Joel L. Morrison, Phillip C. Muehrcke, A. Jon Kimerling, and Stephen C. Guptill. *Elements of Cartography*. Sixth Edition. John Wiley & Sons, 1995.

For more information on topics related to this lesson, refer to ARC/INFO's online help system under *Cartography-->Map display and query using ARCPLOT* and *Working with Tables-->Using INFO-->Using reports*. Also see the online *Command References* for ARCPLOT and INFO.

project status

The project is now complete! In the next lesson, you'll have a chance to create an ARC/INFO menu interface to query and display your database. This interface will allow those with a minimal knowledge of GIS and ARC/INFO to use this technology in their work.

workspace contents You added a number of files to the DATA directory during this lesson:

data	land	strm
border.map	clipcov	info
buffcov	georef01	log
bufro100	geoutm02	streams.lin
clipcov	info	streams.tab
covlist	label.err	strmat03
elimcov	landat05	strmbd02
final.rep	landbd04	strmgn01
finalcov	landcn	
info	landcn.gra	
inlanbuf	landcn02	
intro.aml	landnode.gra	
lab.map	landcp07	
labmap.key	landdg01	
labplot.key	landds10	
landcn	landed	
landsoil	landed03	
landtr	landem08	
landuse	landmj09	
landuse.key	landtr	
linkcov	landtr06	
log	linkcov	
luat10	log	
northarr	luat10	
projdb.aml	node.err	
projdb.menu	ticcov	
rd.key		
rd.lut		
roads		
sewerbuf		
sewers		
sites.map		
sites.gra		
soils		
streams		
streams.lin		
streams.tab		
strmbuf		
template		
ulogo		

task summary   Here is a summary of the completed project tasks.

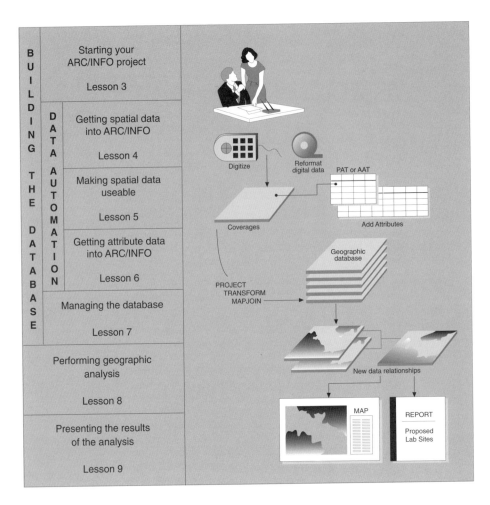

Lesson 10 Customizing ARC/INFO

This lesson introduces you to the ARC Macro Language (AML), the language used to customize ARC/INFO. AML can be used throughout the ARC system to perform a variety of tasks. AML provides a full set of programming capabilities that allow you to

- Automate frequently performed actions

- Create your own commands

- Provide startup utilities for new users or for operations that require specific command settings

- Develop menu-driven user interfaces designed to meet the needs of end users

There are two types of AML files: command macros and menus. Macros organize a sequence of ARC/INFO commands into easily performed, sophisticated geoprocessing operations. Menus can provide an easy-to-use interface that employs a mouse to select desired menu choices.

In this lesson, you'll create a menu-driven application. This application will make it easier for an inexperienced ARC/INFO user to access the geographic database you've developed and to display and query the potential lab sites. Specifically, you'll see

- What's in an AML
- Types of AML menus
- Anatomy of an AML program
- How to create an AML macro
- How to develop a menu-driven user interface

The estimated time needed to complete this lesson is 2 hours.

What's in an AML

You can create AML programs that are composed exclusively of commands from ARC and its subsystems. This is a great convenience and time-saver, particularly if you execute the same sequence of commands many times. However, this is only the beginning of what AML offers. You can also develop menus that allow end users to apply ARC/INFO to meet their specific needs.

AML programs are text files named according to the conventions of the host operating system. Although not mandatory, names usually end in .AML (e.g., WINDOW.AML, TEST.AML). This .AML suffix adds clarity and makes file printing, transfers, and so on, easier.

running an AML program   AML programs are executed by issuing the &RUN directive along with the name of the program to be run. AML programs can be run interactively from the command line, as an executable line in another AML program, or as the result of an AML menu selection. When invoking an AML program, you don't have to specify the .AML suffix. For example, the following two statements are equivalent—both invoke the AML program COMPARE.AML:

```
Arc: &RUN COMPARE.AML
Arc: &RUN COMPARE
```

An AML program runs until the &RETURN directive is encountered. When a program is ended with &RETURN, control returns to the previous input source, usually the terminal.

EXERCISE

Execute a command file

One of the most basic functions that AML provides is the ability to combine a series of ARC commands that must be performed regularly. In many production environments, where a database is being built or updated, each coverage in the database flows through a well-defined series of operations. The geographic data is first input into the computer, either by digitizing or converting data, topology is created, attribute data is added to each coverage, then finally, all the adjacent coverages for each layer are brought together to create a contiguous database.

But before all the coverages are brought together, each undergoes the same series of steps to reach the map joining stage. This is where AML can help streamline the process. With AML, you can create macros to set up the appropriate editing environment in ARCEDIT, to create topology and add attributes once the editing is completed, to join the coverages of each layer in the database, and to display the results of any analysis that was performed on the database.

In this exercise, you'll execute a command file containing ARCPLOT commands that display the potential lab sites and the road network. Before proceeding with the exercise, move to your local DATA workspace and copy the necessary files as follows:

Start ARC/INFO.

UNIX
Windows NT

```
% arc
(You are already in ARC)
```

UNIX

Windows NT

```
Arc: w /yourname/ugis/data
Arc: &sys cp /yourname/ugis/aml/ex*.* .
Arc: w <drive>:\yourname\ugis\data
Arc: &sys copy <drive>:\yourname\ugis\aml\ex*.*
```

HELP

If you have not completed the exercises in Lessons 4 through 9, you also need to copy the coverage, FINALCOV, provided in the RESULTS directory.

UNIX
Windows NT

```
Arc: copy ../results/finalcov finalcov
Arc: copy ..\results\finalcov finalcov
```

In the workspace is a file named EX1.AML which contains a sequence of ARCPLOT commands to display the desired coverages. The file contains the following commands:

```
ARCPLOT
SHADESET COLOR
MAPEXTENT TEMPLATE
ARCS TEMPLATE
ARCLINES ROADS RD-CODE ROADS.LUT
RESELECT FINALCOV POLY SUITABLE = 1
POLYGONSHADES FINALCOV 1
&return
```

Notice that all the commands in the file, except the last one, are ARCPLOT commands. The last command, &RETURN, is an AML directive that terminates the program. Before running the AML program, use the &STATION directive to establish the display device and terminal type.

Arc: **&STATION <name>**

Now run the program to display the coverages on the screen. Use the &RUN directive to execute the AML.

Arc: **&RUN EX1**

Your graphic display will look something like this:

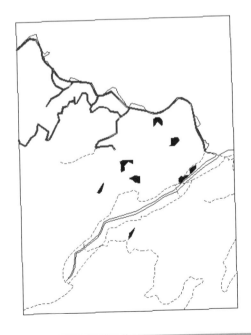

Understanding GIS—The ARC/INFO Method

In this format, the AML program functions exactly like entering the commands interactively from the keyboard. Notice that once the AML program terminates, the Arcplot: prompt appears. At this point, you could enter more ARCPLOT commands or quit ARCPLOT and return to ARC. The next part of this exercise requires ARCPLOT, so don't quit yet.

A system file called a watch file can be used to capture commands entered interactively from the keyboard. A watch file writes all user input and program output to the specified file. The &WATCH directive opens a watch file.

Arcplot: **&WATCH MY.WAT**

All commands and program output are sent to the watch file. Issue the following commands:

Arcplot: **CLEAR**
Arcplot: **CLEARSELECT**
Arcplot: **RESELECT FINALCOV POLY SUITABLE = 1**
FINALCOV polys : 8 of 628 selected.
Arcplot: **POLYGONSHADES FINALCOV SUITABLE**
Arcplot: **LINECOLOR RED**
Arcplot: **POLYGONS TEMPLATE**

Now turn the watch file off.

Arcplot: **&WATCH &OFF**

Now, as you've done in previous lessons, you can use the AML directive &POPUP to view the file you just created.

Arcplot: **&POPUP MY.WAT**

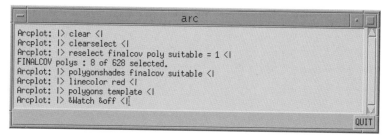

Quit from the popup window when you finish viewing the file.

The &CONV_WATCH_TO_AML directive (&CWTA) converts a watch file to an AML program. It creates an AML file containing only the commands that were entered by the user.

```
Arcplot: &USAGE &CWTA
Usage: &CONV_WATCH_TO_AML <watch_file> <AML_FILE> {&COORDINATES}
Arcplot: &CWTA MY.WAT MY.AML
```

The AML file can now be run to repeat the command sequence that was previously executed from the keyboard. Run the AML you just created.

```
Arcplot: &RUN MY
FINALCOV polys  : 8 of 628 selected.
```

You can see how AML can save a lot of typing when a series of commands needs to be executed again and again. This is just one example of the power of AML.

For the next exercise, quit from ARCPLOT.

```
Arcplot: QUIT
Leaving ARCPLOT...
```

END

AML menus

In addition to command files, AML provides the ability to create menu-based interfaces for your applications. Menus provide an exciting, visual means of integrating ARC/INFO into the way you do your work. Menus typically list a set of choices on the terminal from which a selection can be made. This selection usually results in the execution of an ARC or operating system command, an AML program, or even another menu. There are seven types of menus that can be created in AML: pulldown, sidebar, matrix, form, key, tablet, and digitizer.

pulldown menus   A pulldown menu appears as a bar across the top of the screen. A selection from the menu bar

might result in the display of a submenu, or second level of choices.

These choices are seemingly 'pulled down' from the menu bar above; explaining the name, pulldown menu. You can select from these choices as well.

EXERCISE **Display coverages with a pulldown menu**

Menus allow new or inexperienced users to perform complex operations without having to know the actual command or command sequences required to do so. This exercise uses a pulldown menu to display and list attributes of coverages in the database.

From the `Arc:` prompt, run EX1.AML to start ARCPLOT and again display the boundary coverage, road network, and potential lab sites for the study area.

Arc: **&RUN EX1**

Now, from the `Arcplot:` prompt, display the menu, EX2.MENU using the &MENU directive. Similar to the naming convention for AML programs, AML menus typically have a .MENU suffix which can be optionally specified on the command line.

Arcplot: **&MENU EX2**

The menu displayed on the screen looks like this:

Selecting the Draw column displays a submenu containing a list of coverages that you can draw.

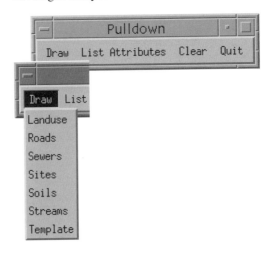

Select **Draw** from the pulldown menu and then **Streams** from the submenu to display the STREAMS coverage.

To clear the graphics display, select **Clear**.

Notice that the Clear choice in the pulldown menu does not contain a submenu of choices. It clears the graphics display.

Select **List Attributes**. Choose a coverage whose attributes you want to display.

HELP

The attribute listing displays in a popup window if your station file sets the AML directive &FULLSCREEN &POPUP. Otherwise, the display appears in the dialog area. You must close the popup window to terminate the display and continue.

---

anatomy of a pulldown menu

A menu file is a text file you create with your operating system's text editor. The format of the menu file is what determines how a menu is displayed, which choices are included, and what action is taken when a selection is made. The pulldown menu file, EX2.MENU, looks like this:

```
1   Sample pulldown menu
Draw
   Landuse   POLYGONSHADES LANDUSE LU-CODE LANDUSE.LUT
   Roads     ARCLINES ROADS RD-CODE ROADS.LUT
   Sewers    ARCLINES SEWERS SYMBOL
   Sites     POLYGONSHADES FINALCOV 1
   Soils     POLYGONSHADES SOILS SUIT SOILS.LUT
   Streams   ARCLINES STREAMS STRM-CODE STREAMS.LUT
   Template ARCS TEMPLATE
'List Attributes'
   Landuse   LIST LANDUSE POLY
   Roads     LIST ROADS ARC
   Sewers    LIST SEWERS ARC
   Sites     LIST FINALCOV POLY
   Soils     LIST SOILS POLY
   Streams   LIST STREAMS ARC
Clear
Quit
```

menu type codes   The first line of all menu files consists of a menu type code (a number from 1 to 7 identifying the menu type), followed by optional text that you can use for documentation or identification purposes. There can be only one such line in a menu file; it must be the first line, and it may not continue onto the next line. In EX2.MENU, the menu type code of 1 indicates that the menu file displays as a pulldown menu. The menu type codes are:

> 1 - Pulldown menu
> 2 - Sidebar menu
> 3 - Matrix menu
> 4 - Key menu
> 5 - Tablet menu
> 6 - Digitizer menu
> 7 - Form menu

menu statements   The remainder of the file consists of statements that define the menu choices and the action each choice performs. Because a pulldown menu can contain submenus, the positioning of the statements determines whether a choice is to appear on the top menu bar, or as a choice on a submenu. If you want the choice to appear on the top menu bar, then the statement must begin in the first column of the line; if the choice is to be part of a submenu, then the statement is indented leaving the first column blank. So, Landuse, Roads, Sewers, Sites, Soils, Streams, and Template are all subchoices of the Draw choice in the menu bar of EX2.MENU.

```
Draw
 Landuse  POLYGONSHADES LANDUSE LU-CODE LANDUSE.LUT
 Roads    ARCLINES ROADS RD-CODE ROADS.LUT
 Sewers   ARCLINES SEWERS SYMBOL
 Sites    POLYGONSHADES FINALCOV 1
 Soils    POLYGONSHADES SOILS SUIT SOILS.LUT
 Streams  ARCLINES STREAMS STRM-CODE STREAMS.LUT
 Template ARCS TEMPLATE
```

A statement typically has two parts: the visible choice that's displayed in the menu and the action carried out upon the selection of that choice. The action to be performed can be an ARC/INFO command, an AML macro, or another AML menu; for example,

```
Landuse   POLYGONSHADES LANDUSE LU-CODE LANDUSE.LUT
```

The visible choice displayed in the menu is 'Landuse' which, when selected, executes the ARCPLOT POLYGONSHADES command.

If the visible choice contains any blank characters, it must be quoted. For example, the selection 'List Attributes' is quoted:

```
List Attributes'
  Landuse   LIST LANDUSE POLY
  Roads     LIST ROADS ARC
  Sewers    LIST SEWERS ARC
  Sites     LIST FINALCOV POLY
  Soils     LIST SOILS POLY
  Streams   LIST STREAMS ARC
```

There are, however, two instances when a statement only has one part. The first is when the choice has an associated submenu (e.g., Draw and List Attributes above). The second is when the first part of the statement is also the desired action to be executed. For example, the following statement lines

```
Clear
Quit
```

contain only one word because they function as both the visible choice displayed in the menu and as the operation to be performed.

For a complete description of the other menu types, see online help under *Customizing ARC/INFO-->AML (ARC Macro Language) --> Form menus*.

When you are finished select **QUIT** from the menu.

END

Anatomy of an AML program

AML is an interpretive language. Each command line, entered from either the keyboard or an AML file, is interpreted by the AML processor, which performs variable substitution, logical branching, and looping before the command is executed by the current ARC program.

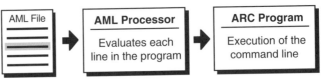

Each line of an AML program passes through the AML processor before the current ARC program executes it.

AML is a flexible language. You can combine host operating system commands, ARC/INFO commands, and AML elements to perform complex operations. There are three types of AML elements:

- Directives
- Functions
- Variables

You will find that AML is similar in principle and functionality to many high-level programming languages in its ability to execute actions such as branching, variable manipulation, and argument transfer.

EXERCISE   **Use AML directives, functions, and variables**

An AML directive tells the AML processor to perform some action or determine the flow of control. AML variables and functions perform text substitution, but in slightly different ways. In this exercise, you'll add directives, functions, and variables to the AML program presented in the first exercise to create a more flexible macro. You'll modify EX1.AML, creating a new AML named EX3.AML.

Understanding GIS—The ARC/INFO Method

```
┌─────────┐
│  HELP   │
└─────────┘
```
If you don't know how to use your operating
system's text editor, copy a finished version of the AML from the
RESULTS directory as follows:

UNIX   Arc: **&sys cp ../results/ex3.aml .**
Windows NT   Arc: **&sys copy ..\results\ex3.aml ex3.aml**

Using your operating system's text editor, edit EX1.AML as follows:

Text editors read carriage returns differently. If you are using
Windows NT and experience difficulty reading EX1.AML, try editing
the file using a different text editor. Be sure to save EX3.AML in
MS-DOS text format and clear the file before running it.

- Delete the line that contains the command SHADESET COLOR
- Add the lines of AML code shown in bold text below
- Save the changes to a new file called EX3.AML

```
/* EX3.AML - displays coverages from the database. The user
/* is prompted for an &STATION file and whether color or
/* black and white shades are to be used.

ARCPLOT
&setvar dev := [response 'Enter a station file']
&type Setting station file to %dev%...
&station %dev%
SHADESET [getchoice color bw -prompt ~
   'Select Color or Black & White shades:']
MAPEXTENT TEMPLATE
ARCS TEMPLATE
ARCLINES ROADS RD-CODE ROADS.LUT
RESELECT FINALCOV POLY SUITABLE = 1
POLYGONSHADES FINALCOV 1
&return
```

Now instead of a command file containing ARCPLOT commands,
you have added AML directives, functions, and variables to create an
AML program. At this point, don't worry if you don't understand the
changes made to the AML file; they are discussed in greater detail on
the following pages. For now, run the new program and notice the
differences in the way the AML program now functions.

Arc: **&RUN EX3**

Recall that in the first exercise, the &STATION directive had to be
issued at the Arc: prompt before the AML file was run. Now the
program prompts you to enter a station file. At the prompt, enter the
name of your station file, replacing <station> below (e.g., 9999).

```
Enter a station file: <station>
```

The program responds by returning the following message:

```
Setting station file to <station>...
```

A menu appears on the screen prompting you to select a shadeset file.

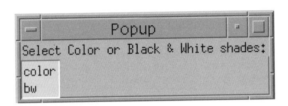

After you make the appropriate choice, the boundary coverage, road network, and potential lab sites are drawn on the screen. The difference between color and black and white will be more obvious in the exercise at the end of this lesson.

HELP   Don't worry if the AML you edited does not execute properly. You may have incorrectly edited the AML file. For example, we made an error in our edits. Here's what happened when we tried to execute the AML:

```
Arc: &RUN EX3
AML ERROR   - Missing Function delimiter(s) ']'
              line 5 of file EX3.AML
AML MESSAGE - Stopping execution of AML file due to ERROR condition
              line 5 of file EX3.AML
```

These messages results from the missing bracket ( ]) in line 5 of our AML.

```
/* EX3.AML - displays coverages from the database.  The user
/* is prompted for the &STATION file and whether color or
/* black and white shades are to be used.
ARCPLOT
&setvar dev := [response 'Enter a station file'
&type Setting station file to %dev%...
&station %dev%
```

Here's the line with the error:

We located the error and fixed it using the system's text editor.

```
&setvar dev := [response 'Enter a station file']
```

By adding a few AML commands to the program, you've created a user interface to ARCPLOT that interactively prompts the user for the station file and the shadeset file to be used.

Running this AML program requires little knowledge of the actual ARCPLOT commands used to create the display and can help the inexperienced user to perform complex operations. Before continuing with this lesson, end the ARCPLOT session.

Arcplot: **QUIT**

END

components of EX3.AML

The changes you made to the AML macro show how an AML program can be modified to create a much more flexible macro. Prompting the user for input eliminates the need to *hard code* parameters needed to run the program. This means the same macro can handle a variety of different graphic display devices. However, it also requires that the user know a little more about the graphic environment.

comment statements

When writing AML programs, it's important to include documentation that explains what the program does and how it performs those tasks. Comments make the program much easier to update. AML provides a special comment symbol—a forward slash followed by an asterisk (/*)—for you to use to document your programs. Text following a comment symbol is ignored by the AML processor. Comments can be placed anywhere in the program. The first three lines you added to EX3.AML are comment statements.

An AML program does not pass blank lines and comment lines to the ARC/INFO program that is running.

```
/* EX3.AML - displays coverages from the database. The user
/* is prompted for an &STATION file and whether color or
/* black and white shades are to be used.
```

AML directives

If a command begins with an ampersand (&), the AML processor recognizes it as a directive. AML directives tell the AML processor to perform some action. Information entered on a directive line is never passed directly to a program. Instead, directives instruct AML to perform the desired AML operation. For example, directives can be used to run an AML, as shown previously, or to type a message to the terminal.

```
&type Setting station file to %dev%...
```

AML variables   AML variables can be assigned a wide variety of data types:

- Character strings
- Integers
- Real numbers
- Boolean expressions
- Expressions that evaluate to any of the above

The &SETVAR directive sets a variable. For example, the variable dev is assigned a value as follows:

```
&setvar dev := [response 'Enter a station file']
```

The variable is assigned the value entered to the right of the assignment operator (:=), in this case, the value returned by the AML RESPONSE function. The assignment operator is an optional parameter. So, the following lines of code are equivalent:

```
&setvar dev := [response 'Enter a station file']
&setvar dev = [response 'Enter a station file']
&setvar dev [response 'Enter a station file']
```

Percent signs (%) identify variable references. (Generally, the only time percent signs do not surround a variable is when the variable is set with the &SETVAR directive.) For example, the variable containing the name of the station file is referenced with the name of the variable surrounded by percent signs:

```
&station %dev%
```

When the AML processor encounters percent signs, it substitutes the value of the variable for the variable reference. The modified command line is then passed to ARC or an ARC subsystem.

For example, if 9999 is the current value of the variable dev when the following line is encountered,

```
&station %dev%
```

the AML processor substitutes the value 9999 for the variable, and the following line is executed:

```
&station 9999
```

AML functions

A function performs a more complex substitution than does a variable. When the AML processor encounters the square brackets [ ], it evaluates the function contained in the brackets and returns the value of the function.

The value a function returns depends on which function is used. Functions can return a number, a character string, or a Boolean value. Normally, the returned value is assigned to a variable or used as part of a command line. A function does not usually act as a command by itself.

In the program EX3.AML, the variable dev is assigned the value returned by the RESPONSE function:

```
&setvar dev := [response 'Enter a station file']
```

When the AML processor encounters the RESPONSE function, it displays the prompt string and waits for the user to enter a response to the prompt.

```
Enter a station file: 9999
```

The variable is then set to the response entered by the user. After the function evaluates, the command line would look like this:

```
&setvar dev := 9999
```

where the value 9999 is substituted for the RESPONSE function.

GET functions

In AML, there are several functions that display a list of choices on the screen from which a selection can be made. These functions are prefixed with the word GET. One example is the GETCHOICE function that was used in EX3.AML to allow the user to choose color or monochrome shades. Evaluating the function causes a menu of choices to appear on the screen. The user selects one of the choices, which is returned as the value of the function.

This line of code

A list of choices and a prompt are
the arguments to GETCHOICE.

```
SHADESET [getchoice color bw -prompt ~
  'Select Color or Black & White shades:']
```

displays the following menu:

If the user selects COLOR, the function substitutes the value COLOR on the command line. The following command then executes in ARCPLOT:

```
SHADESET COLOR
```

line continuation

When writing an AML program, it's sometimes necessary to continue a command over more than one line. AML provides a special line continuation character. Place a tilde (~) at the end of the line to be continued and finish typing the command on the following line. The AML processor interprets both lines as one; for example,

```
SHADESET [getchoice color bw -prompt ~
  'Select Color or Black & White shades:']
```

line separation

In ARC/INFO, the semicolon (;) functions as a line separation symbol. Whenever it's necessary to enter more than one command on a line, separate each command with a semicolon. The separation symbol is useful for creating menu options that require that more than one statement be executed.

The previous exercise did not use a separation symbol. The following example shows how to enter several commands on a single command line to perform a series of operations in ARCEDIT:

```
Arcedit: EDITFEATURE ARC; SELECT MANY;
DRAWSELECT
```

Commands execute in the order in which they appear.

Getting more out of AML

The previous section showed how directives, functions, and variables can enhance an AML macro. This section goes one step further to introduce more complex concepts such as

- Using local and global variables
- Passing arguments to an AML
- Creating logical expressions to alter the flow of control
- Obtaining information from the current program
- Looping operations to repeat command sequences

local and global variables

AML supports two kinds of user-defined variables: local and global. Everything you can do with a local variable you can also do with a global variable. There are, however, important distinctions. A global variable is set the same as a local variable, except a period (.) precedes the variable name.

```
Arc: &setvar .coverage := ROADS
```

In this case, the global variable .COVERAGE is established.

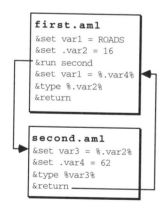

```
first.aml
&set var1 = ROADS
&set .var2 = 16
&run second
&set var1 = %.var4%
&type %.var2%
&return
```

```
second.aml
&set var3 = %.var2%
&set .var4 = 62
&type %var3%
&return
```

The scope of a global variable is greater than that of a local variable. What this means is that a local variable is known only to the AML program in which it was created, whereas a global variable can be accessed by all AML programs. The figure to the left illustrates the point. FIRST.AML sets two variables: VAR1, a local variable, and .VAR2, a global variable. Because .VAR2 is global, it can be referenced in SECOND.AML. When SECOND.AML is run, it references the value of .VAR2 and assigns it to the local variable VAR3. Additionally, SECOND.AML creates the global variable .VAR4. Because it is defined locally, VAR3 cannot be accessed by FIRST.AML. However, because .VAR4 was defined as a global variable, FIRST.AML can now reference it.

EXERCISE

Create an AML macro

Suppose you decide that EX3.AML needs further enhancements. Instead of prompting the user for a station file, you want it specified on the command line when the program is run. And, because some users' terminals obscure the coverage display with the menu and dialog, you want the AML program to define the display such that the menu, dialog, and graphics don't overlap.

The first thing to do is to break up the problem into smaller pieces and solve them one at a time. Here is the list of things you need to do:

- Replace the interactive prompt for the station file and pass it as an argument to the program.

- Control the graphics area on nonworkstation terminals so that it does not overlap the dialog or the menu.

For this exercise, you'll edit EX3.AML and save the changes to EX4.AML.

HELP
    If you don't want to edit EX3.AML, you can copy a completed version of EX4.AML from the RESULTS directory. To copy EX4.AML to your workspace

UNIX   Arc: **&sys cp ../results/ex4.aml .**
Windows NT   Arc: **&sys copy ..\results\ex4.aml ex4.aml**

This is EX3.AML as it currently looks:

```
/* EX3.AML - displays coverages from the database. The user
/* is prompted for an &STATION file and whether color or
/* black and white shades are to be used.

ARCPLOT
&setvar dev := [response 'Enter a station file']
&type Setting station file to %dev%...
&station %dev%
MAPEXTENT TEMPLATE
SHADESET [getchoice color bw -prompt ~
   'Select Color or Black & White shades:']
ARCS TEMPLATE
ARCLINES ROADS RD-CODE ROADS.LUT
RESELECT FINALCOV POLY SUITABLE = 1
POLYGONSHADES FINALCOV 1
&return
```

passing arguments   The &ARGS directive is the means by which arguments are passed to a program. When the program is run, the tokens, or arguments to the program, are placed on the command line after the name of the AML. Each token is assigned to the corresponding variable following the &ARGS directive in the program; for example,

```
Arc: &run some.aml   token1   token2   token3

/* SOME.AML - illustrates how arguments
/* are passed to a program.

&args variable1 variable2 variable3
```

Arguments passed to the program are assigned to the corresponding variable following the &ARGS directive in the program.

To pass the station file name as an argument to the program, you must change the way the station file is set. Instead of explicitly setting the variable with the &SETVAR directive, the assignment is made with the &ARGS directive. Using your operating system's text editor, edit EX3.AML as follows:

■ Delete the following lines in the AML that prompt the user for the station name.

```
&setvar dev := [response 'Enter a station file']
&type Setting station file to %dev%...
```

■ Replace the deleted lines with the &ARGS directive positioned at the top of the file as shown in bold text below:

```
/* EX4.AML - displays coverages from the database. The user
/* is prompted for an &STATION file and whether color or
/* black and white shades are to be used.

&args dev
ARCPLOT
```

■ Save the changes to a new file named EX4.AML.

When this program is run, the station file name is placed after the name of the AML program on the command line. If, for example, the user enters the following command line,

```
Arc: &RUN EX4 9999
```

the token '9999' is passed as an argument to the program and variable dev is assigned the value 9999.

But setting station file variable this way presents a problem. You need to make sure that the user actually enters a value for the station file. Otherwise, the display environment and terminal device will not be established, causing an error when ARCPLOT attempts to draw graphics on the screen. The problem can be broken into two parts. First, how do you verify that the user entered a station file? Second, if one was not entered, how do you stop execution of the program and return an error message to the user? One way to solve the problem is to alter the flow of control in the program and execute the ARCPLOT commands only if a station file is entered.

flow of control

Statements in an AML program are executed in the order in which they appear in the file unless an explicit change in the flow of control is specified. You can control the actions the program takes by using the AML flow-of-control directives. These directives allow you to perform logical branching and execute commands only if certain criteria are met. In this exercise, you want the program to execute only if a station file has been specified.

&IF statements

One directive that alters the flow of control in an AML program is the &IF directive. The form of the &IF directive is,

```
&IF <logical_expression> &THEN <statement>
   &ELSE <statement>
```

where the &THEN <statement> is executed when <logical_expression> is true, and the &ELSE <statement> is executed when it is false.

A logical expression is one that returns a Boolean value: true or false. AML provides a function, the NULL function, that checks whether a variable has a value. This function has the form:

```
[null %variable%]
```

If the variable is null or blank, .TRUE. is returned by the function; otherwise, .FALSE. is returned.

FYI

In AML, an expression that returns a Boolean value returns the word TRUE or FALSE with a period (.) before and after the word. For example, .TRUE. is returned if the value of the expression is true and .FALSE. if the expression is false.

The problem of determining whether the user has entered a station file is solved by combining a logical expression with the &IF directive and is summarized as follows: if a station file is not entered, then issue a message to the user; otherwise, execute the program. Converting this to AML is a simple process of substituting the logical expression, the &THEN statement, and the &ELSE statement into the form of the &IF directive.

By using the NULL function to create the logical expression, the &IF directive can be coded and inserted into the program. Use your operating system's text editor to make the following changes to EX4.AML:

■ Insert into EX4.AML the following lines shown in bold text below.
■ Save the changes made to the file.

```
&args dev
&if [null %dev%] &then
  &return Usage: &RUN EX4 <station_file>
&else &do
  ARCPLOT
  &station %dev%
  SHADESET [getchoice color bw -prompt ~
    'Select Color or Black & White shades:']
  MAPEXTENT TEMPLATE
  ARCS TEMPLATE
  ARCLINES ROADS RD-CODE ROADS.LUT
  RESELECT FINALCOV POLY SUITABLE = 1
  POLYGONSHADES FINALCOV 1
&end  /* else do
&return
```

Indenting statements following an &THEN or &ELSE makes them easier to read and interpret.

AML allows one statement to be executed as a result of a logical expression. If you want to execute several statements—as in the &ELSE condition above—group them with an &DO block as shown. An &DO block delimits the beginning of a block of statements that represent a single action to the AML processor.

&DO blocks end with the &END directive and can have variants that serve to iterate through the &DO group, performing an action repeatedly until an escape condition is met. The example uses the simple form of the &DO block where all the statements between the &DO and the &END are executed only once. We discuss &DO loops in greater detail later in this lesson.

Now try running the program without specifying a station file:

```
Arc: &RUN EX4
Usage: &RUN EX4 <station_file>
Arc:
```

Notice that if no station file is entered, the usage line is returned to the user and the program ends.

the [SHOW] function

The next problem to solve is the dialog, graphics, and menu overlap on nonworkstation terminals. This requires setting the map limits, or drawing area, in ARCPLOT. Unfortunately, not all display devices are the same size, so you can't explicitly set a display size in the program and expect it to work for every terminal. You need to be able to query ARCPLOT to find out the size of the screen. The SHOW function can do just that.

During an ARC/INFO session, ARC and its subsystems keep track of information about environments that have been set. You can access much of this information using the SHOW function. The value returned by the function can be assigned to a variable or used directly as an argument to a command.

In ARCPLOT, you can obtain the page size by using the PAGESIZE option of the SHOW function.

Use the &TYPE directive to display the results of the SHOW function at the terminal.

```
Arcplot: &TYPE [show pagesize]
14.02559,9.239665
```

Your page size will likely be different.

The returned value will, of course, depend on the display device, but the format of the output is always the same. The maximum x- and y-dimensions can be displayed separately using the EXTRACT function. EXTRACT returns a specified element from a list of elements separated by blanks or commas. Nesting the two functions, SHOW and EXTRACT performs the operation in one step. For example, the following command line returns the first element, in this case, the x-dimension.

```
Arcplot: &TYPE [extract 1 [show pagesize]]
14.02559
```

The same can be done to return the y-dimension.

```
Arcplot: &TYPE [extract 2 [show pagesize]]
9.239665
```

Before proceeding with this exercise, exit ARCPLOT.

```
Arcplot: QUIT
```

controlling the graphic display

Now that you have a way of obtaining the screen dimensions, you can adjust the size of the graphics display using the ARCPLOT MAPLIMITS command to prevent the display, menu, and dialog from overlapping on nonworkstation terminals. In this part of the exercise, you'll modify EX4.AML by adding the SHOW function to control the size of the graphics display.

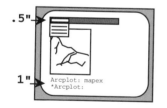

The pulldown menu bar requires about one-half of an inch at the top of the screen. Subtracting .5 from the maximum y-value will leave enough room for the menu. By default, ARCPLOT displays four lines of dialog on the terminal. Four lines of dialog require about an inch of space at the bottom of the terminal. So a minimum y-value of 1 is required. Using the calculated screen dimensions, the map limits are set as follows:

```
&setvar .xmax := [extract 1 [show pagesize]]
&setvar .ymax := [extract 2 [show pagesize]] - .5
MAPLIMITS 0 1 %.xmax% %.ymax%
MAPPOSITION CEN CEN
```

These lines of code can be inserted into the program to control the size of the graphics display.

Use your text editor to make the following changes to EX4.AML:

- Add the lines shown below in bold text.
- Save the changes made to the file.

```
&args dev
&if [null %dev%] &then
  &return Usage: &RUN EX4 <station_file>
&else &do
  ARCPLOT
  &station %dev%
  SHADESET [getchoice color bw -prompt ~
    'Select Color or Black & White shades:']
  MAPEXTENT TEMPLATE
  /* set map limits to screen size
  &setvar .xmax := [extract 1 [show pagesize]]
  &setvar .ymax := [extract 2 [show pagesize]] - .5
  MAPLIMITS 0 1 %.xmax% %.ymax%
  MAPPOSITION CEN CEN
  ARCS TEMPLATE
  ARCLINES ROADS RD-CODE ROADS.LUT
  RESELECT FINALCOV POLY SUITABLE = 1
  POLYGONSHADES FINALCOV 1
&end  /* else do
&return
```

Now when the program runs, the graphics are centered in an area one inch from the bottom and one-half of an inch from the top of the display window. Run EX4.AML, replacing 'station' with the name of your station file.

Arc: **&RUN EX4 <station>**

Before proceeding with this lesson, exit ARCPLOT.

Arcplot: **QUIT**

In the next exercise, you'll learn how this AML can be joined with the menu presented earlier in the lesson to create an application that starts ARCPLOT and displays coverages in the specified display area.

■ END

looping mechanisms   The control method used to repeatedly execute a series of statements in AML is the &DO loop. AML provides six variations of the &DO loop, three of which are discussed in this lesson. These are:

- The counted loop—a loop that executes a specific number of times from a starting value to an end value.

- The &DO &WHILE loop—a loop that executes as long as a certain test condition is met.

- The &DO &LIST loop—a loop that executes until each item in a list of items has passed through the loop.

counted loop   The first type of loop is the counted loop. The counted loop is used when a number of statements need to be executed a specific number of times. The form of the counted loop is:

```
&DO <index_var> := <start_value> &TO <end_value>
```

Suppose you want to execute a number of statements ten times. This is done using a counted loop.

```
&do index := 1 &to 10
    /* perform some operation 10 times
    &run operation.aml
&end
```

AML internally increments the value of the variable index and ends the loop when it completes the specified number of iterations.

&DO &WHILE loop   The &DO &WHILE loop functions as long as a specified logical expression is true. The form of the &DO &WHILE loop is as follows:

```
&DO &WHILE <expression>
```

where <expression> is any logical expression that evaluates to .TRUE. or .FALSE. The loop repeats as long as the expression is true; for example,

```
&setvar done := .false.
&do &while not %done%
    &run operation.aml
    &setvar done := [query 'Do you want to quit' .true.]
&end
```

The loop continues to execute as long as the Boolean expression is true (i.e., done = .false.). Upon each iteration of the loop, the user is asked whether or not to end the loop.

&DO &LIST loop The final loop variant discussed here is the &DO &LIST loop. The &DO &LIST loop has the form:

```
&DO <index_var> &LIST <list>
```

where <index_var> is a variable assigned the value of the first item in the list on the first loop iteration; subsequently, it's assigned the value of the second token, and so on, until the list is exhausted. For example, if you had a list of line coverages to be drawn in ARCPLOT, you could use the &DO &LIST loop to display them all on the screen.

```
&do coverage &list ROADS STREAMS CONTOURS
    ARCS %coverage%
&end
```

The loop would first draw the ROADS coverage, then the STREAMS coverage, and finally the CONTOURS coverage. Because the CONTOURS coverage is the last token in the list, the loop ends.

Developing a user interface

You have seen how AML programs are written and how a menus are created. This section shows how the two can be integrated to create a user interface.

Creating a user interface is a cyclical process that begins with a design phase, proceeds to a coding phase, and then to testing and debugging phases. At any point, it may be necessary to return to the design phase to modify the application.

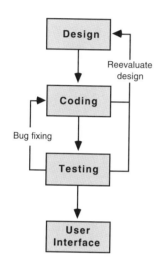

In the design phase, the requirements of the interface are identified. During this phase, several questions are asked. For example: What kinds of operations are going to be performed? What will the system look like? Will the system be designed for a specific application, or will it need to include more general capabilities? All these questions, and more, should be answered before any coding is done.

The coding phase converts the design requirements of the application into actual AML programs and menus. During this step, you'll undoubtedly encounter problems that will require redesigning certain parts of the interface.

The last step is testing and debugging your programs. This is one of the most important steps in developing a user interface. For the interface to be effective, it must be relatively free of bugs. This phase sometimes uncovers limitations of the user interface that require additional design and coding work.

EXERCISE   **Combine AML programs and menus**

Suppose that, after assessing the needs of the potential users of the database, you have found the interface needs three additional capabilities. You want to add the ability to

- Execute the menu from the AML program
- Zoom in on a specified area of the database
- Query the coverages in the database

This exercise combines the menu and AML program presented in earlier exercises to form an application that displays the coverages contained in the database. The AML programs and menu for this exercise have been provided for you and are prefixed with EX5. No editing of files is required.

calling the menu   To execute the menu from the AML program only requires that the &MENU directive be added to the end of the program. You execute EX5.AML by using &RUN.

```
Arc:  &RUN EX5.AML  9999
```

or

add the bold line to EX4.AML and &RUN EX4.AML.

The line shown in bold text below illustrates how this is done:

```
&args dev
&if [null %dev%] &then
   &return Usage: &RUN EX5 <station_file>
&else &do
   ARCPLOT
   &station %dev%

   .

   .

   .

   &menu ex5
&end  /* else do
&return
```

┌─────────┐
│ HELP   │
└─────────┘
        List the contents of EX5.MENU on the screen as you follow along with the rest of this exercise. This will allow you to see how all the pieces fit together, and how the subprograms are called from EX5.MENU. Use the following command:

```
Arc:  &POPUP EX5.AML
```

adding a zoom function

At first glance, adding a zoom function to the menu seems relatively easy; it only requires changing the map extent and drawing the coverages. But how do you know which coverages have been drawn on the screen already? Before the program can draw the coverages, it needs to know which coverages are *active*.

drawing coverages on the screen

One way of solving this problem is to define variables that indicate the status of each coverage. If the coverage is active (already drawn on the screen), the variable will have a value of ON; otherwise, the variable will be blank. You can expand the existing menu to provide On (drawn) and Off (not drawn) choices for each coverage. If you select On, the coverage is drawn on the screen, becoming an active coverage. If you select Off, the coverage is cleared from the screen and is no longer active. The menu looks like this:

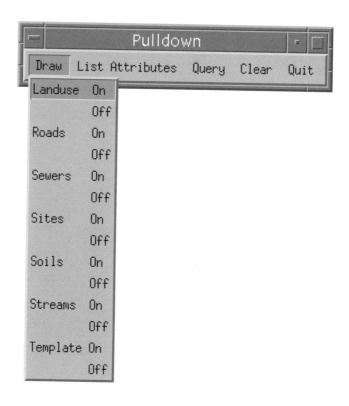

A coverage is made active (turned on) by making the appropriate menu selection. This selection causes the menu to do two things. First, the coverage status variable is updated to indicate that the coverage is active. Then, the coverage is drawn on the screen with the appropriate ARCPLOT command. For example, the menu statement to activate the LANDUSE coverage is as follows:

The menu selection sets the status variable and draws the coverage.

```
Draw
  'Landuse On' &setvar .landuse ON; POLYGONSHADES ~
              LANDUSE LU-CODE LANDUSE.LUT
```

First the global variable .LANDUSE is set to ON. Then the ARCPLOT command, POLYGONSHADES, is issued to draw the coverage. Statements that draw the other coverages are written similarly.

Turning a coverage off requires three things: resetting the status variable to indicate that the coverage is off, clearing the screen, and redrawing the active coverages. Because this is a more complex set of commands, part of it is combined in a separate AML called EX5REDRW.AML. This AML clears the screen, then uses the NULL function to determine the active coverages that must be redrawn. The AML is written as follows:

```
CLEAR
&if ^ [null %.landuse%] &then
    POLYGONSHADES LANDUSE LU-CODE LANDUSE.LUT
&if ^ [null %.soils%] &then
    POLYGONSHADES SOILS SUIT SOILS.LUT
&if ^ [null %.finalcov%] &then
    POLYGONSHADES FINALCOV 1
&if ^ [null %.roads%] &then
    ARCLINES ROADS RD-CODE ROADS.LUT
&if ^ [null %.sewers%] &then
    ARCLINES SEWERS SYMBOL
&if ^ [null %.streams%] &then
    ARCLINES STREAMS STRM-CODE STREAMS.LUT
&if ^ [null %.template%] &then
    ARCS TEMPLATE
&return
```

The ^ is a logical operator meaning NOT.

The statement in EX5.MENU to turn the LANDUSE coverage off is shown in bold type here:

```
Draw
   'Landuse    On' &setvar .landuse ON; POLYGONSHADES ~
                   LANDUSE LU-CODE LANDUSE.LUT
   '            Off' &setvar .landuse = ; &run ex5redrw
```

The global variable .LANDUSE is set to null, then EX5REDRW.AML is run to redraw the active coverages.

Now that you have a way of telling which coverages are active (i.e., coverage status variables), adding the zoom function becomes an easy task—change the map extent, then draw the active coverages. The zoom function is added to the bottom of the Draw column as shown below:

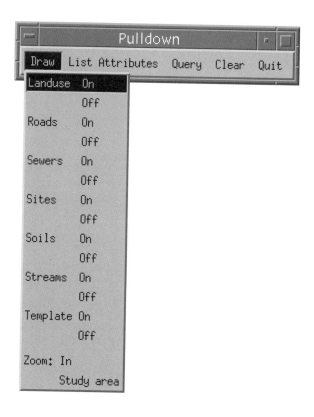

The lines of code that must be added to the Draw pulldown menu for the zoom function are shown below:

```
'Zoom:   In' &type Enter two diagonal corners of ~
the zoom area; MAPEXTENT *; &r ex5redrw
    '           Study area' MAPEXTENT LANDUSE; &r ex5redrw
```

Selecting 'Zoom: In' from the menu prompts you to enter two opposing corners of a box defining the zoom area. The ARCPLOT MAPEXTENT command displays the graphics cursor and waits for the user to identify the new area to view. Once set, all active coverages are redrawn using EX5REDRW.AML. An additional menu option, Zoom: Study area, returns the display to the entire study area. This option resets the map extent to the LANDUSE coverage and redraws all active coverages.

adding a query function　　The query function identifies a feature in a coverage and lists its attributes. For example, you could identify the land use or soil type of a particular area, or determine whether a stream is classified as major or minor. To perform the query operation, the menu can be modified by adding a new pulldown column after the List Attributes column:

You can perform the query using the ARCPLOT IDENTIFY command along with the appropriate coverage name and feature class.

The following text added to the menu file will create a Query column:

```
Query
    Landuse IDENTIFY LANDUSE POLY *
    Roads   IDENTIFY ROADS ARC *
    Streams IDENTIFY SEWERS ARC *
    Sites   IDENTIFY FINALCOV POLY *
    Soils   IDENTIFY SOILS POLY *
    Streams IDENTIFY STREAMS ARC *
```

This method presents a problem because if the coverage is not already drawn on the screen, the user cannot select features. But this problem has already been solved. As with the zoom function, the coverage status variables (e.g., .LANDUSE) can indicate whether the coverage can be queried. If the coverage is active, the query can be performed; if it is not active, an error message is returned.

So instead of directly performing the IDENTIFY from the menu, an AML that uses the &IF directive to verify that the coverage is active is called. For example, the following lines identify a land use polygon:

Check whether the coverage is active before identifying a land use polygon.

```
&if [null %.landuse%] &then &do
  &type The coverage is not an active coverage.  Please
  &type activate the coverage using the 'Draw' column.
&end
&else IDENTIFY LANDUSE POLY *
&return
```

In the above AML code, the IDENTIFY is performed only when the coverage is active as indicated by the coverage status variable, in this case, LANDUSE.

This particular application could include a separate AML to query each coverage and run the appropriate one depending upon the coverage you want to query. However, it may not be efficient to have one AML for each operation you want to perform. The following AML, EX5QRY.AML, shows how one AML can query any of the coverages:

The coverage name and feature class to identify are passed as arguments to the program.

```
&args cover feature
&severity &error &ignore
&type \\\\
&if [null [value .%cover%]] &then &do
   &type The coverage is not an active coverage. Please
   &type activate the coverage using the 'Draw' column.
&end
&else &do &until %aml$sev% = 0
   /* the aml$sev reserved variable is used to confirm
   /* that a feature has been located.  The loop
   /* terminates once a feature has been identified.
   &type \Point to the feature to identify
   IDENTIFY %cover% %feature% *
&end
&return
```

For the AML to work with all coverages, the coverage name and feature class are passed as arguments to the program. The program uses these arguments to identify a feature in the specified coverage.

Run the application to see how it works. At the `Arc:` prompt enter:

`Arc: &RUN EX5 <station_file>`

replacing <station> with the name of your station file.

To change the viewing area, select **Draw** and choose **Zoom: In**.

With the screen cursor, enter opposing corners of a box that defines the area to be viewed. The zoom area will then be drawn on the screen. To reset the viewing area to the whole study area:

Select **Draw** and choose **Zoom: Study area**.

To query the land use type of a particular area, you must first make the LANDUSE coverage an active coverage.

Select **Draw** and choose **Landuse On**. To perform the query, select **Query** and choose **Landuse**.

Position the screen cursor inside the land use polygon you want to identify. The land use information is displayed.

Try using the menu on your own to see how the interface works. For example, see what happens when you try to query a coverage that is not drawn on the screen.

When you finish using the menu, select **Quit** to leave the menu and exit ARCPLOT.

END

Summary

The ARC Macro Language (AML) is the language through which you communicate in the ARC environment. AML provides full programming capabilities and a set of tools to tailor the user interface of your application. AML can be used throughout the ARC system to perform a variety of tasks. AML allows you to automate frequently performed actions, create your own commands, provide startup utilities to help new or inexperienced users perform operations that require specific command settings, and develop menu-driven user interfaces to meet the needs of end users.

This lesson introduced you to some of the basic capabilities of AML for making your GIS projects more efficient. You saw how AML programs organize a sequence of ARC/INFO commands into sophisticated geoprocessing operations, and how AML menus provide the basis for combining these operations into a structured, easy-to-use, graphical user interface. Specifically, you saw how:

- AML automates a process by providing the ability to string together ARC commands.

- A menu provides an alternative method for executing commands.

- Directives, functions, and variables create more flexible AML programs.

- AML programs and menus integrate to create a user interface.

The following table summarizes some of the syntactical features of AML:

Feature	Represented by	Example
Variable	%	%.xmax%
Directive	&	&args dev
Function	[ ]	[null %dev%]
Line separation	;	EF ARC; SELECT ONE
Line continuation	~	&type hello ~ there

The figures on the following pages illustrate some of the AML capabilities that this lesson discussed.

AML Program Summary

Comment statements - used to document the program

&ARGS - allows the program to accept arguments

NULL - expression indicating whether the variable is blank

&IF - flow of control directive to perform logical branching

&DO - delimits a block of statements that can be performed repeatedly

&STATION - sets the terminal and display device

GETCHOICE - displays a menu of choices from which a selection can be made

&DALINES - sets the number of dialog lines

&SETVAR - creates a variable

SHOW - queries a program returning information about a specified environment

&END - terminates an &DO block

VARIABLES - used for value assignment; global variables are preceeded by a period and can be passed between AML programs

&RETURN - terminates the AML program

```
/* EX4.AML - displays coverages from the
/* database.  The user is prompted for an
/* &STATION file and whether color or black
/* and white shades are to be used

&args dev
&if [null %dev%] &then
    &return Usage: &RUN EX4 <station_file>
&else &do
    ARCPLOT
    &station %dev%
    &dalines 4
    SHADESET [getchoice color bw -prompt ~
    'Select Color or Black & White shades:']
    MAPEXTENT TEMPLATE
    /* set map limits to screen size
    &setvar .xmax := [extract 1 [show pagesize]]
    &setvar .ymax := [extract 2 [show pagesize]] - .2
    MAPLIMITS 0 1 %.xmax% %.ymax%
    MAPPOSITION CEN CEN
    ARCS TEMPLATE
    ARCLINES ROADS RD-CODE ROADS.LUT
    RESELECT FINALCOV POLY SUITABLE = 1
    POLYGONSHADES FINALCOV 1
&end  /* else do
&return
```

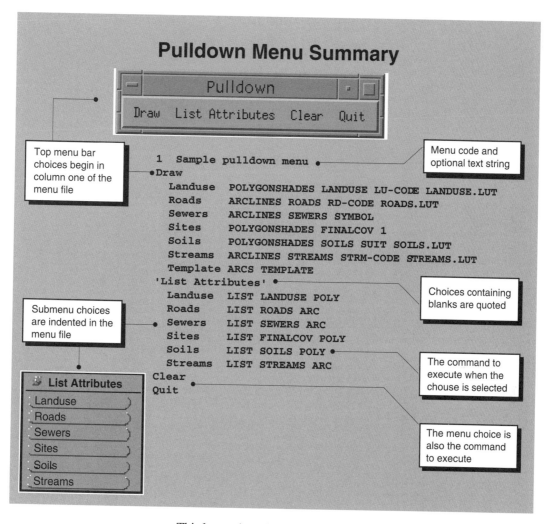

Pulldown Menu Summary

Top menu bar choices begin in column one of the menu file

Menu code and optional text string

Submenu choices are indented in the menu file

Choices containing blanks are quoted

The command to execute when the chouse is selected

The menu choice is also the command to execute

```
1  Sample pulldown menu
Draw
   Landuse   POLYGONSHADES LANDUSE LU-CODE LANDUSE.LUT
   Roads     ARCLINES ROADS RD-CODE ROADS.LUT
   Sewers    ARCLINES SEWERS SYMBOL
   Sites     POLYGONSHADES FINALCOV 1
   Soils     POLYGONSHADES SOILS SUIT SOILS.LUT
   Streams   ARCLINES STREAMS STRM-CODE STREAMS.LUT
   Template ARCS TEMPLATE
'List Attributes'
   Landuse   LIST LANDUSE POLY
   Roads     LIST ROADS ARC
   Sewers    LIST SEWERS ARC
   Sites     LIST FINALCOV POLY
   Soils     LIST SOILS POLY
   Streams   LIST STREAMS ARC
Clear
Quit
```

List Attributes
- Landuse
- Roads
- Sewers
- Sites
- Soils
- Streams

This lesson introduced the basic capabilities of AML. AML, however, offers much more. With AML, users can build a GIS dashboard to control the working environment. Multiple menus—and multiple menu types—can be displayed on the screen simultaneously. AML menus can make use of interactive, visual features like buttons, slider bars, check boxes, and icons (e.g., the menu system used in Lesson 1). The possibilities are almost unlimited.

For more detailed information about AML, refer to online help under *Customizing ARC/INFO-->AML* and *Customizing ARC/INFO -->Using FormEdit*. You will also find the online *Command References* for AML helpful.

What next?

Congratulations! You've completed a simplified version of the type of GIS application project that takes 12 months for most GIS users. You've learned a lot. Now where do you go from here?

Besides experience, you'll need more training to become a truly effective user of GIS. Additional training falls into three areas: using ARC/INFO, applying GIS solutions, and managing a GIS organization. This section provides some guidance on how to proceed.

ARC/INFO classes

ESRI has a comprehensive education program to support users of its family of vector and raster GIS software products. The curriculum includes 12 courses covering introductory and advanced topics related to using ARC/INFO software.

In the United States, classes are offered at the ESRI Learning Center at Redlands, California, and at ten ESRI regional training facilities across the country. In addition, a network of 500 ESRI-authorized instructors teaches classes in association with ESRI's international subsidiaries and distributors in 72 countries around the world.

For more information about classes in the United States, contact:

ESRI Learning Center
380 New York Street
Redlands, California 92373-8100
Telephone (909) 335-8233; Fax: (909) 335-8233
E-mail: edu_registration@esri.com.
Internet: www.esri.com

Outside the United States, contact your local ARC/INFO distributor for course offerings and class schedules.

Introduction to ARC/INFO

This five-day course teaches the basics of GIS and ARC/INFO. Designed around a typical GIS project, the course illustrates GIS concepts, functions, and considerations. It prepares students to conduct their own pilot projects. Students receive specific instruction in the basic operation of ARC, ARCEDIT, ARCPLOT, and TABLES software.

Advanced ARC/INFO
This course gives students who need to broaden their range of skills the hands-on experience they need. Students learn techniques for relating and managing tabular data in ARC/INFO, modeling linear data, creating and using regions, creating and editing symbols, displaying images, creating annotation, and producing quality map products.

Customizing ARC/INFO with AML
This five-day course introduces students to the functionality of the ARC Marco Language (AML) and its associated menu interfaces. It's designed for ARC/INFO users who want to increase productivity and programmers who want to create large applications using AML. Using the basic programming concepts, techniques, and practices learned in class, students design an application, then build menus and write AML programs to implement it.

Using ARC GRID with ARC/INFO
This five-day course gives students the hands-on experience and technical background they need to understand raster GIS and perform cell-based modeling using ARC/INFO GRID software. The course emphasizes using GRID for editing, managing, analyzing, and displaying geographic data. Topics include an in-depth discussion of the operators, functions, commands, and conversion routines that make up the Map Algebra that GRID uses to analyze cell-based data. Students use GRID tools for dispersion, least-cost path, and spatial coincidence modeling of real-world problems.

ARC/INFO Database Design
This five-day course teaches methods for designing an ARC/INFO database and strategies for determining project scope, resource requirements, and user's needs. Students learn a generic process for building a well-designed, integrated database using both conceptual and physical design steps. Database considerations such as scale, resolution, coordinate systems, and map projections are discussed.

ARC/INFO Software Extensions
Using ARC NETWORK, Using ARC TIN, Using ARC COGO, Using ArcStorm , and *Using ArcScan* are five, one-day courses offered the same week. Students can register for any number of days. These five courses address topics related to ARC/INFO's optional software extensions and are described as follows:

Using ARC NETWORK ™
This one-day course will interest experienced ARC/INFO users whose applications deal with the movement of goods and services through spatial networks. Lectures and online exercises teach the ARC/INFO NETWORK tools for analyzing optimal paths (e.g., routing vehicles), distributing resources to centers, assigning demand to sites, locating sites based on demand and distance, geocoding addresses, and estimating the interaction potential between population and centers of attraction.

Using ARC TIN ™
This one-day course is intended for all ARC/INFO users who analyze and display surface-derived data in their GIS applications. The class covers using the triangulated irregular network (TIN) and lattice data models for generating surfaces from sample points and discusses the advantages of each. Topics include editing and filtering surfaces and generating contours, cross sections, and visibility and perspective drawings.

Using ARC COGO ™
This one-day course teaches the collection of tools for automating survey data. Students learn the interactive entry and data conversion methods for automating survey data. Students also learn to use the tools for adding features to a COGO coverage and the tools for generating reports about COGO coverages. Other topics include entering traverses, adding curves, setting COGO environments and tolerances, and using COGO attributes.

Using ArcStorm ™
ArcStorm (ARC Storage Manager) is a comprehensive database manager for spatial information. This one-day course teaches how to access and maintain coverages and INFO™ files stored in ArcStorm databases. Students also learn how ArcStorm manages tables stored in proprietary database management systems. Topics include handling complex transactions, managing transactions and maintaining a historic record, creating historical views of the database, and performing database rollbacks.

Using ArcScan ™
ArcScan is a set of software tools that provide raster-to-vector conversion and raster editing capabilities. This one-day course teaches students how to create vector data from scanned raster imagery. In addition, students learn how to geometrically correct images, georeference images, use raster editing tools, convert raster data to vector data, use automated tracing tools, and create soft-and hard-copy raster displays.

self-study workbooks

ARC Macro Language—
Developing ARC/INFO menus and macros with AML™

This self-study workbook is essential reading for professionals, researchers and college students who want to build ARC/INFO applications. It teaches the ARC Macro Language (AML™) in the context of accomplishing practical ARC/INFO tasks. The workbook covers the basics for those who are either new to programming or using AML and teaches the advanced techniques that those who already use AML want to know. *ARC Macro Language—Developing ARC/INFO menus and macros with AML* is full of tips and tricks for using AML to its potential.

To order the *ARC Macro Language—Developing ARC/INFO menus and Macros with AML* or additional copies of *Understanding GIS—The ARC/INFO Method* call (800) 447-9778

ArcTools menu interface

Throughout this workbook, you've applied the ARC/INFO command language to perform various GIS tasks. As an alternative, a series of menu systems named ArcTools is available. ArcTools is a general purpose, menu-based interface to ARC/INFO designed to get new users started quickly and to make all users more productive at performing common geoprocessing tasks. Common operations such as mapping, query, data automation, and analysis are implemented through a series of AML-based tools and menus.

You can get acquainted with ArcTools by working through the ArcTools tutorial in the *Getting Started* users' guide. Also refer to online help under *Getting started-->Working with ArcTools*.

documentation

Continue using the training and concepts guides and online help introduced in this workbook. They contain a tremendous amount of information for learning and using ARC/INFO.

Getting Started covers the ARC/INFO data model and introduces the online tutorials that cover basic ARC/INFO concepts and teach ArcTools.

Two of the printed books included with your ARC/INFO software cover key GIS and mapping concepts. *ARC/INFO Data Management* describes spatial data concepts and how they are implemented by ARC/INFO. *Map Projections & Coordinate Management* introduces the concepts behind mapping and map projections and defines the technical characteristics that define maps and map accuracy.

Online help covers all aspects of the ARC/INFO, including the use of extension products such as ArcStorm and GRID. Online help provides software documentation, concepts, step-by-step procedures and command references in an easy-to-use format. Online help also includes online versions of all the printed documents included in the ARC/INFO package, except this workbook.

regional and local user groups

In addition to attending formal training courses, it's invaluable to establish relationships with other users who are performing similar applications work. In particular, we recommend that you get involved with your regional or local ARC/INFO User Group.

Many users meet as regional or local groups to exchange ideas, data, AML macros, and procedures with each other. Users help each other by sharing information. Get in touch with other GIS individuals involved in applying ARC/INFO in your area. User groups exist in the U.S., Canada, Australia, and throughout Europe and Asia. In addition, the Higher Education User Group is open to those who teach and use ARC/INFO at the college and university level.

In the United States, users interested in getting involved in a regional or local ARC/INFO User Group should call ESRI at 909-793-2853 and ask for the User Group Coordinator, or contact the ESRI regional office for their area. Outside the United States, users should contact their ARC/INFO distributor.

ESRI regional offices

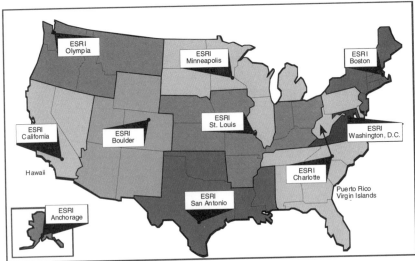

ESRI-Alaska (907) 344-6613

ESRI-California (909) 793-2853

ESRI-Boulder (303) 449-7779

ESRI-Olympia (360) 754-4727

ESRI-St. Louis (314) 949-6620

ESRI-Boston (508) 777-4543

ESRI-Charlotte (704) 541-9810

ESRI-Minneapolis (612) 454-0600

ESRI-San Antonio (210) 340-5762

ESRI-Washington D.C. (703) 506-9515

ESRI on the Internet

Visit ESRI's web site at www.esri.com and get the latest information about GIS software and technology. ESRI provides public forums where ARC/INFO users with varying levels of experience can ask questions and exchange technical information. Discussion threads often occur about various topics. Periodically, ESRI posts release news for users as well. For more information on these services, consult the *ARC/INFO Support Services* brochure packaged with ARC/INFO software.

ESRI User Conference   The ESRI User Conference is held every year in the Spring. This conference is the largest gathering of technical GIS staff in the world. It provides an extraordinary forum to improve your technical, management, and professional skills for working with GIS. The information gained at the technical sessions, demonstrations, and workshops makes attendance at the conference invaluable for both beginning and experienced users.

You're a member of a rapidly expanding field in which the growth of GIS hardware and software is out-pacing the supply of qualified, experienced personnel to run these systems. The knowledge and experience you gain will make you a valuable asset, and you can contribute to real solutions that ultimately affect the way we live.

Welcome to the ARC/INFO user community.

Appendix A Confirming training data installation

If you aren't sure whether the training data was installed on your system, confirm the installation using the following instructions.

To confirm the installation, you must first attach to the TRAINING directory. This directory contains all the coverages and files necessary to complete the lessons in the workbook. Attach to this directory by typing:

UNIX   `%  cd $AIDATA/training/ugis`
Windows NT   `Arc:  &workspace  %aidata%\training\ugis`

HELP

If the UGIS data is not loaded on your system, you can copy the data from the CD packaged with this book.

UNIX

Mount the CD-rom drive on your computer and issue the following commands. (Check with your system administrator, if you do not know how to mount a CD drive.)

```
mkdir<your_name>
cd<your_name>
cp -r <cdrom_device>/unix/ugis ugis
```

Windows NT

Use the Windows NT File Manager to create a directory with your name and copy the data from the nt directory on the CD to the new directory

or

Click on the ARC/INFO icon in the ARC/INFO program group to start ARC.

From the `Arc:` prompt issue the following commands.

```
Arc: cw <yourname>
Arc: w <yourname>
Arc: &sys xcopy <drive:>\nt\ugis\*.*
         ugis\*.* /s/e/v
```

Now list the contents of the directory:

UNIX   `%  ls`
Windows NT `Arc: &sys dir`

The directory should contain the following subdirectories:

AML—contains AML files
DATA—contains the input coverages and files for the exercises
RESULTS—contains coverages and files created by completing an exercise

---

| HELP |

The installation guide, which accompanies the training data tape, recommends that the Sample data set be installed as a top-level directory. On UNIX-based systems, the variable AIDATA contains the pathname where the Sample data is installed. Windows NT systems use the aidata logical. If AIDATA is not set, or if the TRAINING directory does not exist, consult your system administrator. Because the Sample data is not required to run ARC/INFO, it may not have been installed. Refer to the installation instructions which accompanied the Samples CD.

Check our discussion forum at www.esri.com/esribooks. Go to the Understanding GIS (UNIX, Windows NT) conference. You'll find postings of any new information that wasn't available at the time the book was published. You'll also find user discussions relating to the book and CD.

The files and coverages each directory contains are shown on the next page.

```
                              $AIDATA
         ┌──────┬──────────┬──────────┬──────────┐
      demos   icons    training    misc      tour
                                                │
                                              ugis
                              ┌─────────────────┼─────────────────┐
                             aml              data            results
                        adi_zoom.aml      border.map        buffcov
                        adi_zoom.icon     clipcov           bufro100
                        analysis.aml      covlist           elimcov
                        analysis.menu     intro.aml         ex3.aml
                        buffer.aml        labmap.key        ex4.aml
                        buffer.menu       labplot.key       final.rep
                        clear.aml         landcn            finalcov
                        corners32.icon    landtr            georef01
                        draw.aml          landuse           geoutm02
                        draw.menu         landuse.key       inlanbuf
                        drawcover.aml     linkcov           label.err
                        drawother.aml     luat10            lab.map
                        drawother.menu    northarr          landat05
                        ex1.aml           roads             landbd04
                        ex2.menu          sewers            landcn.gra
                        ex5.aml           soils             landcn02
                        ex5.menu          streams           landnode.gra
                        ex5qry.aml        streams.lin       landcp07
                        ex5clr.aml        streams.tab       landdg01
                        ex5redraw.aml     template          landds10
                        focus.aml         ulogo             landed
                        hourgls32.icon    info              landed03
                        inform32.icon                       landem08
                        main.menu                           landmj09
                        modal.aml                           landsoil
                        msinform.aml                         landtr06
                        msinform.menu                        landuse
                        msworking.aml                        my.aml
                        msworking.menu                       my.wat
                        orig32.icon                          node.err
                        othercheck.aml                       rd.key
                        pan32.icon                           sewerbuf
                        projdb.menu                          sites.gra
                        projdb.aml                           sites.map
                        query.aml                            strmat03
                        query.menu                           strmbd02
                        quit.aml                             strmbuf
                        redraw.aml                           strmgn01
                        select.aml                           ticcov
                        select.cpy                           info
                        select.menu
                        stats.aml
                        stats.menu
                        switchcheck.aml
                        tool.aml
                        zoom.menu
                        zoomin32.icon
                        zoomout32.icon
                        zoomsel32.icon
```

Appendix B Project database

The data used for performing geographic analysis and presenting the results in Lessons 8 and 9 are for a hypothetical situation and location. The database provided consists of six data layers: regions of land use, roads, sewer lines, zones of different soil types, streams, and the outline of the study area. Each coverage layer represents thematic data for the same geographic location, as shown by the diagram below.

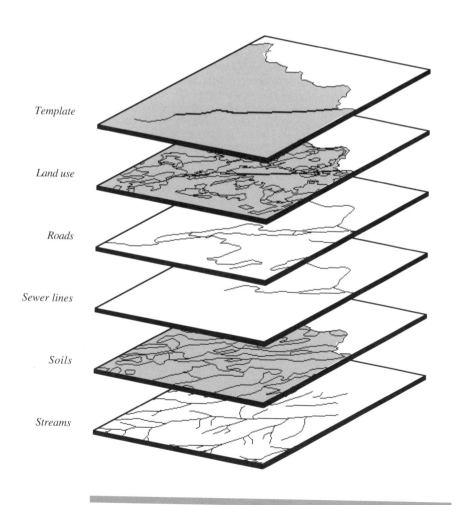

Template

Land use

Roads

Sewer lines

Soils

Streams

coverages   All coverages and their feature attribute tables are located in the following directory:

UNIX   `training/ugis/data`
Windows NT   `\training\ugis\data`

This directory contains a geographic database composed of six related coverages. Each coverage represents a thematic layer of data registered to the same geographic location. The following list describes each coverage and the included feature type.

TEMPLATE	polygons	Defines tics, study area, and coastline.
LANDUSE	polygons	Specifies existing land use codes.
ROADS	arcs	Identifies all roads and codes them.
SEWERS	arcs	Identifies the sewer lines and codes them.
SOILS	polygons	Classifies soils by type and suitability.
STREAMS	arcs	Identifies all streams and codes them.

Each coverage is further described in the pages that follow, including diagrams of each coverage layer, item definitions, and keys to the coded attributes.

automation history   The data was automated into a standardized template with a boundary defined by reference values of latitude and longitude. Longitude values extended from -74° 00' 00" to -73° 58' 30", and latitudes extended from 41° 03' 00" to 41° 04' 30". It was then processed using a fuzzy tolerance of 0.003 inches (digitizer units).

study area   The extreme coordinates of this study area are as follows:

XMIN	YMIN	XMAX	YMAX
4,008.982	4,577.147	6,141.984	7,376.990

projection data   The coordinate system of this data set can be defined using the following values:

```
PROJECTION UTM
UNITS METERS
ZONE 18
XSHIFT -580000
YSHIFT -4540000
```

TEMPLATE

This coverage uses polygons to define the coastline and the boundary of the study area. Each of the related data layers has been clipped with this boundary.

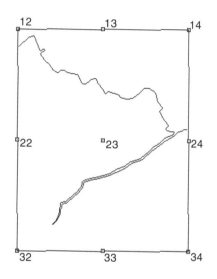

TEMPLATE.TIC   All data layers have the same set of tics. The coordinate values for these nine tics are listed below:

RECORD	IDTIC	XTIC	YTIC
1	12	4,008.982	7,352.600
2	13	5,058.853	7,364.715
3	14	6,109.365	7,376.990
4	22	4,024.895	5,964.872
5	23	5,074.965	5,976.987
6	24	6,125.677	5,989.261
7	32	4,040.805	4,577.147
8	33	5,091.074	4,589.262
9	34	6,141.984	4,601.535

LANDUSE

This coverage layer is composed of 76 polygons describing the land uses for specific regions within the study area.

LANDUSE polygons

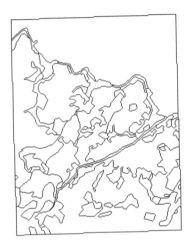

item definitions for LANDUSE.PAT

COLUMN	ITEM NAME	WIDTH	OUTPUT	TYPE	N.DEC
1	AREA	4	12	F	3
5	PERIMETER	4	12	F	3
9	LANDUSE#	4	5	B	--
13	LANDUSE-ID	4	5	B	--
17	LU-CODE	3	3	I	--
20	COST/HA	6	6	I	--

The LU-CODE item is used to store various land use codes, and the COST/HA item lists approximate values of the land. These values were determined by the assessor's office and range from 10,000 to 40,000.

contents of LANDUSE.LUT

The LU-CODE values have been defined in the LANDUSE.LUT lookup table, an INFO file containing three items.

COLUMN	ITEM NAME	WIDTH	OUTPUT	TYPE	N.DEC
1	LU-CODE	3	3	I	--
4	LABEL	12	12	C	--
16	SYMBOL	3	3	I	--

coding classifications   The LU-CODE attribute stores one of seven land use categories for each region. Note that these codes can also be used to distinguish land and water.

RECORD	LU-CODE	LABEL	SYMBOL
1	100	Urban	14
2	200	Agriculture	7
3	300	Brushland	8
4	400	Forest	3
5	500	Water	4
6	600	Wetlands	5
7	700	Barren	15

ROADS

This coverage layer has 45 lines that define each road in the area. Their attribute values can be used to differentiate between improved and semi-improved road conditions.

ROADS arcs

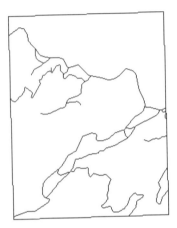

The outline of the study area is not part of this coverage.

item definitions for
ROADS.AAT

COLUMN	ITEM NAME	WIDTH	OUTPUT	TYPE	N.DEC
1	FNODE#	4	5	B	-
5	TNODE#	4	5	B	-
9	LPOLY#	4	5	B	-
13	RPOLY#	4	5	B	-
17	LENGTH	4	12	F	3
21	ROADS#	4	5	B	-
25	ROADS-ID	4	5	B	-
29	RD-CODE	1	1	I	-

contents of
ROADS.LUT

The RD-CODE values have been defined in the ROADS.LUT lookup table, an INFO file containing three items.

COLUMN	ITEM NAME	WIDTH	OUTPUT	TYPE	N.DEC
1	RD-CODE	1	1	I	-
2	LABEL	14	14	C	-
16	SYMBOL	3	3	I	-

coding classifications

The RD-CODE uses two values to differentiate road conditions.

RECORD	RD-CODE	LABEL	SYMBOL
1	1	Improved	10
2	2	Semi-improved	78

Understanding GIS—The ARC/INFO Method

SEWERS

This coverage layer uses six arcs to describe all sewer lines in the study area. Their attribute values can be used to differentiate primary and secondary lines.

SEWERS arcs

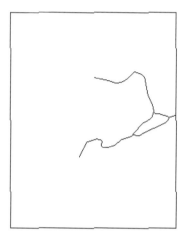

The outline of the study area is not part of this coverage.

item definitions for
SEWERS.AAT

COLUMN	ITEM NAME	WIDTH	OUTPUT	TYPE	N.DEC
1	FNODE#	4	5	B	-
5	TNODE#	4	5	B	-
9	LPOLY#	4	5	B	-
13	RPOLY#	4	5	B	-
17	LENGTH	4	12	F	3
21	SEWERS#	4	5	B	-
25	SEWERS-ID	4	5	B	-
29	DIAMETER	2	2	I	-
31	SYMBOL	3	3	I	-

coding classifications
for SEWERS.AAT

The primary sewer lines have a larger diameter than the secondary ones, so they can be differentiated by their DIAMETER values (60 and 45, respectively) or their SYMBOL values (1 and 77, respectively).

SOILS

The study area contains 43 soil polygons classified by soil type and suitability for development.

SOILS polygons

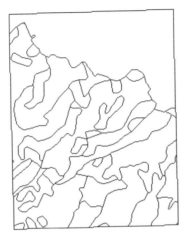

item definitions for
SOILS.PAT

COLUMN	ITEM NAME	WIDTH	OUTPUT	TYPE	N.DEC
1	AREA	4	12	F	3
5	PERIMETER	4	12	F	3
9	SOILS#	4	5	B	–
13	SOILS-ID	4	5	B	–
17	SOIL-CODE	3	3	C	–
20	SUIT	1	1	I	–

coding classifications
for SOILS.PAT

The SOIL-CODE represents a specific type of soil. These are listed below, along with their associated suitability rating.

SOIL-CODE	SUIT
Id1	2
Id3	1
Ko	3
Ns1	2
Ns2	1
Ns3	1
Sg	3
Ss	2
Tn4	2

contents of SOILS.LUT   The SUIT values have been defined in the SOILS.LUT lookup table, an INFO file containing three items.

COLUMN	ITEM NAME	WIDTH	OUTPUT	TYPE	N.DEC
1	SUIT	1	1	I	-
2	LABEL	16	16	C	-
18	SYMBOL	3	3	I	-

coding classifications
for suitability   The SUIT codes represent the soil's suitability for developing foundations.

RECORD	SUIT	LABEL	SYMBOL
1	0	Not Suitable	0
2	1	Poor Suitability	72
3	2	Mod Suitability	44
4	3	Good Suitability	44

STREAMS

This coverage layer uses 106 arcs to describe all streams in the study area. Their attribute values can be used to differentiate major and minor streams.

STREAMS arcs

The outline of the study area is not part of this coverage.

item definitions for
STREAMS.AAT

COLUMN	ITEM NAME	WIDTH	OUTPUT	TYPE	N.DEC
1	FNODE#	4	5	B	-
5	TNODE#	4	5	B	-
9	LPOLY#	4	5	B	-
13	RPOLY#	4	5	B	-
17	LENGTH	4	12	F	3
21	STREAMS#	4	5	B	-
25	STREAMS-ID	4	5	B	-
29	STRM-CODE	1	1	I	-

contents of
STREAMS.LUT

The STRM-CODE values have been defined in the STREAMS.LUT lookup table, an INFO file containing three items.

COLUMN	ITEM NAME	WIDTH	OUTPUT	TYPE	N.DEC
1	STRM-CODE	1	1	I	-
2	LABEL	6	6	C	-
8	SYMBOL	3	3	I	-

coding classifications

This item uses codes values to differentiate major and minor streams.

RECORD	STRM-CODE	LABEL	SYMBOL
1	1	Major	16
2	2	Minor	8

Appendix C Map sheets

Use the reference grid of latitude and longitude to locate the study area in real-world coordinates. There are a total of nine tics, with ID values as indicated.

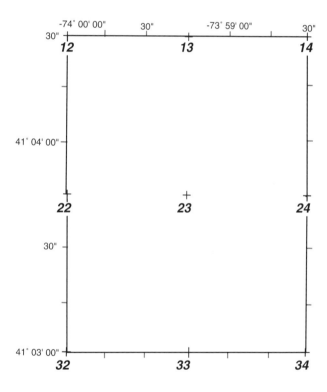

∇ FYI Depending on the map projection, lines of latitude and longitude are not necessarily straight lines on a base map. Don't interpolate these values by measuring along straight lines drawn between the known tics printed on your map. Refer *Map Projections & Coordinate Management*.

Database status chart

Use this chart to track the status of your database. Check off the appropriate box as each step is completed. The processing for the STREAMS coverage occurs in the advanced exercises in Lessons 4 through 6.

Coverage name	Digitized/ converted	Topology created	Edited	Attributes added	Projected	Transformed to real-world coordinates	Mapjoined
SOILS	√	√	√	√	√	√	√
LANDUSE	☐	☐	☐	☐	☐	☐	☐
STREAMS	☐	☐	☐	☐	√	√	n/a
SEWERS	√	√	√	√	√	√	√
ROADS	√	√	√	√	√	√	√

Land use map manuscript *This edge will be up when mounted on the digitizer.*

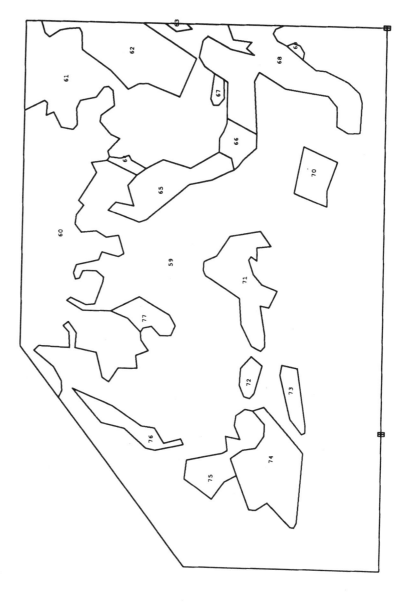

Map layout for final map

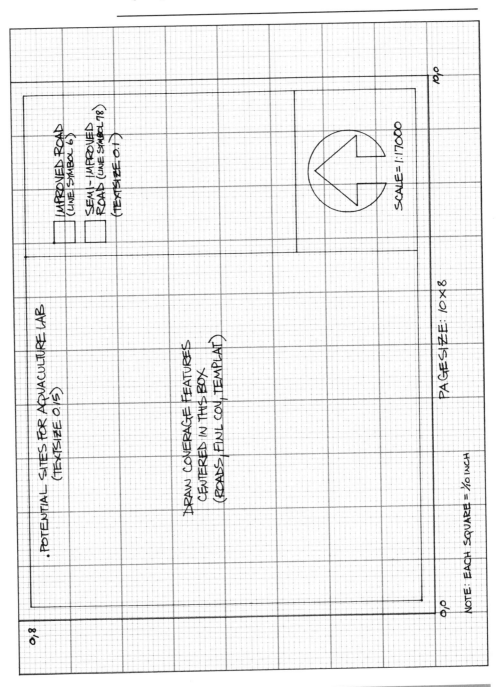

Appendix D Answers to written exercises

Following are the answers to the written exercises contained in Lessons 2, 3, 4, 5 and 9.

Lesson 2

EXERCISE Define map features

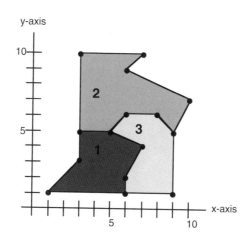

Polygon	x,y pairs
1	1,1 3,3 3,5 5,5 7,4 6,2 6,1 1,1
2	3,5 3,10 7,10 6,9 10,7 9,5 8,6 6,6 5,5 3,5
3	6,1 6,2 7,4 5,5 6,6 8,6 9,5 9,1 6,1

Lesson 2

EXERCISE   **Generate topology**

Roads map

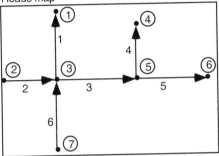

Arc	From node	To node
1	3	1
2	2	3
3	3	5
4	5	4
5	5	6
6	7	3

Path from Node 6 to Node 1

Arc #	5	3	1		
Direction	−	−	+		

+ = from- to to-node

− = to- to from-node

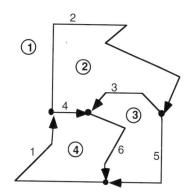

polygon	# of arcs	list of arcs
2	3	2, 3, 4
3	3	3, 5, 6
4	3	1, 4, 6

arc	left polygon	right polygon
1	1	4
2	1	2
3	3	2
4	2	4
5	1	3
6	3	4

Lesson 2

EXERCISE   Organize the data

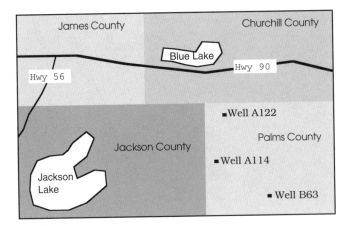

layer	feature type
LAKES	POLYGON
HIGHWAYS	LINE
WELLS	POINT
COUNTIES	POLYGON

Lesson 2

EXERCISE Use the identifier to connect features with attributes and to relate two tables

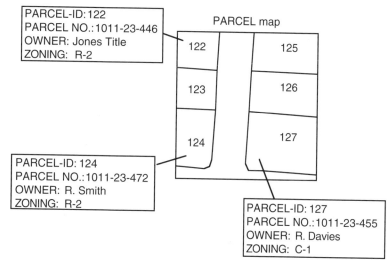

PARCEL-ID:122
PARCEL NO.:1011-23-446
OWNER: Jones Title
ZONING: R-2

PARCEL map

PARCEL-ID: 124
PARCEL NO.:1011-23-472
OWNER: R. Smith
ZONING: R-2

PARCEL-ID: 127
PARCEL NO.:1011-23-455
OWNER: R. Davies
ZONING: C-1

Assessor's parcel list

ID	PARCEL NO.	OWNER	ZONING
122	1011-23-446	Jones Title	R-2
123	1011-23-440	Jones Title	R-1
124	1011-23-472	R. Smith	R-2
125	1011-23-547	S. Brown	R-2
126	1011-23-511	J. Stevens	C-1
127	1011-23-455	R. Davies	C-1

STREET	VALUE	PARCEL NO.
Orange	101,000	1011-23-547
Lemon	145,000	1011-23-455
Orange	98,500	1011-23-446
Orange	128,000	1011-23-511
Lemon	139,000	1011-23-472
Orange	100,500	1011-23-440

PARCEL NO.	OWNER	ZONING
1011-23-446	Jones Title	R-2
1011-23-440	Jones Title	R-1
1011-23-472	R. Smith	R-2
1011-23-547	S. Brown	R-2
1011-23-511	J. Stevens	C-1
1011-23-455	R. Davies	C-1

Lesson 3

EXERCISE   Identify the required data layers for the project

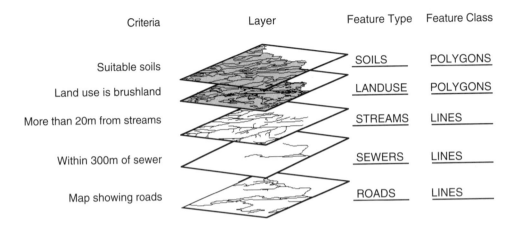

Criteria	Layer	Feature Type	Feature Class
Suitable soils		SOILS	POLYGONS
Land use is brushland		LANDUSE	POLYGONS
More than 20m from streams		STREAMS	LINES
Within 300m of sewer		SEWERS	LINES
Map showing roads		ROADS	LINES

Lesson 3

EXERCISE   Create a master TIC file

Tic-ID	x-coordinate	y-coordinate
12	-74° 00' 00"	41° 04' 30"
13	-73° 59' 15"	41° 04' 30"
14	-73° 58' 30"	41° 04' 30"
22	-74° 00' 00"	41° 03' 45"
23	-73° 59' 15"	41° 03' 45"
24	-73° 58' 30"	41° 03' 45"
32	-74° 00' 00"	41° 03' 00"
33	-73° 59' 15"	41° 03' 00"
34	-73° 58' 30"	41° 03' 00"

Lesson 4

EXERCISE

Prepare map manuscript for automation

Your prepared map manuscript should look something like this:

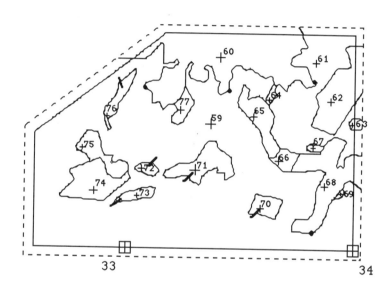

Lesson 5

EXERCISE Identify edits to be made

You should have been able to identify the following errors:

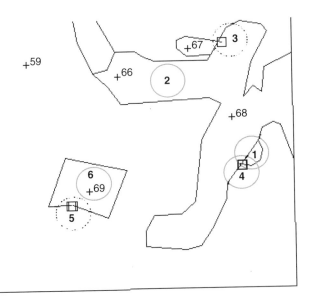

1 Missing label point
2 Polygon with two label points due to a missing arc
3 Dangling node due to an overshoot arc
4 Dangling node due to an undershoot arc
5 Dangling nodes due to an unclosed island polygon
6 Label point with wrong label User-ID

Lesson 9

EXERCISE   List the required information to be displayed on the map

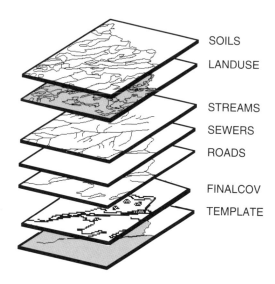

SOILS
LANDUSE

STREAMS
SEWERS
ROADS

FINALCOV
TEMPLATE

List here the three prominent coverages that will be included in the map:

ROADS

FINALCOV

TEMPLATE

Lesson 9

EXERCISE   Lay out the final map

The coordinates of the area where the coverage features will be drawn	
minimum x-coordinate:	0.25
minimum y-coordinate:	0.25
maximum x-coordinate:	6.75
maximum y-coordinate:	7.75

Map element	x-coordinate	y-coordinate
The upper left corner of the top legend box	7.0	7.2
The lower left corner of the first title line	0.8	7.4

Appendix E ARC/INFO sample maps

This appendix contains maps illustrating GIS applications—from natural resource studies to regional planning. The maps were created using many of the same procedures and ARC/INFO commands used in this workbook. They exemplify many of the components of map layout and design. We thank the ARC/INFO users who allowed us to reprint their maps.

LANDSCAPE QUALITY ASSESSMENT MAP

765 kv Transmission Line Corridor Siting Project
Selected View Points of Part of the New Castle, Virginia Quad

National Forest

Private Holdings

Town of New Castle

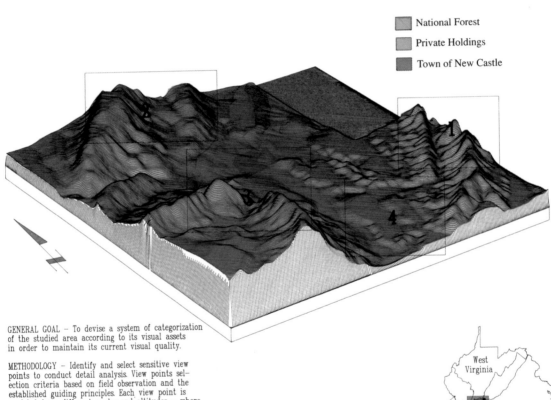

GENERAL GOAL – To devise a system of categorization
of the studied area according to its visual assets
in order to maintain its current visual quality.

METHODOLOGY – Identify and select sensitive view
points to conduct detail analysis. View points selection criteria based on field observation and the
established guiding principles. Each view point is
modeled from different angles and altitudes – where
the volume of viewers is often identified to be high.
Attribute information such as general land uses and
cultural features is integrated in the study through
either overlay or draping techniques.

TECHNIQUE – This map is created in Arc/Info. The TIN
module was used to convert a USGS 7.5 minutes quad
DEM (of New Castle, Virginia) to a Arc/Info lattice
file. The map was plotted on a HP 7585 type B plotter.

West
Virginia

Virginia

Study Area

Quad Location

Understanding GIS—The ARC/INFO Method

Sensitive View Points

This sensitive area includes the Lick Mt. and the Broad Run Mt. which are within the Jefferson National Forest. The highest peak is 2400 feet above sea level. The area has a interesting terrain with ridges and valleys. Powerlines should avoid this area.

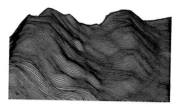

Most dominating land feature when travel along the state routes 311, 42, 611 is the this Nutters Mt. With an elevation of more than 2800 feet. Powerlines should not be designed to silhouette against the sky.

With the Johns Creek Mt. and the Sinking Creek Mt. on the north and south side, the scenic valley in between, has a relatively high level of human settelement with a traditional rural landscape. In addition, several vista points with panoramic views are identified when travel along the State Rt. 42.

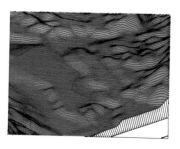

This is the valley region with the historic town New Castle at its north. Craig Creek runs through this valley. Powerlines and transmission towers should avoid this area.

Landscape Quality Assessment Map

Landscape Architecture Department, Virginia Polytechnic Institute, Blacksburg, Virginia, by Shaoli Huang

ARC/INFO software was used to combine satellite imagery and visual simulation techniques to assess landscape quality along the Appalachian Trail. The visual models were based on U.S. Geological Survey 7.5-minute digital elevation model files with some points added to increase resolution. The models were then processed with filters and VIP selection. Visibility analysis was performed using a linear feature coverage that contained the study area of the Appalachian Trail. The output coverage will be used to select vista points along the trail. A series of three-dimensional views was plotted as if seen from these vista points.

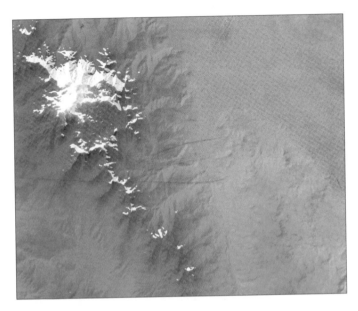

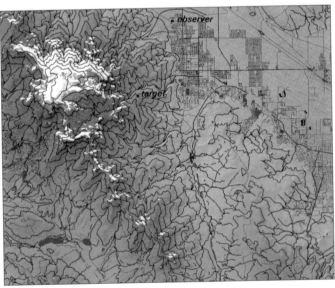

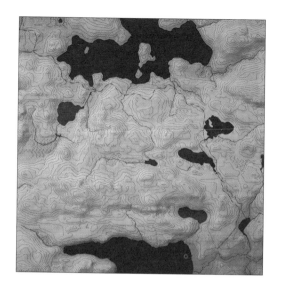 

▲ **Left: Color-shaded Contour Map of Algonquin Provincial Park**
Environmental Systems Research Institute, Inc., Redlands, California, by Chuck Payne
This map illustrates how color shading based on elevation and afternoon sun can further enhance the readability of a shaded contour map. The shading was done by classifying the lattice surface model into approximately 50 elevation bands. Each elevation band was assigned a color based on the hue saturation value (HSV) color model. Hill-shading values, based on an illumination source in the northwest, were applied to adjust the color values for each location.

▲ **Right: Gray-shaded Contour Map of Algonquin Provincial Park**
Environmental Systems Research Institute, Inc., Redlands, California, by Chuck Payne
This map illustrates how gray shading based on elevation and afternoon sun can enhance the readability of contour maps. Gray shading was done by classifying the lattice surface model into 175 elevation bands; each was then assigned a shade of gray. Hill-shading values, based on an illumination source in the northwest, were also applied to adjust the gray values for each location. These maps were created from a lattice generated from data provided by the Ontario Ministry of Natural Resources.

◄ **Planimetric Maps of Mt. San Jacinto and Palm Springs**
Environmental Systems Research Institute, Inc., Redlands, California, by Chuck Payne
These planimetric maps were created from six U.S. Geological Survey 1:24,000 digital elevation models joined to form a single lattice. The lattice was modeled for late spring snow cover, and color shaded by elevation and afternoon sun. It was plotted with vector data from streams, transportation, and 250-meter contours.

THREE-DIMENSIONAL ANALYSIS
TCE PLUME AT SUBSITE #1

A multi-dimensional view of the contaminant plums provides a more complete delineation of the problem for planning the cleanup and monitoring efforts, and for communicating the nature of the contamination to public officials and other interested parties. This analysis was constructed by generating a vertical grid and contouring well log data. The three-dimensional views were generated in VIEW.

LOG CONC (PPB)		GEOLOGY
0.75-1.25	2.75-3.25	CLAY
1.25-1.75	3.25-3.75	SAND
1.75-2.25	3.75-4.25	SAND/AQUIFER
2.25-2.75	GT 4.25	

HORIZONTAL SECTION

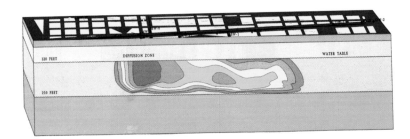

VERTICAL SECTION

Groundwater Contamination—Plume Analysis Project

U.S. Environmental Protection Agency, Kansas City, Kansas, by Walt Foster and Vickie Hale

Shown here are the results of a pilot project conducted to determine how a GIS could replace traditional hand analysis of contaminated aquifers. Existing site and subsite maps were converted to GIS coverages; well locations were integrated into the site coverages; and well sample data, converted from paper and database files, were related to the appropriate locations. The GIS surface analysis functions were used to create a triangulated irregular network from the mean concentrations of each pollutant at each well. Data values were converted to logs and contours generated by the GIS. Further analysis was conducted to develop vertical and three-dimensional characterizations of the plume.

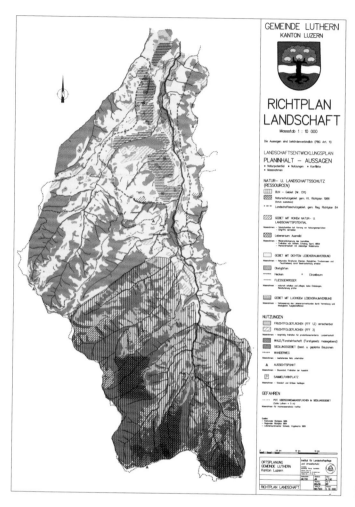

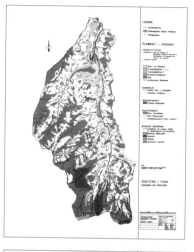

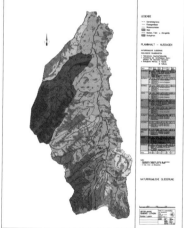

Landscape Development Map and Masterplan of a Community in the Swiss Alps

Institute for Landscape Planning and Environmental Protection, Uster, Switzerland, by Sepp Wanner

Each community in Switzerland requires a master development plan and, therefore, needs special planning maps. These maps are examples of landscape development maps and show the master plan for a community in the Alps. Top right: Richtplan Landschaft: landscape development map, showing regions of higher and lower nature and landscape potential. Top left: Naturräumliche Gliederung: structure of natural areas, basic map. Bottom right: Vegetation/Faune: vegetation/fauna basic map.

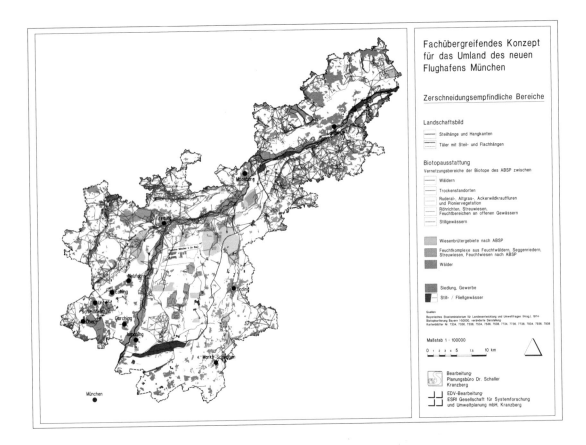

Fachübergreifendes—Konzept für das Umland des Neuen Flughafens München

ESRI–Germany, by Dr. Jörg Schaller

Shown on this and the following page are draft maps (yet unpublished) for a comprehensive regional planning study covering aspects of ecology, transportation, and urban development in an area influenced by the new Munich airport. The study was requested by the Bavarian State Ministry for Regional Development and Environmental Affairs and carried out by a team of consultants.

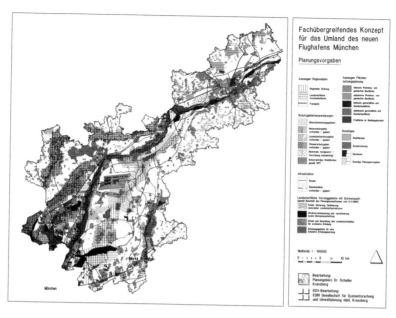

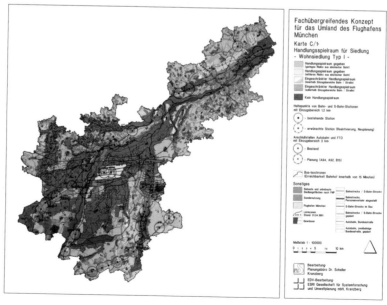

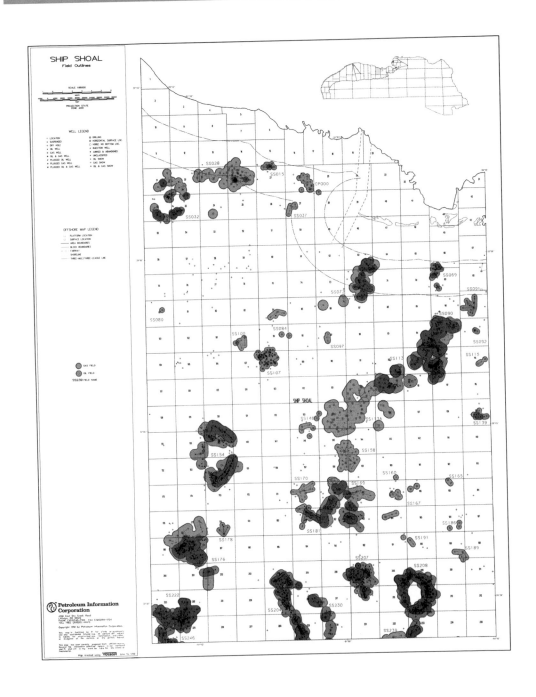

Understanding GIS—The ARC/INFO Method

◀ ## Ship Shoal Field Outlines

Copyright 1991 Petroleum Information Corporation, Denver, Colorado, by Richard E. Evans

This map shows the general trend of oil and gas fields in the offshore Gulf of Mexico ship shoal area. Wells were posted from data contained in the Petroleum Information Exploration Systems Division offshore well location (OWL) file. Custom data translation programs were used to import OWL file data directly into ARC/INFO coverages. Field outlines were processed in three steps by a set of macros. First, a subset of wells and platforms for an individual field and commodity were reselected out from master coverages. These coverages were used to create buffer zones with a radius proportional to the extent (boundary) of the selected coverages. Second, these buffer zones were joined together into a single coverage for the field. Attribute items were populated to identify each polygon with the proper commodity and field name. Finally, the arcs were smoothed to yield an aesthetically pleasing outline. This coverage was then used either as the source of flat file data, for insertion into a library, or to build a master coverage. The features, borders, legends, and tics of this map were created with automated map generation procedures by Petroleum Information Corporation.

Spatial Distribution of Operable Forest Resources

U.S. Department of Agriculture—Forest Service, Starkville, Mississippi, by Ronald W. Carraway and David L. Evans

This map illustrates using GIS for integrating data from various sources to determine resource availability. The land area from the SPOT classification was selected by the following hypothetical harvestable constraints: (1) within 500-meter road buffer, (2) not within 50-meter stream buffer, and (3) not within 50-meter wetland buffer. All unselected areas are shown in white. The soil erosion hazard and average slope percent are low in this study area.

▶

Spatial Distribution of
Operable Forest Resources

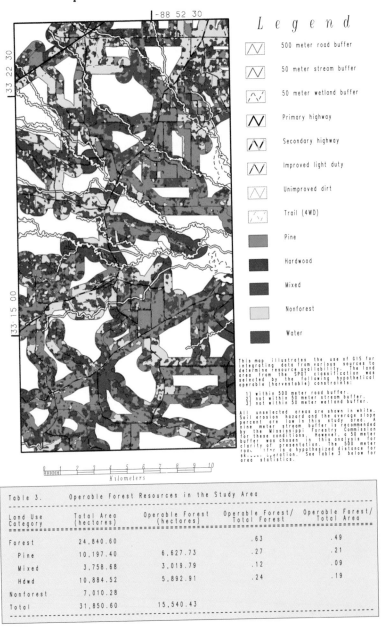

Legend

⌒⌒ 500 meter road buffer

⌒⌒ 50 meter stream buffer

⌒⌒ 50 meter wetland buffer

⌒⌒ Primary highway

⌒⌒ Secondary highway

⌒⌒ Improved light duty

⌒⌒ Unimproved dirt

⌒⌒ Trail (4WD)

▨ Pine

▨ Hardwood

▨ Mixed

▨ Nonforest

▨ Water

This map illustrates the use of GIS for integrating data from various sources to determine resource availability. The land area from the SPOT classification was selected by the following hypothetical operable (harvestable) constraints:

1) within 500 meter road buffer.
2) not within 50 meter stream buffer.
3) not within 50 meter wetland buffer.

All unselected areas are shown in white. Soil erosion hazard and the average slope percent are low in this study area. A nine meter stream buffer is recommended by the Mississippi Forestry Commission for these conditions. However, a 50 meter buffer was chosen in this analysis for clarity of presentation. The 500 meter road buffer is a hypothesized distance for skidder operation. See Table 3 below for area statistics.

Table 3.	Operable Forest Resources in the Study Area			
Land Use Category	Total Area (hectares)	Operable Forest (hectares)	Operable Forest/ Total Forest	Operable Forest/ Total Area
Forest	24,840.60		.63	.49
Pine	10,197.40	6,627.73	.27	.21
Mixed	3,758.68	3,019.79	.12	.09
Hdwd	10,884.52	5,892.91	.24	.19
Nonforest	7,010.28			
Total	31,850.60	15,540.43		

Land use maps
Washoe County Department of Comprehensive Planning, Reno, Nevada
Sun Valley Existing Land Use (Page E-14) and Sun Valley Planned Land Use (Page E-15) are two in
a series of five maps prepared as part of the county's comprehensive plan.

▶

Assessor Book Boundaries
Washoe County Department of Comprehensive Planning, Reno, Nevada
Assessor Book Boundaries (Page E-16) is an index map used to locate a parcel and identify which
assessor's map should be referenced. This map was created by dissolving on book number (the first
three digits of the assessor's parcel number). The county has more than 103,000 parcels, so this is a
useful tool for the public as well as for county staff.

▶

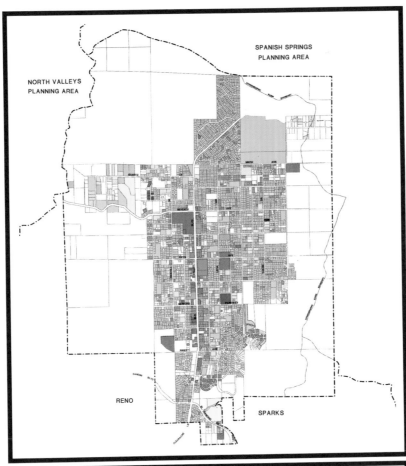

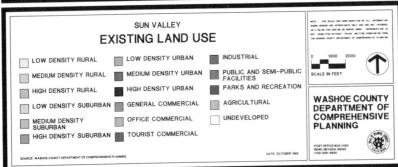

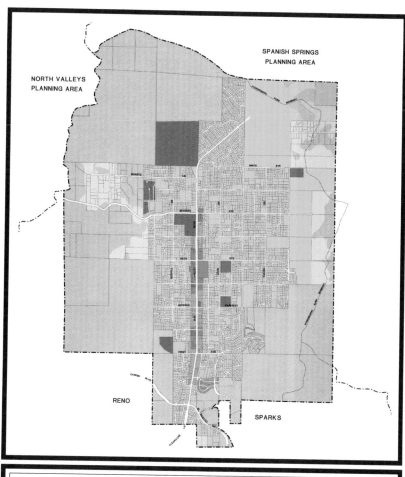

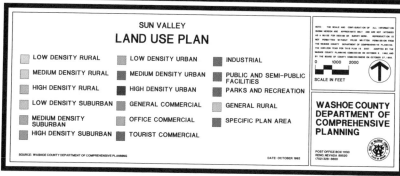

SUN VALLEY
LAND USE PLAN

LOW DENSITY RURAL

MEDIUM DENSITY RURAL

HIGH DENSITY RURAL

LOW DENSITY SUBURBAN

MEDIUM DENSITY
SUBURBAN

HIGH DENSITY SUBURBAN

LOW DENSITY URBAN

MEDIUM DENSITY URBAN

HIGH DENSITY URBAN

GENERAL COMMERCIAL

OFFICE COMMERCIAL

TOURIST COMMERCIAL

INDUSTRIAL

PUBLIC AND SEMI-PUBLIC
FACILITIES

PARKS AND RECREATION

GENERAL RURAL

SPECIFIC PLAN AREA

SOURCE: WASHOE COUNTY DEPARTMENT OF COMPREHENSIVE PLANNING

DATE: OCTOBER 1992

SCALE IN FEET

0   1000   2000

**WASHOE COUNTY
DEPARTMENT OF
COMPREHENSIVE
PLANNING**

POST OFFICE BOX 11130
RENO, NEVADA 89520
(702) 328-3600

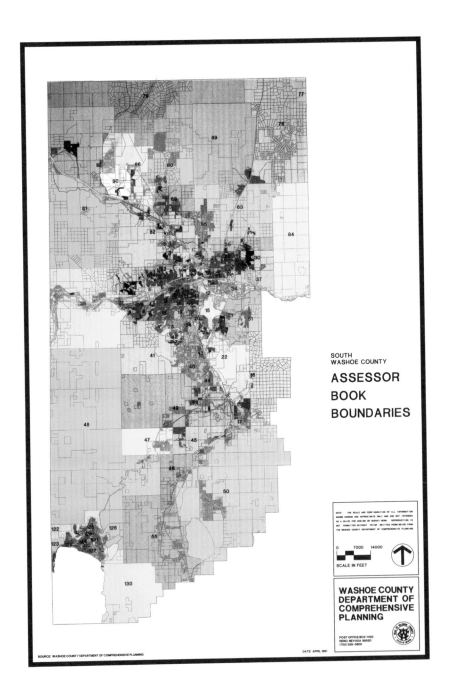

SOUTH
WASHOE COUNTY

ASSESSOR
BOOK
BOUNDARIES

WASHOE COUNTY
DEPARTMENT OF
COMPREHENSIVE
PLANNING

POST OFFICE BOX 11130
RENO, NEVADA 89520
(702) 328-3600

0   7000   14000

SCALE IN FEET

DATE: APRIL 1991

SOURCE: WASHOE COUNTY DEPARTMENT OF COMPREHENSIVE PLANNING

Appendix F License Agreement

Important: Read carefully before opening the sealed media package

ENVIRONMENTAL SYSTEMS RESEARCH INSTITUTE, INC. (ESRI), IS WILLING TO LICENSE THE ENCLOSED SOFTWARE, DATA, AND RELATED MATERIALS TO YOU ONLY UPON THE CONDITION THAT YOU ACCEPT ALL OF THE TERMS AND CONDITIONS CONTAINED IN THIS LICENSE AGREEMENT. PLEASE READ THE TERMS AND CONDITIONS CAREFULLY BEFORE OPENING THE SEALED MEDIA PACKAGE. BY OPENING THE SEALED MEDIA PACKAGE, YOU ARE INDICATING YOUR ACCEPTANCE OF THE ESRI® LICENSE AGREEMENT. IF YOU DO NOT AGREE TO THE TERMS AND CONDITIONS AS STATED, THEN ESRI IS UNWILLING TO LICENSE THE SOFTWARE, DATA, AND RELATED MATERIALS TO YOU. IN SUCH EVENT, YOU SHOULD RETURN THE MEDIA PACKAGE WITH THE SEAL UNBROKEN AND ALL OTHER COMPONENTS TO ESRI.

ESRI License Agreement

This is a license agreement, and not an agreement for sale, between you (Licensee) and Environmental Systems Research Institute, Inc. (ESRI). This ESRI License Agreement (Agreement) gives Licensee certain limited rights to use the software and related materials (Software, Data, and Related Materials). All rights not specifically granted in this Agreement are reserved to ESRI and its Licensors.

Reservation of Ownership and Grant of License:

ESRI and its Licensors retain exclusive rights, title, and ownership to the copy of the Software, Data, and Related Materials licensed under this Agreement and, hereby, grant to Licensee a personal, nonexclusive, nontransferable, royalty-free, worldwide license to use the Software, Data, and Related Materials based on the terms and conditions of this Agreement. Licensee agrees to use reasonable effort to protect the Software, Data, and Related Materials from unauthorized use, reproduction, distribution, or publication.

Proprietary Rights and Copyright:

Licensee acknowledges that the Software, Data, and Related Materials are proprietary and confidential property of ESRI and its Licensors and are protected by United States copyright laws and applicable international copyright treaties and/or conventions.

Permitted Uses:

Licensee may install the Software, Data, and Related Materials onto permanent storage device(s) for Licensee's own internal use.

Licensee may make only one (1) copy of the original Software, Data, and Related Materials for archival purposes during the term of this Agreement unless the right to make additional copies is granted to Licensee in writing by ESRI.

Licensee may internally use the Software, Data, and Related Materials provided by ESRI for the stated purpose of GIS education.

Uses Not Permitted:

Licensee shall not sell, rent, lease, sublicense, lend, assign, time-share, or transfer, in whole or in part, or provide unlicensed Third Parties access to the Software, Data, and Related Materials or portions of the Software, Data, and Related Materials, any updates, or Licensee's rights under this Agreement.

Licensee shall not remove or obscure any copyright or trademark notices of ESRI or its Licensors.

Term:

The Agreement shall automatically terminate without notice if Licensee fails to comply with any provision of this Agreement. Licensee shall then return to ESRI the Software, Data, and Related Materials. The parties hereby agree that all provisions that operate to protect the rights of ESRI and its Licensors shall remain in force should breach occur.

Limited Warranty:

THE SOFTWARE, DATA, AND RELATED MATERIALS CONTAINED HEREIN ARE PROVIDED "AS-IS," WITHOUT WARRANTY OF ANY KIND, EITHER EXPRESS OR IMPLIED, INCLUDING, BUT NOT LIMITED TO, THE IMPLIED WARRANTIES OF MERCHANTABILITY AND FITNESS FOR A PARTICULAR PURPOSE.

ESRI does not warrant that the Software, Data, and Related Materials will meet Licensee's needs or expectations, that the use of the Software, Data, and Related Materials will be uninterrupted, or that all nonconformities, defects, or errors can or will be corrected. ESRI is not inviting reliance on the Software, Data, and/or Related Materials for planning or analysis purposes, and Licensee should always check actual data.

Limitation of Liability:

ESRI shall not be liable for direct, indirect, special, incidental, or consequential damages related to Licensee's use of the Software, Data, and Related Materials, even if ESRI is advised of the possibility of such damage.

No Implied Waivers:

No failure or delay by ESRI or its Licensors in enforcing any right or remedy under this Agreement shall be construed as a waiver of any future or other exercise of such right or remedy by ESRI or its Licensors.

Order for Precedence:

Any conflict between the terms of this Agreement and any FAR, DFAR, purchase order, or other terms shall be resolved in favor of the terms expressed in this Agreement, subject to the government's minimum rights unless agreed otherwise.

Export Regulation:

Licensee acknowledges that this Agreement and the performance thereof are subject to compliance with any and all applicable United States laws, regulations, or orders relating to the export of data thereto. Licensee agrees to comply with all laws, regulations, and orders of the United States in regard to any export of such technical data.

Severability:

If any provision(s) of this Agreement shall be held to be invalid, illegal, or unenforceable by a court or other tribunal of competent jurisdiction, the validity, legality, and enforceability of the remaining provisions shall not in any way be affected or impaired thereby.

Governing Law:

This Agreement, entered into in the County of San Bernardino, shall be construed and enforced in accordance with and be governed by the laws of the United States of America and the State of California without reference to conflict of laws principles. The parties hereby consent to the personal jurisdiction of the courts of this county and waive their rights to change venue.

Entire Agreement:

The parties agree that this Agreement constitutes the sole and entire agreement of the parties as to the matter set forth herein and supersedes any previous agreements, understandings, and arrangements between the parties relating hereto.

Glossary

AAT   Arc attribute table. A table containing attributes for a line coverage. At a minimum, AATs contain the following items (columns):

FNODE#   from-node sequence number
TNODE#   to-node sequence number
LPOLY#   left-polygon sequence number
RPOLY#   right-polygon sequence number
LENGTH   length in coverage units
Cover#   arc internal sequence number (record number)
Cover-ID   arc feature ID

See also *feature attribute table.*

AML   The ARC Macro Language. A high-level, algorithmic language that provides full programming capabilities and a set of tools for building menus to tailor user interfaces for specific applications. Features include the ability to create on-screen menus from text files, to use and assign variables, and to get and use map or page unit coordinates. AML includes an extensive set of directives and in-line functions that can be used interactively or in AML programs (macros) as well as functions that report on the status of ARC/INFO command parameters.

analysis   See *model* and *spatial analysis.*

annotation   1. Descriptive text used to label coverage features. It is used for display, not for analysis.
2. One of the feature classes in a coverage used to label other features. Information stored for annotation includes a text string, the location at which it is displayed, and a text symbol (color, font, size, etc.) for display. More than one subclass of annotation can be created for a coverage. See also *TAT.*

arc
1. A string of x,y coordinate pairs (vertices) that begin at one location and end at another. Connecting the arc's vertices creates a line.
2. A coverage feature class used to represent linear features and polygon boundaries. One line feature can contain many arcs. Arcs are topologically linked at their endpoints (nodes) and to the areas (polygons) on either side. Arcs start and end at a node and can define areas to the left and right of their direction of travel (determined arbitrarily at the time of data capture). The descriptive attributes of arcs are stored in the arc attribute table (AAT). See also *node*.

arc—node topology
The coordinate and topological data structure ARC/INFO uses to represent linear features and polygon boundaries. Arcs represent lines, or define areas, and are split where they intersect with other arcs. Nodes represent the beginning and ending vertices of each arc. Arcs that share a common node are connected. Polygons are defined by a series of arcs. Arcs have left and right polygons.

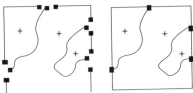

Arcs connect at a common node.

ArcStorm
ArcStorm (Arc Storage Manager) is a data storage facility and transaction manager for ARC/INFO data. ArcStorm manages a feature-oriented database that can be closely integrated with database systems supported by ARC/INFO's DATABASE INTEGRATOR.

ArcStorm database
An ArcStorm database is a collection of libraries, layers, INFO tables, and external DBMS tables. Data stored in an ArcStorm database benefit from the transaction management and data archiving capabilities of ArcStorm

ArcTools
ArcTools is a collection of ARC/INFO productivity tools implemented through an AML-based graphical user interface. ArcTools provides a user-friendly approach to commonly used ARC/INFO operations and functions.

area   A closed figure (polygon). A homogeneous area bounded by one or more arc features. Examples: states, counties, lakes, land use areas, and census tracts. Polygons represent areas in ARC/INFO coverages.

ASCII   American Standard Code for Information Interchange. A set of codes for representing alphanumeric information (e.g., a byte with a value of 77 represents a capital M). Text files, such as those created with the text editor of a computer system, are often referred to as *ASCII files*.

attribute   1. A characteristic of a geographic feature described by numbers or characters, typically stored in tabular format, and linked to the feature by a user-assigned identifier (e.g., the attributes of a well, represented by a point, might include depth, location, and gallons-per-minute). 2. A numeric, text, or image data field in a relational database table that describes a spatial feature such as a point, line, node, area, or cell.

attribute table   An INFO or other tabular file containing rows and columns. Descriptive attributes about some object, such as a geographic feature, are contained in each row. The same column in each row represents the same attribute. See also *feature attribute table*.

ROAD-TYPE	SURFACE	WIDTH	LANES	NAME
2	Asphalt	48	4	N Main St
1	Concrete	60	4	Hwy 42
4	Asphalt	32	2	Elm St

Row

Column

base map   A map containing geographic features, used for locational reference.

bit   The smallest unit of information that a computer can store and process. A bit has two possible values, 0 or 1, which can be interpreted as YES/NO, TRUE/FALSE, or ON/OFF. See also *byte*.

BND The coverage or grid boundary file, which contains the minimum bounding rectangle (i.e., xmin,ymin and xmax,ymax) of all coordinates for arcs and label points in a coverage. See also *coverage extent*.

Boolean expression 1. Boolean - a type of expression that reduces to a true or false (logical) condition. A Boolean operator is a keyword that specifies how to combine simple logical expressions into complex expressions. Boolean operators negate a predicate (NOT), specify a combination of predicates (AND), or specify a list of alternative predicates (OR). For example: DEPTH > 100 *AND* GPM > 500.
2. Loosely, but erroneously, used to refer to logical expressions such as *DEPTH greater than 100*. See also *feature selection by attribute*.

border arcs Arcs that surround the outer edge of a polygon coverage and create its boundary. In LIBRARIAN, the tile boundary arcs that split a polygon coverage between tiles.

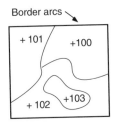

buffer A zone of a specified distance around coverage features. Both constant- and variable-width buffers can be generated for a set of coverage features based on each feature's attribute values. The resulting buffer zones form polygons—areas that are either inside or outside the specified buffer distance from each feature. Buffers are useful for proximity analysis (e.g., find all stream segments within 300 feet of a proposed logging area).

Constant Width   Variable Width

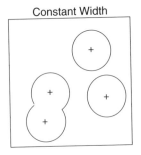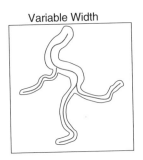

byte   A memory and data storage unit composed of contiguous bits, usually eight. For example, file sizes are measured in bytes or megabytes (one million bytes). Bytes contain values of 0 to 255 and most often represent integer numbers or ASCII characters (e.g., a byte with an ASCII value of 77 represents a capital M). A collection of bytes (often 4 or 8 bytes) represents real numbers and integers larger than 255. See also *bit*.

CAD   Computer-aided design. An automated system for the design, drafting, and display of graphically oriented information.

Cartesian coordinate system   A two-dimensional, planar coordinate system in which x measures horizontal distance and y measures vertical distance. Relative measures of distance, area, and direction are constant throughout the Cartesian coordinate plane. An x,y coordinate defines every point on the plane.

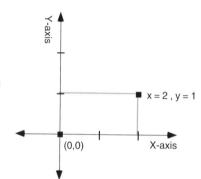

cell   The basic element of spatial information in a grid data set. Cells are always square. A group of cells forms a *grid*. Cells store values that can be related to the value attribute table (VAT).

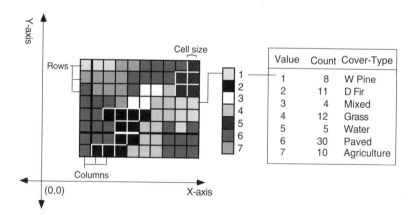

character   1. A letter (e.g., a, b, c, or d), number (e.g., 1, 2, or 3), or special graphic symbol (e.g., *, †, or −) treated as a single unit of data.
2. A data type that refers to text columns in an attribute table (such as an item called NAME).

clip   The spatial extraction of those features from one coverage that reside entirely within a boundary defined by features in another coverage (called the clip coverage)—clipping works much like a *cookie cutter*.

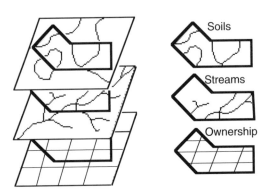

Clipping of layers in a database

COGO   1. Abbreviation of the term *COordinate GeOmetry*. Land surveyors use COGO functions to enter survey data, to calculate precise locations and boundaries, to define curves, and so on.
2. The name of the coordinate geometry software product for ARC/INFO.

column   A vertical field in an attribute table.

ROAD-TYPE	SURFACE	WIDTH	LANES	NAME
2	Asphalt	48	4	N Main St
1	Concrete	60	4	Hwy 42
4	Asphalt	32	2	Elm St

Column

command   A specific instruction to a computer program, issued by the user to perform a desired action.

connectivity The topological identification of arcs that connect at a node. Within a linear network, the from- and to-node numbers for each arc define connectivity. So, arcs that share a common node are connected.

contiguity The topological identification of adjacent polygons by recording the left and right polygons of each arc.

continuous data A surface in which each location has a value. Typically represented by a tin or lattice (e.g., surface elevation).

coordinate An x,y location in a Cartesian coordinate system or an x,y,z location in a three-dimensional coordinate system. Coordinates represent locations on the Earth's surface relative to other locations. Planar coordinates describe a two-dimensional x,y location in terms of distance from a fixed reference. See also *vector* and *Cartesian coordinate system.*

coordinate geometry Used to construct mathematical/geometric models of a design and its environment. See also *COGO*.

coordinate system A system used to measure horizontal and vertical distances on a planimetric map; in ARC/INFO, a system with units and characteristics defined by a map projection. A common coordinate system is used to spatially register geographic data for the same area.

A coordinate system is usually defined by a map projection, a spheroid of reference, a datum, one or more standard parallels, a central meridian, and possible shifts in the x- and y-directions to locate x,y positions of point, line, and area features in a coverage.

Cover# A unique sequence number automatically generated by ARC/INFO for each coverage feature. This internal number is used to access coverage features and describe topological relationships them. It is often referred to as the *record number*.

Cover-ID An item found in PATs, NATs and AATs. The item in which feature IDs are recorded for points, polygons, arcs, and nodes. The user-assigned integer number that identifies a coverage feature. See also *feature ID* and *User-ID*.

coverage   1. A digital version of a map forming the basic unit of vector data storage in ARC/INFO. A coverage stores map features as primary features (such as arcs, nodes, polygons, and label points) and secondary features (such as tics, map extent, links, and annotation). Associated feature attribute tables describe and store attributes of the map features.

2. A set of thematically associated data considered as a unit. A coverage usually represents a single theme, or layer, such as soils, streams, roads, or land use.

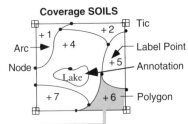

Coverage SOILS

SOILS.PAT

AREA	PERIMETER	SOILS#	SOILS-ID	SOIL	CLASS	SUIT
-36.0	24.0	1	0	—	—	—
3.0	9.0	2	1	A3	113	High
2.5	8.5	3	2	C6	95	Low
15.0	15.0	4	3	B7	212	Moderate
4.0	8.5	5	4	B13	201	Moderate
2.0	4.5	6	5	Z22	86	Low
5.5	12.0	7	6	A6	77	High
4.0	7.0	8	7	A1	117	Moderate

coverage extent   Also known as *BND*, the bounding limits of a coverage defined by two coordinates (xmin,ymin and xmax,ymax) which form the lower-left and upper-right corners of a rectangle just large enough to enclose all coverage arcs and label points. In ARCPLOT and ARCEDIT, map extent is often set from the coverage extent.

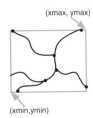

(xmax, ymax)

(xmin,ymin)

coverage units   The units (e.g., feet, meters, inches) of the coordinate system in which a coverage is stored.

cursor
1. A graphic pointer used with a mouse to point to a location on a terminal screen.
2. An internal pointer to a record in a table. The record to which the cursor points is available for display, query, and update operations.

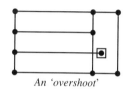

Parcel-No	Owner
11-115-001	Brown, D.
11-115-002	Greene, J.
11-115-003	Smith, L.
11-115-003	Cleaver, T.
11-115-003	Koop, C.

dangling arc
An arc having the same polygon on both its left and right sides and having at least one node that does not connect to any other arc— usually the result of an overshoot during digitizing.

An 'overshoot'

dangle length
Minimum length allowed for dangling arcs during the CLEAN process. CLEAN removes dangling arcs that are shorter than the dangle length.

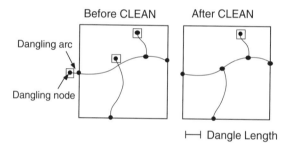

Before CLEAN   After CLEAN

Dangling arc

Dangling node

⊢—⊣ Dangle Length

dangling node
The endpoint of a dangling arc. Often identifies where a polygon doesn't close properly (e.g., undershoot), where arcs don't connect properly, or where an arc was digitized past its intersection with another arc (i.e., overshoot). A dangling arc is not always an error. For example, dangling arcs can represent cul-de-sacs in street centerline maps.

An 'undershoot'

data conversion
The translation of data from one format to another. Data conversion occurs when data is transferred from one system to another. ARC/INFO supports data conversion from many geographic data formats such as DLG, TIGER, DXF, and DEM.

data model
1. The result of the conceptual design process. A generalized, user-defined view of the data related to applications.
2. A formal method of arranging data to mimic the behavior of the real-world entities they represent. Fully developed data models describe data types, integrity rules for the data types, and operations on the data types. ARC/INFO coverages and grids use a georelational data model, a hybrid data model that combines spatial data (in coverages or grids) and attribute data (in tables). Other data models used in ARC/INFO include tins, images, and the relational model for tabular data.

database
1. A logical collection of interrelated information, managed and stored as a unit, usually on some form of mass-storage system such as magnetic tape or disk. A GIS database includes data about the spatial location and shape of geographic features recorded as points, lines, areas, pixels, grid cells, or tins as well as their attributes.

DATABASE INTEGRATOR (DBI)
The ARC/INFO software's link to relational database management systems (RDBMS). DBI enables ARC/INFO users to access existing commercial databases and take advantage of the power and capabilities of the RDBMS.

database management systems (DBMS)
A set of computer programs for organizing the information in a database. Often abbreviated *DBMS*. Typically, a DBMS contains routines for structuring a database in a standard format and providing tools for data input, verification, storage, retrieval, query, and manipulation.

datum
A set of parameters and control points used to accurately define the three-dimensional shape of the Earth (e.g., as a spheroid). The corresponding datum is the basis for a planar coordinate system. For example, the North American Datum for 1983 (NAD83) is the datum for map projections and coordinates within the United States and throughout North America.

DBMS
Database management system.

DBMS table
See *attribute table*.

DEM
Digital elevation model.
1. A topographic surface arranged in a data file as a set of regularly-spaced x,y,z locations where z represents elevation.
2. An elevation database for elevation data by map sheet from the National Mapping Division of the U.S. Geological Survey (USGS).
3. The format of the USGS digital elevation data sets.

descriptive data
Tabular data describing the geographic characteristics of map features. Can include numbers, text, images, and CAD drawings about features. ARC/INFO stores descriptive data in feature attribute tables and in related tables.

digital elevation model
See *DEM*.

digitize
1. To encode map features as x,y coordinates in digital form.
2. To employ a digitizing tablet to record x,y or x,y,z values for map features. Lines are traced to define their shape. A digitizer button, pressed periodically along the line, records x,y coordinates. So, a *digitized* line is a series of x,y coordinates.

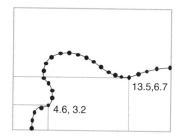

digitizer
1. A device that consists of a table and a cursor with crosshairs and keys used to record the locations of map features as x,y coordinates.
2. Title of the person using the device to automate maps.

digitizing
See *digitize*.

DIME
See *GBF/DIME*.

directory   A location on a disk containing a set of data files and other directories (subdirectories). Operating systems use directories to organize data. Directories are organized in a tree structure in which each branch on the tree represents a subdirectory. The location of a directory is specified with a *pathname* (e.g., /disk/project_db/tile202/soilscov).

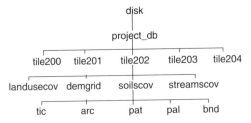

dissolve   The process of removing boundaries between adjacent polygons that have the same values for a specified attribute.

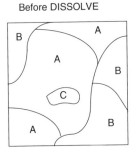 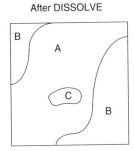

DLG   1. Digital Line Graph files from the U.S. Geological Survey (USGS), including data from the base map categories such as transportation, hydrography, contours, and public land survey boundaries.
2. The digital format standards published by USGS for exchanging cartographic data files and for which the USGS delivers Digital Line Graph data sets.

double-precision Refers to a high level of coordinate accuracy based on the possible number of significant digits that can be stored for each coordinate. ARC/INFO data sets can be stored in either single- or double-precision coordinates. Single-precision coverages store up to 7 significant digits for each coordinate, retaining a precision of 1 meter in an extent of 1,000,000 meters. Double-precision coverages store up to 15 significant digits per coordinate (typically 13 to 14 significant digits), retaining the accuracy of much less than one meter at a global extent. See also *single-precision*.

DXF Data Exchange Format. A format for storing vector data in ASCII or binary files; used by AutoCAD and other CAD software and convertible to ARC/INFO coverages.

dynamic segmentation The process of computing the locations of events on linear features at run time. Event features are not stored in the geometry of the coverage—they are derived as needed. Dynamic segmentation provides an alternative to using pseudo nodes to segment arcs to record attributes. Route-system features and event handling commands provide the dynamic segmentation capability within ARC/INFO.

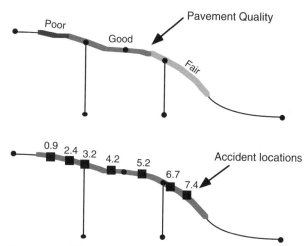

The process of dynamically locating events on linear features—that is, straight from attribute tables of events for which distance measures are available. This is done without changing the underlying data structure. Both point and linear events can be located on routes.

edge matching	An editing procedure to ensure that all features that cross adjacent map sheets have the same edge locations. Links connect the locations in one coverage to the matching feature locations in the adjacent coverage.

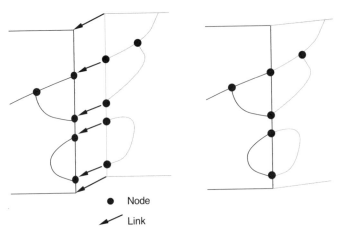

● Node

↙ Link

edit	To correct errors within, or modify, a computer file, a geographic data set, or a tabular file containing attribute data.
environment	A set of parameters defining various display, editing, and data manipulation conditions that remain active during a session until explicitly changed by the user.
equation item	An arithmetic expression used in place of an item name in an ARC/INFO command. Equation items can be used in most places instead of an item name. For example, to list feature areas, a user could specify LIST AREA; to list areas in acres instead of square feet, a user could specify LIST AREA / 43560.
Equator	The parallel of reference, 0° north or south.
event	Attributes that occur along linear features. Their position is defined in terms of route and measure coordinates. There are three event types: linear, continuous, and point. Closure of the left lane on route I-10 from milepost 1.5 to 2.1 is a linear event. A continuous event is a type of linear event where the start position is the same as the end position of the previous event, so only the end position is recorded. Point events are attributes that occur at a point along a route. An accident occurred at the 6.3 milepost on route I-10 is a point event.
external file	INFO stores data in files in a database; however, database information can be stored in files outside of the database. These files are referred to as external files. For example, feature attribute tables are stored as external INFO data files maintained in the coverage directory.

external polygon   *See universe polygon.*

feature attribute table   A table used to store attribute information for a specific coverage feature class. ARC/INFO writes the first several items of these tables. Feature attribute tables supported for coverages include:

*Cover.*PAT for polygons or points
*Cover.*AAT for arcs
*Cover.*NAT for nodes
*Cover.*RAT for routes
*Cover.*SEC for sections
*Cover.*TAT for annotation (text)

where *Cover* is the coverage name.

feature class   1. The type of feature represented in a coverage. Coverage feature classes include arcs, nodes, label points, polygons, tics, annotation, links, boundaries, routes, and sections.
2. The type of representation for a map feature. Often called an object, an entity, or a geographic phenomenon. When referring to map data, feature classes include points, lines, areas, and surfaces. One or more coverage features are used to model map features; for example, arcs and nodes can be used to model linear features such as street centerlines.

feature selection by attribute   *See logical selection.*

feature ID   An identification number assigned to each coverage feature by the user. It is used as the key to relate the feature to its corresponding record in the feature attribute table and to additional tabular data. Used interchangeably with *User-ID.*

file   A set of related information that a computer can access by a unique name (e.g., a text file, a data file, a DLG file). Files are the logical units managed on disk by the computer's operating system. Files may be stored on tapes or disks.

font   A logical set of related patterns representing text characters or point symbology (e.g., A,B,C, etc.). A font pattern is the basic building block for markers and text symbols. After the desired patterns are placed in fonts, you can build any symbol you desire.

```
Courier    AaBbCc012!@#&
```
Helvetica AaBbCc012!@#&
Times   AaBbCc012!@#&

format   The pattern into which data are systematically arranged for use on a computer. A file format is the specific design of how information is organized in the file. For example, ARC/INFO has specific, proprietary formats used to store coverages; DLG, DEM, and TIGER are geographic data sets in particular formats available for many parts of the United States.

from-node   Of an arc's two endpoints, the one first digitized.

From-node   To-node

fuzzy tolerance   In ARC/INFO, a distance, measured in coverage units, that defines the coordinate resolution of all arcs in any coverage that results from the CLEAN operation or a topological overlay operation such as UNION, INTERSECT, or CLIP. It is the smallest distance between all arc coordinates. The fuzzy tolerance is an extremely small distance used to resolve inexact intersection locations due to limited arithmetic precision of computers. Fuzzy tolerance values typically range from 1/10,000 to 1/1,000,000 times the width of the coverage extent.

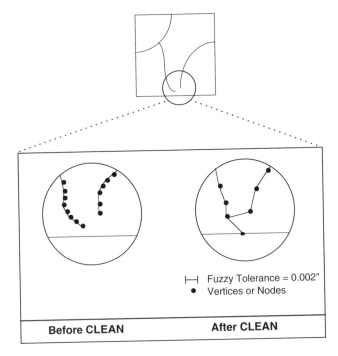

Fuzzy Tolerance = 0.002"
• Vertices or Nodes

Before CLEAN   **After CLEAN**

GBF/DIME   For the 1980 census, the U.S. Census Bureau produced Geographic Base Files (GBF) and Dual Independent Map Encoding (DIME) files, containing census geographic statistical codes and coordinates of line segments for most metropolitan areas. DIME files provide a schematic map of a city's streets, address ranges, and geostatistical codes relating to the Census Bureau's tabular statistical data. DIME was replaced by TIGER for the 1990 Census.

geocode   The process of identifying a location by one or more x,y coordinates from another location description such as an address. For example, an address can be matched against a TIGER street network to determine the location of a home.

geographic data   The locations and descriptions of geographic features. The composite of spatial data and descriptive data.

geographic database   A collection of spatial data and related descriptive data organized for efficient storage and retrieval by many users.

geographic data set   One of seven geographic data types supported by ARC/INFO. Geographic data sets in ARC/INFO include coverages, grids, DBMS tables, tins, images, lattices, and CAD drawings.

geographic object   A user-defined geographic phenomenon that can be modeled or represented using geographic data sets in ARC/INFO. Examples of geographic objects include streets, sewer lines, manhole covers, accidents, lot lines, and parcels. A geographic or map feature.

georeference   To establish the relationship between page coordinates on a planar map and known real-world coordinates.

georelational model   A geographic data model that represents both spatial features and their related descriptive data. RDBMS tables store descriptive data, which are associated, or related, to features by the feature ID.

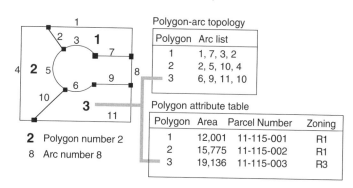

GIS   Geographic information system. An organized collection of computer hardware, software, geographic data, and personnel designed to efficiently capture, store, update, manipulate, analyze, and display all forms of geographically referenced information.

global positioning system   A satellite-based device that records x,y,z coordinates and other data. GPS devices can be taken into the field to record data while driving, flying, or hiking. Ground locations are calculated by signals from satellites orbiting the Earth.

GPS   See *global positioning system*.

grain tolerance   A parameter controlling the distance between vertices on curves. Grain tolerance restricts the number of vertices and the distance between them on arcs representing curves. The smaller the grain tolerance, the closer vertices can be. The grain tolerance is different from a densify tolerance which has no effect on shape.

Grain tolerance used to spline curves.   *Densify tolerance used to add vertices, but shape is maintained.*

Large grain   *Small grain*   *Densify straight lines*

graphical user interface   Also known as *GUI*. A graphical method of controlling how a user interacts with a computer to perform various tasks. Instead of issuing commands at a prompt, the user performs desired tasks by choosing from 'a dashboard' of options presented by the GUI on the display screen. These are in the form of pictorial buttons (icons) and lists. The user interacts with the system using a mouse to point-and-click. Some GUI tools are dynamic and the user must manipulate a graphical object on the screen to invoke a function; for example, moving a slider bar back and forth to determine the value of a parameter for a particular operation (e.g., setting the scale of a map).

graphics display terminal   A computer terminal used to view and manipulate spatial information. A graphics terminal can also be used for graphic input (e.g., during feature selection), digitizing and editing, and so on.

graphics page   That area on the graphics display device reserved for map display, or the plotter page area. Page units are typically in centimeters or inches instead of real-world coordinates such as meters or feet. Maps are composed on the graphics page.

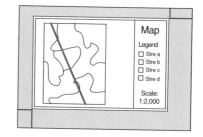

GRASS   Geographical Resource Analysis Support System. A public-domain raster GIS modeling product of the U.S. Army Corps of Engineers' Construction Engineering Research Laboratory (CERL).

grid   1. A raster geographic data set for use with ARC/INFO's GRID software. An x,y location references each grid cell. Cells store values The value attribute table (VAT) stores additional attributes of the cell. 2. One of many data structures used to represent map features. A raster-based data structure composed of cells of equal size arranged in columns and rows. The value of each cell, or group of cells, represents the value of the feature. (Also called *raster*.)

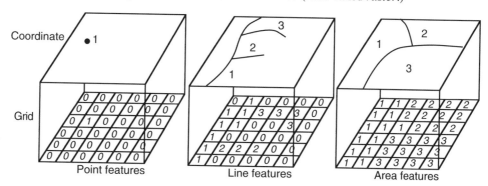

GRID   An ARC/INFO software product that provides a fully-integrated raster (cell-based) geoprocessing system for use with ARC/INFO. GRID supports a Map Algebra spatial language that allows sophisticated spatial modeling and analysis.

grid cell   A discretely uniform unit that represents a portion of the Earth, such as a square meter or square mile. Each grid cell has a value that corresponds to the feature or characteristic at that site, such as a soil type, census tract, or vegetation class. See also *cell*.

GUI   See *graphical user interface*.

hardware   The physical components of a computer system—the computer, plotters, printers, terminals, digitizers, and so on.

identity   The topological overlay of a coverage with a polygon coverage that computes the geometric intersection of the two coverages. The output coverage preserves all the input features plus those portions of the polygon coverage that overlap the input coverage. Input features, preserved in the output data set, receive attributes of the polygons they intersect. See also *intersect* and *union*.

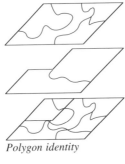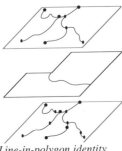

Polygon identity   *Line-in-polygon identity*

identity link   A coverage link whose from-location is the same as its to-location. Used to control rubber sheeting and adjustment operations. Identity links act as nails to hold down the point location during adjustment. See also *link*.

image   A graphic representation or description of an object, typically produced by an optical or electronic device. Common examples include remotely sensed data such as satellite data, scanned data, and photographs. An image is stored as a raster data set of binary or integer values that represent the intensity of reflected light, heat, or another range of values on the electromagnetic spectrum. Remotely sensed images are digital representations of the Earth.

image catalog   An organized set of spatially referenced, possibly overlapping, images that can be accessed as one logical image. An image catalog is a group of images on disk, each referenced by a record in an INFO data file. At a minimum, items in the data file include the image pathname and the bounding coordinates xmin,ymin and xmax,ymax.

IMAGE INTEGRATOR   A collection of image management and display tools in ARC/INFO that allows vector and raster data to be displayed concurrently. IMAGE INTEGRATOR commands georeference images to real-world coordinates, display images, and manage image catalogs.

INFO   A tabular DBMS used by ARC/INFO to store and manipulate feature attribute and related tables.

INFO database   The contents of a set of INFO data files, feature attribute tables, and related files stored in each ARC/INFO workspace under a subdirectory named INFO. This subdirectory contains all feature attribute tables for the set of coverages contained in the workspace.

interface   A hardware and software link that connects two computer systems, or a computer and its peripherals, for data communication.

internal number   A unique sequence number that is automatically generated by ARC/INFO for each coverage feature. The internal number is used as a direct-access record number for the feature. The internal number is also used to describe topological relationships between coverage features. It is often referred to as the *record number* or *Cover#*.

intersect   The topological integration of two spatial data sets that preserves features that fall within the spatial extent common to both input data sets. See also *identity* and *union*.

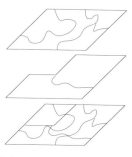

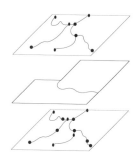

Polygon intersect   *Line-in-polygon intersect*

item
In an attribute table, a *field* of information commonly displayed as a column. A single attribute from a record in an INFO data file.

Item

Area	Perimeter	Cover#	Cover-ID	Stand-No
30	21	2	101	I–1604
68	52	3	1001	I–1623
32	19	4	23	I–2004

Record

item indexing
A means of accelerating logical queries and tabular 'relates' by creating a modified binary tree (B-tree) index. Binary searches of indexed items are often faster than linear searches.

join
See relational join.

label point
A coverage feature class stored as a single x,y location and used to represent point features (e.g., well sites, telephone poles, mountain peaks), or to assign feature IDs to polygons. When representing point features, the x,y location of the label point describes the location of the feature. When identifying polygons, the label point can be located anywhere within the polygon. Point features have a feature attribute table called a *PAT*. In a single coverage, label points can represent points or assign polygon IDs, but not both. One coverage cannot have feature attribute tables for both point and polygon features. See also *PAT* and *point*.

latitude-longitude
A spherical reference system used to measure locations on the Earth's surface. Latitude and longitude are angles measured from the Earth's center to locations on the Earth's surface. Latitude measures angles in a north-south direction. Longitude measures angles in the east-west direction.

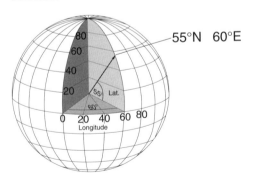

55°N 60°E

lattice   A surface representation that uses a rectangular array of points spaced at a constant sampling interval in the x and y directions relative to a common origin. A lattice is stored as a grid, but differs in that it represents the value of the surface only at the mesh points of the lattice rather than the value of the cell area surrounding each mesh point.

```
+ + + + + + + +
+ + + + + + + +
+ + + + + + + +
+ + + + + + + +
+ + + + + + + +
+ + + + + + + +
```

layer   A logical set of thematic data described and stored in a map library. Layers organize a map library by subject matter (e.g., soils, roads, and wells), and extend over the entire geographic area defined by the spatial index of the map library. See also *map library*.

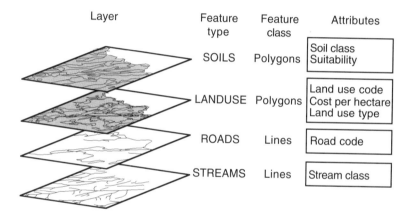

legend   1. The reference area on a map that lists and explains the colors, symbols, line patterns, shadings, and annotation used on the map. The legend often includes the scale, origin, orientation, and other map information.
2. The symbol key on a map used to describe and explain a map's symbols.

LIBRARIAN   A set of software tools used to manage and access large geographic data sets in a map library. A *map library* is a collection of spatial tiles used to spatially partition large areas and layers used to thematically organize geographic data. LIBRARIAN commands create and define a map library, move data in and out of a library, query the data in a map library, and display the results of a query. See also *map library*.

line   1. A set of ordered coordinates that represents the shape of geographic features too narrow to be displayed as an area at the given scale (e.g., contours, street centerlines, or streams), or linear features with no area (e.g., state and county boundary lines). 2. A single arc in a coverage. 3. A line on a map (e.g., a neatline).

linear feature   A geographic feature that can be represented by a line or set of lines. For example, rivers, roads within a pizza delivery area, and electric and telecommunication networks are all linear features. Linear features are represented in ARC/INFO by arcs or by the route-system feature class.

line-in-polygon   A spatial operation in which arcs in one coverage are overlaid with polygons of another coverage to determine which arcs, or portions of arcs, are contained within the polygons. Polygon attributes are associated with corresponding arcs in the resulting line coverage.

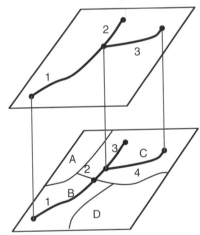

Line ID	Old Line	Poly
1	1	B
2	1	C
3	2	C
4	3	C

line symbol A special symbol with which coverage arcs are drawn. For example here are three line symbols:

link A coverage feature class. Links are two-point segments that represent from- and to-locations for the rubber sheeting adjustment process.

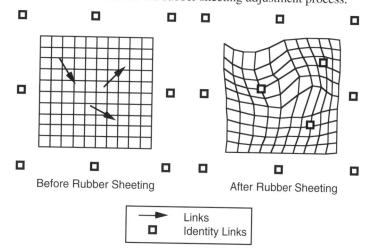

Before Rubber Sheeting   After Rubber Sheeting

→ Links
□ Identity Links

log file Coverage or workspace history file containing a list of all commands used to operate on a coverage or all commands used in the workspace.

logical selection The process of selecting a subset of features from a coverage using logical selection criteria that operate on the attributes of coverage features (e.g., AREA GT 16000). Only those features whose attributes meet the selection criteria are selected. Also known as *feature selection by attribute*.

longitude See *latitude-longitude*.

lookup table 1. A special tabular data file containing additional attributes for features stored in an associated feature attribute table. The table can be an external attribute table or an INFO table that describes coverage features. 2. A special lookup table in which numeric item values are classified into categories. For example, well depth can be recorded explicitly in the feature attribute table, but displayed and used as a set of classes, such as 0 to 250 feet, 251 to 500 feet, and so on. An INFO lookup table contains at least two items: the relate item and an item named either SYMBOL or LABEL.

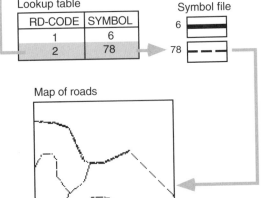

ROADS.AAT

ROAD#	ROAD-ID	RD-CODE
1	1	1
2	2	2
3	3	2
4	4	1
5	5	2
6	6	1

Lookup table

RD-CODE	SYMBOL
1	6
2	78

Symbol file

Map of roads

The maximum value for each class is listed for the relate item; for example,

Lookup table

DEPTH	SYMBOL	Description
0	0	0 feet
250	3	1 to 250 feet
500	4	251 to 500 feet
750	6	501 to 750 feet
1000	8	751 to 1000 feet
9999	9	Over 1000 feet

macro   A text file containing a sequence of commands that can be executed as one command. Macros can be built to perform frequently used, as well as complex, operations. The ARC Macro Language is used to create macros for ARC/INFO. See also *AML*.

many-to-one relate   A relate in which many records in one table are related to a single record in another table. A goal in relational database design is to use many-to-one relates to reduce data storage and redundancy.

NAME	ROAD_CLASS
MAIN	1
OAK	3
ELM	1
SMITH	1
ORANGE	1
WALTON	3
15TH	4
1ST	5

ROAD_CLASS	TEXT	SYMBOL
1	Residential	11
2	Alley	21
3	Major	33
4	Ramp	19
5	Freeway	35

Example of a many-to-one relate.

map   An abstract representation of the physical features of a portion of the Earth's surface graphically displayed on a planar surface. Maps display signs, symbols, and spatial relationships among the features. They typically emphasize, generalize, and omit certain features from the display to meet design objectives (e.g., railroad features might be included in a transportation map but omitted from a street map).

map extent   1. The rectangular limits (xmin,ymin and xmax,ymax) of the area of the Earth's surface you want to display using ARC/INFO. Map extent is specified in the coordinate system of the coverage or other geographic data set used. Typically, the extent of your geographic database (or a portion of it defined by zoomed-in view) defines the map extent for display.
2. The geographic extent of a geographic data set specified by the minimum bounding rectangle (i.e., xmin,ymin and xmax,ymax).

map library   An organized, uniformly defined collection of spatial data partitioned by layers and tiles into component parts. Map libraries organize geographic data spatially as a set of tiles and thematically as a set of layers. The data in a map library are indexed by location for optimal spatial access.

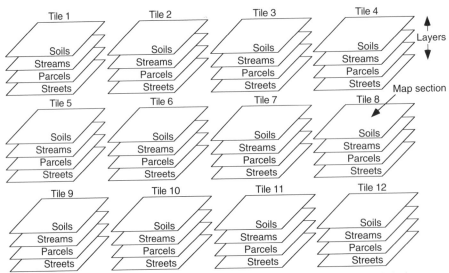

A map library organizes coverages spatially by tiles and thematically by layer. Individual coverages for each layer within a tile are called map sections.

map limits   The rectangular area on the graphics page in which geographic features are displayed. All geographic data are drawn within the map limits, and no geographic data is drawn outside the map limits. Map titles and legends can be drawn outside the map limits.

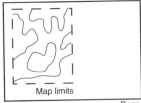

map projection
A systematic conversion of locations on the Earth's surface from spherical to planar coordinates. Because the earth is three-dimensional, some method must be used to depict a map in two dimensions. A mathematical model that transforms the locations of features on the Earth's surface to locations on a two-dimensional surface. Some projections preserve shape; others preserve accuracy of area, distance, or direction. See also *coordinate system*.

Map projections project the Earth's surface onto a flat plane. However, any such representation distorts some parameter of the Earth's surface be it distance, area, shape, or direction.

map query
The process of eliciting information from a GIS by asking questions of the geographic data. Query can be spatial or logical. Spatial query is the process of spatially selecting features (e.g., select all features within 300 feet of another; point at a set of features to select them). Logical query is the process of selecting features whose attributes meet specific logical criteria (e.g., select all polygons whose value for AREA is greater than 10,000 or select all streets whose name is 'Main St'). The query process involves selecting a set of features, then performing additional operations with those features—drawing them with assigned symbols, listing their attributes or summarizing attribute values (e.g., calculating the total or average value of an item).

map scale
The extent of reduction needed to display a representation of the Earth's surface on a map. A statement of a measure on the map and the equivalent measure on the Earth's surface, often expressed as a representative fraction of distance, such as 1:24,000 (one unit of distance on the map represents 24,000 of the same units of distance on the Earth). Map scale can also be expressed as a statement of equivalence using different units; for example, 1 inch = 1 mile or 1 inch = 2,000 feet.

map-to-page transformation
The process of positioning and scaling a map on a graphic page. It controls how coverage coordinates are transformed into graphics on the display screen or plotter page. (Coverages are not maps; they contain the unscaled coordinates that ARC/INFO uses to draw maps.)

map units
The coordinate units in which a geographic data set (e.g., a coverage) is stored in ARC/INFO. Map units can be inches, centimeters, feet, meters, or decimal degrees.

marker symbol
A symbol used to represent a point location such as an airport: ✈

meridian	A line running vertically from the north pole to the south pole along which all locations have the same longitude. The Prime Meridian (0°) runs through Greenwich, England. From the Prime Meridian, measures of longitude are negative to the west and positive to the east up to 180° halfway around the globe.

Meridians of longitude

minimum bounding rectangle	The rectangle defined by the map extent of a geographic data set and specified by two coordinates: xmin,ymin and xmax,ymax.
minimum mapping units	The minimum sizes or dimensions for features to be mapped as lines or areas for a given map scale. For example, long narrow features such as streams and rivers will be represented as lines if their width is less than .10 inch. If a polygon is smaller than .125 inch on a side, it will be represented as a point.
model	1. An abstraction of reality. A procedure run on a database to derive a measure or a set of measures. A set of clearly defined analytical procedures used to derive new information. A model is structured as a set of rules and procedures to derive new information that can be analyzed to aid in problem solving and planning. Analytical tools in a geographic information system (GIS) are used for building spatial models. Models can include a combination of logical expressions, mathematical procedures, and criteria, which are applied for the purpose of simulating a process, predicting an outcome, or characterizing a phenomenon. The terms *modeling* and *analysis* are often used interchangeably. Analysis is the process of identifying a question or issue to be addressed, modeling the issue, investigating model results, and making interpretations about the results including a recommendation about the issue being addressed. Modeling is more limited in scope; it is the process of simulation, prediction, or description. 2. Data representation of reality; for example, spatial data models include arc-node, georelational, raster (grid), and tin. See also *spatial modeling* and *spatial analysis*.
modeling	See *model, spatial analysis* and *spatial modeling*.
mouse	A hand-controlled hardware device for interacting with a computer terminal or entering data from a digitizer. Moving the mouse across a surface moves a cursor across a computer screen. A mouse is used to make selections and position the cursor to fields in computer forms when interacting with graphical user interfaces. A digitizer mouse is used to trace features and enter x,y coordinates of features.

NAT   Node attribute table for a coverage. Stores attribute information about a node. At a minimum, NATs contain the following items:

ARC#   Internal number of an arc to which a node is attached
Cover#   Node internal number
Cover-ID   Node feature ID

See also *feature attribute table*.

neatline   A border line commonly drawn around the extent of a map.

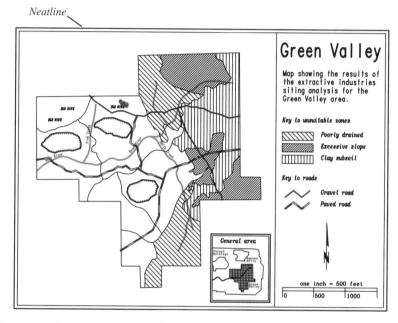

network   1. An interconnected set of arcs representing possible paths for the movement of resources from one location to another. 2. A coverage representing linear features containing arcs or a route-system. 3. When referring to computer hardware systems, a local area network or a wide area network.

NETWORK   The ARC/INFO software product that performs address matching/ geocoding, allocation, routing, and pathfinding across linear networks.

node   1. The beginning and ending locations of an arc. A node is topologically linked to all arcs that meet at the node. The point at which arcs (lines) in a polygon network connect. Nodes carry information about topology of the polygons.

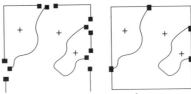

Arcs connect at a common node.

2. In graph theory, the location at which three or more lines connect.
3. The three corner points of each triangle in a tin. Every sample point input to a tin becomes a node in the triangulation. A triangle node is topologically linked to all triangles that meet at the node.

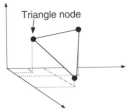

node match tolerance   The minimum radial distance within which two nodes will be joined (matched) to form one node.

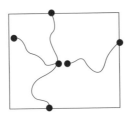

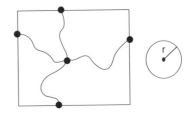

Before node matching   *After node matching*

one-to-many   A type of relate connecting a unique value in one file to many records (that have the same value) in another file.

Parcel-No	Zoning
101-21-002	R1
101-21-003	R1
101-21-004	R1
101-21-005	R4
101-22-001	MR

Parcel-No	Owner	Address
101-21-002	Smith, A	112 Main
101-21-003	Brown, T	114 Main
101-21-003	Brown, B	114 Main
101-21-003	Acme Bank	2103 1st
101-21-004	Lyle, L	116 Main

operating system (OS)   Computer software designed to allow communication between the computer and the user. The operating system controls the flow of data, the application of other programs, the organization and management of files, and the display of information.

overshoot   That portion of an arc digitized past its intersection with another arc. See also *dangling arc*.

An 'overshoot'

pan   To move the viewing window up, down, or sideways to display areas in a geographic data set which, at the current viewing scale, lie outside the viewing window. See also *zoom*.

parallel   1. A property of two or more lines that are separated at all points by the same distance.
2. A horizontal line encircling the Earth at a constant latitude. The Equator is a parallel whose latitude is 0°. Measures of latitude range from 0° to 90° north of the Equator and from 0° to -90° to the south.

Parallels of latitude

PAT   1. Point attribute table. 2. Polygon attribute table. A coverage can have either a point attribute table or a polygon attribute table, but not both. At a minimum, PATs contain the following items:

AREA   polygon area in coverage units. Set to 0 for point features
PERIMETER   perimeter in coverage units. Set to 0 for point features
Cover#   Internal number of polygon or point
Cover-ID   Feature ID of polygon or point

See *feature attribute table*.

pathname   The path to a file or directory location on a disk. Pathnames are always specific to the computer operating system. Computer operating systems use directories and files to organize data. Directories are organized in a tree structure; each branch on the tree represents a subdirectory or file. Pathnames indicate locations in this hierarchy.

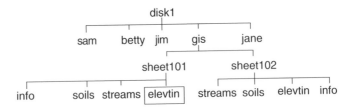

The UNIX pathname to elevtin for sheet 101 is: */disk1/gis/sheet101/elevtin.*

peripheral device   A hardware device not part of the central computer. Examples are digitizers, plotters, and printers.

pixel   A contraction of the words *picture element*. The smallest unit of information in an image or raster map. Referred to as a cell in an image or grid.

point   1. A single x,y coordinate that represents a geographic feature too small to be displayed as a line or area; for example, the location of a mountain peak or a building location on a small-scale map.
2. A label point feature in a coverage. In ARC/INFO, label points are used either to represent point features in a point coverage or to assign IDs to polygons in a polygon coverage.

point-in-polygon   A spatial operation in which points from one coverage are overlaid with a polygon coverage to determine which points fall within the polygon boundaries. Points assume the attributes of the polygons within which they fall.

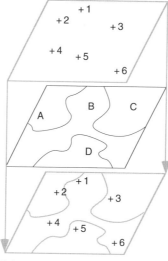

Point ID	V1	V2	V3	Poly ID	V6	V7
1	1	1	1	B	1	1
2	2	2	2	A	2	2
3	3	3	3	C	3	3
4	4	4	4	B	1	1
5	5	5	5	D	5	5
6	6	6	6	B	1	1

Point-in-polygon overlay

polygon   A multisided figure that represents an area on a map. An areal feature defined by the arcs that make up its boundary. Every polygon contains one label point inside its boundary. Polygons have attributes that describe the geographic feature they represent. See also *area*.

polygon overlay   A process that merges spatially coincident polygons from two coverages, and their attributes, to create a third coverage that contains new polygons and describes new relationships.

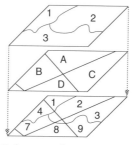

Newcover	Cover1	Cover2
1	1	A
2	2	A
3	2	C
4	1	B
5	2	B
6	2	D
7	3	B
8	3	D
9	3	C

Polygon overlay

precision Refers to the number of significant digits used to store numbers. Precision is important for accurate mapping. Coordinate precision specifies how many significant digits are available for coordinate values. There are single- and double-precision coordinates in ARC/INFO. See also *single-precision* and *double-precision*.

projection See *map projection*.

projection file 1. A coverage file that stores the parameters for the map projection and coordinate system of a geographic data set (e.g., a coverage). 2. A text file containing input and output projection parameters that can be used to convert a geographic data file from one coordinate system to another.

pseudo node A node where two, and only two, arcs intersect, or a single arc that connects with itself. Pseudo nodes can be used to subdivide an arc to mark the location of an attribute change along a linear feature. However, the route-system data model can store the information associated with linear features without modifying the underlying linear data.

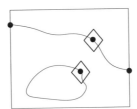

Examples of pseudo nodes in a coverage.

quadrangle (quad) Typically refers to a map sheet published by the U.S. Geological Survey, in the 7.5-minute quadrangle series or the 15-minute quadrangle series. Also known as a *topographic* or *topo* map.

query See *map query*.

raster A cellular data structure composed of rows and columns. Groups of cells represent features. The value of each cell represents the value of the feature. Image data is stored using this structure. See also *grid*.

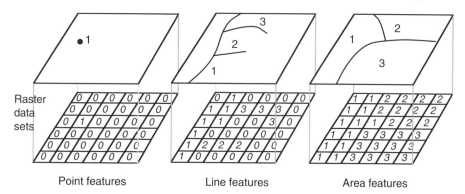

Point features   Line features   Area features

RAT Route attribute table. There is one RAT for each route-system in a coverage named *<cover>.RAT<subclass>* where subclass is the name of the route-system. An RAT stores route attributes. An RAT contains a minimum of two items:

Subclass#   Internal sequence number (record number) of the route
Subclass-ID User-assigned ID number of the route

See also *route-system, section, SEC,* and *feature attribute table.*

RDBMS Relational database management system. A database management system with the ability to access data organized in tabular files that can be related to each other by a common field (item). An RDBMS has the capability to recombine the data items from different files, providing powerful tools for data usage. See also *relate*.

record 1. In an attribute table, a single 'row' of thematic descriptors.

Area	Perimeter	Cover#	Cover-ID	Stand-No
30	21	2	101	I–1604
68	52	3	1001	I–1623
32	19	4	23	I–2004

Record

2. A logical unit of data in a file. For example, there is one record in the ARC file for each arc in a coverage.

region A coverage feature class used to represent a spatial feature as one or more polygons. Many regions can be defined in a single coverage. Regions have attributes (PAT) that describe the geographic feature they represent.

relate   An operation that establishes a temporary connection between corresponding records in two tables using an item common to both. Each record in one table is connected to those records in the other table that share the same value for the common item. A relate gives access to additional feature attributes that are not stored in a single table.

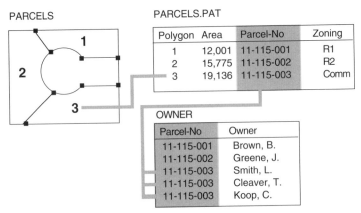

Conceptual view of a relate between PARCELS.PAT and OWNER.

relate key   The common set of columns used to relate two attribute tables. The column in the table to be related *from* is called the *foreign key*. The column in the table to be related *to* is called the *primary key*.

Example of primary and foreign relate keys.

relational database   A method of structuring data as collections of tables that are logically associated to each other by shared attributes. Any data element can be found in a relation by knowing the name of the table, the attribute (column) name, and the value of the primary key. See also *relate, relate key,* and *relational join.*

relational join   The operation of relating and physically merging two attribute tables using their common item.

Before relational join

AREA	PERIMETER	LOTS#	LOTS-ID
200	175	2	120
350	98	3	121
300	91	4	122
350	97	5	123

LOTS-ID	PARCEL-NO	OWNER	ZONING
121	11-221-15	Brown	R2
122	11-221-16	Smith	R1
123	11-221-17	Jones	R1

After relational join

AREA	PERIMETER	LOTS #	LOTS-ID	PARCEL-NO	OWNER	ZONING
200	175	2	120	—	—	—
350	98	3	121	111-221-15	Brown	R2
300	91	4	122	111-221-16	Smith	R1
350	97	5	123	111-221-17	Jones	R1

remote sensing   Acquiring information about an object without contacting it physically. Methods include aerial photography, radar, and satellite imaging.

resolution   1. Resolution is the accuracy at which a given map scale can depict the location and shape of map features. For example, at a map scale of 1:63,360 (1 inch = 1 mile), features smaller than .10-mile long or wide only measure .10-inch wide or long on the map. The larger the map scale, the higher the possible resolution. As map scale decreases, resolution diminishes and feature boundaries must be smoothed, simplified, or not shown at all. For example, small areas may have to be represented as points.

2. Distance between sample points in a lattice.
3. Size of the smallest feature that can be represented in a surface.
4. The number of points in x and y in a grid or lattice (e.g., the resolution of a U.S. Geological Survey one-degree DEM is 1201 x 1201 mesh points).

RMS error   The root mean square error (or tic registration error) is calculated when tics are used to register a map on the digitizer and during the TRANSFORM operation. The RMS value represents the amount of error between the original and new coordinate locations. The lower the RMS error, the more accurate the digitizing or transformation. To maintain highly accurate geographic data, keep the RMS under 0.004 inches. For less accurate data, the value may be as high as 0.008. See also *tic*.

route   A feature class in ARC/INFO that is part of the route-system data model. Routes represent linear features. A route is an ordered collection of sections. Sections define which arcs belong to the route, the direction of the route, and the measurement system used to address positions along it. The route attribute table (RAT) stores route attributes. See also *route-system* and *section*.

route attribute table   See *RAT*.

route-system   A collection of routes representing separate instances of a common linear entity is called a route-system. For example, a collection of bus routes within a city would be termed a BUS route-system. A single line coverage can contain many route-systems, differentiated by name. For example, a road coverage can contain a BUS route-system, a HIGHWAY route-system and PIZZA delivery route-system. Both an RAT and an SEC exist for each route-system. Attributes of the features that make up a route-system are called *events*.

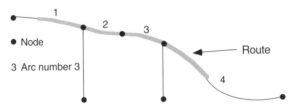

Routes are ordered collections of arcs or parts of arcs used to represent linear features. This route is defined on top of four arcs. Routes do not have to begin and end at nodes. Notice how the route's start- and endpoints fall within the arcs.

Sections are the arcs, or portions of arcs, used to define each route. They form the infrastructure of route-systems much like arcs form the infrastructure of polygons.

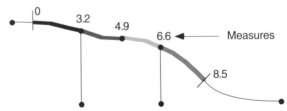

Many events can be positioned along routes. Attributes that contain distance measurements, such as milepost numbers or addresses, can be used to locate events such as accidents or pavement quality.

row   1. A record in an attribute table.

Area	Perimeter	Cover#	Cover-ID	Stand-No
30	21	2	101	I–1604
68	52	3	1001	I–1623
32	19	4	23	I–2004

→ row

2. A horizontal group of cells in a grid, or pixels in an image.

1	1	2	1	4	1
5	1	5	3	6	1
3	5	3	5	2	5
6	6	4	6	2	4
2	3	2	3	3	3
5	4	5	4	5	2
4	4	4	2	1	4

→ row

rubber sheeting   A procedure to adjust the features of a coverage in a nonuniform manner. Links representing from- and to-locations are used to define the adjustment. See also *link*.

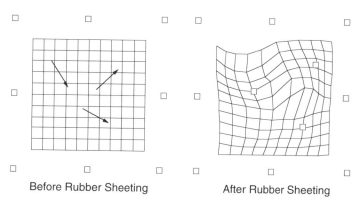

Before Rubber Sheeting   After Rubber Sheeting

scale   See *map scale*.

scale bar   A map element that shows the map scale graphically.

Scale = 1:55,000

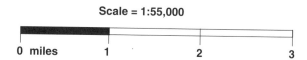

0 miles   1   2   3

scanning   The process of data input in raster format with a device called a *scanner*. Some scanners also use software to convert raster data to vector data.

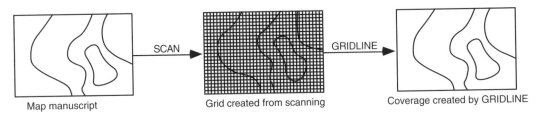

Map manuscript   Grid created from scanning   Coverage created by GRIDLINE

scratch file   A temporary file holding intermediate calculations; for example, when calculating arc intersections, building feature topology, and so on.

SEC   Section table for the section feature class in a coverage. Part of a route-system that defines which arcs constitute a route and calibrates measures along the route for dynamic segmentation of events. The SEC holds attributes about sections. The section table is named *<cover>.SEC<subclass>* where subclass is the name of the route-system. At a minimum, the SEC for a route-system in a coverage contains the following items:

ROUTELINK#	Internal sequence number (record number) of the route to which the section belongs. Relates to Subclass# in the RAT.
ARCLINK#	Internal sequence number (record number) of the arc to which the section belongs. Relates to Cover# in the AAT.
F-POS	From-position. Location along the arc, recorded as a percentage of its total length, at which the section begins (e.g., F-POS = 50% for a section beginning at the midpoint of an arc).
T-POS	To-position. Location along the arc, recorded as a percentage of its total length, at which the section ends (e.g., the T-POS = 100% for a section that ends at an arc's to-node).
F-MEAS	From-measure. The route-system measure at which the section begins. Uses the same measurement units in which event data is recorded.
T-MEAS	To-measure. The measure of the route-system at which the section ends.
Subclass#	The internal sequence number (record number) of each section.
Subclass-ID	User-assigned feature ID for each section.

See also *feature attribute table*.

section   A feature class in ARC/INFO that is a component of the route-system data model used to implement linear features or routes. An arc, or part of an arc. Sections keep track of: (1) how much of an arc is part of the route; (2) what direction the route traverses the arc; and (3) the measuring system defined for the route. See also *route* and *SEC*.

shade symbol   A pattern used to shade polygons in ARC/INFO. Shade symbol patterns include crosshatch, repeating, and solid fill.

single-precision   Refers to a level of coordinate accuracy based on the number of significant digits that can be stored for each coordinate. Single-precision numbers store up to 7 significant digits for each coordinate, retaining a precision of ±5 meters in an extent of 1,000,000 meters. Double-precision numbers store up to 15 significant digits (typically 13 to 14 significant digits), retaining the accuracy of much less than one meter at a global extent. ARC/INFO data sets can be stored as either single- or double-precision coordinates. See also *double-precision*.

sliver polygon   A small areal feature commonly occurring along the borders of polygons following the overlay of two or more coverages.

LANDUSE   SOILS

Overlay of LANDUSE and SOILS

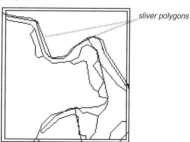

sliver polygons

slope   A measure of change in surface value over distance, expressed in degrees or as a percentage. For example, a rise of 2 meters over a distance of 100 meters describes a 2% slope with an angle of 1.15°. Mathematically, slope is referred to as the first derivative of the surface.

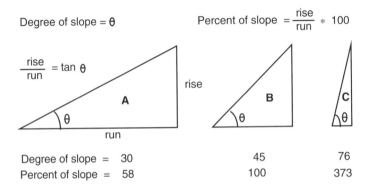

Degree of slope = θ Percent of slope $= \dfrac{rise}{run} * 100$

$\dfrac{rise}{run} = \tan \theta$

| Degree of slope = | 30 | 45 | 76 |
| Percent of slope = | 58 | 100 | 373 |

snapping   The process of moving a feature to coincide exactly with coordinates of another feature within a specified snapping distance, or tolerance.

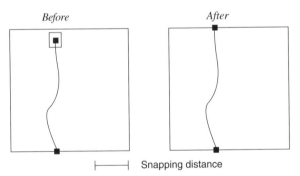

Before   *After*

├───┤ Snapping distance

Example of snapping nodes to arc features within a given feature snapping tolerance.

spatial analysis   The process of modeling, examining, and interpreting model results. Spatial analysis is the process of extracting or creating new information about a set of geographic features. Spatial analysis is useful for evaluating suitability and capability, for estimating and predicting, and for interpreting and understanding.

Spatial analysis is often referred to as *modeling*. In GIS, there are four traditional types of spatial analysis: spatial overlay and contiguity analysis, surface analysis, linear analysis, and raster analysis.

spatial data Information about the location and shape of, and relationships among, geographic features, usually stored as coordinates and topology.

spatial indexing A means of accelerating coverage drawing, spatial selection, and feature identification by generating feature-based indexes for one or more feature classes of a coverage.

spatial object See *geographic object*.

spatial modeling Analytical procedures applied with a GIS. There are three categories of spatial modeling functions that can be applied to geographic data objects within a GIS: (1) geometric models, such as calculating the Euclidean distance between objects, generating buffers, calculating areas and perimeters, and so on; (2) coincidence models, such as polygon overlay; and (3) adjacency models (pathfinding, redistricting, and allocation). All three model categories support operations on geographic data objects such as points, lines, polygons, tins, and grids. Functions are organized in a sequence of steps to derive the desired information for analysis. See also *model*.

SQL Structured Query Language. A syntax for defining and manipulating data from a relational database. Developed by IBM in the 1970s, it has become an industry standard for query languages in most relational database management systems.

station file An AML file containing commands needed to establish the environment for graphic display and graphic input. Typically, station files contain commands that define the DISPLAY device, the AML &TERMINAL device, the type of DIGITIZER, if any, and the method to be used for COORDINATE input.

subclass A specific annotation, route, or section feature class within a coverage. For example, a road coverage may have three route-systems stored as subclasses for mail delivery, street cleaning, and garbage pickup.

surface A representation of geographic information as a set of continuous data in which the map features are not spatially discrete; that is, there is an infinite set of values between any two locations. There are no clear or well-defined breaks between possible values of the geographic feature. Surfaces can be represented by models built from regularly or irregularly spaced sample points on the surface. See also *surface model*.

surface model Digital abstraction or approximation of a surface. Because a surface contains an infinite number of points, some subset of points must be used to represent the surface. Each model contains a formalized data structure, rules, and x,y,z point measurements that can be used to represent a surface. The TIN software package supports two data models for representing surfaces: tins and lattices. See also *lattice, tin,* and *TIN*.

symbol A graphic pattern used to represent a feature. For example, line symbols represent arc features; marker symbols, points; shades symbols, polygons; and text symbols, annotation. Many characteristics define symbols, including color, size, angle, and pattern. See also *text symbol, marker symbol, shade symbol,* and *line symbol*.

symbol environment Defines the types of map symbols and their characteristics during a graphic display session in ARC/INFO. There are four types of active map symbols: line, marker, shade, and text.

TAT Text attribute table for an annotation subclass in a coverage. The TAT is named *<cover>.TAT<subclass>* where subclass is the name of the annotation subclass in the coverage. At a minimum, a TAT for an annotation subclass contains two items:

Subclass# Internal sequence number (record number) for each annotation string

Subclass-ID User-assigned ID number for each annotation string

See also *feature attribute table*.

template 1. A coverage containing common feature boundaries, such as land-water boundaries, for use as a starting place in automating other coverages. Templates save time and increase the precision of spatial overlays.
2. A map template containing neatlines, North arrow, logos, and other cartographic map elements for a common map series.
3. An empty tabular data file containing only item definitions.

terminal A device, usually a display monitor and a keyboard, used to communicate with the computer.

text symbol A text style defined by font, size, character spacing, color, and so on, used to label maps and coverage features in ARC/INFO; for example,

Text symbol 1
Text symbol 2
Text symbol 3

Thiessen polygons Polygons whose boundaries define the area that is closest to each point relative to all other points. Thiessen polygons are generated from a set of points. They are mathematically defined by the perpendicular bisectors of the lines between all points. A tin structure is used to create Thiessen polygons.

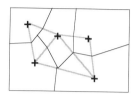

theme A collection of geographic objects defined by the user. Geographic objects are organized logically into groups of layers or *themes*. Examples of themes include streets, wells, soil types, and streams. In ARC/INFO, themes are represented by a coverage, one of its feature classes, and a set of corresponding attributes; or by another geographic data set such as a grid, image, or tin.

thematic data See *descriptive data*.

tic Registration or geographic control points for a coverage representing known locations on the Earth's surface. Tics allow all coverage features to be recorded in a common coordinate system (e.g., Universal Transverse Mercator [UTM] meters or State Plane feet). Tics are used to register map sheets when they are mounted on a digitizer and to transform the coordinates of a coverage (e.g., from digitizer units [inches] to UTM meters).

TIC file The coverage file used to store tic coordinates and tic IDs for a coverage. An INFO data file in the coverage named *Cover*.TIC.

tic match tolerance The maximum distance allowed between an existing tic and a tic being digitized. If this distance is exceeded, the digitizing error is considered unacceptable and the map must be registered over again. The tic match tolerance is used to ensure a low RMS error during map registration on a digitizer.

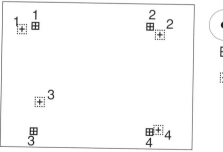

TIGER   The Topologically Integrated Geographic Encoding and Referencing data format used by the U.S. Census Bureau to support census programs and surveys. It was used for the 1990 census. TIGER files contain street address ranges along lines and census tract/block boundaries. This descriptive data can be used to associate address information and census/demographic data with coverage features.

tile   The spatial unit by which geographic data is organized, subdivided, and stored in a map library. Tiles subdivide the area covered by a map library and organize the library data by location (e.g., counties might be the tiles in a statewide database). A tile can be a regular, geometric shape (e.g., a map sheet), or an irregular shape, such as a county boundary. See also *LIBRARIAN*.

tin   Triangulated irregular network. A surface representation derived from irregularly spaced sample points and breakline features. The tin data set includes topological relationships between points and their proximal triangles. Each sample point has an x,y coordinate and a surface, or z-value. These points are connected by edges to form a set of nonoverlapping triangles used to represent the surface. Tins are also called *irregular triangular mesh* or *irregular triangular surface model*.

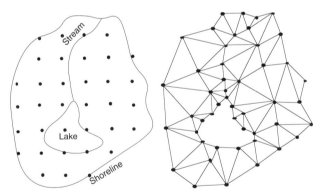

TIN   The ARC/INFO software product used for surface representation, modeling, and display.

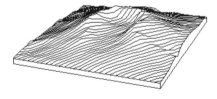

TOL file   A coverage file that contains processing tolerances (fuzzy, tic match, dangle length) and editing tolerances (weed, grain, edit distance, snap distance, and node snapping distance). ARC/INFO uses TOL file values as defaults in many automation, editing, and processing operations.

to-node   Of an arc's two endpoints, the one last digitized. See also *from-node*.

From-node   To-node

topographic map   1. A map containing contours indicating lines of equal surface elevation (relief), often referred to as *topo maps*.
2. Often used to refer to a map sheet published by the U.S. Geological Survey in the 7.5-minute quadrangle series or the 15-minute quadrangle series.

topology   The spatial relationships between connecting or adjacent coverage features (e.g., arcs, nodes, polygons, and points). For example, the topology of an arc includes its from- and to-nodes, and its left and right polygons. Topological relationships are built from simple elements into complex elements: points (simplest elements), arcs (sets of connected points), areas (sets of connected arcs), and routes (sets of sections, which are arcs or portions of arcs). Redundant data (coordinates) are eliminated because an arc may represent a linear feature, part of the boundary of an area feature, or both. Topology is useful in GIS because many spatial modeling operations don't require coordinates, only topological information. For example, to find an optimal path between two points requires a list of the arcs that connect to each other and the cost to traverse each arc in each direction. Coordinates are only needed for drawing the path after it is calculated.

transformation   The process that converts coordinates from one coordinate system to another through translation, rotation, and scaling. ARC/INFO supports these transformations: similarity, affine, piecewise linear, projective, NADCON datum adjustment using minimum-derived curvature transformation, and a polynomial transformation to warp grids and images.

triangulated irregular network   See *tin*.

undershoot   An arc that does not extend far enough to intersect another arc. See also *dangling arc*.

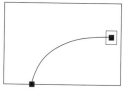

An undershoot

union	A topological overlay of two polygonal spatial data sets which preserves features that fall within the spatial extent of either input data set; that is, all features from both coverages are retained. See also *intersect* and *identity*.

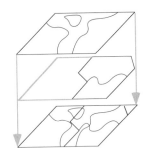

universe polygon The first record in a polygon attribute table. It represents the area beyond the outer boundary of the coverage. It's the only polygon that never has a label point, and so has a User-ID value of 0. Its area equals the negative sum of all the polygons in the coverage. Also referred to as the *external polygon*.

User-ID A user-assigned identifier (ID) for a feature in a coverage. Feature attribute tables store the User-IDs along with the locational data for a feature class in a coverage. User-ID is used interchangeably with *feature-ID* and *Cover-ID*

vector A coordinate-based data structure commonly used to represent linear map features. Each linear feature is represented as a list of ordered x,y coordinates. Attributes are associated with the feature (as opposed to a raster data structure, which associates attributes with a grid cell). Traditional vector data structures include double-digitized polygons and arc-node models.

vertex One of a set of ordered x,y coordinates that constitute a line feature.

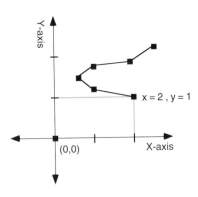

watch file A text file that records all nongraphic input and output during an ARC/INFO session. Watch files can be edited and converted to AML programs, which may be executed to 'replay' the session.

weed tolerance   The minimum allowable distance between any two vertices along an arc. Weed tolerance is a parameter that can be set before adding arc features. When adding new arcs, if an input vertex is within the weed distance from the last vertex, it is disregarded. When weeding existing arcs, it is the tolerance used by the Douglas-Peucker algorithm.

• Vertices digitized along the arc

Weed tolerance

• Vertices digitized along the arc

Weed tolerance

As arcs are digitized, vertices are deleted if they fall within the weed distance of existing vertices.

Existing arcs can be generalized using the Douglas-Peucker algorithm for line generalization.

workspace   A directory containing geographic data sets for use with ARC/INFO. A workspace contains an INFO directory for the feature attribute tables. ARC/INFO workspaces have three primary uses: as user work areas, to store all the map sections for each tile in a map library, and as automation workspaces to store all the versions of a single coverage as it progresses through the coverage automation process.

z-value   The elevation value of a surface at a particular x,y location. Also, often referred to as *spot values* or *spot elevations*.

zoom   To display a region smaller than the full extent of the spatial data set to enlarge it and show greater detail.

Index

Arc (cont.)
  topology
    defined 2-10 thru 2-11
    constructing 5-8, 5-9, 5-11, 5-57 thru 5-59,
      5-61, 7-47
    undershoot 4-11, 5-3, 5-48, 5-64, 5-66

ARC 1-10
  starting xvii, 3-21, 4-17
  stopping *See* QUIT

Arc attribute table *See* AAT

ARC Macro Language *See* AML

Arc-node topology *See* Arc, topology

ARCEDIT 4-1, 4-9, 4-26 thru 4-27, 6-8
  saving *See* SAVE
  starting 4-18
  stopping *See* QUIT
  used in Chapters 4, 5, and 7

ARCLINES 6-31, 6-33, 9-14

ARCPLOT 1-13, 3-22, 4-43, 5-23, 6-20
  starting 4-48
  stopping *See* QUIT
  used in Chapters 4, 6, 7, 8, and 9

ARCS 4-48, 6-31, 6-33, 9-54, 9-55

ARCSNAP 5-40 thru 5-41, 5-46, 5-65, 5-66

Area *See* Polygon

Area definition *See* Topological relationships

ASELECT 8-30, 8-47

Attribute
  adding to PAT or AAT 2-22 thru 2-27, 6-1 thru 6-4,
    6-15 thru 6-30, 6-32, 8-9, 8-27 thru 8-28, 9-16
  adding values to INFO data file 6-12 thru 6-15, 6-22
    thru 6-24, 6-26 thru 6-29, 8-33, 8-42, 8-47, 8-48
  characteristics of 6-5 thru 6-11, 8-27
  coding
    as a range of values 3-11
    as unique values 2-17, 3-11 thru 3-12, 6-5, 6-12
      thru 6-14, 6-22 thru 6-24, 9-16, 9-19
    storage space requirements 2-20 thru 2-24, 3-12,
      6-6, 6-26
  defined 1-10, 2-21 thru 2-27, 2-30, 3-11, 3-20, 5-62,
    6-31

Attribute (cont.)
  displaying
    in ARC 5-13, 5-59, 6-19, 6-24
    in ARCPLOT 6-20 thru 6-21, 6-30, 8-14 thru
      8-15, 8-24 thru 8-25, 9-33 thru 9-34, 9-44 thru
      9-45, 9-50, 9-54
    in INFO 6-14, 6-23, 6-29, 6-33, 8-13, 9-20
  in database design 3-1 thru 3-3, 3-5, 3-11, 6-10, 6-25
  identifying 3-6 thru 3-7
  modifying 6-15, 6-33, 8-50
  table *See* Feature attribute table

BACKCOVERAGE (BACKCOVER) 7-31

BACKENVIRONMENT (BACKENV) 7-32

BND *See* Coverage, boundary

BOX 9-14, 9-48, 9-49, 9-54, 9-55

BUFFER 8-6, 8-12, 8-14, 8-51

Buffer generation *See* Analysis

BUILD 5-2, 5-9 thru 5-15, 5-55 thru 5-59,
  5-63 thru 5-65, 7-45

CALCULATE
  in ARCEDIT 5-52, 5-66
  in ARCPLOT 8-32 thru 8-34, 8-42, 8-51
  in INFO 7-47

CLEAN 5-2, 5-9 thru 5-15, 5-46, 5-55 thru 5-59,
  5-63 thru 5-65

CLEAR 6-31, 7-4, 7-48, 8-40, 8-47, 9-31, 9-36, 9-51

CLEARSELECT 8-40

Clip 7-30 thru 7-32, 7-55

CLIP 4-8, 7-21, 7-31, 8-15

COGO x

Command usage
  conventions 4-12
  displaying 4-12
  examples 4-12, 4-13

COMMANDS
  in ARC 4-13
  in ARCEDIT 5-28
  in GENERATE 4-47